Homelessness and the Built Environment

Homelessness and the Built Environment provides a practical introduction to the effective physical design of homes and other facilities that assist unhoused persons in countries identified as middle- to high-income. It considers the supportive role that design can play for unhoused persons and other users and argues that the built environment is an equal partner alongside other therapies and programs for ending a person's state of homelessness. By exploring issues, trends, and the unique potential of built environments, this book moves the needle of what is possible to assist people experiencing trauma.

Examining important architectural and interior architectural design considerations in detail within emergency shelters, transitional shelters, permanent supportive housing, day centers, and multi-service complexes such as space planning choices, circulation and wayfinding, visibility, lighting, and materials and finishes, it provides readers with both curated conclusions from empirical knowledge and experienced designers' perspectives.

Homelessness and the Built Environment is an imperative and singular reference for interior designers, architects and building renovation sponsors, design researchers and students forging new discoveries, and policy makers who seek to assist communities affected by homelessness.

Jill Pable is a professor and chair of the Interior Architecture & Design Department at Florida State University. Her research focuses on the design of environments for people experiencing trauma and she leads Design Resources for Homelessness, a non-profit research communication organization at designresourcesforhomelessness.org

Yelena McLane is an assistant professor in the Interior Architecture & Design Department at Florida State University. She explores relationships between interior configurations and users' experiences within spaces, and social influences upon these relationships. Her recent scholarship focuses on resident perceptions of community spaces in permanent supportive housing.

Lauren Trujillo has a BS and an MFA in interior design and has served as an adjunct instructor in interior design and art history at several colleges. She is a licensed interior designer in Florida and is a LEED GA. Her research interests include intercultural design and education.

Homelessness and the Built Environment

Designing for Unhoused Persons

Jill Pable, Yelena McLane, and Lauren Trujillo

Routledge
Taylor & Francis Group

NEW YORK AND LONDON

First published 2022
by Routledge
52 Vanderbilt Avenue, New York, NY 10017

and by Routledge
2 Park Square, Milton Park, Abingdon, Oxon, OX14 4RN

Routledge is an imprint of the Taylor & Francis Group, an informa business

© 2022 Taylor & Francis

Library of Congress Cataloging-in-Publication Data
Names: Pable, Jill, author. | McLane, Yelena, author. | Trujillo, Lauren, author.
Title: Homelessness and the built environment : designing for unhoused
    persons / Jill Pable, Yelena McLane, Lauren Trujillo.
Description: 1 Edition. | New York : Routledge, 2021. | Includes
    bibliographical references and index. |
Identifiers: LCCN 2020051570 (print) | LCCN 2020051571 (ebook) |
    ISBN 9780367232627 (hardback) | ISBN 9780367232443 (paperback) |
    ISBN 9780429279027 (ebook)
Subjects: LCSH: Homelessness—United States. | Poor—United States—
    Social conditions. | Public housing—United States. | Architecture,
    Domestic—United States.
Classification: LCC HV4505 .P223 2021 (print) | LCC HV4505 (ebook) |
    DDC 363.5/969420973—dc23
LC record available at https://lccn.loc.gov/2020051570
LC ebook record available at https://lccn.loc.gov/2020051571

Cover image courtesy of SkidRobot.

ISBN: 978-0-367-23262-7 (hbk)
ISBN: 978-0-367-23244-3 (pbk)
ISBN: 978-0-429-27902-7 (ebk)

Typeset in Univers
by Apex CoVantage, LLC

Contents

■ Contents

Foreword

Around the world, communities are striving to answer the question, "How do we end homelessness and how do we keep it ended?" The solutions are as dynamic, varied, and multidimensional as the root causes of homelessness.

One important through line of successful solutions, no matter where in the world you live and work, is human-centered design. To bring an end to homelessness, we must center the needs of the people who are experiencing homeless as we design both the system that serves them *and* the built environment in which that system is deployed.

This first-of-a-kind book explores the latter aspect, detailing the evidence showing that architecture and interior design can enhance services in ways that better support people experiencing the crisis of homelessness. This book leads an important conversation that, by and large, has been missing from the global conversations around homelessness. While the housing and homeless services sector in high-income countries works to apply concepts of harm reduction and trauma-informed care to program delivery, rarely is that application extended to art, architecture, and interior design. The work of authors Jill Pable, Yelena McLane, and Lauren Trujillo fills in this void.

The themes explored by this book challenge the prevalent stigma that people who are experiencing homelessness "should be grateful" for any housing or services offered to them, and calls us to new heights in honoring the full humanity of our neighbors in need. Those of us who are housed dignify ourselves with functionality and amenities in our own dwellings, and we must extend that dignity to those who are experiencing homelessness. We extend this dignity by asking people who are experiencing homelessness what is it that they need and want in a built environment, listening well to their answers, and then meeting those needs and desires to the best of our ability and capacity.

As Richard Buchanan, editor of *Design Issues*, once wrote,

> Human-centered design is fundamentally an affirmation of human dignity. It is an ongoing search for what can be done to support and strengthen the dignity of human beings as they act out their lives in varied social, economic, political, and cultural circumstances.[1]

Take note of his insight that design work is ongoing, and, as people and context change, so too will the designs that surround them need to evolve. This is hard work, but it is the right thing to do, and it will lead to good results.

Beyond the humanity, dignity, and inherent rights of people experiencing homelessness is a very practical consideration. "Reduction in returns to homelessness" is a metric tracked by many high-income countries, meaning how many people cycle back to homelessness once housed. Multiple episodes of homelessness are unfortunately a common occurrence.[2] While services are an important part of reducing returns to homelessness, we should also consider the extent to which a thoughtfully designed built environment can reduce returns to homelessness. As authors Pable, McLane, and Trujillo note in Chapter 5, "one's psychological state, emotional state, and the physical environment are more closely connected than previously surmised." The research indicates that the built environment has an underutilized potential to help, or conversely to hinder, a person's therapeutic journey. Considering the possibility for impact on individual outcomes and system-wide metrics provides a further impetus for us to contemplate the themes explored in this book.

Yet, beyond the exploration of interesting concepts, we must also move to apply the themes to our work as it relates to serving people who are experiencing homelessness. It is my hope that the actionable insights, both large and small, presented in this book will be broadly applied across many sectors. From art, architecture, and interior design to housing and homeless services, we all have a role to play in reaching a permanent end to homelessness, and we should take the opportunity to enhance our role by acting on the principles presented in *Homelessness and the Built Environment*.

Lydia Stazen
Executive Director, Institute of Global Homelessness
www.ighomelessness.org
Chicago – August 2020

Acknowledgements

This book was the direct result of much generosity of time and expertise on the part of numerous architects and designers, scholars, non-profit professionals, and experts with whom the authors were fortunate to meet and correspond and whose works this book showcases. This project would not have been possible without their many insights and observations. We are sincerely grateful to:

- Alex Campbell and Mallori Hamilton of Nelson Worldwide
- BLOCK project, Seattle, Washington
- Bob Duncan of Duncan Wisniewski Architecture
- Chloe Anderson of Holland Harvey Architects, London, UK
- Collaborative House, LLC, Los Angeles, California
- Camillin Denny Architects, Brighton, UK
- Catholic Housing Services, Seattle, Washington
- Clemons Rutherford Architects, Tallahassee, Florida
- Drew Adams and Janna Levitt of LGA Architectural Partners and ERA Architects, Toronto, Canada
- Edward Rafailovitc
- Environmental Works Community Design Center, Seattle, Washington
- Alejandro Aravena, Elemental, Chile
- Erin Mayer of True Worth Presbyterian Night Shelter, Fort Worth, Texas
- Facing Homelessness, Seattle, Washington
- Homeless Transition Village, Fayetteville, Arkansas
- HOPE Community, Tallahassee, Florida
- ICON
- Jacob Reiter of Kearney Comprehensive Emergency Services Center, Tallahassee, Florida
- Jamie Castillo of HKS, Fort Worth, Texas
- Jeff Cornelison
- Jim Reese and Jennifer Hutchison of Atlanta Mission, Atlanta, Georgia
- Jimaylya Topsy Harry Centre, Mount Isa, Australia
- Jonathan Farrell of the Committee on Temporary Shelter, Burlington, Vermont
- Joshua Wheeler and Sue Buchanan of MGS Architects, Melbourne, Australia
- Wade Killefer, Killefer Flammang, Santa Monica, California
- Lawrence Scarpa of Brooks+Scarpa, Los Angeles, California

- Laura Rossbert of Shopworks Architecture, Denver, Colorado
- Lindsey Slater, volunteer, Design Resources for Homelessness
- Lorcan O'Herlihy of Lorcan O'Herlihy Architects, Los Angeles, California
- Matthew Smith of The Booth Centre, Southampton, UK
- Michael Maltzan of Michael Maltzan Architecture, Inc., Los Angeles, California
- Mobile Loaves & Fishes, Austin, Texas
- Norix Furniture
- Paul Memmott of Aboriginal Environments Research Centre & Indigenous Design Place, University of Queensland, Brisbane, Australia
- People Oriented Design and Indij Design, Cairns, Australia
- Podshare, Los Angeles, California
- Skid Row Housing Authority, Los Angeles, California
- Sonya Keep of Brisbane Common Ground, Brisbane, Australia
- Stephen Luoni, University of Arkansas Community Design Center, Fayetteville, Arkansas
- Tomi Gomory, School of Social Work, Florida State University
- Trinity Winchester House, Winchester, UK

We would also like to recognize Design Resources for Homelessness, a non-profit organization, for partnering with the authors on this project.

Obtaining and securing photographer permissions for this book required a substantial effort. We acknowledge the following photographers and organizations who donated their work to this publication:

- Andrew Latreille
- Ben Rahn/A-Frame
- Bob Glatt
- Cas Allan
- Chris Matterson
- Elvert Barnes
- Garrett Rowland
- Mary E. Nichols
- Matthew Staver
- Michael Marzik
- Nicholas Worley
- Nicolas Boullosa
- Paul Vu
- SkidRobot
- Suzanne Furst
- Tara Wujcik
- Trevor Mein

It was a distinct pleasure to work with the editorial team at Routledge. Their support and professionalism helped us to navigate both the manuscript writing and production phases of the project.

■ Acknowledgements

We also extend our deepest gratitude to our families for their understanding and patience over the past several years, and to the many individuals served by the organizations featured in this book, as well as those who are unserved, whose stories and circumstances we sought to convey with dignity and respect.

NOTES

1. Buchanan R. Human Dignity and Human Rights: Thoughts on the Principles of Human-Centered Design. *Design Issues*. 2001; 17(3): 35–39.
2. Anucha, U. Conceptualizing Homeless Exits and Returns: The Case for a Multi-dimensional Response to Episodic Homelessness. *Critical Social Work*. 2005; 6(1): 1–17.

1   Introduction

Jill Pable

We live at a time of both great progress and change, where technology and science make possible advancements that stand poised to transform our culture in ways we cannot yet foresee. However, this time is also haunted by tragedies and short-comings that hold us back from realizing our full cultural potential. Poverty plagues millions, as do crime, income inequality, violence, and lack of education. This book concentrates on one problem, homelessness, yet addresses many other problems while doing so, as homelessness encapsulates, causes, exacerbates, or is a conse-quence of many societal issues: racism, substance abuse, housing inadequacies, and untreated mental illness, to name a few.[1] As one city leader observes, "home-lessness is a symbol of the failures of all our institutions" (Gumbel, 2018, para. 22). This introductory chapter will establish the current context of homelessness and its frequency and causes, and set the tone for the chapters that follow by making the case that architectural design is an indivisible part of the restorative experience, and why the time has come for the role and contribution of the built environment to be discussed. It concludes with an explanation of the uses of this book and its intended target audiences.

Although homelessness is interrelated with many societal problems, any dis-cussion of homelessness reveals its array of unique characteristics:

- In contrast to problems like poor education or lack of sanitation, the causes of homelessness are oftentimes controversial and exclusively attributed by some to an individual's personal weaknesses or personal failings (whether accurate or not). This can create stereotyping, anger, or indifference toward afflicted persons, and this prejudice is at least partially to blame for the inconsistent or inadequate attention and funding to remedy the problem.
- For someone who has lost their housing, their new status as 'homeless' can bring them to fundamentally reconsider who they are as a person, reacting to both internal and external cues. As summarized in remarks by the United National Human Rights Council, "people denied water or food are rarely treated as a social group in the way homeless people are. Those who are homeless are subject to stigmatization, social exclusion and criminalization" (United Nations Human Rights Council, 2015, p. 3).

- Homelessness can be a high-stakes predicament. Unlike a lack of education or loss of a job, lack of shelter can bring with it immediate health hazards or even death from exposure, if weather or climate conditions are severe and options for sleeping on a friend's sofa or in a vehicle do not present themselves. Homelessness demands the person's immediate attention and negatively impacts their ability to attend to long-term solutions (Mullainathan and Shafir, 2013).

- Long-term homelessness also brings significant hazards, such as an increased chance of degraded physical and mental health (National Health Care for the Homeless Council, 2018). A 2010 study of unhoused or inadequately housed Canadian citizens found that men and women had a 32 percent and 60 percent chance, respectively, of living to 75, which is below the Canadian average age expectancy of 81.1 (Ubelacker, 2018). Children who experience homelessness are more likely to develop learning disabilities, putting them behind their peers in their mental and social growth to an extent that can last a lifetime (Firth, 2014).

- For a community, the presence of a homeless population takes a toll on park services, detox centers, emergency rooms, ambulance services, and police protection. In 2012, the director of the U.S. Department of Housing and Urban Development identified that a chronically unhoused person can cost their community between $30,000 and $50,000 per year through their use of these services (Moorhead, 2012).

- Seldom discussed, but inherent to the persistence and pervasiveness of homelessness is the loss of human potential, with hundreds of thousands of creative minds squandered as persons scramble for food, shelter, and general survival on a daily basis. People, properly cultivated and supported, can help advance a society more effectively and quickly as engaged, productive citizens offering their energy and wisdom. Prompted by his mission of helping impoverished people with services such as sewage and water treatment, GISS Technologies CEO Rob Corra undertook a thought experiment about this question. Although actual numbers are difficult to predict, he reasoned that, if one examines the 2.1 billion people currently living in extreme poverty worldwide, it is statistically likely that more than 730,000,000 of these persons have IQ scores between 120 and 176, which range from 'superior', akin to the intellect of Bill Gates, to 'super genius' (Leonardo DaVinci). Thanks to poverty and its associated problems, we collectively lose the intellectual potential of more than 200 million people with superior intelligence or better and almost 70,000 who could be as smart as Einstein (Corra, 2015).

The agencies and organizations that minister to and shelter unhoused persons similarly encounter many hurdles as they offer their care.

- Organizations often contend with precarious, inconsistent budgets that are dependent on donors and grants.
- Some supportive housing, shelters and similar facilities must use repurposed buildings, which may be wildly unsuitable to actual needs. (We have seen one

shelter that offers emergency shelter within a windowless warehouse located under an interstate exchange.)

- Organizations offering assistance are sometimes so busy trying to help people to exit homelessness (often the largest and most complex crisis of their clients' lives) that they have little time to attend to structural changes that could make their work more successful, such as the effectiveness of their physical facilities. In the words of one provider, there is no 'slack' in the workload that permits reflection and progress.

- There is often an over-supply of unhoused clients whom providers must turn away or for whom aid is delayed. Need often outstrips capacity: if every emergency shelter bed and transitional housing bed were filled in the 32 U.S. cities studied in the 2016 Mayors' Report on Hunger and Homelessness, over 34,000 persons in need would still be unsheltered on any given night (U.S. Conference of Mayors, 2016).

The stakes of homelessness are large for the people who are unhoused and the societies they live in, and the hurdles are difficult for organizations on the front lines of assisting these persons. In such a situation, you would want those forces that lend aid to have every advantage, harnessing every possible asset in order to effectively lift people from their crisis so that they could rejoin society as respected, productive citizens just as soon as possible. This book makes that case that built environments – that is, the architecture and interior design of places that assist unhoused persons and the staff that help them – are one of those potential assets, and one that is currently undervalued and underutilized. Although architecture and design are not the entire source of the solution to homelessness, this book will press the case that built environments can operate alongside therapies, support programs, and other aids to usher people along to a better future as quickly and effectively as possible. Ideas and discoveries from fields ranging from psychology to social work are converging on this very notion, identifying the built environment as one of the critically necessary determinants of health (Office of Disease Prevention and Health Promotion, 2018). This book will discuss these notions in further detail in Chapters 5, 6 and 7.

THE FREQUENCY OF HOMELESSNESS

Before exploring the potential role of architecture and design in this introductory chapter, it is helpful to discuss the nature of homelessness in general, for any good problem must first be understood before it can be confronted effectively. An in-depth explanation of the history of homelessness and its architectural characteristics can be found in Chapter 2.

Being without a physical home is pervasive and persistent, and is a problem that affects the citizens of countries worldwide. It occurs in high-income as well as in low-income countries alike.[2] However, defining homelessness is not as simple as it seems, as one culture's standards of habitation may differ widely from another's, with traditional huts viewed as more than adequate in some locales, whereas seemingly more advanced brick and mortar structures may be perceived as wanting in other places. The Institute of Global Homelessness has proposed a universal definition of homelessness as "lacking access to minimally adequate housing"; although factually accurate, however, this definition does not capture the damage to a person's psyche and loss of a sense of social belonging that may come with losing one's home (United Nations Human Rights Council, 2015). Owing in part to these variables, there are no confirmed statistics about the global extent of homelessness;[3] however, more than 1 billion people live in informal settlements worldwide (United Nations Human Rights Council, 2015), and 100 million people likely have no housing whatsoever (Institute on Global Homelessness, 2017).

High-income countries such as the United States, Canada, and the United Kingdom are similarly beset with homelessness. The January 2016 annual 'point in time' count identified that 544,084 people experienced homelessness on a single night (U.S. Conference of Mayors, 2016), roughly equal to the population of Tucson, Arizona. Although homelessness has been declining for a period of several years nationally in the United States (a 12.9 percent decrease from 2009 to 2016), increases in some cities contradict these trends. Cities and certain areas, in fact, vary greatly in the size of their homeless populations. Seattle, Portland, and Hawaii, for example, each declared a state of emergency concerning homelessness in 2015. In 2016, Los Angeles reported a 20 percent increase in a single year with 58,000 people (Gumbel, 2018), and, on one night in December of 2017, a record high of 63,000 men, women, and children slept in New York City shelters. Three quarters of these persons were members of unhoused families (Routhier, 2018).

Significant populations of unhoused persons also exist in middle- and high-income countries other than the United States, according to organizations that keep records. These findings are shown in 1.1. Many sources agree that the face

1.1
Conservative estimates of number of persons experiencing homelessness in middle and high-income countries, 2016–2017.

Country	Estimate of unhoused persons, year recorded	Source	Notes
United States	544,000, 2016	Department of Housing and Urban Development: requires communities to submit these counts as part of their application for federal homeless assistance funds	Indicates a 12.9 percent decrease from 2009 to 2016; however, selected city increases contradict this trend
Canada	150,000, 2017	Homeless Hub (2017)	28,000 are estimated to be homeless on any given night
United Kingdom	78,930, 2017	Homeless Link (2018)	2,830 young people aged 16–24 were accepted and classified as statutory homeless
Australia	116,000, 2016	Australian Census: www.aph.gov.au/About_Parliament/Parliamentary_Departments/Parliamentary_Library/FlagPost/2018/March/Homelessness_in_Australia; Crothers (2018)	Indicates a 14 percent increase over 5 years from 2011 to 2016

of homelessness is changing, with women and families with children becoming more frequent in some areas (Crothers, 2018; Hillard, 2018; Kusmer, 2001; U.S. Conference of Mayors, 2016).

THE REASONS FOR HOMELESSNESS

People become homeless for many reasons. However, the lack of affordable housing as one of these causes is growing in frequency. For example, nearly all officials in the 23 cities that contributed to the U.S. Mayors' Report in 2016 identified the need for housing assistance and affordable housing as the most needed resource (U.S. Conference of Mayors, 2016). Rising rental rates coupled with lack of housing stock can mean vacancy rates of only 2 percent in high-demand areas such as Los Angeles (Gumbel, 2018). Such conditions are forcing citizens who operate on the edge of solvency out of permanent housing and into friends' homes, shelters, or tents. The measure of affordability for housing has long been defined by the United States Housing Act of 1937 standard (Pub L No. 93–383, 88 Stat 653), which identifies that 30 percent of one's monthly adjusted income is the threshold for affordable housing costs. This level of affordability is becoming less common. By 2008, half of renter households paid more than 30 percent of their income in rent in the U.S., and one-quarter paid more than 50 percent, as revealed by a Harvard University study (Joint Center for Housing Studies of Harvard University, 2010). The National Low Income Housing Coalition reported that, as of 2018, no state in the U.S. had sufficient affordable rental housing for persons of the lowest economic capability, and that the U.S. needs 7.2 million affordable rental homes in total to correct this problem (National Low Income Housing Coalition, 2018).

Lack of affordable housing is not the only reason for current levels of homelessness, however. Underemployment or unemployment tied to disappearance of low-skilled jobs and lack of job training has exacerbated poverty, which in turn affects the frequency of homelessness (Jencks, 1994; National Coalition for the Homeless, 2018). Many unhoused persons also suffer from mental disabilities, and their presence among the unhoused can be tied in part to a lack of alternative social safety nets put in place after the closing of mental institutions in western countries beginning in the mid-1950s, a deinstitutionalization process that has been called a "psychiatric 'Titanic'" (Frontline, 2005; Torrey, 2008). Declining welfare benefits have also contributed to strife, as have common coping strategies such as drug and alcohol abuse. The increase in opioid use disorders since the 1990s has also affected the population of unhoused persons, as access to even basic healthcare for them is more challenging than for those with homes (National Alliance to End Homelessness, 2017). These conditions can prompt violence that results in a criminal record – which, in a vicious circle, makes employment and housing that much harder to obtain. This common co-occurrence of multiple challenges has led to the recognition of 'persons with complex needs' as a group often afflicted by home loss and the need for 'complex care' strategies that effectively assist them (National Center for Complex Health and Social Needs, 2017).

RESPONSES TO HOMELESSNESS

The response to homelessness by governmental and societal agencies and organizations in the United States has been historically less than coherent, an issue explored in further detail in Chapter 2. In general, however, organized efforts to combat homelessness have been marked not by specific legislation or theory, but instead by a de facto system of services reflecting "[the] vicissitudes of funding, differing approaches among federal departments, and unique territories staked out within the advocacy community" (Leginski, 2007, pp. 1–7). In the recent past, agencies often differed on the intended goal: was it to end homelessness, end chronic homelessness, or revise current efforts with the goal of being more effective (Leginski, 2007)? Since 2007, consensus has grown about the effectiveness and viability of 'housing first' approaches, whereby a person is provided shelter *before* being drug and alcohol free, and otherwise 'ready' for housing (Department of Housing and Urban Development, 2014). The housing first model is also taking hold in Sweden and the United Kingdom (Clapham, 2017). In the U.S., this change in approach has led to increased construction of permanent supportive housing and a decrease in transitional housing types usually intended for habitation for up to 1 year. Even with an estimated 3,000 emergency shelters currently operating in the United States, the need continues (Homeless Shelter Directory, 2018).

In sum, the causes of homelessness depend to a point on who you ask. For some members of the public, homelessness is caused by personal weakness and the attendant failure to secure work and a home. However, for a growing collection of researchers and organizations, bolstered by empirical study and documented experience of persons who are unhoused, homelessness is often a natural outcome of collective forces that offer a compromised playing field, coupled with crisis-reactive biological and other personal forces that make it difficult to keep pace with society. As the United Nations Humans Rights Council describes, homelessness occurs "when housing is treated as a commodity rather than as a human right" and is "symptomatic of the failure of governments to address growing inequalities in income, wealth and access to land and property and to effectively respond to the change of migration and urbanization" (United Nations Human Rights Council, 2015, p. 4.) Whatever its cause, its immediacy and impact are undeniable both to the individual and to their community.

WHO ARE PERSONS EXPERIENCING HOMELESSNESS?

For most people, exposure to homelessness comes in the form of a public encounter with someone who is sleeping in a doorway or seeking spare change. To investigate this population in depth, however, is to encounter a shadow culture present among us, but seldom apparent in extent. Only sometimes visible due to the stigma it brings and often denying it to themselves, people share friends' sofas or sleep at work, rent motel rooms, sleep in vehicles, or squat in abandoned or substandard buildings. Some live in the woods behind big box retail stores or under overpasses, and others band together in protective groups of makeshift structures to ward off real or perceived threats of violence. 'Living rough' outside can be a risky lifestyle, exposing a person to significant violence and crime. In a 2018 National Public Radio audio story, two women who were new to homelessness in Los Angeles's skid row neighborhood were warned by support agency workers to not borrow money from anyone as they live on the street. This is because they will then be 'owned', with negative consequences and obligations. Another woman in skid row was required to regularly give her entire monthly benefits check to the gangs that serve as 'landlords' of the sidewalk where she lived (Hillard, 2018).

Historically speaking, women in the United States were not known to be homeless in large numbers before the 1990s. Chapter 2 discusses the changes in the identities of unhoused persons in the United States over the three centuries of its settlement, and how early groups of itinerant working men gave way in frequency to African Americans and the working class during the Great Depression, and then to the contemporary period characterized by single men and women of diverse age ranges, persons with mental disabilities, and families with children (Kusmer, 2001). Indeed, it is only within the last several decades that persons without housing have diversified to a great extent, encompassing groups that previously had found societal protection from homelessness. Chapter 3 explores in greater detail key contemporary groups of people who are experiencing homelessness, including single men and women, victims of domestic violence, the elderly, veterans, adolescents on their own or aging out of the foster care system, persons with mental disabilities, families with children, persons recently released from incarceration, and persons from indigenous populations. Each of these groups may be best served by unique architectural features in their built environments. It should also be said, although people can be classified into a group, each individual also comes from a distinct set of circumstances and complex needs that can blur these categories. For instance, a victim of domestic violence may have children; a veteran may suffer from a mental disability such as PTSD. In order to bring such persons to life, Chapter 3 provides a representation of people's 'back stories' from each of these groups.

ARCHITECTURAL RESPONSES: AN INTRODUCTION

The architecture and design of homeless shelters are far more neglected in the literature than other sectors with which they share some similarities – hospitals, schools, dormitories, and prisons. With the exception of architect and professor Sam Davis's 2004 work *Designing for the Homeless: Architecture That Works*, the architecture and design issues facing shelters and day centers have not been examined in detail. Permanent supportive housing, in contrast, has more in common with traditional apartment buildings and, therefore, enjoys a more liberal base of knowledge from which to devise an architectural program, but more work is needed on the integration of support services with these projects. These and similar details are explored more fully in Chapter 2, which discusses past initiatives undertaken by organizations such as the American Society of Interior Designers and the American

Institute of Architects. The choice of location for shelters and supportive housing – critically important in its consideration of transportation, connectivity to services, and neighborhood acceptance – has been explored in books such as *Homeless Shelter Design: Considerations for Shaping Shelters and The Public Realm* (Graham, Walsh, & Sandalack, 2008). Such site selection considerations will not be deeply explored within these chapters, as the focus here is on the design of the buildings themselves.

Environments for unhoused persons differ in important ways from similarly functional spaces. For example:

- Although day centers, shelters, and supportive housing often serve unhoused persons with mental disabilities, these projects typically require fewer restrictions than in- or out-patient mental facilities. Safety is a higher priority in day centers and shelters than in a typical apartment building, but it is best when such secured facilities look 'normal'. Doing so can reduce the stigma associated with looking too 'institutional'.
- Facilities for unhoused persons must accommodate the great variety of personal and circumstantial characteristics in the populations they serve. The diversity of needs calls for more specialized architectural features than current standard apartment projects offer, such as space plans that help victims of violence feel they would not be accosted from behind and playgrounds for children that are resistant to kidnapping by incensed partners. Sleeping spaces for some populations may call for security-influenced solutions such as partial-wall 'pods' instead of full wall-height apartments.
- The need for proximate support services makes these spaces somewhat akin to refugee centers, yet with more freedom and permeability in their space planning. Support services typically exceed what is offered in a dormitory or apartment complex and can in some cases include medical clinics, barber and beauty shops, training rooms, community gathering spaces, courtrooms, and mailrooms. A more complete discussion of these features is presented in Chapters 7 through 11.

As with all architectural projects, design effectiveness is linked to the extent of support the physical space lends to the host organization's policies. Accordingly, architectural forms for housing and facilities that help unhoused persons have followed the evolution of support approaches in recent decades. For example, the *continuum of care* model that emerged in the 1980s mapped out a pathway for unhoused persons, starting with emergency shelters, moving to transitional shelters for 3–12 months, and then progressing to the destination of supportive housing. Both emergency shelters and supportive housing as distinct types have continued in the United States to the present. However, following the withdrawal of funding by federal and other funders, transitional shelters have largely been discarded in lieu of housing types that follow the *housing first* model, which skips transitional shelters. Housing first (and its variant, *rapid rehousing*) ideally ushers unhoused persons directly from emergency shelters to permanent housing forms (usually apartments) or permanent supportive housing (also usually apartments, but with on-site case managers and similar support services), without barriers to entry such as sobriety, treatment, or service participation requirements (Department of Housing and Urban Development, 2014). Day centers where unhoused persons can study, shower, do laundry, take classes, or engage in other activities are typically open during daylight hours, but may operate alongside night housing. Other housing styles, such as single resident occupancy units (SROs), saw a decrease several decades ago, but are now rebounding somewhat in popularity. These and similar forms are discussed further in Chapters 8, 9, and 11. Specific aspects of architecture and interior design, including site selection, space planning, lighting, color, and product specifications, are discussed in Chapter 7.

ARCHITECTURAL PROJECTS FOR UNHOUSED PERSONS: A PERFECT STORM

This book is premised upon the idea that the design of housing and facilities for unhoused persons must address needs and conditions that do not impact other design projects. These bear mentioning, as the design practitioner should understand from the outset the challenges they may face in undertaking these types of projects:

- Projects that serve unhoused persons can be politically volatile. People disagree as to how unhoused persons should be accommodated and assisted. 'Not in my backyard' (NIMBY) concerns of nearby property owners often emerge, especially during the site selection phase. Political tides can wax and wane, which can compromise partnerships and attract media scrutiny.
- Homelessness becomes more visible to the average citizen in times of greater turmoil and change (Leginski, 2007). The operable outcome is that, when a city realizes it has a problem, it wants a solution right away. This can compress and pressurize project time schedules as organizers move to respond quickly, which can compromise needed learning and reflection time in architectural programming.
- Budgets for projects can be both small and inconsistent, and they are often dependent on continuing grants. Public–private partnerships can increase available funding, yet bring additional (and at times, disparate) voices and priorities to the table.
- With low profit margins, project infrequency, and challenging conditions, architectural and design firms may not have experience or expertise in shelter or supportive housing or day center building types. (Permanent supportive housing is less afflicted by this issue.) The situation causes designers to often reinvent the wheel, or base their decisions on visits to similar projects nearby that may not offer effective solutions.
- Finally, facilities for unhoused persons are often subject to heavy, damaging use by a sometimes crushing number of users. Furnishings, finishes, and

equipment must be capable of withstanding significant abuse that can be exacerbated by users' mental instabilities, yet still must offer an atmosphere that supports the human spirit and is sufficiently acceptable so that people will make use of the facility. Diseases can be spread quickly. Pest infestations such as bedbugs are common, and some facilities must be cleaned multiple times a day.

THE TIMING OF THIS BUILT ENVIRONMENT AND HOMELESSNESS DISCUSSION

Several factors suggest that the timing is right for an examination of the intersection of homelessness recovery and the built environment. At the time of this writing, an acute tension between economic and social forces yields near daily headlines about the inadequacies of housing and similar support facilities in major metropolitan areas throughout the United States. A global refugee crisis is adding pressure on services and housing in many European countries, fostering a stirring of nationalist sentiments echoed by leaders in nations including the United States, Italy, the United Kingdom, and Turkey, to name but a few. Politicians' emphasis on corporations' success ahead of that of private citizens has led to a surge in income inequality. The minimum wage continues to fall relative to a rising cost of living, leading persons on the margins to lose their homes, while the gentrification of cities incentivizes landlords to evict. Rent-controlled apartments in high-cost cities are becoming a thing of the past (Barker, Silver-Greenberg, Ashford, & Cohen, 2018). Compounding these issues, the COVID-19 virus pandemic has made health conditions for people in crisis worse, especially as places people in crisis access and inhabit often compel close human contact. Taken together, these and similar forces are concentrating the public's focus on homelessness and a search for viable solutions.

Meanwhile, research in the fields of neuroscience, cognitive psychology, social work, and related areas are shedding light on the perceptions and motivations that can afflict unhoused persons, including how scarcity affects their reasoning, and hormone imbalances impair judgement. Research is confirming that adverse childhood experiences, including those associated with lack of shelter, may affect a person throughout their adult life, affecting decision-making and their ability to be a fully actualized individual (Centers for Disease Control and Prevention, 2016). These and similar discoveries are starting to establish a baseline of knowledge about mental and behavioral health issues associated with homelessness.

It is also now well understood that physical places are a social and physical determinant of health (Office of Disease Prevention and Health Promotion, 2018; Shepley & Pasha, 2017), and yet research is only now starting to address what this means for the design of the built environment. Some design and health organizations are moving to fill this gap, such as the Center for Health Design and the National Center for Complex Health and Social Needs, which has held national conferences to confront co-occurring issues such as poverty, discrimination, healthcare, and crime that many unhoused persons face (Needs, 2017). Creative fields, including architecture and interior architecture/design, are turning their attention to strategies for promoting human well-being. Among the products of this movement is the WELL Building Standard, a voluntary building certification system that identifies and confirms the links between built environment features and human health, such as air and water quality, light, human movement, and the ability to sense and build community (International Well Building Institute, 2017). The WELL Building Standard's intersections with built environments for unhoused persons are discussed in Chapter 6.

This book is also well timed for the ongoing evolution within the social work and psychology practitioner communities that develop and advocate therapies and care strategies for unhoused persons. What was once an accepted practice of top–down, authoritative methods of governing interactions with persons who have lost their homes has now largely been discredited. Taking its place is the concept of trauma-informed care marked by an approach of empowerment, internal motivation, and lower-barrier entry to support services (Substance Abuse and Mental Health Services Administration, 2014). Notably, the built environment has been identified as one factor of opportunity in trauma-informed care principles. A similar philosophy termed psychologically informed environments is now emerging in the United Kingdom, which also counts physical environment among its tools for healing (Keats, Maguire, Johnson, & Cockersell, 2012). Chapter 6 discusses the ramifications of these movements for built environments.

Prompted by the 24/7 news media cycle, the availability of social media, and a heightened visibility of social ills, groups and movements are now emerging that are targeting societal shortcomings that affect people of lower economic means. Poverty, income inequality, water shortages, natural disasters, the environment, health emergencies, and homelessness are among these issues. Early and prominent among them was the 2011 Occupy Movement, whose slogan "We are the 99%" sought to bring attention to growing income equality in the United States and other countries. At the time of this writing, the Black Lives Matter movement is successfully shining a light on long-standing inequities and mortal dangers that Black and African American persons face on a regular basis.

Within the design fields, awareness has grown about the need for practitioners to provide services for people other than the wealthy, marked, for example, by a 2007 Smithsonian Cooper-Hewitt National Design Museum exhibit entitled "Design for the Other 90%" in New York City (Smithsonian Cooper-Hewitt National Design Museum, 2018). Other movements have also gained ground, including the SEED Network (2020), the Design Other 90 Network (Smithsonian Cooper-Hewitt Design Museum, 2020), Auburn University's Rural Studio (Takepart, 2018), and Design Corps (Spatial Agency, 2020). More broadly, discussions around specialized design subfields, variably called public design, social design, or social betterment design, are engaging people through conferences, publications, and group action. A certain sense of anxiousness and urgency permeates these efforts. In 2018, for example, the group What Design Can Do launched a series of events in Amsterdam, São Paulo, and Mexico, broadly aimed at a diverse array of social issues including climate change, sex trafficking, and clean energy, recognizing that "the power of design and creativity [can] transform society," and that "money, governments or science can't solve complex global issues on their own" (What Design Can Do, n.d., para. 1). Specific to intersections of homelessness and the potential of design, the 2018 Design Week Portland event in Oregon offered a gathering called "Homelessness is Not Normal," asserting that "design can "help to lead the way" (Portland Design Week, 2018).

As further evidence of the rising awareness of design for all and its movement into the mainstream, architect Shigeru Ban was awarded the Pritzker Prize in 2014 for his work on the design of inexpensive temporary housing for refugees. Noted Ban, "architects are not building temporary housing because we are too busy building for the privileged people. … I'm not saying I'm against building monuments, but I'm thinking we can work more for the public" (Pogrebin, 2014, para. 11). Two years later, the 2016 Pritzker Prize was awarded to Alejandro Aravena, architect creator of 'half-houses', deliberately partially completed homes in Chile that invite low-income residents to finish the work by themselves (Rhodes, 2016).

These global and local events, organizations, recognitions, and publications point to the growing realization that design practitioners are no longer content to sit on the sidelines, waiting for clients to discover the innovative solutions that design can bring to social problems. Rather, the age is marked by a certain restlessness with inaction on the part of governments and other influential groups. Innovation characterizes this age of grassroots, experimental design solutions, detailed in Chapter 13. Time will tell which direction will take hold and make effective inroads into addressing homelessness. This book intends to aid this process, bringing clarity and research-bolstered knowledge to the table in service to the unhoused, who are arguably the neediest among us.

THE CASE FOR AN EXAMINATION OF MIDDLE- AND HIGH-INCOME COUNTRIES' RESPONSES

Homelessness is indiscriminate in its affliction of high-, middle-, and low-income countries. As authors, we have made the conscious choice to confine this book's content to architectural design and homelessness as it exists in middle- and high-income countries. This is for several reasons. First, as noted above, the definitions of homelessness vary significantly with cultural norms (United Nations Human Rights Council, 2015), which complicates the process of discussing acceptability of built environments at the global level. One country's bamboo lean-to structures may be perfectly acceptable climatically and culturally, whereas such structures would be entirely inappropriate in other places. Second is that relative wealth in middle- and high-income areas yields more resources and ideas to which we might respond, and more research and media evidence exists from which to identify and evaluate design ideas. Third, middle- and high-income countries hold together as a group more cohesively in their cultural living expectations, available building materials, and the like, permitting comparisons and discussions that may move the collective dialogue forward. You must, of course, start somewhere, and we sense that progress made may eventually influence lower-income settings as well. Researchers are not turning their backs on the deeply troubling global refugee populations that too often live in substandard temporary camps; this topic is receiving attention in other recent and ongoing projects (Bianchi & Hedenskog, 2016; Jacobson, Bruderlein, Pollock, & Weizman, 2014). Regarding this related but separate discussion, we do wish to share our uneasiness about any suggestion that refugee camps should be made permanent. As with the forms of homelessness that we address in this book, refugees must be met with programs and housing solutions that recognize individual dignity and effect a rapid and effective transition into the full expression of civic life.

THE READERS AND NEEDS THIS BOOK ADDRESSES

There are many books about homelessness, including those that discuss therapy methods, others that offer deeply moving personal narratives, and books that analyze historical and current assistance policies. This book focuses on the nature, potential, and practical strategies of the design of homes and related facilities constructed to assist unhoused persons so that they can recover quickly and effectively. It is an outgrowth of the work of the non-profit organization Design Resources for Homelessness, created and facilitated by this book's first author. Its website (designresourcesforhomelessness.org) offers research-informed information including case studies of successful design projects, research summaries, databases of design practitioners, and model projects. This book is a companion to this website information and serves the same purpose, yet expands on its ideas in a more comprehensive fashion. Specifically, this book's intent is fourfold:

- To act as a curator and translator of research-based information, making available and accessible practical information that can be applied to new and renovation building projects to increase their effectiveness.
- To serve as a catalyst for new connections across disciplines and among practitioners, support organizations, and researchers who share the same purpose of improving the lived experience of unhoused persons as they exit their crisis.
- To offer researchers and advanced students a launching pad into extended in-depth inquiry, providing a useful collection of orientation materials, analyses, overview of emerging theories and frameworks, and bibliography for further use.
- To examine, for the first time, the architectural responses to homelessness at a global scale spanning middle- and high-income countries on multiple continents, with the express intent of sharing good ideas more effectively.

With these goals as a springboard, we have crafted this book to be useful to a variety of readers:

- *Design practitioners and project consultants*: Architects, interior architects/designers, graphic and other design practitioners, product specifiers, consultants in environmental psychology and social work, and others engaged in architectural projects that seek to assist unhoused persons.
- *Support/advocacy organizations*: Groups that are renovating or building new housing and/or facilities including permanent supportive housing, day centers, and shelters.
- *Researchers*: Scholars in fields ranging from architecture and interior architecture/design to those in environmental psychology, social work, communications, and facilities management, and others such as epidemiologists and physicians who interface with the needs of unhoused persons and the built spaces that support them.
- *Students and educators*: Learners and educators seeking to expand their understanding of public design or to engage in design work in this area. The interior design higher education accreditation organization Council for Interior Design Accreditation (CIDA) requires that design educators expose their students to how social and economic contexts inform design decisions, which may include "human responses to hardship and stress" (Council for Interior Design Accreditation, 2018, p. 16). The National Architectural Accrediting Board (NAAB) requires that students understand that architectural design can create a civilized place by making communities more livable (National Architectural Accrediting Board, 2015).
- *Policy makers*: Leaders in governmental and other contexts at national, state, county, or city levels who face the challenges of supporting unhoused persons in their midst and interface with support organizations that lend this aid.

The challenges presented by homelessness are significant. As an important element of a necessarily wide societal response, the architecture and interior design of shelters, service centers, transitional housing, and other related facilities should effectively anticipate and accommodate a diverse array of users' needs. To that end, the creators of such housing must understand these requirements and challenges and be prepared to integrate that understanding into their designs. In the words of Buckminster Fuller, "You never change things by fighting the existing reality. To change something, build a new model that makes the existing model obsolete" (Sieden, 2011, p. 358). The existing reality of homelessness must be changed. This book seeks to provide a needed context in which designers, support organizations, researchers, and others may base their most important work – effectively helping those who arguably need it the most.

NOTES

1. Following the lead of other sources in the homelessness literature, this book will avoid referring to people with the label of 'homeless person', but will instead adhere to less stigma-inducing terms such as a 'person experiencing loss of housing' or an 'unhoused

person'. Although the distinction may seem small, the intent is to avoid having one's very identity altered and harnessed with an inalterable new state laced with the sense of want and failure.

2. In this book, we will use the terminology of low-, middle-, and high-income countries instead of 'first-world' and 'third-world' countries in an effort to avoid the stereotyping this confers. Arguably, calling developing countries 'third-world' is insulting and was a dated system that imprecisely grouped the U.S., Western Europe, and their allies into 'first-world', the Communist Bloc countries into 'second-world', and the remaining nations were assigned to 'third-world' (Silver, 2015).

3. The Institute on Global Homelessness was initiated in 2014 (www.ighomelessness.org/) as a partnership of DePaul University and DePaul International. It is hoped that its mission of supporting an emerging global movement to end homelessness may at last reckon with its frequency and distribution.

BIBLIOGRAPHY

Angelou, M. (1993). *Wouldn't take nothing for my journey now*. New York: Random House.

Barker, K., Silver-Greenberg, J., Ashford, G., & Cohen, S. (2018, May 20). The eviction machine churning through New York City. *New York Times*.

Bianchi, M., & Hedenskog, L. (2016, January 1). *What home is for a refugee without one*. (IKEA, Producer) Retrieved April 28, 2018, from IKEA Highlights 2016: www.ikea.com/ms/en_US/this-is-ikea/ikea-highlights/Home-for-a-refugee/index.html

Centers for Disease Control and Prevention. (2016). *Adverse Childhood Experiences (ACEs)*. Retrieved 28 2018, April, from Violence Prevention: www.cdc.gov/violenceprevention/acestudy/index.html

Chiland, E. (2017, August 16). *LA County will pay homeowners to build granny flats for the homeless*. (V. Media, Producer) Retrieved May 29, 2018, from Curbed Los Angeles: https://la.curbed.com/2017/8/16/16157282/los-angeles-homeless-housing-accessory-dwelling-granny-flat

Clapham, D. (2017). *Accommodating difference: evaluating supported housing for vulnerable people*. Bristol, UK: Policy Press.

Cooper-Hewitt National Design Museum. (2018, May 29). *Design for the other 90%*. Retrieved May 29, 2018, from Design for the other 90%: http://archive.cooperhewitt.org/other90/other90.cooperhewitt.org/about/index.html

Corra, R. (2015, September 3). *The effect of poverty, poor sanitation, unclean water, and hunger on the world*. Retrieved June 1, 2018, from Loss of human intellectual potential: https://www.linkedin.com/pulse/loss-human-intellectual-potential-rob-corra/

Council for Interior Design Accreditation. (2018, January 1). *Professional standards 2018*. Retrieved May 30, 2018, from Council for Interior Design Accreditation: https://accredit-id.org/wp-content/uploads/2018/01/Professional-Standards-2018_Final.pdf

Crothers, J. (2018, March 14). Homelessness growing worse in Australia, census data shows. *ABC News Online*. Melbourne, Australia.

Davis, S. (2004). *Designing for the homeless: architecture that works*. Oakland, CA: University of California Press.

Department of Housing and Urban Development. (2014). *Housing first in permanent supportive housing*. Department of Housing and Urban Development, HUDExchange. Washington, DC: Department of Housing and Urban Development.

Firth, P. (2014, January 1). *Homelessness and academic achievement: the impact of childhood stress on school performance*. Retrieved June 1, 2018, from Firesteel: http://firesteelwa.org/2014/09/homelessness-and-academic-achievement-the-impact-of-childhood-stress-onschool-performance/

Frontline. (2005, May 10). *Deinstitutionalization: a psychiatric "Titanic."* (WGBH Educational Foundation) Retrieved June 1, 2018, from Frontline: www.pbs.org/wgbh/pages/frontline/shows/asylums/special/excerpt.html

Get Domestic Violence Help. (2018). *Domestic violence success stories*. Retrieved June 8, 2018, from Get Domestic Violence Help: www.getdomesticviolencehelp.com/domestic-violence-success-stories.html

Graham, J. R., Walsh, C., & Sandalack, B. (2008). *Homeless shelter design: considerations for shaping shelters and the public realm*. Calgary, Alberta, Canada: Detselig Enterprises.

Gumbel, A. (2018, March 16). The sorriest urban scene: why a US homelessness crisis drags on. From *The Guardian, Los Angeles Outside in America*. Retrieved April 28, 2018, from: www.theguardian.com/us-news/2018/mar/16/us-homelessness-crisis-los-angeles-politicians

Hillard, G. (2018, June 1). *Women of LA's skid row tell their stories through the anger, despair on their faces*. (N. P. Edition, Producer) Retrieved June 1, 2018, from National Public Radio National: www.npr.org/2018/06/01/614455357/women-of-las-skid-row-tell-their-stories-through-the-anger-despair-on-their-face

Homeless Hub. (2017, 1 1). *How many people are homeless in Canada?* Retrieved May 28, 2018, from Homeless Hub: www.homelesshub.ca/about-homelessness/homelessness-101/how-many-people-are-homeless-canada

Homeless Link. (2018). *Statutory homelessness data October–December 2017 (Q4)*. Homeless Link. London: Homeless Link.

Homeless Shelter Directory. (2018, January 1). *More about our directory*. Retrieved May 29, 2018, from Homeless Shelter Directory: www.homelessshelterdirectory.org/

Institute on Global Homelessness. (2017, January 1). *Regions*. (I. o. Homelessness, Producer) Retrieved May 29, 2018, from IGHub: https://ighhub.org/regions

International Well Building Institute. (2017, January 1). *Welcome to WELL v2*. Retrieved June 1, 2018, from International WELL Building Institute: www.wellcertified.com/

Jacobson, H.Z., Bruderlein, C., Pollock, N., & Weizman, E. (2014). *Humanitarian architecture*. New York: Artbook.

Jencks, C. (1994, June 13). *Perspective on homelessness*. Retrieved June 1, 2018, from *Los Angeles Times*: http://articles.latimes.com/1994-06-13/local/me-3543_1_daytime-homelessness

Joint Center for Housing Studies of Harvard University. (2010). *The state of the nation's housing 2010*. Harvard University, Graduate School of Design. New York: President and Fellows of Harvard College.

Keats, H., Maguire, N., Johnson, R., & Cockersell, P. (2012). *Psychologically informed services for homeless people*. Department for Communities and Local Government. Southampton, UK: Spy Design & Publishing.

Kusmer, K. (2001). *Down and out, on the road: the homeless in American history*. New York: Oxford University Press.

Leginski, W. (2007). Historical and contextual influences on the U.S. response to contemporary homelessness. In G. L. Deborah Dennis (Ed.), *Toward understanding homelessness: the 2007 national symposium on homelessness research* (pp. 1-1–1-36). Washington, DC: Department of Health and Human Services and U.S. Department of Housing and Urban Development.

Loudenback, T. (2017, March 12). Crazy-high rent, record-low homeownership, and overcrowding: California has a plan to solve the housing crisis, but not without a fight. *Business Insider*.

Moorhead, M. (2012, January 1). *HUD secretary says a homeless person costs taxpayers $40,000 a year*. Retrieved June 1, 2018, from Politifact: www.politifact.com/truth-o-meter/statements/2012/mar/12/shaun-donovan/hud-secretary-says-homeless-person-costs-taxpayers/

Mullainathan, S., & Shafir, E. (2013). *Scarcity: why having too little means so much*. New York: Henry Holt.

National Alliance to End Homelessness. (2017, November 3). *Homelessness and the opioid crisis: background, funding and resources*. (N. A. Homelessness, Producer) Retrieved June 1, 2018, from Resources: https://endhomelessness.org/resource/homelessness-opioid-crisis-background-funding-resources/

National Architectural Accrediting Board. (2015). *Procedures for Accreditation*. Washington, D.C.: National Architectural Accrediting Board.

National Center for Complex Health and Social Needs. (2017, January 1). *What is complex care?* (N. C. Needs, Producer) Retrieved May 29, 2018, from National Center for Complex Health and Social Needs: www.nationalcomplex.care/our-work/what-is-complex-care/

National Coalition for the Homeless. (2018, January 1). *Employment and income*. Retrieved June 1, 2018, from Building a movement to end homelessness: http://nationalhome-less.org/issues/economic-justice/

National Health Care for the Homeless Council. (2018, January 1). *What is the relationship between health, housing and homelessness?* Retrieved June 1, 2018, from National Health Care for the Homeless Council: www.nhchc.org/faq/relationship-health-housing-homelessness/

National Low Income Housing Coalition. (2018, January 1). *The gap: a shortage of affordable rental homes*. (N. L. Coalition, Producer) Retrieved June 1, 2018, from No state has an adequate supply of affordable rental housing for the lowest income renters: http://nlihc.org/gap?smid=nytcore-ios-share

Needs, N. C. (2017, January 1). *A relationship-based approach can transform health care*. Retrieved April 28, 2018, from www.nationalcomplex.care/

Office of Disease Prevention and Health Promotion. (2018). *Determinants of health*. (U.S. Department of Health and Human Services) Retrieved 28 2018, April, from Healthypeople.gov: www.healthypeople.gov/2020/about/foundation-health-measures/determinants-of-health

Phippen, J. W. (2016, December 5). What caused the deadly Oakland warehouse fire? *The Atlantic*, p. 1.

Pogrebin, R. (2014, March 24). Pritzker Architecture Prize goes to Shigeru Ban. *New York Times*.

Portland Design Week (2018, April 18). *Homelessness is not normal*. Retrieved April 28, 2018, from Design Week Portland: www.designweekportland.com/events/homelessness-is-not-normal

Rhodes, M. (2016, January 13). *Get to know Alejandro Aravena, the Pritzker Prize winner who builds half-finished homes*. Retrieved May 30, 2018, from Wired: www.wired.com/2016/01/get-to-know-alejandro-aravena-this-years-pritzker-prize-winner/

Routheir, G. (2018, January 1). *State of the homeless 2018*. Retrieved May 29, 2018, from Coalition for the Homeless: www.coalitionforthehomeless.org/state-of-the-homeless-2018/

Shepley, M. M., & Pasha, S. (2017). *Design for Mental and Behavioral Health*. London: Routledge.

SEED Network. (2020). Design for the common good. Pacific Rim Community Design Network. Retrieved November 5, 2020: https://seednetwork.org/design

Silver, M. (2015, January 4). *If you shouldn't call it the third world, what should you call it?* (N. P. Radio, Producer) Retrieved June 1, 2018, from Goats and Soda: Stories of life in a changing world: www.npr.org/sections/goatsandsoda/2015/01/04/372684438/if-you-shouldnt-call-it-the-third-world-what-should-you-call-it

Smithsonian Cooper Hewitt Design Museum. (2020). Design Other 90 Network. Retrieved November 5, 2020: www.designother90.org/

Spatial Agency. (November 8, 2020). Design Corps. Retrieved November 8.2020 from http://spatialagency.net/database/design.corps

Substance Abuse and Mental Health Services Administration. (2014, January 1). *SAMHSA's concept of trauma and guidance for a trauma-informed approach*. SAMHSA, SAMHSA Trauma and Justice Strategic Initiative. Rockville, MD: SAMHSA.

Takepart. (2018, May 29). *This $20K house makes homeownership possible for the impoverished*. (Takepart, Producer, & Participant Media) Retrieved May 29, 2018, from Takepart: www.takepart.com/article/2014/01/03/rural-studio-auburn-university-affordable-housing-impoverished

Torrey, E. F. (2008). *Out of the shadows: confronting America's mental illness crisis*. New York: Wiley.

U.S. Conference of Mayors. (2016). *U.S. Conference of Mayors' Report on Hunger and Homelessness*. New York: U.S. Conference of Mayors.

Ubelacker, S. (2018, May 3). Homeless have a much shorter life expectancy, study suggests. *The Globe and Mail*. Retrieved June 1, 2018, from: www.theglobeandmail.com/news/national/homeless-have-a-much-shorter-life-expectancy-study-suggests/article1204019/

United Nationals Educational, Scientific and Cultural Organization and Centre de Sciences Humaines. (2011). *Urban policies and the right to the city in India*. New Delhi: UNESCO House.

United Nations Human Rights Council. (2015). *Report of the Special Rapporteur on adequate housing as a component of the right to an adequate standard of living, and on the right to non-discrimination in this context*. United Nations, General Assembly. New York: United Nations.

van der Ryn, S. (2005). *Design for life: the architecture of Sim Van der Ryn*. Layton, UT: Gibbs Smith.

What Design Can Do. (n.d.). *Who we are: new ideas for a better world*. Retrieved from What Design Can Do: www.whatdesigncando.com/about-wdcd/

TEACHING MATERIALS

Lauren Trujillo

Key Terms

Built environments
Continuum of care
Day centers
Housing first
"Living rough"
Permanent supportive housing
Person experiencing a loss of housing

Psychologically informed
   environments
Rapid rehousing
Single residency units (SROs)
Trauma-informed care
Unhoused person

Discussion Questions

1. Prior to reading the author's explanation of the confluence of factors that may lead someone to lose their home, what did you think was the main cause of homelessness? If applicable, how has your opinion of people in this situation changed after reading this chapter?
2. In your community, do you see persons experiencing a loss of housing? Every community is different.
   a. Do you believe it is a result of unaffordable housing, suboptimal community support, ineffective policies, or some other cause or combination of causes? Discuss your beliefs.
   b. Based on your current level of understanding, describe one strategy you believe would assist this situation.
   c. Do you know how your community interfaces with, assists, or represents this group of people? If so, do you think this approach is effective? If you do not know, how could you find out?
3. The author of this chapter writes, "homelessness becomes more visible to the average citizen in times of greater turmoil and change." Do you think that homelessness is more visible in your community now than it has been in the past? Why or why not?
4. In this overview, the author introduced several topics such as the reasons for homelessness, responses to homelessness, and the effects on the people experiencing homelessness, as well as the community at large.
   a. Which of these topics do you have pre-existing knowledge of or familiarity with?
   b. Which ones do you know very little about?

This chapter provided an overview of homelessness and the potential of design. Discuss gaps in knowledge on this subject that you want to learn more about.

2 A Short History of Homelessness and its Architectural Responses

Yelena McLane

Knowledge of the past helps us to identify how contemporary strategies for addressing homelessness might be based upon flawed systems and inherited assumptions. The historical contexts of homelessness – its causes, popular attitudes towards it, government policies intended to address it, and architectural responses to those policies – must then be our starting point. Through much of Western history, *homelessness* was thought of as a social malady extending from extreme poverty. The concomitant view of *homeless persons* as extrinsic others who ran a "disorderly course of life" (Vagrancy, n.d.) is reflected in the myriad epithets by which they have been referred: beggars, bums, idlers, indigents, itinerants, drifters, tramps, floaters, hobos, wanderers, rolling stones, mendicants, vagrants, and vagabonds. These terms invoke varying senses of geographic mobility, itinerant labor, alternative lifestyle choices, criminality, and overall low economic status reflecting the extent to which the "the construction of modern states and imperial structures [led to] the formation of subcultures among the poor, rapidity of urbanization, and responses to poverty through welfare, charity, and prosecution" (Ocobock, 2008, p. 2). Today, the word *homeless* covers an array of problems associated with poverty and need, including "social dislocation, extreme poverty, seasonal and itinerant work, and unconventional ways of life" (Hopper & Baumohl, 1996, p. 3). Since the early 1980s, the word *homelessness* has generally referred to a condition of extreme poverty that leads persons to being unhoused (i.e., "on the streets") or to live in overcrowded shelter-like accommodations or itinerant tent camps (Hulchanski, 2009). The marked evolution of the interrelationship of homelessness and larger societal forms over time led us to organize this chapter around five economic periods: the pre-industrial era, the industrial era, the modern period of the first half of the twentieth century, the "service economy" of the second half of the twentieth century, and the "human economy," which continues into our time.

Each major wave of homelessness is associated with a period during which geographic regions and countries undergo significant economic and social changes. Proceeding chronologically through the perceived causes of and responses to homelessness reveals the structural and individual factors that unify and distinguish the periods (Beck & Twiss, 2018). Structural factors include institutional laws, customs, and rules of behavior that define a society, which may be rooted in religion, government policies, economics, popular attitudes towards welfare, and access to education and healthcare services. Individual factors include the state of one's mental health, the extent to which one's habits of personal responsibility, industriousness, or virtuousness affect moral standing (both in one's own eyes and in others' eyes), and the direct economic or social consequences of behaviors perceived as vices (e.g., inconstancy, drinking to excess) or extending from idleness or physical weakness (Coleman & Fopp, 2014). A combination of factors led to policy and legal responses – from criminalization (subjecting individuals to incarceration and compulsory labor), to providing temporary seasonal employment for a minimal wage, to pathologizing the phenomenon by treating individuals as an afflicted subclass to be managed by governmental, religious, or charitable organizations (Ocobock, 2008; Whitehead, 2013; Willse, 2015). Attitudes and policies towards the poor and homeless in turn prompted architectural responses tied to these organizations and their institutional goals, management styles, and rules.

Henri LeFebvre (1984) advanced the notion that architectural spaces were manifestations of ideology. Bill Hillier and Julienne Hanson, in *The Social Logic of Space* (1988), further asserted that built environments reflect existing social structures, arranging "space by means of buildings, boundaries, paths, markets, zones, and so on, so that the physical milieu of that society also takes on a definite pattern" (p. 27), planning and constructing "physical environments and spatial forms" towards more "efficient, pleasurable, and supportive" functions (p. 28). Michael Foucault (1995) explored the nature of power and surveillance that determined the design of prisons and broader society (Piro, 2008). Building upon this body of research, we assert that architectural responses to homelessness – from historical workhouses, almshouses, and casual wards to contemporary shelters and transitional housing – reflect the economic values, public perceptions (both informed and uninformed), moral priorities, and welfare-related social science that, in combination, motivate a community to take action.[1]

In this chapter, we briefly recount attitudes towards homelessness reflected in historical "poor laws," policies, and social welfare practices in England (later the United Kingdom), the United States, Canada, Australia, New Zealand, and South Africa, which in turn manifested in specific and instructive architectural forms.

THE PRE-INDUSTRIAL ERA

The English Old Poor Law and Parish-Based Systems of Poor Support

The history of poverty goes hand in hand with the history of homelessness. Both extend from related conditions: macroeconomics (depression, recession, disease or famine leading to mass itinerancy); compromised individual or collective social or financial status (systemic racism, disinheritance, loss of a means of subsisting); and the personal inability to work due to physical infirmity or psychological problems (Mollat, 1986, pp. 5–6). In medieval Europe, poverty was widespread and perceived as a common and inescapable condition (Beck & Twiss, 2018; Mollat, 1986; Ocobock, 2008).

Homelessness was primarily an urban phenomenon in medieval Europe. In the countryside, feudal landlords were dependent upon their vassals and responsible for taking care of the needy. Judaism and Christianity emphasized charity and collectivity, obligating the faithful to support the most vulnerable. Towards the end of the twelfth century, economies shifted away from barter-based gift and service exchanges to transactions based on cash. A significant population increase accompanied this shift, particularly in towns (Little, 1983). Towns offered more opportunities, but the risk of misfortune was greater, especially at the bottom of the urban economy, where work was low-paying and irregular (Little, 1983, p. 28). This, together with frequent food shortages, made vagrancy a common feature of urban communities.

The weakening of feudal support structures, combined with a general recognition among elites that growing populations of the desperately poor posed a threat to "social order," prompted the ecclesiastical, aristocratic, and merchant classes to enlist these individuals into specific economic services or assume direct financial responsibility for those most in need. One early English law was the Act for the Relief of the Poor (the Elizabethan Poor Act, or "Old Poor Law") from 1601, which recognized how poverty went hand in hand with economic issues such as low wages and unemployment.

The Old Poor Law regulated laborers' movement and wages and compelled work. Premised on the notion that individuals were morally culpable for their hardships, Poor Laws found one's ability (or inability) to work determinative of one's "worthiness to receive aid from others," whether the person was "unfit for work, unable to find work, or unwilling to engage in work" (Mollat, 1986, p. 295). Categories emerged – the "worthy" poor (unable to work and, therefore, deserving of alms) and the "unworthy" poor (unemployed, able-bodied individuals undeserving of assistance; Beck & Twiss, 2018). For able-bodied beggars, failing to work was a crime meriting harsh punishment (Beck & Twiss, 2018, p. 16).

The Old Poor Law placed the responsibility on local parishes to finance, support, and care for the sick and destitute (Morrison, 1999). Those who could not care for themselves and had nowhere to live had to seek help in bridewells (prisons for petty offenders), almshouses (homes for the "worthy poor"), or infirmaries (hospitals for the sick or lame). These were typically repurposed structures away from public view, down back streets, at the edge of town, or in the country. Their dour appearances reflected the Poor Law's intent to punish those who refused to work while providing a bare minimum to the worthy poor (Beck & Twiss, 2018). The architecture of new workhouses and almshouses was plain and functional, although larger institutions in prominent areas at times assumed the "formality and the pretension of grandeur" of contemporary civic architecture (Morrison, 1999, p. 3). Interiors were basic and often did not allow for the supervision or control of inmates or for health considerations such as heat or ventilation.[2]

The Destitute and the Indigenous People in the Colonies

Expansion of European economic interests through overseas colonialism offered one solution for endemic poverty. Having begun as opportunities for the pursuit of wealth, colonies soon faced the same problems of how to address the old, injured, and desti-tute. American, Australian, and New Zealand colonists modeled their responses on the Elizabethan Poor Act (Coleman & Fopp, 2014; Meltsner, 2012; Memmott & Nash, 2016; Ocobock, 2008). The abundance of land needing cultivation and a correspondingly high demand for laborers, when combined with a Protestant ethic emphasizing hard work, thrift, prudence (Howard, 1791), and efficiency (Webber, 2003), prompted particularly harsh treatment of the poor and unemployed. Idleness was treated as a moral failing and crime against the community. St. Paul's admonition that "he who will not work shall not eat" informed many approaches to public aid, which, when given at all, was given reluctantly and only to the "worthiest" (and almost exclusively white) residents (Beck & Twiss, 2018; Meltsner, 2012). Receipt of such charity was a personal shame accepted only as a last resort.

Colonial authorities treated Native Americans and the indigenous peoples of Canada, Australia, and New Zealand as outsiders to be displaced or conquered (Ocobock, 2008; Christensen, 2016). Forced from their lands and confronted with aggressive policies aimed at dismantling traditional lifestyles, many indigenous people were left without a means of supporting themselves. White colonizers also imposed their views and morals, including the notion that poverty, idleness, and homelessness (even when the direct result of military-enforced dislocation) reflected low morals. Policy responses towards indigenous people found wandering or idle ranged from neglect, to monitoring by law enforcement, to forced con-struction work on projects run by government entities or private land developers (Coleman & Fopp, 2014, p. 13; Ocobock, 2008, p. 14).

Similarly, in colonial Africa, poverty and homelessness were rooted in the history of land use and agrarian community practices (Morrow, 2010). The indig-enous Khoikhoi people lost their cattle and hunting lands to the colonizers in the late 1700s and were forced to work for Dutch and English landowners to survive (Atmore & Marks, 1974). In response to labor shortages and the need to control vagrancy, local authorities in the Cape Colony controlled movements of enslaved indigenous persons and new European migrants by instituting "pass laws" in the early eighteenth century. Travel between towns and settlements required a writ-ten pass from local authorities (South African History Online, 2011). As a result, during the pre-industrial era, vagrancy and homelessness among white, black, and other ethnic populations in South Africa went unnoticed. After the official emancipation of slaves in 1834, the Cape government proposed a Vagrancy Act, nominally forbidding any form of "vagrancy," but in essence benefitting large-scale farmers by securing a labor supply under a purported policy of crime control (Watson, 2012). Although this formal ordinance was ultimately rejected, other laws led to similar results.

THE INDUSTRIAL ERA

English New Poor Law and Workhouses

In the nineteenth century, the increase of wealth in industrialized Britain and the colonies only exacerbated the problems of poverty and vagrancy (Ocobock, 2008). Conventional wisdom held that, "the moral depravity of the poorest class" was at the root of this social ailment (Jordan, 1974). The Poor Law Amendment Act of 1834, referred to in its time as the "New Poor Law," was, despite its name, fundamentally based upon the Old Poor Law of 1601. Influenced by the writings of Poor Law Commissioner George Nicholls and the Rev. John Thomas Becher, the New Poor Law ensured that only the most destitute would be admitted to a shelter or offered help (Ocobock, pp. 2, 6–9). Parishes were compelled to pool funds and build workhouses rather than support individuals with food, fuel, and clothing. Hundreds of facilities became part of a unified government scheme coordinated from London. Some established under the Old Poor Law were retained, and many new "model" workhouses, such as the 1824 workhouse in the town of Southwell, were built to purpose (see 2.1).

These were managed by category of inmates, with adults divided into those unable to work (the "blameless") and those capable of work but unemployed (the "idle and profligate able-bodied"; Meltsner, 2012, p. 7; Morrison, 1999, p. 120; National Trust, n.d.). Inmates were further segregated by sex. Each received food, clothes, and lodgings in exchange for some kind of work, including tedious chores such as breaking rocks, grinding bones, or "picking oakum" (unknotting old tar-soaked ropes). Children stayed in isolated dormitories away from their families and received a rudimentary education while also working. This intentionally harsh regime was intended to yield both "moral" and physiological improvement. It was widely believed that "motivating" the poor to pursue all avenues of self-support before seeking charity would save the person from degeneracy.[3]

Despite the ostensibly charitable nature of workhouses, living conditions were similar to those in prisons. Spatial layouts originated in late eighteenth-century prison buildings in which inmate segregation was a means of regulating behavior and maintaining control. Visual and physical access from a central location to as many spaces as possible prompted three main architectural approaches: the courtyard, radial, and corridor plans (Morrison, 1999).[4] This also allowed for efficient surveillance and upkeep with as few resources as possible.

Whereas workhouses provided long-term accommodations for poor vagrants, casual wards served as short-term shelters (typically for a single night) and provided

2.1
The workhouse in the town of Southwell, England, 1824, designed by the architect William Adams Nicholson and the Rev. John Thomas Beecher to accommodate up to 158 inmates from 62 regional parishes. The building was called "Beecher's Workhouse" through much of the nineteenth century and the "Greet House" in the twentieth century.

2.2

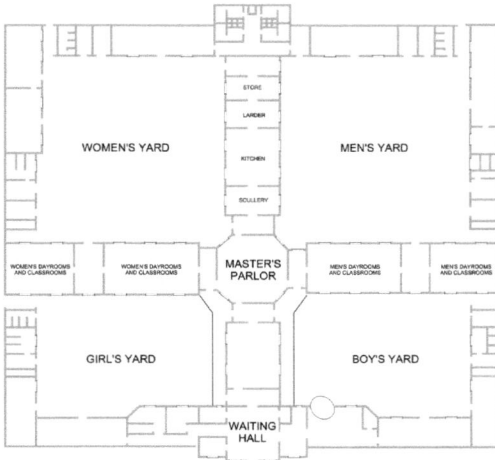

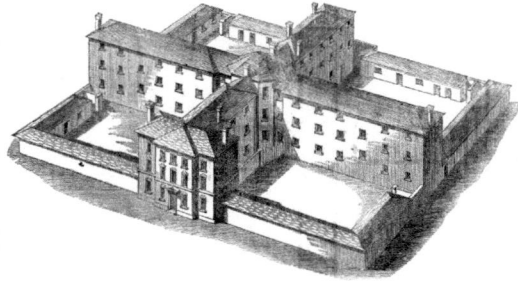

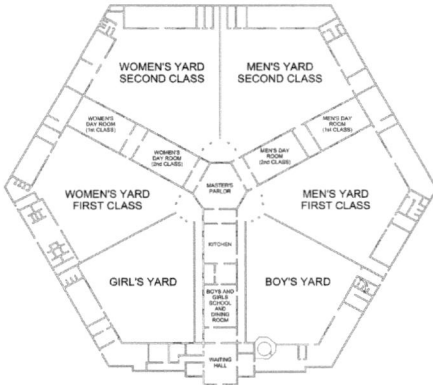

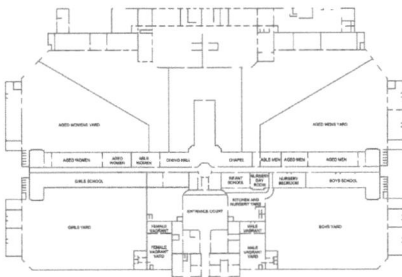

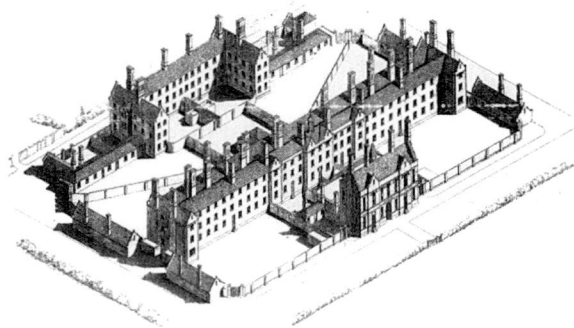

Workhouse types: courtyard plan and radial plan (also called y-plan) developed by architect Sampson Kempthorne (typical for the first half of nineteenth-century England) and corridor plan by the architect R. P. Browne for the Greenwich Union Workhouse, ca. 1840 (later Saint Alfege's hospital).

a meal for the "casuals" (including itinerants and wayfarers) in exchange for work. Many urban homeless preferred these basic accommodations to workhouses (Rosen, 2012), even though they had to wait outside until spaces became available. Men and women were separated, sleeping in large rooms with two inclined straw-strewn boards on either side with a passage in the middle (Henry Mayhew, as cited in Rosen, 2012). Sometimes those admitted had to bathe before going to the dormitories.

2.3
Luke Fildes,
Applicants for Admission to a Casual Ward (1874).

The system was based on shaming and fear. Although able adults could leave the workhouse at will, with no means to support themselves most chose to remain (Morrison, 1999). Towards the end of the century, the conditions deteriorated further. According to an influential 1909 Poor Law report by Sidney and Beatrice Webb, the "overcrowding, insanitation, filth, neglect, and gross indecency … were simply indescribable" (Webb & Webb, 1909, p. 44). The system of workhouses, almshouses, and casual wards existed in England and other parts of the United Kingdom through the 1920s.

Pauper Support System in the United States

Homelessness has also been an enduring feature in American history.[5] Until the twentieth century, assistance to vagrants and paupers in colonial America and the United States was indistinguishable from support offered to all low-income people (Leginski, 2007) and based on a residential work model comparable with that in England. Rather than being parish-based, however, responses were organized at the city and county levels with aid from local charities that engaged civic and private-sector partners in building "poorhouses" (American vernacular for workhouses), almshouses, and poor farms (Meltsner, 2012, pp. 24–27).

In Massachusetts, for instance, the problem of pauperism was acute, and expenditures for the poor increased from $20,000 to $75,000 between 1801 and 1820. In response, the state legislature established a committee chaired by Josiah Quincy, the future Mayor of Boston, to find solutions for the problem. The Quincy committee identified two classes: the *impotent poor*, incapable of work due to old age, infancy, sickness, or disability; and the *able poor*, who could perform some degree of work and for whom houses of industry were recommended. It also developed four ways of aiding the poor: *outdoor relief*, which offered supplies, food, fuel, and financial support to poor families in their own homes; *pauper auctions*, by which care for an individual's needs were provided for by the lowest bidder, who in turn would be paid by the town for their support (Kelso, 1969); *bidding the local poor as a group out to the lowest bidder*, a town-wide contract system where one entity or person bid to take care of all of the community's poor; and *poorhouses* or *houses of industry* (Eastman & McGrath, n.d.). At the time, Massachusetts had the most poorhouses in the country, and its system subsequently emerged as a template for shaping American social policy towards poverty (Meltsner, 2012; Wagner, 2005).

Poorhouses were publicly funded buildings that conformed to two models: domestic and institutional (Meltsner, 2012). The domestic was more fitting for rural communities – typically organized around farm-type structures housing fewer residents. Institutional poorhouses were usually located on inexpensive public or private lands on the outskirts of town. Similar to English models, they were masonry structures that could shelter more residents, keep the sexes apart, and provide separate accommodations for children and the sick.

The Leveret Street Almshouse in Boston (1800), designed by the architect Charles Bullfinch in the Neoclassical style, was a rare example of stately

2.4
The Leverett Street Almshouse, Boston, Massachusetts (1800) designed by Charles Bulfinch. The three-story façade was organized with a taller pedimented central section decorated with elongated windows separated by pilasters with three marble arches. The flanking wings appear as two five-bay structures with individual entrances.

architecture in a class of generally dour buildings. The three-sectioned façade suggested that male and female inmates resided on opposite sides of the grand vestibule (Meltsner, 2012). The law required that the institution accommodate not only the "worthy" destitute, but also the "unworthy" poor and criminals, which led to severe overcrowding and inadequate segregation, severe wear and tear, and resulting demolition of the building in 1825. The Leveret Street Almshouse was, however, highly influential on design of similar institutions in the United States well into the twentieth century.

The Poor and the Indigenous Poor Support Systems in the Commonwealth Nations and in South Africa

Canada, Australia, and New Zealand were initially formed as colonies of the British Empire and are now sovereign members of the Commonwealth of Nations. Today, all three belong to the group of developed nations in which large population groups enjoy high standards of living and where respect for human rights and well-being are the top policy priorities. The indigenous peoples that historically lived in these territories, and who lost their lands to the colonizers, experience higher rates of social, economic, and health inequality, which is reflected in greater instances of homelessness relative to non-indigenous populations, which, of course, also experience homelessness at concerning rates (Anderson & Collins, 2014; Christensen, 2016). The dislocation of Indigenous peoples from their ancestral lands not only led to physical homelessness but extends to include "spiritual homelessness" for situations in which indigenous people are displaced from knowledge, rituals, and kinship relationships, a displacement from which poverty can precipitate (Memmott, Long, Chambers, & Spring, 2003, p. 5). Although individual stories of unhoused Indigenous persons in each of the geographic locations differ, the causes and reasons for its continuance today are rooted in these peoples' historic social and cultural vulnerability within the territories of former colonies (Memmott et al., 2003).

Starting in the late eighteenth century, the Canadian government, representing the Crown and the Indigenous people of the First Nations, signed a series of treaties under which the latter gave up large portions of their territories in exchange for reserve lands, annual payments, and hunting and fishing rights. These terms were systematically unfulfilled by the government and accompanied by a policy of aggressive assimilation (Christensen, 2016). In accordance with the Indian Act of 1876, Indigenous peoples were relocated to reserves while their children were placed in residential schools run by Christian religious organizations (Menzies, 2010), in which children often experienced systematic physical, sexual, and psychological abuse. These policies lasted until the 1980s, and the resulting traumas make those who went through the system more vulnerable to "threatening social conditions" leading to homelessness (Menzies, 2010). The practices of confining Indigenous persons on reserves and leaving them without the means of maintaining traditional lifestyles or connections to extended family and land, culturally sensitive education, and employment opportunities further contributed to the disproportionate homelessness among Canada's Indigenous people.

As in North America, ever since the British claimed the *terra nullius* (*empty land*), homelessness has been woven into the social fabric of Australia (Coleman & Fopp, 2014; Memmott & Nash, 2016) and New Zealand (Groot & Peters, 2016). The earliest homeless populations were the Aboriginal people who lost access to their lands and connection to their spiritual homes when they were displaced by European settlers. The settler governments of both colonies imposed British concepts of title and ownership, and the resulting alienation meant that, by the mid-1800s, a combination of the British Crown and private trading companies had "purchased" nearly all rights to occupy and exploit the lands and seas (Durie, 2005; Groot & Peters, 2015). From the mid-1800s, many activities associated with poverty and homelessness were criminalized, and government responses focused on controlling and removing to workhouses and asylums the destitute, the infirm, and those in need of "moral correction" (Coleman & Fopp, 2014, pp. 13–14).

By the beginning of the nineteenth century, the tiny outpost established by the Dutch East India Company at the Cape of South Africa in 1652 had grown into a sprawling multiracial colony in which a minority of European settlers occupied a position of privilege and authority over a larger population of slaves and an indeterminate number of native inhabitants who were largely deprived of their cattle and grazing and hunting lands (Atmore & Marks, 1974). The discovery of diamonds and gold after the 1860s brought an influx of skilled white workers from Europe and Australia, increased land competition, and led to rapid industrialization. Profiteers pushed white and black farmers off their lands, from which a new cohort of landless farm tenants emerged (Davie, 2015). In the midst of these transformations, the numbers of destitute white farmers and diamond diggers increased and were perceived as an offence to public dignity. Compared with the description of the living conditions of London poor from *Bitter Cry of Outcast London*, "a mere eight feet square and passageways crawling with vermin," Cape Town slums teemed with mixed-race poor "even more depraved than London's 'residuum'" (*Cape Times*, January 21, 1896, as cited in Davie, 2015, pp. 40–41). Similar to the other colonial settings, English-style vagrancy laws became the basis for dealing with the needy whites and mandated confining them to workhouses, while destitute black populations were left to the meager devices of their segregated communities.

THE MODERN ERA

By the turn of the twentieth century, leading social philosophers and reformers such as Thomas Hill Green and Henry Sidgwick sought to shift convention, arguing that the root of vagrancy was poverty, rather than genetic character flaws or a predisposition to laziness (Humphries, 1999, pp. 110–111). This laid the groundwork for a proliferation of studies in psychology, sociology, and economics, and work programs aimed at addressing the endemic poverty that continued through the interwar years of economic depression and mass homelessness in the United Kingdom, Europe, Canada, and the United States. Concurrently, however, the pseudo-science of eugenics emerged at many colleges and universities, and organizations such as the British Eugenics Education Society and the American Eugenics Society sought to influence welfare policies by asserting that poverty and its associated ills proliferated through genetics. Among other similar bodies, the New York-based Eugenics Record Office gathered biological, medical, and social information about the American population from 1910 to 1939 (data about headaches, "crooked feet," drinking, and instances of venereal diseases) in hopes that it would help to identify "tramp tendencies" (Welshman, 2013). As Tim Cresswell (2001) described, "observers sought to encode the bodies of tramps as pathological, as diseased and genetically unsound" (p. 114). This was a moment in the social history of homelessness that led to its being viewed as a societal pathology in need of eradication. In 1914, a Model Eugenical Sterilization Law in the United States proposed to authorize sterilization of the "socially inadequate" – persons supported in institutions or "maintained wholly or in part by public expense." The law encompassed the "feeble-minded, insane, criminalistic, epileptic, inebriate, diseased, blind, deaf, deformed, and dependent" – including "orphans, ne'er-do-wells, tramps, the homeless and paupers" (Laughlin, 2020/1914). At the time the Model Law was published, twelve states had already enacted sterilization laws, and similar laws followed in Canada[6] and Australia.[7]

At the turn of the century through the 1930s, most cities in the United States sought to address the vagrancy problem by constructing local poorhouses based upon institutional building models adapted from hospital and prison designs, or erecting clusters of unlocked huts referred to as "tramp dwellings." In 1929, with the onset of the Great Depression, the need for such housing rapidly increased while the resources for new buildings and maintenance drastically diminished (Cresswell, 2001). By 1932, millions of Americans, hard-working men and women, had lost their homes and had to travel from place to place in search of employment. Some moved in with relatives, and, as unit densities soared, squatting became the norm. Others found shelter in one of the increasing numbers of buildings vacated after a business had closed, and families clustered in shantytowns near soup kitchens. Termed "Hoovervilles" (after Herbert Hoover, who was president of the United States when the Depression started and deemed culpable), at the height of the Depression, there were hundreds of these shelter camps across the country, with hundreds of thousands of people living in them. These settlements generally consisted of tents and shacks. Authorities did not officially recognize these Hoovervilles and occasionally removed the occupants for trespassing, but they were largely tolerated out of necessity. Under the social welfare programs of President Franklin Roosevelt's New Deal, including the Federal Emergency Relief Administration (FERA) and the Works Progress Administration (WPA), unemployment and homelessness were alleviated through government-based jobs for skilled and unskilled laborers and assistance with reentering the rental housing market. President Roosevelt recognized that adequate housing was not only an individual need, but a societal need, and he declared the "right of every family to a decent home" in his 1944 State of the Union address (Roosevelt, 1944, para 69).

2.5
Homeless man
sitting in front
of shack in
shantytown known
as Hooverville,
Seattle, Washington,
October 27, 1931.

In Australia and New Zealand, the situation was very similar to that in the United States. The depressions of the 1890s and 1930s resulted in thousands of workers losing their jobs. Dilapidated infrastructure and overcrowded living conditions led to mass homelessness (Parliamentary Library Research Paper, 2014). Those who had to be "on the road" in search of work were mistrusted and treated with little sympathy (*Waikato Times*, 2013). Aboriginal people's housing conditions were particularly poor (Howden-Chapman, Bierre, & Cunningham, 2013). The post-World War II economic boom in Australia and New Zealand prompted a break from the trend of vilifying the poor and itinerant, as the government assumed a greater role in providing employment and affordable housing opportunities for those in need (Coleman & Fopp, 2014). The social objectives were increasing the number of available jobs and opening paths to home ownership, which, in combination, were perceived as the best protections against poverty and homelessness.

The policy silence and programmatic inactivity around the systematic causes of homelessness – individuals' personal health, economic situation, and social status – perpetuated the problem (Coleman & Fopp, 2014, p. 15). Homelessness persisted among economically disadvantaged populations, indigenous persons, and descendants of enslaved persons, engendering a class of the "permanent poor" (Brown, 2016; Groot & Peters, 2016). The social welfare programs that originated in the Depression-era 1930s and continued in the post-war period (both in the United States and in other parts of the world) were a turning point in the process of recognizing that this was not a moral or genetic problem. Coordinated efforts with multiple support organizations and community partners were key to addressing the complex problems that produce and arise from homelessness. Starting in the 1950s, the unilateral parish- or city-based workhouse model fell out of favor, and in its place a network of housing, food, health, vocational training, and spiritual and emotional support experts sought to improve the circumstance of the homeless person or family through specialized interventions.

THE SERVICE ECONOMY

Throughout the 1950s and 1960s, with increased urbanization, the total numbers of homeless persons increased compared with the war years, but declined relative to the Depression era, leading to the perception that the problem was on the way to being solved (Rossi, 1990). Poverty was ghettoized in urban centers, while the wealthy retreated into suburban, gated communities. Those homeless who remained in public were stereotyped as unredeemable alcoholic men who resisted relief (Bahr & Caplow, 1974). In many American cities, police and magistrates applied vagrancy laws against "habitual drunkards" or "whoever willfully makes or causes to be made any loud, boisterous and unseemly noise or disturbance to the annoyance of the peaceable residents nearby" (Footet, 1956, pp. 605, 610). The laws aimed to banish "bums" from city centers, to perform a form of social sanitation and as a means of controlling "suspicious" persons (Footet, 1956, p. 613) until a number of civil cases brought in the United States legal system began questioning the constitutionality of these laws. The Supreme Court declared those unconstitutional in 1972 (Yeamans, 1968).[8] In society, however, fear of the disorderly and criminal potential of the homeless persisted, perpetuated in part by news media's fixation on violent crime and race-centric incidents and government emphasis on arresting, disciplining, and institutionalizing its most marginalized citizens rather than rehabilitation (Ocobock, 2008, pp. 26–27; Welshman, 2013).

The intersection of homelessness and the inadequacy of mental-health services and hospital capacity during this period is also important to observe. Between 1955 and 1985, New York State "dumped" more than 125,000 low-income patients from mental-health hospitals into the city (Sullivan & Burke, 2013, p. 912). Among the most serious aspects of deinstitutionalization was the inadequacy of aftercare services for the newly discharged. "Former" patients often received little or no rehabilitative, socialization, or vocational support as they attempted to reenter society (Malone, 1982, pp. 761–767).[9]

Another factor that contributed to increased numbers of homeless persons was the gradual disappearance of affordable housing options in major cities with high population densities. An example of this is single-room occupancies (SROs) – small, furnished single rooms with a bed, chair, and sometimes a small desk, with a shared bathroom down the hall. Until the twentieth century, SROs housed a broad, socioeconomically diverse population. In 1926, the *New York Times* editorialized that, "the perfect apartment, at least in New York, is probably in a residential hotel"

(Groth, 1999, pp. 20–24). This was the default urban housing option for single, working-class men (and, to a much lesser extent, working-class women; Blackburn, 1996; Groth, 1999; Sullivan & Burke, 2013). By the mid-1950s, however, New York housing policy had turned against SROs, and the city sought actively to eliminate these units and their associations with the poor.

> There were terribly deteriorated buildings … which could be incredibly valuable if they were rented to young professionals … [Landlords forced residents to leave] by creating unimaginably dreadful conditions[.] They turned the heat off, they let units to prostitutes [and] drug dealers. Some hired thugs to simply throw tenants out.
>
> (Dr. Anthony Blackburn as cited in Sullivan & Burke, 2013, p. 911;
> see also Blackburn, 1996; Gladwell, 1993)

By 1985, more than 100,000 units had been eliminated, with nothing to replace them (Blackburn, 1996). In 1983, the New York City Department of Housing Preservation and Development sought to reverse course with its Certificate of No Harassment (CONH) policy, but individuals placed through these programs had no permanent rights to their SROs, and rising rents drove them into the streets (Sullivan & Burke, 2013, pp. 917–918). Although most historic housing options for homeless persons were in mass dormitories or barrack-type spaces, SROs within a multi-unit building appeared to be a more dignified yet affordable option to house homeless individuals (Sullivan & Burke, 2013).

Prior to the 1980s, the primary assistance to the homeless was in the form of soup kitchens run by charities or religious organizations. These were typically located in "skid row" neighborhoods, offering basic meals and sometimes shelter for the night. The programs were independently funded and operated, and few offered a comprehensive program of health and vocational support for their homeless and near-homeless populations (Burt et al., 2002). The public, elected officials, and government agencies increasingly saw homelessness as an endemic problem for which existing models were inadequate. The United Nations announced that 1987 would be the International Year of Shelter for the Homeless.

In the United States, legislative action culminated with the Homeless Persons Survival Act (McKinney Homeless Assistance Act) of 1987, which addressed emergency, preventive, and long-term approaches to managing homeless populations. Most of the attention was focused on the emergency component, while the preventive and long-term support were sidelined (Leginski, 2007). Concurrently, research and evaluation efforts led to a growing awareness of the multiple needs of homeless persons, which laid the foundation for new, more systematic approaches to service. The model identified the varying needs of the homeless populations at the community level, rather than following legislative mandates or top–down theoretical speculation (Leginski, 2007, pp. 1–7). In the early 1990s, the U.S. Department of Housing and Urban Development endorsed this *continuum of care* approach (Burt et al., 2002) as a grant-funding requirement, emphasizing the importance of community self-determination. Under this model, distinct programs support persons unable to pay for housing. A brief overview of the housing types is shown in 2.6,

2.6
Continuum of care housing types.

Housing Type	Description	Residents	Financing
Emergency shelter	Duration of stay: one night with daily readmissions Design: women's/men's quarters, large dormitory-style sleeping Services: food/hot meals, social/case management, medical triage	Least able to pay: families (most often single parent), single persons, seniors, young adults Indiscriminate admissions for people suffering from drug addiction, alcoholism, or mental disabilities	Public and private funds, donations
Transitional shelter	Duration of stay: typically, 6 months, can be up to 2 years Design: gender separated, dormitory-style sleeping to smaller 6–8 resident rooms Services: food services, case management, social services, development of life skills and job training/placement assistance	Least able to pay residents participating in social support programs to help them become independent: families (most often single parent), single persons, seniors, young adults Residents must be "clean" and free from drug or alcohol use and be actively working with support services	Public and private funds, donations
Transitional housing	Duration of stay: up to 2 years Design: approximate independent living situations in a variety of forms such as SRO buildings or shared residences (boarding houses) Services: food services, case management, social services, development of life skills and job training/placement assistance available, but not always on-site	Residents with some income and ability to pay for housing; families, single persons, seniors, young adults Residents must be free from drug or alcohol use and be actively working with support services	Public and private funds, donations
Permanent supportive housing	Duration of stay: no limit Design: supports independent living in SRO or larger apartment buildings, shared residences (boarding houses), or single-family houses Services: case management, social services, development of life skills and job training/placement assistance available, but not always on-site	Residents with some income and ability to pay for housing Residents must be "clean" and free from drug or alcohol use and be actively working with support services	Public and private funds, donations

Housing Type	Description	Residents	Financing
Public housing	Duration of stay: no limit Design: independent living, often low-rise apartment buildings Services: case management, social services, development of life skills and job training/placement assistance available, but not always on-site	Residents with some income and ability to pay for housing; expected to spend 30 percent of their income on rent	Public and private funds, donations; tax dollars allocated by state and federal governments Often supported by non-profit community development corporations

2.6

(Continued)

although policies vary greatly among individual facilities. The most widely used programs will be discussed in greater detail in subsequent chapters.

The continuum of care model has, however, come under criticism for its "techno-conceptual" rubrics, in which vulnerable persons are managed not as individuals, but as populations that must conform to government and non-profit organizations' views as to what constitutes "progress" and "success" in managing and exiting homelessness (Willse, 2015, p. 21; see also Beck & Twiss, 2018). Its bureaucratized approach often focuses on the assumed needs of a generic homeless person or family without accounting for the specific circumstances that led them to lose their home or that preclude them from exiting homelessness (i.e., having lost a job or income, having no close family members who could help, or chronic alcohol or drug use).

Government-based programs outside of the United States faced similar problems. Two examples were Australia's Homeless Persons Assistance Act (1974, the year in which the first shelters for women escaping domestic violence were established) and Support Accommodation Assistance Program (1985; Coleman & Fopp, 2014, p. 14). This extended in part from the changing demographics of the homeless, who were becoming more and more visible: women escaping violent relationships (identified in the 1970s); young people (1980s); families with children and older Australians (early 1990s); people with housing affordability issues (late 1990s on); the working poor; and single older women (Coleman & Fopp, 2014, p. 17). The Supported Accommodation Assistance Program was the first comprehensive national approach to homelessness in Australia under which Crisis Accommodation Program funding could be used to "build, buy, lease, renovate, or convert dwellings for short-term crisis accommodation" to provide support to persons transitioning to independent living (Chesterman, 1989, p. 10).

Overall, the record of successfully addressing the specific care and housing needs for unhoused persons is mixed. As the scale of the problem has grown (Dennis, Locke, & Khadduri, 2007; Henry et al., 2018; Institute of Global Homelessness, 2019), contemporary buildings for the poor (often clinical in atmosphere, inefficient, and poorly constructed) struggle to meet demand and suffer aesthetically even by comparison with the solid brick and mortar poorhouses and workhouses built in the nineteenth and early twentieth centuries (Meltsner, 2012). The seemingly modern concept of "affordable housing" – idealized as private, able to be personalized living spaces for low-income and homeless persons – has been around in the form of shacks and lean-tos assembled from scrap and available "on demand." Travelers' camps and Hoovervilles differed little from present-day iterations found along skid row (Leginski, 2007). Although the economy from the 1960s to the 1990s focused on providing services to a widening array of consumers, this coincided with a marginalizing of the poor and the disadvantaged by their being denied rehabilitation, health services, education, and economic support. From the perspective of these disadvantaged persons, we might equally term this period a disservice economy, a model that left many out of work and on the streets.

THE HUMAN ECONOMY

Economists Keith Hart, Jean-Louis Laville, and Antonio Cattani have described the current economy as *human* – characterized by a renewed interest in people as individuals, their needs and interests, and their overall physical and psychological well-being in confrontation with a variety of social problems in their "institutional complexity" (Hart, Laville, & Cattani, 2010). These values are reflected in consumers' service expectations and in the frameworks that businesses adopt, including organizations that support homeless populations. In the present day, most aid efforts have shifted their focus away from the individual characteristics of the homeless person, which in the past determined one's worthiness to be helped, to external factors including poverty, unemployment, lack of access to affordable housing, domestic violence, and physical and mental health. This has also been a period of realization that persons experiencing homelessness are diverse – adolescents, veterans, elderly persons, crime victims, indigenous persons, and families – and that support organizations and other stakeholders must develop flexible solutions to offer more individualized support and accommodations.

The questionable progress achieved under the continuum of care approach led to the development of an alternative to "managing" homelessness by excluding "unworthy" care recipients (Beck & Twiss, 2018). Federal programs such as Rapid Re-Housing, which aims to help individuals and families that do not need intensive and ongoing social services support to quickly exit homelessness (United States Interagency Council on Homelessness, 2018), the Common Ground Community founded by Rosanne Haggerty in 1990, or Pathways Housing First founded by Sam Tsemberis in 1992 allow homeless persons to be placed directly into permanent housing that provides intensive treatment and support (Tsemberis, Gulcur, & Nakae, 2004) rather than moving through different "levels" of housing, with each inching them closer to independent living. The field has moved rapidly to adopt Housing First as the preferred intervention, particularly in response to ending chronic homelessness (Leginski, 2007) both for individuals and families (Eibinder & Tull, 2005; Lanzerotti, 2004), in the United States, Canada, Europe, and Australia (Padgett, Henwood, & Tsemberis, 2016).

The model for implementing Housing First in multiple sites and countries is not always consistent, and may differ with regard to whether it includes social service components, or it can be any sort of affordable housing facility other than an overnight emergency shelter. Although Housing First is recognized as a successful model and a crucial component that allows people to secure permanent housing, it has several limitations. Some vulnerable population groups, such as persons diagnosed with mental illness, people who are active drug users, and people who have experienced chronic homelessness, do not thrive in this model because they need more, ongoing support than it often offers (Noble, 2015; Woolley, 2016). In the rush to adopt and fund Housing First, funding and support for emergency shelters has decreased, even as the need for such shelters has not (Capps, 2017).

THE ROLE OF DESIGN

Starting in the early 1980s, numerous professional design organizations joined the conversation and sought ways of being more involved in exploring alternative architectural and design solutions to help solve the homelessness crisis. In the United States, the National Association of Home Builders put it most succinctly:

> We do not need to accept homelessness. We are an able people. It is time to build. It is our job to build housing, to build community, to build people. It is our job to house the homeless. Let's do it.
>
> (Hayes, 1988, p. 10)

The American Institute of Architects (AIA), at both national and chapter involvement, introduced the issue to its membership in 1984, and it was the centerpiece discussion at conferences held in 1986 and again in 1988 (Greer, 1986). Through the AIA's Search for Shelter program, its members were able to get individual commissions, take upon pro bono projects, or offer professional services on temporary or permanent supportive housing for homeless populations (American Institute of Architects, 1989; Leavitt, 1988). In 1988, the American Society of Interior Designers (ASID) produced a training manual as an encouragement and a guide for local chapters involved in community projects to benefit unhoused persons. These recommendations included increasing awareness, advocating in the community, participating in the legislative process, creating new knowledge, supporting actual projects (public housing, shelters, etc.), and collaborating with other professionals (American Society of Interior Designers, Independent Housing Services San Francisco, 1988, p. v).[10] The Royal Institute of British Architects (RIBA) has been actively involved with legislative policy development initiatives, grassroots research, and community development projects that help to address the affordable housing crisis and homelessness (Royal Institute of British Architects, n.d.). Yet, at the turn of the century, homelessness remained a growing problem for virtually every country in the world, with a conservative estimate that more than 100 million people were homeless and over 1 billion people were inadequately housed (Commission on Human Rights, 2005).

With increased attention to human rights and dignity and greater awareness of the severity of the homeless problem, especially in larger metropolitan areas, architects and designers initiated public interest design movements such as the Association for Community Design (ACD), Social Economic Environmental Design (SEED) Network, and Public Architecture. We also have witnessed more small, independent initiatives that help designers to engage with support organizations and their clients and advocate for public work. For example, the Design for Humanity Initiative is a research program initiated by the Institute of International Humanitarian Affairs (IIHA) at Fordham University. Similarly, the UN Migration Agency (IOM) participated in Design with the Other 90%, a series of exhibitions organized by the Cooper-Hewitt, Smithsonian Design Museum devoted to demonstrating that design can be a powerful force in transforming communities and saving lives (Smith, n.d.). The One Percent Project: A Collaboration to End Homelessness, a project and a discussion series, was initiated in 2019 by Portland Design Week (Design Portland, 2020).

CONCLUSION

As this brief historical overview has revealed, homelessness is a complex social problem caused and exacerbated by a multitude of historical, individual, economic, and social factors. Societal transitions often result in large numbers of citizens losing access to a means of supporting themselves and the onset of mass homelessness. The means of addressing it are often reflected in policies, social control methods, and architectural conventions adapted from religious, medical, and penal contexts. Endemic homelessness disproportionately affects persons against whom larger discriminatory behaviors are directed (persons suffering from physical infirmity or mental illness, ethnic minorities, emotionally or sexually abused persons). Designing for the particular needs of these groups is an emerging and vitally necessary undertaking.

NOTES

1. The vocabulary used to describe the buildings and institutions associated with aiding the poor and the homeless is anachronistic and nuanced. The English "workhouse" was a building (at times combined with inmate residences) where able-bodied "vagrants, paupers, and petty criminals" were forced to work, often alongside the "deserving poor," including children, who were frequently interred together with incarcerated residents (Meltsner, 2012). "Casual wards" were overnight shelters that offered a place to sleep and a meal in return for work. These primarily served a clientele of urban homeless unwilling to go to "workhouses." The policy to deal with such short-term applicants was "to make the vagrant's life so disagreeable that he would hesitate to come back" (Longmate, 2012). The "almshouse" was for the "virtuous elderly, sick or disabled," but often also accommodated able-bodied residents. The distinction between workhouses and almshouses is somewhat blurred, and the two terms eventually became interchangeable. Over time, the vernacular "poor house" came to be used for both, and "workhouse" disappeared from use with the institution itself (ibid.)
2. One exception was the original Bridewell Hospital, which, like other pre-modern prisons was segregated by sex, but in which offenders could intermingle with visitors delivering

money, food, or other necessities. Bridewell also provided medical care, bathtubs, straw bedding, and regular clothes-washing to help prevent the spread of disease.

When the prison reformer John Howard visited Bridewell in 1789 he praised the prison for its facilities: "Each sex has a workroom and a night-room. They lie in boxes, with a little straw on the floor … There are many excellent regulations in this establishment. The prisoners have a liberal allowance, suitable employment, and some proper instruction; but the visitor laments that they are not more separated … no other prison in London has any straw or bedding. … There are, very properly, solitary cells for the Bridewell boys, in which one was confined and employed in beating hemp" (Howard, 1791, p. 127).

Bridewell Hospital in London was originally Bridewell Palace built by Thomas Wolsey in 1523 for Henry VIII. The palace was located on the Fleet River and named after an adjacent holy well dedicated to St. Bride. In 1553, Edward VI gave the palace to the City of London for the housing of vagrants and homeless children and for the punishment of petty offenders and "disorderly women." The City converted the palace into a prison, hospital, and workrooms. It later became known as Bridewell Royal Hospital and Bridewell Prison. The prison closed in 1855, and the buildings were demolished in 1863–1864.

3. Under social theories derived from misapplication of Darwin's concepts of natural selection, providing poor or homeless persons with food and shelter through less punitive means could contribute to personal enfeeblement and subsequent societal degradation. In an observation typical of its time, the English evolutionary biologist Edwin Ray Lankester posited that, "any new set of conditions which renders a species' food and safety very easily obtained, seems to lead to degeneration" (Lankester, 1880, p. 33). Urban degeneration theories took inspiration from biological models, and social welfare programs based in workhouses served to extract undesirable individuals who were perceived as a threat to social heath and weakening the fortitude of a community (Ocobock, 2008, p. 23). This idea parallels with today's views that offering assistance to homeless persons may lead to their 'shelterization', or 'learned helplessness', which may lead to their unwillingness or incapability to take care of themselves.

4. Much of this was inspired by Jeremy Bentham's utilitarian model of the panopticon, a circular structure with a round observation tower in the center to allow a small number of guards to constantly watch a large number of prisoners (Bentham, 2017/1791).

5. Writers such as Caton (1990) and Kusmer (2002) describe at least five waves of mass homelessness in the United States: colonial (after King Philip's War of 1675–1676 against Native Americans who responded to encroachments of English land acquisitions by attacking more than twenty towns and burning several of them to the ground; Meltsner, 2012, p. 9); pre-industrial (the result of the economic depression of 1819–1821, which threw thousands out of work and substantially reduced trade at a time when industrialization increased productivity and put many out of work (Meltsner, 2012, pp. 22, 23); post-Civil War (veterans coming 'home' with what is now recognized as post-traumatic stress disorder, followed by the Depression of 1873 and the economic dislocations of 1893–1896); the period of the Great Depression; and contemporary economic dislocation, which continues at profoundly concerning levels (Leginski, 2007, pp. 1–2).

6. Among other examples, the Sexual Sterilization Act (Alberta, 1928) created a Eugenics Board that could authorize the sexual sterilization of inmates of mental hospitals who were proposed for release, if it was determined that there was a risk of transmitting "disability" to their children. Over 2,800 individuals were sterilized under this Act (www. thecanadianencyclopedia.ca/en/article/eugenics).

7. Three "Mental Deficiency Bills" were presented to the Australian Parliament (1926, 1929, and 1939). Each aimed to institutionalize a sterilization program aimed at populations determined to be "inefficient," which included "slum dwellers, homosexuals, prostitutes, alcoholics," and persons with "small heads and with low IQs." Australia's Aboriginal population also fell within this group. The first two attempts to enact the bills failed owing to political instability, not thanks to any significant opposition. The third was passed unanimously, but never enacted because of the outbreak of World War II and the moral clarity

brought about by subsequent knowledge of the Holocaust and Nazi eugenics racial policies (https://theconversation.com/eugenics-in-australia-the-secret-of-melbournes-elite-3350).

8. In 1972, the issue reached the United States Supreme Court in the case of *Papachristou v. City of Jacksonville*. In a 7–0 decision, the Supreme Court ruled that the Jacksonville Vagrancy Ordinance was too vague for citizens to understand what sorts of conduct were illegal. The ordinance was also found to have criminalized innocent behavior and invested too much power in the hands of authorities (Ellickson, 1996). Overnight, vagrancy laws such as the one employed by the city of Jacksonville were invalidated (Ocobock, 2008, p. 26).

9. For example, studies have consistently estimated that, even today, almost half of all individuals with schizophrenia or bipolar disorder are receiving no treatment for their mental illness at any given time. According to National Institute of Mental Health estimates, in the United States, approximately 3.5 million such individuals are receiving no treatment (see, e.g., https://mentalillnesspolicy.org/consequences/percentage-mentally-ill-untreated.html).

10. Over subsequent years, many AIA chapters remained actively engaged as participants in a Homelessness Task Force managed jointly with the Housing Development Consortium, ASID maintains a "State of the Nation's Housing" report, and these and many other organizations participate in the annual observation of Affordable Housing Week.

REFERENCES

American Institute of Architects. (1989). *The search for shelter workbook*. Washington, DC: The American Institute of Architects.

American Society of Interior Designers; Independent Housing Services San Francisco. (1988). *The homeless: living on hope*. New York: American Society of Interior Designers.

Anderson, J. T., & Collins, D. (2014). Prevalence and causes of urban homelessness among indigenous peoples: a three-country scoping review. *Housing Studies*, *29*(7), 959–976.

Atmore, A., & Marks, S. (1974). The imperial factor in South Africa in the nineteenth century: towards a reassessment. *The Journal of Imperial and Commonwealth History*, *3*(1), 105–139. doi:10.1080/03086537408582423

Australian Government. (2008). *The road home: a national approach to reducing homelessness*. *White Paper*. Canberra: Department of Families, Housing, Community Services and Indigenous Affairs.

Bahr, H., & Caplow, T. (1974). *Old men drunk and sober*. New York: New York University Press.

Beck, E., & Twiss, P. (2018). *The homelessness industry: a critique of U.S. social policy*. Boulder, CO and London: Lynne Rienner.

Bentham, J. (2017/1791). *Panopticon: the inspection house*. Whithorn, UK: Anodos Books.

Berger, J. (1991). *Keeping a rendezvous*. New York: Random House.

Blackburn, A. J. (1996). *Single room living in New York City: a report*. New York: Department of Housing Preservation and Development.

Brown, D. (2016). Tūrangawaewae kore: nowhere to stand. In E. J. Christensen, *Indigenous homelessness* (pp. 331–360). Manitoba: University of Manitoba Press.

Bullen, J., & Reynolds, F. (2014). Reforming the service system. In C. Chamberlain, G. Johnson, & C. Robinson, *Homelessness in Australia: an introduction* (pp. 273–292). Sydney: New South Publishing, Council to Homeless Persons, and University of New South Wales Press.

Burt, M. R., Pollack, D., Sosland, A., Mikelson, K. S., Drapa, E., Greenwalt, K., … Smith, R.. (2002). *Evaluation of continuums of care*. Washington, DC: The Urban Institute.

Capps, K. (2017, June 30). The disappearing downtown shelter. *CityLab*. Retrieved from www.bloomberg.com/news/articles/2017-06-30/housing-first-and-the-disappearing-downtown-shelter

Caton, C. (1990). *Homeless in America*. New York: Oxford University Press.

Chesterman, C. (1989). *Homes away from home: supported accommodation assistance program review.* Canberra: Commonwealth State and Territory Welfare Ministers.

Christensen, J. (2016). Introduction; Indigenous homelessness: Canadian context. In E. J. Peters & J. Christensen, *Indigenous homelessness: perspectives from Canada, Australia, and New Zealand* (pp. 15–23). Winnipeg, Manitoba: University of Manitoba Press.

Coleman, A., & Fopp, R. (2014). Homelessness policy: benign neglect or regulation and control? In C. Chamberlain, G. Johnson, & C. Robinson, *Homelessness in Australia: an introduction* (pp. 11–29). Sydney: New South Publishing, Council to Homeless Persons, and University of New South Wales Press.

Commission on Human Rights. (2005). Economic, social, and cultural rights: report of the Special Rapporteur on adequate housing as a component of the right to an adequate standard of living, Miloon Kothari. United Nations. New York: Economic and Social Council. Retrieved from www.ohchr.org/EN/Issues/Housing/Pages/AnnualReports.aspx

Cresswell, T. (2001). *The tramp in America.* London: Reaktion Books.

Davie, G. (2015). *Poverty knowledge in South Africa: a social history of human science, 1855–2005.* Cambridge: Cambridge University Press.

Davis, S. (2004). *Designing for the homeless.* Berkley, Los Angeles, and London: University of California Press.

Dennis, D., Locke, G., & Khadduri, J. (2007). *Toward understanding homelessness: the 2007 National Symposium on Homelessness Research.* Washington, DC: Department of Health and Human Services & U.S. Department of Housing and Urban Development.

Design Portland. (2020). The 1% Project. Retrieved from Design Portland Festival: https://designportland.org/festival/2020/schedule/the-1-project

Durie, M. H. (2005). *Ngā Tai Mataū: tides of Māori endurance.* Melbourne, Australia: Oxford University Press.

Eastman, W. D., & McGrath, K. (n.d.). Quincy report. Retrieved from Primaryresearch.org: http://primaryresearch.org/quincy-report/

Eibinder, S. D., & Tull, T. (2005). *The housing first program for homeless families: empirical evidence of long-term efficacy to end and prevent family homelessness.* Los Angeles, CA: Beyond Shelter.

Ellickson, R. C. (1996). Controlling chronic misconduct in city spaces: of planning, skid rows, and public-space zoning. *Yale Law Journal, 105*(5), 1210–1211.

Erebus Consulting Partners. (2004). *National evaluation of the Supported Assistance Accommodation Program (SAAP IV), Final Report.* Canberra: Commonwealth of Australia.

Footet, C. (1956). Vagrancy-type law and its administration. *University of Pennsylvania Law Review, 104,* 603–650.

Foucault, M. (1995). *Discipline and punish: the birth of the prison* (A. Sheridan, Ed.) New York: Pantheon Books.

Gladwell, M. (1993, April 24). N.Y. hopes to help homeless by reviving single room occupancy hotels. *Los Angeles Times.* Retrieved from www.latimes.com/archives/la-xpm-1993-04-25-mn-27098-story.html

Greer, N. (1986). *Housing the homeless.* Washington, DC: American Institute of Architects.

Groot, S., & Peters, E. (2016). Indigenous homelessness: New Zealand context. In E. J. Peters & J. Christensen, *Indigenous homelessness: perspectives from Canada, Australia, and New Zealand* (pp. 323–328). Winnipeg, Manitoba: University of Manitoba Press.

Groth, P. (1999). *Living downtown: the history of residential hotels in the United States.* Berkley, Los Angeles, and London: University of California Press.

Hart, K., Laville, J.-L., & Cattani, A. D. (2010). *The human economy* (K. Hart, J.-L. Laville, & A. D. Cattani, Eds.) Cambridge, UK: Polity.

Hayes, R. (1988). *Builders examine the many faces of homelessness.* Washington, DC: National Coalition for the Homeless.

Henry, M., Mahathey, A., Morrill, T., Robinson, A., Shivji, A., & Watt, R. (2018). The 2018 Annual Homeless Assessment Report (AHAR) to Congress. Washington, DC: U.S. Department of Housing and Urban Development, Office of Community Planning and Development.

Hevesi, D. (1999, April 25). Building homes for the single homeless. *New York Times*. Retrieved from www.nytimes.com/1999/04/25/realestate/building-homes-for-the-single-homeless.html

Hillier, B. (2007). *Space is the machine*. London: University College London.

Hillier, B., & Hanson, J. (1988). *The social logic of space*. Cambridge, New York, and Melbourne: Cambridge University Press.

Hopper, K., & Baumohl, J. (1996). Redefining the cursed word. In J. Baumohl, *Homelessness in America*. Phoenix, AZ: Oryx Press.

Howard, J. (1791). *An account of the principal lazarettos in Europe: with various papers relative to the plague, together with further observations on some foreign prisons and hospitals, and additional remarks on the present state of those in Great Britain and Ireland* (Vol. 2). London: J. Johnson, C. Dilly, & T. Cadell. Retrieved from https://books.google.com/books?id=RBhPAAAAYAAJ&printsec=frontcover#v=onepage&q=each%20sex&f=false

Howden-Chapman, P., Bierre, S., & Cunningham, C. (2013). Building inequality. In M. Rashbrooke, *Inequality – A New Zealand crisis* (pp. 112–123). Wellington, NZ: Bridget Williams Books.

Hulchanski, D. (2009). Homelessness in Canada: past, present, future. In *Growing home: housing and homelessness in Canada* (pp. 1–13). Calgary: Growing Home: Housing and Homelessness in Canada.

Humphries, R. (1999). *No fixed abode: a history of responses to the roofless and rootless in Britain*. London: Macmillan.

Institute of Global Homelessness. (2019). *State of homelessness in countries with developed economies*. Chicago, IL: Institute of Global Homelessness.

Jordan, B. (1974). *Poor parents: social policy and the "cycle of deprivation."* London: Routledge & Kegan Paul.

Kelso, R. W. (1969). *History of public poor relief in Massachusetts: 1620–1920*. Montclair: Patterson Smith. Retrieved from http://primaryresearch.org/pauper-auction/

Kusmer, K. L. (2002). *Down and out, on the road: the homeless in American history*. Oxford and New York: Oxford University Press. Retrieved from https://books.google.com/books?id=xpJ3ME7vHuEC&printsec=frontcover&source=gbs_ge_summary_r&cad=0#v=onepage&q&f=false

Lankester. (1880). Degeneration: a chapter in Darwinism. Retrieved from https://books.google.com/books?id=mgEFAAAAYAAJ&printsec=frontcover#v=onepage&q=easily%20obtained%2C%20seems%20to%20lead%20to%20degeneration&f=false

Lanzerotti, L. (2004). *Housing First for families: research to support the development of a Housing First for families training curriculum*. Los Angeles, CA: The National Alliance to End Homelessness.

Laughlin, H. (2020/1914, n.d.). Laughlin's Model Law. Retrieved from Harry Laughlin and Eugenics, A Selection of Historical Objects from Harry H. Laughlin Papers, Truman State University: https://historyofeugenics.truman.edu/altering-lives/sterilization/model-law/

Leavitt, J. (1988, October). Housing Acts and architects, editorial. *Progressive Architecture*, p. 9.

Lefebvre, H. (1984). *The production of space*. Oxford, UK and Cambridge, MA: Blackwell.

Leginski, W. (2007). Historical and contextual influences on the U.S. response to contemporary homelessness. In *Toward Understanding Homelessness: The 2007 National Symposium on Homelessness Research* (pp. 1.1–1.36). Arlington, VA: Department of Health and Human Services and U.S. Department of Housing and Urban Development. Retrieved from www.huduser.gov/portal/publications/homeless/homeless_symp_07.html

Little, L. K. (1983). *Religious poverty and the profit economy in medieval Europe*. Ithaca, NY: Cornell University Press.

Longmate, N. (2012, December 17). *The Victorian casual ward* (B. Rosen, Ed.) Retrieved from Victorian History: http://vichist.blogspot.com/2012/12/the-victorian-casual-ward.html

Malone, M. (1982). Homelessness in a modern urban setting. *Fordham Urban Law Journal*, *10*(4), 749–781. Retrieved from https://ir.lawnet.fordham.edu/ulj/vol10/iss4/8

Meltsner, H. (2012). *The poorhouses of Massachusetts: cultural and architectural history*. Jefferson, NC and London: McFarland.

Memmott, P., Long, S., Chambers, C., & Spring, F. (2003). Categories of Indigenous 'homeless' people and good practice responses to their needs. Melbourne: Australian Housing and Urban Research Institute. Retrieved from www.ahuri.edu.au/research/final-reports/49

Memmott, P., & Nash, D. (2016). Indigenous homelessness: Australian context. In E. J. Peters & J. Christensen, *Indigenous homelessness: perspectives from Canada, Australia, and New Zealand* (pp. 213–220). Winnipeg, Manitoba: University of Manitoba Press.

Menzies, P. (2010). Intergenerational trauma from a mental health perspective. *Native Social Work Journal*, *7*, 63–85.

Mollat, M. (1986). *The poor in the Middle Ages* (A. Goldhammer, Trans.) New Haven, CT and London: Yale University Press.

Morrison, K. (1999). *The workhouse: a study of poor-law buildings in England*. Swindon, UK: English Heritage at the National Monuments Record Centre.

Morrow, S. (2010). The homeless in historical context. *Development South Africa*, *27*(1), 51–62. doi:10.1080/03768350903519341

National Trust. (n.d.). *The workhouse concept*. Retrieved from www.nationaltrust.org.uk/the-workhouse-southwell/features/the-workhouse-concept

Noble, A. (2015). *Beyond Housing First: a holistic response to family homelessness in Canada*. Toronto, Canada: Raising the Roof. Retrieved from https://homelesshub.ca/resource/beyond-housing-first-holistic-response-family-homelessness-canada

Ocobock, P. (2008). Introduction. In A. L. Beier & P. Ocobock, *Cast out: vagrancy and homelessness in global and historical perspective* (pp. 1–34). Athens, OH: Ohio University Press.

Padgett, D. K., Henwood, B. F., & Tsemberis, S. J. (2016). *Housing First: ending homelessness, transforming systems, and changing lives*. Oxford & New York: Oxford University Press.

Parliamentary Library Research Paper. (2014, July 17). Homelessness in New Zealand. Retrieved from New Zealand Parliament: www.parliament.nz/en/pb/research-papers/document/00PLEcoRP14021/homelessness-in-new-zealand#RelatedAnchor

Parsell, C., & Marston, G. (2012). Beyond the 'at risk' individual: housing and the eradication of poverty to prevent homelessness. *Australian Journal of Public Administration*, *71*(1), 33–44.

South African History Online. (2011, March 21). Pass laws in South Africa 1800–1994. Retrieved from South African History Online: www.sahistory.org.za/article/pass-laws-south-africa-1800-1994

Piro, J. M. (2008). Foucault and the architecture of surveillance: creating regimes of power in schools, shrines, and society. *Educational Studies*, *44*(1), 30–46. doi:10.1080/00131940802225036

Roosevelt, F. D. (1944, January 11). State of the Union Address text. Retrieved from Franklin D. Roosevelt Presidential Library and Museum: www.fdrlibrary.org/address-text

Rosen, B. (2012, December 17). The Victorian casual ward. Retrieved from Victorian History: http://vichist.blogspot.com/2012/12/the-victorian-casual-ward.html

Rossi, P. H. (1990). The old homeless and the new homelessness in historical perspective. *American Psychologist*, *45*(8), 954–959. doi:doi.org/10.1037/0003–066X.45.8.954

Royal Institute of British Architects. (n.d.). Housing matters. Retrieved from RIBA: www.architecture.com/knowledge-and-resources/knowledge-landing-page/housing-matters

Smith, C. E. (n.d.). About Design with the Other 90%: cities. Retrieved from Design Other 90 Network: www.designother90.org/

Sullivan, J. B., & Burke, J. (2013). Single-room occupancy housing in New York City: the origins and dimensions of a crisis. *CUNY Law Review, 17*(1), 901–931. doi:10.31641/clr170104

Tsemberis, S., Gulcur, L., & Nakae, M. (2004). Housing first, consumer choice, and harm reduction for homeless individuals with a dual diagnosis. *American Journal of Public Health, 94*(4), 651–656.

United States Interagency Council on Homelessness. (2018, August 15). Rapid re-housing. Retrieved from www.usich.gov/solutions/housing/rapid-re-housing/

Urban Institute: National Center for Charitable Statistics. (2018, December 13). The nonprofit sector in brief 2018. Retrieved from National Center for Charitable Statistics: https://nccs.urban.org/publication/nonprofit-sector-brief-2018#highlights

Vagrancy. (n.d.). The new world of words; or universal English dictionary (1706). In *Oxford English Dictionary*. Retrieved from www.oed.com/view/Entry/221039?redirectedFrom=vagrancy#eid

Wagner, D. (2005). *The poorhouse: America's forgotten institution*. Lanham, MD: Rowman & Littlefield.

Waikato Times. (2013, December 2). The futile life of the tramps. *Waikato Times*, p. 14. Retrieved from www.pressreader.com/new-zealand/waikato-times/20131201/282187943812881

Watson, R. L. (2012). *Slave emancipation and racial attitudes in nineteenth-century South Africa*. Cambridge, New York, Melbourne, Madrid, Cape Town, Singapore, São Paulo, Delhi, and Mexico City: Cambridge University Press.

Webb, S., & Webb, B. (1909). *The break up of the Poor Law: being part one of the Minority Report of the Poor Law Commission*. London, New York, Sydney, and Calcutta: Longmans, Green.

Webber, M. (2003). *The Protestant ethic and the spirit of capitalism* (T. Parsons, Trans.) New York: Dover.

Welshman, J. (2013). *Underclass: a history of the excluded since 1880*. London, New Delhi, and New York, Sydney: Bloomsbury.

Whitehead, J. (2013). *Underclass: a history of the excluded since 1880* (2nd ed.). London, New Delhi, New York, and Sydney: Bloomsbury.

Willse, C. (2015). *The value of homelessness: managing surplus life in the United States*. Minneapolis, MN and London: University of Minnesota Press.

Woolley, E. (2016, February 26). What are the limitations of Housing First? Retrieved from Homeless Hub: www.homelesshub.ca/blog/what-are-limitations-housing-first

Yeamans, R. (1968). Constitutional attacks on vagrancy laws. *Stanford Law Review, 20*(4), 782–793.

TEACHING MATERIALS

Lauren Trujillo

Key Terms

Affordable housing

Almshouses

Casual wards

Continuum of care model

Hooverville

Housing First model

Human economy

Individual factors of homelessness

Infirmaries

Pauperism

Permanent poor

Poor Laws

Spiritual homelessness

Single-Room Occupancies (SROs)

Structural factors of homelessness

Vagrancy

Workhouses/poorhouses

Worthy poor/unworthy poor

Discussion Questions

1. After reading this chapter, do you think having a better understanding of the history of homelessness, its causes, and societal responses makes the development of a solution to homelessness easier or more complex? Why?

2. Which events and societal responses from history do you think had the biggest impact on how homelessness is viewed by society today?

3. Review the images of the courtyard, radial, and corridor plan workhouses and answer the following questions:

    a. What physical features of the architecture (walls and windows, for example) might help those in charge regulate behavior and maintain control?

    b. For each plan, trace the path one might walk throughout the course of the day. Describe what that walk might feel like. You might consider how the walls, which are nearly 2 feet thick, might sound or feel or how the small, inward facing windows might restrict views. How do you think this routine shaped the overall experience of inmates and staff who spent time in these spaces?

    c. Imagine that you are spending time in these buildings with other members of your family. How do the buildings promote isolation and separation of family members? Do you think this is an intentional part of the design? How might this isolation and separation shape your experience?

    d. What message do corridors, segregated rooms, small windows, and interiors equipped with only bare necessities communicate? Is it a message of judgement and shame or one that would make someone feel empowered to alter their antisocial behavior (whenever and if possible)?

3   User Types

Yelena McLane

Most of us encounter homeless persons regularly. We see them asking for money at intersections, resting in carrels at public libraries, sitting on benches at bus stops or in parks, pushing shopping carts. Some are elderly men. Some are young women. Some appear to be in poor health. We might note their slow way of moving, an unfocused look in their eyes, the dirtiness of their hands and fingernails. They prefer to hide, to tuck themselves into enclosed spaces, to come out into the open only when they have to. These are, of course, stereotypes. These are abstractions of homelessness that many assume reflect the realities of homelessness. But who *really* are the people who live in the streets? What are their stories? And by what means can built environments help them to overcome their conditions?

REASONS FOR BECOMING HOMELESS

Homelessness typically extends from a confluence of poverty, a lack of available affordable housing, and a shortage of social safety net resources. Townshend and Bolt (as cited in Bloomfield, 2014, pp. 2–3) have detailed three types of homelessness, taking into account initial circumstances, the conditions of being homeless (mobility, duration), and the potential for exiting homelessness: the *generationally homeless* or *multigenerationally homeless* (persons whose parents had experienced homelessness), the *situationally homeless* (persons or families who lost their homes for a period of time), and the *couch-homeless* (homeless persons who stay with friends and family). The circumstances that may lead to homelessness are many: substance abuse, mental illnesses, behavioral disorders, physical disabilities, health problems, an economic crisis, or escaping an abusive environment. Many of these reasons can worsen over time and become obstacles in the way of returning to permanent housing, putting one at risk of becoming chronically homeless. In this section we will describe the three categories in further detail, illustrating each with real-life stories.

Poverty and Displacement

Many people who experience homelessness share stories of troubled childhoods in families with alcoholic, drug-addict, or unhoused parents. Basic needs may have been met only through the intervention of grandparents, relatives, or foster parents. The situation may have been exacerbated by sexual abuse perpetrated by a family member, a friend, or a stranger. The person escaped from an unstable or unsafe home environment only to drop out of school.[1] Without skills or training, the person cannot get or maintain a job. They may develop substance abuse issues. Without a means of supporting themselves, they wind up sleeping in the streets. These persons most often compose the *generationally homeless* category (Bloomfield, 2014). To many people, stories like these are typical of most unhoused persons.

Leonard's story

I was twelve years old. My mother died, and I took an overdose. There was sexual abuse in our family by both my father and his friends. I turned my father in to the police for sexual assault on my younger brother and sister. I hated my father for the trauma he caused me. I never did recover from that trauma. I had three overdoses by the time I was fourteen.

When I was older, I had a battle with street drugs and started drinking a lot. There are a lot of years that are blank due to heavy drinking. I have been obsessed with taking my own life so I would not feel so trapped. I did not plan to live past twenty. Due to excess drinking and drugs, I have often been without a place to live. I had no self-worth. I felt lower than a snake.

(Larsen, 2007, p. 23)

In recent decades there has arisen a very different category termed the *situationally homeless* (Bloomfield, 2014, p. 4). The situationally homeless are most often lower- or middle-class individuals or families. When the economic provider suddenly loses their job or suffers some other significant financial hardship, they can no longer afford the cost of housing. They may have lost their home as the result of a natural disaster, fire, or other unforeseeable circumstance. The stories that emerge from this category often begin with a statement that the now unhoused person could never have imagined that they would be without a home:

Noelle's Story

I grew up in a lower-middle-class family. I graduated from college with a degree in business. I developed a good career as a manager in corporate America and raised two great kids – both in college – and thought that life could not get any better.

Then the bottom dropped out.

My company eliminated my department due to the recession. After eleven years, I was sent on my way with ten weeks' severance pay. I searched for a new job, but no corporate jobs were to be had. Nobody would hire me for minimum wage jobs because I was over-qualified. I spent my severance, my savings, my 401K, and my unemployment benefits trying to stay afloat.

[Then] I was evicted from my home. All of my belongings and years of mementos were dumped at the curb. With no options left, I packed up what I could and called the D.C. shelter hotline to find a place to sleep.

(Beaumon, 2010)

Sometimes, individuals who may eventually become homeless owing to *generational* or *situational* circumstances have family, relatives, or friends who allow them to live in their house or apartment for lengths of time. These persons comprise a category termed the *couch-homeless* (Bloomfield, 2014, p. 2). This kind of homelessness is particularly acute among high school and college students.[2] According to a 2017 study of homeless youth in Santa Clara County, California, 17 percent of high school students reported that they did not have stable housing or that they knew someone who was "couch surfing," living in cars, or living on the street (the county had 13,250 registered high school students at the time of the study; Bill Wilson Center, 2017). Of the community college students in the same area, 44 percent reported being in a *couch-homeless* situation or knowing someone in a similar situation (sleeping alternately at relatives' houses, friends' houses, in temporary shelters, or in places not meant for habitation; see 3.1), totaling

3.1
Data on overnight locations for couch surfing.

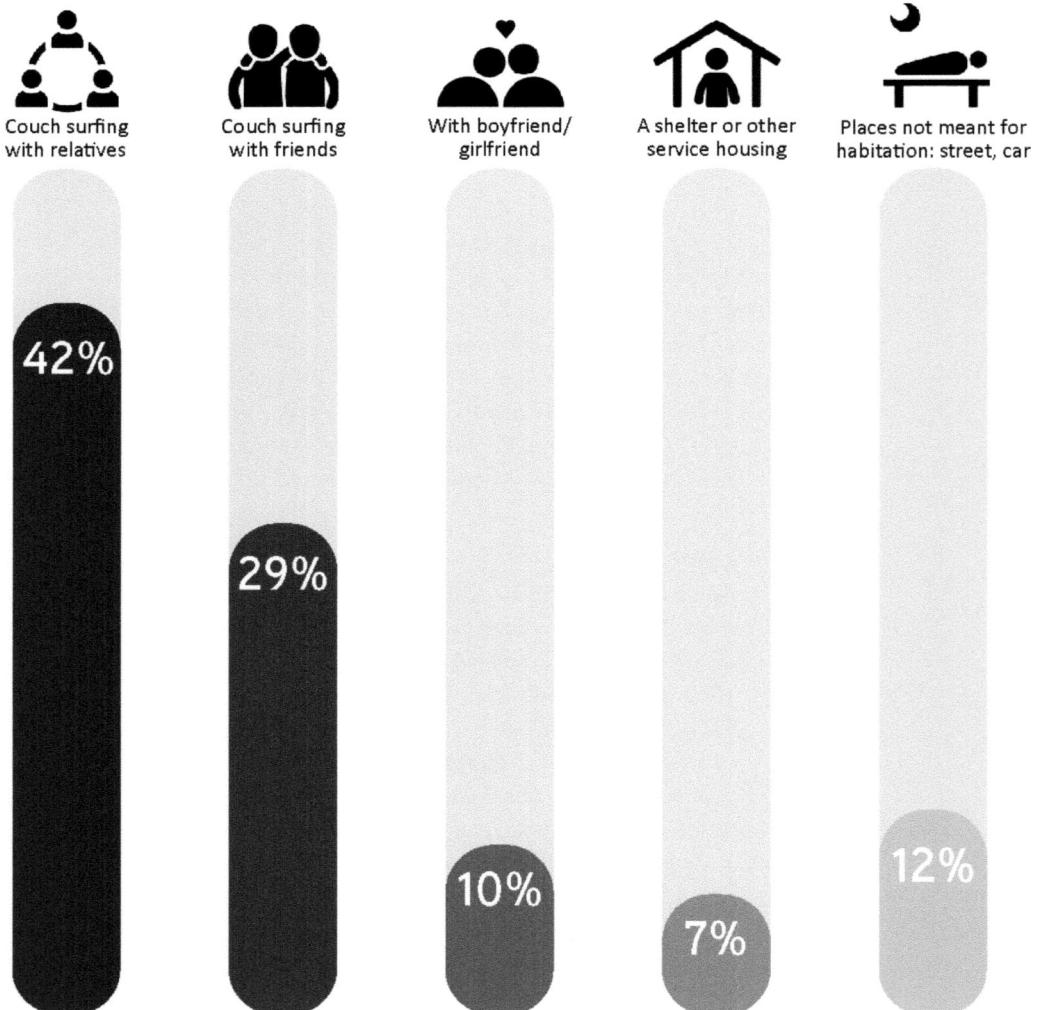

| Couch surfing with relatives | Couch surfing with friends | With boyfriend/ girlfriend | A shelter or other service housing | Places not meant for habitation: street, car |

42%

29%

10%

7%

12%

17,637 young adult students experiencing this form of homelessness sometime over the previous 6 months (ibid., p. 2). Studies from Connecticut, Pennsylvania, and Wisconsin have yielded similar data (Cutuli, 2018; Goldrick-Rab, Richardson, Schneider, Hernandez, & Cady, 2018; Youth Catalytics, 2015).

Johnny's Story

Johnny was doing everything right. He graduated from high school in Chicago, becoming the first in his family to finish high school. He started college at a histori-cally black university in Memphis and found a passion producing music. But by the spring of his freshman year, the stability Johnny had grown up with was stripped away after […] his mother had died from heart failure. "It was just a shaky, unstable road after that," he said.

For the next five years, Johnny lived with his oldest brother until being kicked out after an argument. He lived with a mentor until the house caught on fire. He lived with some of his mentor's friends in Memphis. He returned to Chicago and cycled through the homes of other family members and friends of friends. "They let me in," Johnny said, "but it was just weird staying with a bunch of strangers."

(Johnson, 2018, n.p.)

Johnny and young people like him are not often included in official homeless counts. They try to attract as little attention as possible and to place the smallest possible burden on their hosts and others (Niya Kelly, State Legislative Director for the Chicago Coalition for the Homeless, as reported in Johnson, 2018). These accommodations may come at significant personal or emotional costs. There may be safety risks. Some youths are made to give their disability checks or other ben-efits to their hosts. Some girls get trafficked (Johnson, 2018).

Substance Abuse

One of the most common stereotypes about homeless persons is that they are alcohol or drug abusers. Although substance abuse does occur more frequently among homeless persons than among the general population, statistical data reveal that, in the United States, only 38 percent of homeless persons suffer from alcohol abuse, and 25 percent from drug abuse (Fazel, Khosla, Doll, & Geddes, 2008; National Coalition for the Homeless, 2009b; Substance Abuse and Mental Health Services Administration, 2015). In a London-based study, however, two-thirds of respondents identified alcohol or drug abuse as the pri-mary cause of their homelessness (Didenko & Pankratz, 2007). Substance abuse issues often emerge as a result of a person being in the street. "A person might lean on alcohol or other drugs to help get through a tough night or face unpleas-antness during the day – shame, fear, hunger, and pain are just a few of the challenges a homeless person experiences" (Didenko & Pankratz, 2007, p. 10). A homeless person may perceive excessive alcohol and drug consumption as a pathway to being accepted into the homeless subculture. Given the intense feelings of social isolation reported by these persons, the need to be accepted becomes more acute.

James Wright, a distinguished American sociologist who studied poverty and homelessness, has candidly observed that alcohol or drug use within homeless populations can serve "positive functions" for a homeless individual (1989, p. 103). Many drink heavily to ease the miseries of their material, physical, and mental existences. As long as those reasons remain, so too do substance abuse problems. Wright reasons that this is cause for reconsideration:

> While outright sympathy for homeless alcohol and drug abusers may be more than many of us can muster, we should at least be able to understand that these problems are as often rooted in the existential conditions of homelessness as in the moral failings of a person's character.
>
> (1989, p. 103)

Mental Health

Substance abuse is often accompanied by psychological or psychiatric issues. The people we encounter in the streets often show signs of instability. Mental illness has overtaken alcoholism as the most common assumption that people make about homeless persons (Institute of Medicine (US) Committee on Health Care for Homeless People, 1988; Stark, 1985). This assumption is borne out, to some extent, by reality. In 2015, the United States Substance Abuse and Mental Health Services Administration reported that 25 percent of the homeless suffer from a serious mental condition, as opposed to 4.5 percent among the general population (National Institute of Mental Health, 2017). According to a 2008 U.S. Conference of Mayors report, mental illness was the third most cited reason for single adults to have become homeless, noted by 48 percent of respondents.[3] Among homeless families, it was the eighth most reported cause at 12 percent.

As state psychiatric hospitals across the United States closed in the 1950s and 60s without adequate provision for replacement care, the streets became a "psychiatric dumping ground" (Reich & Siegel, 1978; Treatment Advocacy Center, 2016).[4] The long-term nature of severe mental illness can lead to difficulty in obtaining and maintaining employment, observing self-care practices such as personal hygiene, and use of prescribed medicines. Lacking income to afford a place to live and being unable to maintain family or interpersonal relationships from which shared housing arrangements might extend, homelessness often follows.

Beginning in the early 1980s, studies began reporting on the extent of the intersections between mental illness and homelessness, finding that approximately one-third of the homeless population suffered from schizophrenia (28 percent), with schizoaffective disorder (10 percent) and bipolar disorder or major depression (22.5 percent) also widespread (Institute of Medicine (US) Committee on Health Care for Homeless People, 1988; Treatment Advocacy Center, 2016; Wright, 1989). It is notable that, in a 1989 study, the rate of identified mental disorders among homeless women was two times greater than in homeless men (Wright, 1989). Mentally ill homeless persons of all sexes were found to have been treated for their conditions at rates much lower than the general population (Torrey, n.d.).

Mentally ill homeless persons are at a greater risk of robbery or assault (Stark, 1985; Torrey, n.d.). As the *New York Times* reported,

> Seriously mentally ill individuals living in homeless shelters are said to be easy marks for thieves and other criminals who live there ... Those who receive social security disability checks become targets for muggers ... There is a hierarchy among the shelter clients, and the visibly mentally ill are the lowest caste, untouchables among the outcasts.
>
> (Dugger, 1992, n.p.)

Violent attacks on mentally ill homeless individuals resulting in severe bodily injuries or death happen with sad regularity (Torrey, n.d.). Mentally ill women are at greater risk of being sexually assaulted or robbed because, unlike other homeless women who tend to get protection by being with a husband, a partner, or other companion, they are frequently alone (Stark, 1985).

Mental illnesses significantly complicate pathways to recovery and exiting homelessness. Persons suffering from mental illness may encounter greater difficulties with accessing affordable housing than their unaffected counterparts as they struggle to maintain stable incomes and face stigma (both from within and outside the support services community) and a shortage of mental health services.

Self-Neglect and Hoarding

Self-neglect covers a wide range of behaviors related to failing to care for one's personal hygiene, health needs, or material surroundings, and it is often accompanied by compulsive accumulation or hoarding (Anka, Sorensen, Brandon, & Bailey, 2017; Department of Health, 2016). Self-neglect develops from and is perpetuated by lack of access to washing facilities, showers, or clean water, particularly when combined with an obsessive urge to carry as many personal possessions as possible.

Hoarding is characterized by persistent acquisition of and difficulty to discard a large number of possessions, regardless of their value to the owner or others (Andersen, Raffin-Bouchal, & Marcy-Edwards, 2008; Bratiotis et al., 2009; Brown & Pain, 2014; Davis & Edsell-Vetter, 2015). It is typically associated with progressively lower socioeconomic levels and homelessness (Bratiotis, Sorrentino, & Schmalisch, 2011), as it affects overall personal health and well-being and may lead to eviction and social isolation. Research indicates that the mandatory hygiene or cleaning interventions after forcible removal from residences or shelters appear to be ineffective long term (Brown & Pain, 2014), particularly without treatment of the underlying issues. In the United States and in Europe, studies indicate that between 2 and 5 percent of the homeless population may hoard their possessions. The condition typically sets in during the teenage years and worsens as a person ages (Andersen, Raffin-Bouchal, & Marcy-Edwards, 2008; Brown & Pain, 2014).

Physical Health

It is not surprising that people without homes have poorer overall physical health than the general population. Many homeless persons are very ill, and they may suffer from multiple aggravating conditions (Wright, 1989). The underlying conditions may be present before a person becomes homeless, but they are likely to remain untreated and worsen after one enters the street (Schanzer, Dominquez, Shrout, & Caton, 2007). Absence of suitable clothes, inadequate nutrition, minimal medical care, uncertain sleeping arrangements, various self-harming personal habits – particularly when combined with limited access to personal hygiene facilities – a shortage of safe places to administer medicines or other therapies, and medication theft "produce a health profile among the homeless that is an insult to any standard of human decency" (Wright, 1989, p. 110).

People who are unhoused suffer from statistically higher rates of physical trauma (injuries, foot wounds, and dental damage), skin problems, and parasites (head lice, body lice, and scabies) than the housed population (Aspinall, 2014; Institute of Medicine (US) Committee on Health Care for Homeless People, 1988). As many as 46 percent have chronic health problems, including arthritis, high blood pressure, diabetes, and cancer, and 26 percent have acute respiratory diseases such as bronchitis, pneumonia, tuberculosis, and asthma (Nooe & Patterson, 2010). Vision problems, gastrointestinal diseases, sexually transmitted diseases, and HIV/AIDS also occur at elevated rates (Schanzer et al., 2007; Wright, 1989). In his February 2019 State of the State speech, California Governor Gavin Newsom noted outbreaks of hepatitis A in San Diego County, syphilis in Sonoma County, and typhus in Los Angeles County. "Typhus," he said, "a medieval disease. In California. In 2019" (Gorman, 2019, n.p.). These diseases spread quickly and widely among people living outside or in shelters, helped along by sidewalks strewn with waste, crowded living conditions, weakened immune systems, and limited access to health care. Glenn Lopez, a physician with St. John's Well Child & Family Center, who treats homeless patients in Los Angeles County, describes the hygiene situation for people living on the streets as "horrendous." "It becomes just like a Third World environment, where human feces contaminate the areas where they are eating and sleeping," she says (Gorman, 2019, n.p.). Compounding injuries often occur as the result of a person being tired, disoriented, or intoxicated, including falls, beatings, street fights, and car strikes.[5] Severe health conditions may render a person unable to work, lacking the income necessary to maintain stable housing, or in economic distress brought on by medical bills.

In addition to lack of access to healthcare, the unhoused population is notoriously reluctant to seek medical help. Many have had negative experiences with health services that do not comprehend or adapt to their specific needs (O'Carroll & Wainwright, 2019). As a result, they often do not seek help until their health problem becomes acute or life threatening (Wise & Phillips, 2013).

WHO ARE PEOPLE WHO ARE HOMELESS?

Homelessness is an old and complex problem. In Chapter 2, we provided a brief history of how some Western societies have tried to tackle this pervasive dilemma.

Just as the social structures of our communities have become more complex, the faces of homelessness have become more diverse. Although the physical, psychological, and circumstantial challenges that unhoused persons face may be similar, each person has a unique personal history, and the circumstances and conditions that lead an individual to lose their home are always unique. They may be an honorably discharged veteran, a college student, an evicted family, a mentally impaired man, a runaway youth, or a drug-addicted woman. They may be of any race, nationality, class, or ethnicity. They may be from a city, a suburb, or rural area. This diversity converges, however, in two characteristics shared by nearly all unhoused persons – extreme poverty and lack of stable housing – which leads to isolation from traditional support networks provided by families and friends and culminating in a form of social rejection (Wright, 1989). A series of Spotlight Reports that address the architectural needs of various unhoused person groups is available at the Design Resources for Homelessness non-profit organization (2016). The reports provide detailed information that can assist with design programming of projects for families, victims of domestic violence, seniors and youth.

Families with Children

Wage stagnation, shrinking availability of affordable housing options, increasing medical costs, absence of accessible safety nets, and lack of social support expose families to the risk of losing their homes (Biel, Gilhuly, Wilcox, & Jacobstein, 2014, p. 1247). According to the U.S. Department of Housing and Urban Development's 2018 Annual Homeless Assessment Report, over 56,000 respondents with families lack a stable home (Henry et al., 2018).[6] On a single night in January of 2018, an estimated 189,413 adults with children were believed to be homeless – 33 percent of the overall homeless population. According to the report, about nine in ten people experiencing family homelessness were sheltered (164,023 people), while 16,390 families with children were counted in unsheltered locations – living in a car, sleeping rough, or in other places unsuitable for human habitation (Henry et al., 2018).

A typical homeless family consists of a single young woman with two or more children under 6 years of age (Henry et al., 2018). For this population, stress and trauma are "normal" conditions (Biel et al., 2014). Although statistical data show that the majority of homeless households reside in temporary housing, mothers and children living in emergency shelters or other facilities may still lack conditions conducive to healthy parent–child relationships.

> Consider a single parent in her early twenties with a history of significant trauma exposure, newly homeless, and living in a shelter with her two young children. She must spend her days working or looking for work, applying for more stable housing programs, and juggling her own and her children's nutritional needs, health care, and education, all with very limited social support.
>
> (Biel et al., 2014, p. 1248)

Families with children face higher rates of eviction than households without children. The financial hardships that face parents balancing work and caregiving responsibilities without reliable or affordable childcare can lead to lease violations stemming from overcrowding, property damage, noise, or behavior complaints. Families often face stigma after an eviction. They may have to move in with other households or relocate to lower-quality housing in neighborhoods that are unsafe or distressed. This cascading set of hardships, risks, and harms can contribute to prolonged instability, lost employment opportunities, health risks, and poor school performance (Desmond, An, Winkler, & Ferriss, 2013).

Over the last decade, the "working homeless" phenomenon has emerged. One may have a job but still not be able to escape homelessness. According to a 2013 article in the *New York Times*, "more than one out of four families in shelters, 28 percent, include at least one employed adult" in New York City (Navarro, 2013, n.p.; Woolley, 2016). The author noted that they are mostly women who work

> in a variety of low-wage jobs as security guards, bank tellers, sales clerks, computer instructors, home health aides, and office support staff members. At work they present an image of adult responsibility, while in the shelter they must obey curfews and show evidence that they are actively looking for housing and saving part of their paycheck.

Many unhoused families across the United States find themselves in a similar situation:

Cokethia's Story

> Cokethia returned home from work one August evening to discover a letter from her landlord giving her notice that her lease would not be renewed and that she had 30 days to move out.
>
> She knew very well the Atlanta housing market and how easy it was to lose a lease and did her best to avoid this. She ensured that her rent checks were never late and, despite her exhausting work schedule, became a stickler for cleanliness. So strong was her fear of being deemed a "difficult" tenant that she avoided requesting basic repairs. But it appeared that her efforts had been in vain. Her landlord [...] did not provide any explanation, although she later admitted that the house sale was connected to planned gentrification of the area.
>
> Three months after losing her home, Cokethia finally came to a continuum of care services organization for the homeless in Atlanta. She had spent the past several weeks reaching out to emergency family shelters and nonprofits, and the responses were always the same: She first needed to undergo an assessment through a coordinated entry system, and it had to be done in person. She was angry and exhausted, and she was ashamed. But she was desperate, too. A polite case manager conducted Cokethia's assessment. But the meeting did not last long: based on her answers, her "vulnerability score" was too low to receive assistance.
>
> (Goldstone, 2019)

Children and Adolescents

Youth homelessness was not thought to be a widespread phenomenon until the 1980s, when increasing numbers of homeless children made it more visible

(Gaetz, 2014). It is difficult to report total numbers of unaccompanied children and adolescents because this group does not congregate in areas with homeless adults, where the majority of point-in-time counts occur (Perlman, Willard, Herbers, Cutuli, & Eyrich Garg, 2014; United States Conference of Mayors, 2016). The United States Interagency Council on Homelessness estimates that unaccompanied youth make up about 11 percent (or 41,000) of all people experiencing homelessness as individuals on a given night.[7] Most of these young people (88 percent or 36,010 people) were between the ages of 18 and 25, and 12 percent (4,789 people) were under the age of 18. More than half (55 percent) were unsheltered, meaning that they were sleeping in the streets, in cars, or in other places inadequate for human needs (United States Interagency Council on Homelessness, 2018).

When family and home environments are no longer available to young people, and when there are no adequate social safety nets, these people may become homeless (Farrugia, 2016). According to a report produced by the Voices of Youth Count, a national, multicomponent research and policy initiative (Samuels, Cerven, Curry, S., Robinson, & Patel, 2019), youth homelessness begins with "instability and disruptions of home," resulting in family homelessness or transition to foster care. Most youth who participated in the count said that, "their first spell of homelessness grew out of volatile or unsafe family contexts that, over time, erupted into parental rejection, getting kicked out, or fleeing family conflict" (Samuels et al., 2019, p. 4).[8] Another motive was a "desire for independence" (Rosenthal, Mallett, & Myers, 2006). It is often difficult, however, to distinguish the motivations between the two reasons.

3.2
A homeless youth
in upstate New York.

Homeless youth experience a wide array of social, psychological, and health issues, including "incomplete" or "blended" families; mental health problems including anxiety, depression, or aggression; drug use; criminal activity; poverty; family conflict; physical or sexual abuse; "delinquency"; problems with school attendance; low self-esteem; lack of ego control; and ineffective coping strategies (Farrugia, 2016, p. 5). As a result, they often feel lonely and disconnected from others (Kidd, 2004). Relationships that they establish in the street can be so important that they choose not to pursue social services or housing opportunities (Samuels et al., 2019).

Baylee's Story

Seventeen-year-old Baylee lives in San Diego. Her homelessness started when she was just two years old when her mother and two older sisters lost their house. Baylee described these childhood years as "mov[ing] around a lot" between hotels, shelters, apartments of friends, and family. She attributed this instability to her mother's poor health and, as a result, her inability to hold a steady job.

When Baylee was eleven, her mother committed suicide, and Baylee entered foster care. It took two years for the court to approve an out-of-state placement with her father, stepmother, and stepsiblings. Once there, she became the target of ongoing conflict and arguments. Baylee increasingly struggled with her mental health and was hospitalized multiple times for attempting suicide. Upon discharge, her required "safety plan" included talking with her dad. Baylee explained, "Because of my mental health issues, like I told my dad that I needed to talk to him, and he was like, 'No!'" Feeling rejected, she left home. Her dad told her not to return. She never did.

Baylee first stayed in a hotel with a friend [...], but then she moved to an emergency shelter for minors. She could not be there long because her father refused to sign the paperwork. Baylee then began to exchange sex and "do stuff" to pay for a hotel room. Not wanting this to continue and afraid of sleeping outside on the streets, she returned to the shelter. They let her in and the following morning the shelter convinced Baylee's father to sign for her to stay. When we met Baylee, her 21-day limit at the shelter (a federally mandated restriction) was approaching. She was eagerly awaiting acceptance into Job Corps. Baylee felt optimistic that through Job Corps a brighter future was on her horizon.

(Samuels et al., 2019, paras. 1–3)

LGBTQ

Individuals who identify as lesbian, gay, bisexual, transgender, and questioning (or queer)[9] spectrum encounter a particular set of challenges when they enter homelessness.[10] Studies indicate that queer youth are many times more likely to experience homelessness than their heterosexual counterparts. According to a recent report by the Williams Institute, 40 percent of homeless youth served by agencies identify as LGBTQ (Cochran et al., 2002; Choi et al., 2015; Coolhart & Brown, 2017). Surveys also indicate that 68 percent had a history of family rejection, 65 percent had mental health issues (such as depression or anxiety), and 54 percent had a history of family abuse (physical, emotional, or sexual; Choi et al., 2015).

LGBTQ youth face challenges common to all homeless persons while also encountering additional difficulties with finding shelters run by organizations that do not discriminate against them. Anton, an 18-year-old gay male described his experience:

> After they realized I was gay I mean they kind of put me with the girls, where they had like a separation thing. Guys go with girls. Girls go with guys. And I know there was this one kid there that, she was gay and they put her with the guys, so that way she wouldn't be with the girls. I don't know, I just felt like it was really awkward. Because once you find out someone's sexual orientation, you have to shift every-thing because you think that they're gonna like do something sickening or whatever.
>
> (Coolhart & Brown, 2017, p. 233)

Relative to their heterosexual peers, LGBTQ individuals experiencing home-lessness are often at a heightened risk of violence, abuse, exploitation, mental health issues, and unsafe sexual practices (Barrow, 2018; Coolhart & Brown, 2017). According to a 2017 study, the rate of sexual victimization of queer homeless youth was almost two times higher than that of heterosexual youth (59 percent and 33 percent, respectively; National Coalition for the Homeless, 2017).

> Observed one youth, "street kids and foster children were considered fair game for sexual predators since we were already perceived as damaged and worthless. Our worthlessness was undoubtedly compounded by being queer/gender-variant. A man combed the Tenderloin district [of San Francisco] for young runaway boys and street hustlers and would offer them shelter and opportunities for gainful employ-ment if they would f— him in exchange. He fancied himself quite the philanthropist."
>
> (Tenzin, 2010, p. 20)

Shelters are not always safe places for LGBTQ youth. Many have been abused at shelters, especially if placed together with adults. Many LGBTQ youth avoid shel-ters altogether (Coolhart & Brown, 2017; National Coalition for the Homeless, 2017; Siciliano, 2015).[11] They are more likely than their straight counterparts to exchange sexual favors for basic needs – beds, shelters, food, and clothing:

> Survival sex (or sex work) is a desperate, risky behavior born out of isolation and the lack of any tangible resources. It causes negative health outcomes for any homeless youth, but especially for highly vulnerable LGBT homeless young people. Those who have been abused while younger, especially sexually abused males, are particularly prone to taking sexual risks.
>
> (Ray, 2010, p. 187)

Profound traumatic experiences are woven into the very fabric of homeless youth experiences. Such a crisis may be a cause of leaving home and lead to a person's exasperation, exposure to the elements, hunger, and street violence. Environments that support youth trying to exit homelessness must be safe, support socialization, offer privacy for rest and contemplation, allow for person-alization, and give opportunities for addressing needs, education, and recreation, facilitating trust through limiting rules and regulation (Kitchell & Hearn, 2019).

Single Women

Women are the fastest growing homeless group in the Unites States (Arangua, Andersen, & Gelberg, 2005; Henry et al., 2018).[12] According to a point-in-time count presented in the 2018 Annual Homeless Assessment Report, women make up approximately 29 percent of the overall homeless population in the United States (Henry et al., 2018, p. 23). About 30 percent of sheltered individuals and 27 percent of persons sleeping in the streets are women. The proportion among unaccompa-nied youth is higher, at 38 percent (one-third of whom were staying in unsheltered locations; Henry et al., 2018, p. 46).

In a comprehensive study on homeless women conducted by Arangua, Andersen, and Gelberg (2005), 72 percent of homeless women identified as being single or separated from their children. Many cited traumatic personal or social circumstances, reporting disproportionately high rates of victimization, mental ill-nesses, and substance abuse. According to several studies (Jasinski et al., 2005), one out of five women cited sexual and physical abuse as the main reason for their homelessness, whether episodic or prolonged. The path to homelessness often starts with severe physical abuse, including life-threatening episodes in which women's intimate partners threaten to or actually attempt to kill them; emotional, psychological, and verbal abuse; sexual abuse; financial abuse; spiritual abuse; and stalking (Tutty et al., 2013). In many instances, violence started in their child-hood: 32 percent of homeless women experienced rape as children (compared with 9 percent of women in the general population; Ruggiero et al., 2004), and 44 percent suffered from physical abuse as children (compare with 40 percent in the general population; Thompson, Kingree, & Desai, 2004).[13]

Brittany's* Story

He was beating me all the time. I was always covered in bruises. He started beating me because I wouldn't give him money to buy coke. I felt helpless.

He would beat me. I went to work with black eyes. I had to wear sunglasses all the time.

He seemed to get great pleasure showing people what he'd done to me. It was always my eyes, my face, and my neck would be black and blue because he choked me. I would feel so sore. If I didn't go to work he would freak out. There was never remorse.

He'd broken just about every bone in my head, and I couldn't take it. He threw me out a three-story window and I broke my back in three places. I was in a wheel-chair. The doctor said I'll never walk again, but I walked on my own.

(Tutty et al., 2013, p.7)

* The authors have used a fictional name for this story.

Studies conducted over the last 40 years have found that rates of violence against homeless women are many times higher than in the rest of the population. "Physical and sexual violence and exploitation are exceedingly common elements in the lives of homeless women and are a major precipitating factor for homelessness among women" (Wright, Rubin, & Devine, 1998, p. 155; see also Jasinski et al., 2005). Accordingly, 13 percent of unhoused women experienced rape in the last year alone, compared with 3.2 percent of poor housed women; and 34 percent experienced physical abuse in the previous year, compared with 22 percent of poor housed women and 6 percent of women in the general population (Kushel et al., 2003; Potter et al., 1999).

Tamara's Story

Tamara had a job while living on the streets in Washington, D.C. She slept outside the church across from the White House: She would go to Burger King or McDonald's to the bathroom in the morning and wash up to go to work. She would take bags with her possessions to her job and put them in her locker.

Tamara was diabetic. In the morning, she would go to a nearby church where a nun offered to refrigerate her medications. Tamara would come to the church for the shot of insulin every morning and evening. But making it through each day, even with this minimal support, was very difficult: "I had to work. I had to go to work presentable. I couldn't go there looking like I had just slept in the street. Mentally and physically I was stressed out."

She could not sleep fully at night because she was scared and had to be on guard to protect herself from an assault, "so every day I was fighting to keep my sanity. To go to work. After dealing with homeless men trying to have sex with me, trying to take my money, talking to homeless women that's talking out of their head or mental, sleeping in the street hoping that nobody is going to come and kill me in my sleep or a rat is going to come and bite me, and then prepare myself to look presentable, to get to work and talk on a normal, average level among my coworkers and my boss, not to be sleepy, not to looked drained ... It was stressful."

(Jasinski et al., 2005, p. 58)

Veterans

Veterans make up approximately 9 percent of all homeless adults in the United States (approximately 37,800 veterans were experiencing homelessness on a single night in January 2018).[14] The affected groups include those who served in the late Vietnam and post-Vietnam eras, along with veterans returning from deployments in Afghanistan and Iraq (National Alliance to End Homelessness, 2019). Approximately 91 percent, were single men, and 8.5 percent were women. Only 2 percent of veterans experienced homelessness with a family (Henry et al., 2018). Several studies have found that female veterans are at a higher percentage risk to experience homelessness than men (Byrne, Montgomery, & Dichter, 2013).

Among veterans, the strongest predictors of homelessness are low income, chronic psychological issues, and substance abuse (Metraux et al., 2013; O'Connell,

Kasprow, & Rosenheck, 2008). A recent study showed a clear relationship between veterans with PTSD, bipolar disorder, mental illness, and both recent and chronic incidents of homelessness (Copeland et al., 2009). Being unmarried, being African American, and being between the ages of 46 and 55 also correlated with higher levels of homelessness (Tsai, Hoff, & Harpaz-Rotem, 2017). One factor is leaving the protected, regimented military life without the skills needed to function as a civilian, including personal money management. Said one veteran, "I've been so used to [where] I had a place where I could eat, sleep, things like that. It was very secure. Then coming out to where it's not like that anymore" (Metraux et al., 2017, p. 232–233). For many veterans who had enlisted into the military to escape poverty, the service provided only temporary relief, and life after discharge was a "false promise" (Wright, 1989, p. 64).

James's Story

James enlisted in the military hoping to straighten his life out. As a self-described wild child, he grew up in orphanages and foster homes and struggled with addiction to alcohol and drugs. "I was a kid and I was in trouble, and somebody told me maybe I should think about [enlisting] … my buddy and I tried to go into the Marines, they took him, but the Marines wouldn't take me … I had a few problems in life. But the Army ate me right up."

Once out of the Army, James spent some time in prison in Arizona, and that is where he picked up a Bible and his life started to really straighten out. He came back to the Rapid City area [South Dakota] in 2008 and worked at carpentry and landscaping in federal parks. Then he started having some medical problems and [became] homeless.

(Greager, 2017, n.p.)

Women make up a smaller group of homeless veterans, but they often deal with additional issues related to stress and psychological and sexual trauma experienced while in the military (Pavao et al., 2013; Washington et al., 2010).

Sandra's Story

Sandra was an electrician in the Navy for five years, working on F-14 Tomcat fighters at bases in Virginia and California. After she got out of the military, she had her first son and got introduced to meth, which led to her living on the streets of Omaha for a while.

"I don't know what caused it," Sandra said. "The mental condition after I got out of the military. I don't know if it was from the military or what. We're trying to figure that out. […] So meth was a way to stop the nightmares and stop the condition. The mental condition. And I've been battling it ever since. I get three and a half years sober, then I relapse. […] The VA, this is the first time I've gone for help with them. So it's totally a different avenue, we're trying it this way."

Sandra said it wasn't easy being a woman in the military, and talked of "rampant" sexual abuse when she was in. "There's so many women that are hurt physically and mentally in the military. And it's just missed. […] Because you're just so afraid to say anything when you're in the military because you're supposed to be strong."

(Tobias, 2018, n.p.)

Veterans who participated in combat revealed strong connections between their experiences in the military, behavioral and mental health issues (most were diagnosed with PTSD, accompanied by major depression), and losing stable housing (Metraux et al., 2013). Bipolar disorder and traumatic brain injuries are also present. Anger and anxiety are common manifestations of these ailments, resulting in avoidance of public places and social interactions, which lead to straining family relations, reluctance to seek assistance, and difficulties with finding employment. All of these factors contribute to the increased isolation that often accompanies homelessness (Metraux et al., 2013).

According to Michael Green, whose research focuses on the problem of homelessness, it is still not clear why rejoining civilian life is such a challenge for this group or what may help them. Green pointed out, however, that the situation is similar to another population that struggles with community integration: individuals with psychotic disorders, including schizophrenia, adding that "providing housing is a necessary but insufficient means of helping formerly homeless veterans find a place in the world" (Green as cited in Sullivan, 2016, n.p.).

Seniors

As adults age, they become increasingly vulnerable to health problems, job loss, stagnant wages, rising medical bills, and rising housing costs. Any combination of these may lead to a loss of stable housing.[15] Currently, about 44 percent of unhoused adults aged 50 or older had never experienced homelessness before (Lee et al., 2016), but, as the overall population in the United States is aging, numbers of homeless seniors are increasing. In addition to economic circumstances, factors include declining health, struggles with addictions, severed relationships with family members or partners, and structural social issues (inability to perform physical labor, a criminal record, difficulty with navigating social support system, discrimination, or absence of social services; Caton et al., 2005).

Older adults struggling with homelessness face a complex set of challenges: stress, trauma, loneliness and isolation, premature aging, increased rates of physical and mental decline, chronic illness, targeted assaults, trouble accessing benefits, risk of institutionalization, and higher rates of mortality (Crane et al., 2005; Goldberg, Lang, & Barrington, 2016). After becoming street sleepers, many seniors experience difficulties with mobility or accessing shelters located on upper stories of buildings. Even the physical exertion required to stand in line for accommodations can be too much (National Coalition for the Homeless, 2009a).

Carl's story

Each night Carl sleeps sitting up in a sleeping bag on a concrete sidewalk in front of San Diego's Gary and Mary West Senior Wellness Center. "This is my problem right here – trying to get up with two bad knees. I had two surgeries to replace two hips and being cold all night doesn't help." He also cannot sleep well at night because he "doesn't want to get his throat cut." His cane is his only defense in case of attack.

He wakes up at five a.m. each day and walks several blocks to a deli shop to use a bathroom. He showers and eats breakfast at the senior wellness center and then rides a bus for several hours to catch up on sleep.

Carl used to own a restaurant in Chicago and he also worked as a truck driver. He came to San Diego more than two decades ago with a dream to buy a house and retire, but admits to "wasting" the money on hotel stays.

He said he knew other homeless seniors who killed themselves out of desperation. He wants a job to supplement the $800 a month he receives from Social Security, but "who's going to hire you when you're in your 70s?" he asks. "And what are you qualified to do when you got bad health? You can't breathe. You can't see. You can't walk."

Carl wants to get off the streets and searches almost every day for housing. [...] With the aid of a pro bono lawyer, he is trying to convince the Teamsters Union he is entitled to a pension from his truck-driving days. While he awaits that case's outcome, he remains hopeful along with prayer, help and encouragement.

(Sharma, 2019, n.p.)

The average life expectancy for persons experiencing chronic homelessness in the United States is between 42 and 64 years (compared with the national average of 80 years; Culhane, Metraux, & Bainbridge, 2010; National Coalition for the Homeless, 2009a). Acute and chronic medical conditions aggravated by homeless life, mental illness, or substance abuse were the most frequent causes of premature deaths (National Leadership Initiative to End Elder Homelessness, 2011).

Indigenous Populations – Canada, Australia, New Zealand

In the United States, Canada, Australia, and New Zealand, indigenous peoples have suffered under brutal colonization policies of cultural genocide resulting in loss of traditional lands, ways of life, and sense of self-identity (Peters & Christensen, 2016). These policies continue to manifest in discriminatory stereotyping, stigmatizing, inequitable distribution of resources, and denial of educational and economic opportunities. As a result, the rate of indigenous homelessness, especially those who sleep in unsheltered locations, is much higher than that of the general population (City of Toronto, 2018; Australian Institute of Health and Welfare, 2014).[16]

Stella's story

I was 6 years old when I was taken away from my parents and forced into a residential school. The Department of Indian Affairs came to our reserve in the 1950s, taking Native children away and placing them in residential schools to learn the White way of life. In these schools, we were punished for speaking our language. All I remember is being punished for anything and everything. I grew up with a tremendous amount of shame and loss of dignity.

[One time] the nuns had beaten me so badly that my ears would not stop bleeding. The doctor determined that I had permanently lost my hearing in both ears.

When I was older, I moved to the Downtown Eastside [a neighborhood in Vancouver] and found work at a fish plant. Low-income housing [here] is of such sub-standard quality that many prefer to sleep on the streets. Problems include absence of heat, toilets, and running water, mold, bedbug infestations, rats, and illegal practices by landlords including refusal to return deposits, entering rooms without permission, and arbitrary evictions.

It is hard to describe all the different experiences that women [who live here] have [...] the fact that many of us do not know our parents because the legacy of residential schools and colonization has destroyed our families, the chronic and often fatal illnesses such as AIDS and Hepatitis C that break our bodies, the grief of living through the deaths of our missing and murdered sisters, and much more.

But despite the poverty, criminalization, and trauma, we all care for each other and socialize with one another. Whether people are sober or high on drugs, we listen to each other's dreams and desires to make this neighborhood a better place.

(August, 2011, n.p.)

The challenges of indigenous homelessness lie not only in economic and social inequalities, but also in our very understanding of homelessness under Western values, which do not reflect the perspectives of indigenous populations. Indigenous persons, especially those who grew up outside of their community, are often caught in between cultures and do not feel a sense of belonging to either (Thistle, 2017). Solving the homelessness problem does not mean only providing shelter or conditions suitable for human habitation. Emphasis upon and integration with ancestral community connections and support can be key (Distasio et al., 2019).

When discussing indigenous homelessness, it is important to place it in the context of indigenous cultural practices. For example, Indigenous individuals in Canada are often more mobile, traveling regularly between reserves, and have temporary accommodations in more than one community (Patrick, 2014). Accordingly, the Aboriginal Standing Committee on Housing and Homelessness views Indigenous homelessness as a concept that is:

fully described and understood through a composite lens of Indigenous worldviews. These include: individuals, families and communities isolated from their relationships to land, water, place, family, kin, each other, animals, cultures, languages and identities. Importantly, Indigenous people experiencing these kinds of homelessness cannot culturally, spiritually, emotionally or physically reconnect with their Indigeneity or lost relationships.

(Thistle, 2017, p. 6)

Central to this definition of homelessness is the indigenous interpretation of home, which is understood holistically as a sense of "rootedness," or connectedness

Western Concepts	Traditional Indigenous Concepts
House (a building)	Domestic space with hearth and artifacts (may or may not have a shelter depending on season and weather)
Home (one's regularly used house)	Estate or 'country' (contains multiple campsites, resource places, and scattered sites)
Household (those living in a home)	Band (patrician plus spouses, extended family members, and visitors, all maintaining strong relationships)
House design (architecture)	Campsite selection (with access to resources, resource harvesting strategies, and band group invitations to visit and dwell together)

to a community or several communities and their history, and environment – "to human kinship networks; relationships with animals, plants, spirits and elements; relationships with the Earth, lands, waters and territories; and connection to traditional stories, songs, teachings, names and ancestors" (Thistle, 2017, p. 14). In Australia, the traditional Indigenous construct of home is closely associated with what is known as a campsite[17] and included several components – site selection, availability of resources, shelter type, and maintaining familial and kin relations (Memmott, 2015; see 3.3).

Unhoused indigenous persons share many experiences with non-indigenous populations including poverty, substance abuse, and trauma. A physical condition that often characterizes indigenous homelessness is substandard housing and overcrowding (Peters & Christensen, 2016). Overcrowding is a phenomenon that occurs as the result of social and cultural obligations of extended family and kin networks (Greenop & Memmott, 2016). Households sacrifice the comfort of their home for immediate family for these obligations and "are proud to do so" (p. 292). There are, however, negative aspects that come with assuming these obligations: elevated levels of stress associated with sharing household resources, maintaining cleanliness in the house, and disruptive behaviors resulting from drunkenness. Socio-spatial arrangements may help with management of the household while supporting cultural obligations and norms (Greenop & Memmott, 2016).

CONCLUSION

This chapter began with a brief discussion of the main reasons that lead so many individuals into homelessness, such as poverty, displacement, substance abuse, and poor physical and mental health, many of which often go hand in hand with traumatic personal histories. To dispel stereotypes and common misconceptions about unhoused individuals, we discussed different homeless population groups, their concerns, and needs, and offered insights into their lives, perceptions, and priorities through individual stories of hardships, abuse, neglect, loss of dignity, suffering, trauma, fight for survival, and hopes for a safer and better future. Built environments must start from the premise that *empathetic* and *considerate* architecture and design are key to addressing the issues of extreme poverty and personal well-being. Before proceeding with the planning and design of such facilities, architects, designers, and stakeholders must be attuned to the diversity of backgrounds, circumstances, and needs that the unhoused person may bring.

NOTES

1. Chapter 5 details a research study titled "Adverse Childhood Experiences," which convincingly linked early life experiences with later difficulties, including homelessness.
2. See e.g., Goldrick-Rab, Richardson, Schneider, Hernandez, & Cady (2018), published online by the Wisconsin HOPE Lab: https://hope4college.com/reports/
3. The two most reported reasons were substance abuse (68%) and lack of affordable housing (60%; United States Conference of Mayors, 2008).
4. The number of beds in publicly supported psychiatric institutions has been shrinking, and the remaining are reserved for patients with criminal offenses, meaning that it is becoming increasingly difficult for the homeless with serious mental illnesses to find help (Treatment Advocacy Center, 2016).
5. Homeless individuals make up 20–30% of all adult emergency room visits. Homeless patients are admitted to inpatient units five times more often and have average lengths of stay that are longer than these of non-homeless persons. Homelessness is also associated with a shortened lifespan (Schanzer, Dominquez, Shrout, & Caton, 2007).
6. This is a 29% decline compared with the 2010 numbers right after the height of the 2008 recession (Henry et al., 2018).
7. The term *unaccompanied youth* describes "young people under the age of 25 and who are not part of a family with children or accompanied by their parent of guardian during their episode of homelessness" (United States Interagency Council on Homelessness, 2018, p. 1).
8. Over 50% first experienced homelessness between the ages of 16 and 18, and another 21% became homeless during early adolescence, between the ages of 13 and 15. Only 1% of youth reported a first-time experience of homelessness after the age of 21. Interviews do, however, suggest the beginnings of their housing instability occurred far earlier than these statistics imply (Samuels et al., 2019).
9. This category was recognized as such only recently. The word "queer" was adopted to identify those who did not identify with traditional male and female sexual orientation only in the 1980s (Barrow, 2018). Although this group may now be recognized in the cultural mainstream, it remains unaccepted by many, often including family members and friends of persons who identify as queer. As a result, the group remains marginalized, and parents' inability to reconcile a child's queer identity may cause the young person to be forced from home or flee from physical or emotional abuse or because of conflicts with parents about their sexual orientation. This explains the fact that this group is rather young relative to the overall homeless population (Barrow, 2018).
10. Twenty six percent of homeless LGBTQ youth report being forced out of their homes because of their gender identity or sexual orientation (Choi, Wilson, Shelton, & Gates, 2015).
11. In 2016, the Department of Housing and Urban Development (HUD) released a new Gender Identity Rule which ensures equal access to HUD shelter programs for LGBTQ people. This rule, however, will only apply to those shelters and service providers who receive federal funding.
12. Over the past 60 years, the homeless women population increased about ten times from 3% in 1963 to almost 30% today (Henry et al., 2018).
13. We discuss the impact of adverse childhood experiences on adult behaviors and attitudes in Chapter 6.

14. According to the 2018 Annual Homeless Assessment Report, since 2009, the number of veterans experiencing homelessness has dropped by 48.4%.
15. Economic data suggest that about 28% of Americans nearing retirement age (50–64) have no retirement savings. An average balance of those who do is only $150,000, and the median is only $12,000 (Ghilarducci et al., 2015). The economic security of this group was further eroded by the 2007–2010 recession, when many people lost equity in their homes (Joint Center for Housing Studies of Harvard University, 2014). Those who lost their homes became renters, which, in the absence of tenant protections and with ever-rising monthly expenses, put them at the mercy of landlords.
16. It is estimated that about 30,000 Indigenous persons struggle to find shelter each night in Canada. In Toronto, where only 2.5% of the population is of Indigenous ancestry, they make up 64 & of the overall homeless population and 54% of homeless youth (City of Toronto, 2018). In Winnipeg, 66% of the local population experiencing homelessness is Indigenous, with Indigenous youth homelessness at 74% rate (Distasio et al., 2019). In Australia, during a national one-night count, there were an estimated 26,743 Indigenous people experiencing homelessness, or 28% of all the homeless population, in a place where Indigenous people make up only 3% of the total population. The Indigenous homeless youth rate was about 42% of overall homeless youth. Three-quarters of Indigenous people experiencing homelessness were living in severely crowded dwellings (Australian Institute of Health and Welfare, 2014). In Auckland, New Zealand, the majority of homeless were Māori and older than 30 years of age. At the Christchurch City Mission men's night shelter, the most common ethnic groups were Pākehā (53%), Māori (38%), and Pacific (5%); in the women's night shelter, 50% were Pākehā and 41% Māori (New Zealand Parliament, 2014).
17. Campsite is Indigenous clan members' dwelling, distinguished by a name, resources, protection, connections to spiritual and cultural sites (story places, initiation grounds, mourning, etc.), economic activities (harvesting, hunting, getting fresh water, etc.), and bio-social events (birthing, feasting, and person-naming, etc.; Memmott, 2015). Campsites are complex spatial formations connected with other sites and other places of spiritual, cultural, and emotional significance, and to which kinspeople are attached through their social practices and "past habitations and events" memories. The concept of campsite, therefore, is larger than a physical house or a group of houses: "Traditional shelter, humpies, sheds, outstations, and even conventional housing may be regarded as mere artefacts for interim shelter in this more emotionally and culturally charged landscape" (Memmott et al., 2003, p. 14).

BIBLIOGRAPHY

Adelson, N. (2005). The embodiment of inequity: Health disparities in aboriginal Canada. *Canadian Journal of Public Health*, *96*, S45–S61. doi:https://doi.org/10.1007/BF03403702

Andersen, E., Raffin-Bouchal, S., & Marcy-Edwards, D. (2008). Reasons to accumulate excess: older adults who hoard possessions. *Home Health Care Services Quarterly*, *27*(3), 187–216. doi:10.1080/01621420802319993

Anka, A., Sorensen, P., Brandon, M., & Bailey, S. (2017). Social work intervention with adults who self-neglect in England: responding to the Care Act 2014. *The Journal of Adult Protection*, *19*(2), 67–77. doi:10.1108/JAP-11-2016-0027

Arangua, L., Andersen, R., & Gelberg, L. (2005). The health circumstances of homeless women in the United States. *International Journal of Mental Health*, *34*(2), 62–92. doi:10.1080/00207411.2005.11043398

Aspinall, P. J. (2014). *Identifying key vulnerable groups in data collections: vulnerable migrants, gypsies and travelers, homeless people, and sex workers*. Canterbury, UK: Centre for Health Services Studies, University of Kent. Retrieved from https://assets.publishing.

service.gov.uk/government/uploads/system/uploads/attachment_data/file/287805/vulnerable_groups_data_collections.pdf

August, S. (2011). Residential schools and my journey to the Downtown Eastside. Canada: Homeless Hub. Retrieved from www.homelesshub.ca/resource/residential-schools-and-my-journey-downtown-eastside

Australian Institute of Health and Welfare. (2014). *Homelessness among Indigenous Australians. Cat. no. IHW 133.* Canberra: AIHW.

Barrow, S. K. (2018). Scholarship review of queer youth homelessness in Canada and the United States. *American Review of Canadian Studies, 48*(4), 415–431. doi:https://doi.org/10.1080/02722011.2018.1531603

Beaumon, N. (2010, November 25). Homeless … but thankful. National Public Radio. Retrieved from www.npr.org/sections/tellmemore/2010/11/24/131576544/homeless-but-thankful

Biel, M. G., Gilhuly, D., Wilcox, N., & Jacobstein, D. (2014). Family homelessness: a deepening crisis in urban communities. *Journal of the American Academy of Child & Adolescent Psychiatry, 53*(12), 1247–1250. doi:https://doi.org/10.1016/j.jaac.2014.08.015

Bill Wilson Center. (2017). *Hidden in plain sight: documenting homeless youth populations.* Santa Clara, CA: Bill Wilson Center. Retrieved from www.billwilsoncenter.org/news_events/research.html

Bloomfield, M. A. (2014). *My eyes feel they need to cry: stories from the formerly homeless.* East Lansing, MI: Michigan State University Press.

Bratiotis, C., Otte, S., Steketee, G., & Muroff, J. (2009). Hoarding disorder fact sheet. International Obsessive Compulsive Disorder (OCD) Foundation. Retrieved from https://iocdf.org/brochures-and-fact-sheets/B

Bratiotis, C., Sorrentino, C., & Schmalisch, G. (2011). *The hoarding handbook: a guide for human service professionals.* Oxford, New York: Oxford University Press.

Braye, S., Orr, D., & Preston-Shoot, M. (2011). *Self-neglect and adult safeguarding: findings from research.* London: Social Care Institute for Excellence.

Brown, F., & Pain, A. (2014). Developing an approach to working with hoarding: space for social work. *Practice, 26*(4), 211–224. doi:10.1080/09503153.2014.934799

Byrne, T., Montgomery, A., & Dichter, M. (2013). Homelessness among female veterans: a systematic review of the literature. *Women & Health, 53,* 572–596. doi:http://dx.doi.org/10.1080/03630242.2013.817504

Caton, C. L., Dominguez, B., Schanzer, B., Hasin, D., Shrout, P., Felix, A., & Hsu, E. (2005). Risk factors for long-term homelessness: findings from a longitudinal study of first-time homeless single adults. *American Journal of Public Health, 95*(10), 1753–1759. doi:10.2105/AJPH.2005.063321

Choi, S. K., Wilson, B., Shelton, J., & Gates, G. (2015). *Serving our youth 2015: the needs and experiences of lesbian, gay, bisexual, transgender, and questioning youth experiencing homelessness.* Los Angeles, CA: The Williams Institure with Thrue Colors Fund. Retrieved from https://williamsinstitute.law.ucla.edu/research/safe-schools-and-youth/serving-our-youth-2015-the-needs-and-experiences-of-lesbian-gay-bisexual-transgender-and-questioning-youth-experiencing-homelessness/

City of Toronto. (2018). *Toronto street needs assessment.* Toronto, Canada.

Cochran, B. N., Stewart, A., Ginzler, J., & Cauce, A. (2002). Challenges faced by homeless sexual minorities: comparison of gay, lesbian, bisexual, and transgender homeless adolescents with their heterosexual counterparts. *American Journal of Public Health, 92*(5), 773–777.

Coolhart, D., & Brown, M. T. (2017). The need for safe spaces: exploring the experiences of homeless LGBTQ youth in shelters. *Children and Youth Services Review, 82,* 230–238. doi:http://dx.doi.org/10.1016/j.childyouth.2017.09.021

Copeland, L. A., Miller, A., Welsh, D., McCarthy, J., Zeber, J., and Kilbourne, A. (2009). Clinical and demographic factors associated with homelessness and incarceration among VA patients with bipolar disorder. *American Journal of Public Health, 99*(5), 871–877. doi:10.2105/AJPH.2008.149989

Crane, M., Byrne, K., Fu, R., Lipmann, B., Mirabelli, F., Rota-Barte, A., et al. (2005). The causes of homelessness in later life: findings from a 3-nation study. *The Journals of Gerontology: Series B, 60*(3), S152–S159. doi:https://doi.org/10.1093/geronb/60.3.S152

Culhane, D. P., Metraux, S., & Bainbridge, J. (2010). The age structure of contemporary homelessness: risk period or cohort effect? *Penn School of Social Policy and Practice Working Paper*, 1–28. Retrieved from http://repository.upenn.edu/spp_papers/140

Cunnington, L. R. (2007). Living on the edge: 1981–1991. *Visions Journal, 4*(1). Retrieved from www.heretohelp.bc.ca/visions/housing-and-homelessness-vol4/living-on-the-edge

Cutuli, J. J. (2018). Homelessness in high school: population-representative rates of self-reported homelessness, resilience, and risk in Philadelphia. *Social Work Research, 42*(3), 159–168. doi:https://doi.org/10.1093/swr/svy013

Davis, T. H., & Edsell-Vetter, J. (2015). Rethinking hoarding intervention. *Metropolitan Boston Housing Partnership analysis of the Hoarding Intervention and Tenancy Preservation Project*. Retrieved from www.metrohousingboston.org/helping-people-with-hoarding-live-in-healthier-homes/

Davis-Berman, J. (2011). Older women in the homeless shelter: personal perspectives and practice ideas. *Journal of Women & Aging, 23*(4), 360–374. doi:10.1080/08952841.2011.611391

Department of Health. (2016). Care & support statutory guidance. Issued under the Care Act 2014. Retrieved from www.gov.uk/government/publications/care-act-statutory-guidance/care-and-support-statutory-guidance

Design Resources for Homelessness. (2016). Orientation reports. Retrieved from: http://designresourcesforhomelessness.org/people-1/education/

Desmond, M., An, W., Winkler, R., & Ferriss, T. (2013). Evicting children. *Social Forces, 92*(1), 303–327. doi:https://doi.org/10.1093/sf/sot047

Didenko, E., & Pankratz, N. (2007). Substance use: pathway to homelessness? *Visions: BC's Mental Health and Addictions Journal, 4*(1), 9–10. Retrieved from www.heretohelp.bc.ca/visions/housing-and-homelessness-vol4

Distasio, J., Zell, S., McCullough, S., & Edel, B. (2019). *Localized approaches to ending homelessness: indigenizing Housing First*. Winnipeg, CA: Institute of Urban Studies. Retrieved from uwinnipeg.ca/ius/

Dugger, C. W. (1992, January 12). Big shelters hold terrors for the mentally ill. *The New York Times*. Retrieved from www.nytimes.com/1992/01/12/nyregion/big-shelters-hold-terrors-for-the-mentally-ill.html

Farrugia, D. (2016). *Youth homelessness in late modernity: reflexive identities and moral worth*. Singapore: Springer.

Fazel, S., Khosla, V., Doll, H., & Geddes, J. (2008). The prevalence of mental disorders among the homeless in Western countries: systematic review and meta-regression analysis. *PLOS Medicine, 5*(12), e225. doi:10.1371/journal.pmed.0050225

Gaetz, S. (2014). *Coming of age: reimagining the response to youth homelessness in Canada*. Toronto: The Canadian Homelessness Research Network Press.

George, C., Krogh, M., Watson, D., & Wittner, J. (2008). *Homeless over 50: the graying of Chicago's homeless population*. Chicago, IL: Center for Urban Research and Learning: Publications and Other Works. Retrieved from https://ecommons.luc.edu/curl_pubs/21/

Ghilarducci, T., Radpour, S., Fisher, B., & Saad-Lessler, J. (2015). Inadequate retirement account balances for families nearing retirement. New York: Schwartz Center for Economic Policy Analysis. Retrieved from www.economicpolicyresearch.org/resource-library/inadequate-retirement-account-balances-for-families-nearing-retirement

Goldberg, J., Lang, K., & Barrington, V. (2016). *How to prevent and end homelessness among older adults: special report*. Washington, DC, Los Angeles, CA, and Oakland, CA: Justice in Aging. Retrieved from www.justiceinaging.org/homelessness/

Goldrick-Rab, S., Richardson, J., Schneider, J., Hernandez, A., & Cady, C. (2018). *Still hungry and homeless in college*. Madison, WI: Wisconsine Hope Lab, University of Wisconsin–Madison.

Goldstone, B. (2019, August 21). The new American homeless. *The New Republic*. Retrieved from https://newrepublic.com/article/154618/new-american-homeless-housing-insecurity-richest-cities

Gorman, A. (2019, March 8). Medieval diseases are infecting California's homeless: typhus, tuberculosis, and other illnesses are spreading quickly through camps and shelters. *The Atlantic*. Retrieved from www.theatlantic.com/health/archive/2019/03/typhus-tuberculosis-medieval-diseases-spreading-homeless/584380/

Greager, K. (2017, November 14). Native Sun News Today: Homeless veterans in South Dakota share their stories. *Native Sun News Today*. Retrieved from www.indianz.com/News/2017/11/14/native-sun-news-today-homeless-veterans.asp

Greenop, K., & Memmott, P. (2016). We are good-hearted people, we like to share: definitional dilemmas of crowding and homelessness in urban Indigenous Australia. In E. Peters & J. Christensen, *Indigenous homelessness: perspectives from Canada, Australia, and New Zealand* (pp. 270–298). Winnipeg: University of Manitoba Press.

Grenier, A., Barken, R., Sussman, T., & Rothwell, D. (2016). A literature review of homelessness and aging: suggestions for a policy and practice-relevant research agenda. *Canadian Journal on Aging*, *32*(1), 28–41.

Groot, S., Hodgetts, D., Waimarea Nikora, L., & Leggat-Cook, C. (2011). A Māori homeless woman. *Ethnography*, *12*(3), 375–397.

Håkanson, C., & Öhlén, J. (2016). Illness narratives of people who are homeless. *International Journal of Qualitative Studies on Health and Well-Being*, *11*, 32924. doi:10.3402/qhw.v11.32924

Henry, M., Mahathey, A., Morrill, T., Robinson, A., Shivji, A., Watt, R., et al. (2018). *The 2018 annual homeless assessment report (AHAR) to Congress. Part 1: point-in-time estimates of homelessness.* Washington, DC: The U.S. Department of Housing and Urban Development, Office of Community Planning and Development. Retrieved from www.hud.gov/press/press_releases_media_advisories/HUD_No_18_147

Henry, M., Shivji, A., de Sousa, T., & Cohen, R. (2015). *Annual homeless assessment report (AHAR) to Congress.* The U.S. Department of Housing and Urban Development.

Hughes, V. (2007). The truth of the streets and my life thereafter. *Visions Journal*, *4*(1), 25. Retrieved from www.heretohelp.bc.ca/visions/housing-and-homelessness-vol4

Institute of Medicine (US) Committee on Health Care for Homeless People. (1988). *Homelessness, health, and human needs.* Washington, D.C.: National Academies Press. Retrieved from www.ncbi.nlm.nih.gov/books/NBK218236/

Jasinski, J. L., Wesely, J., Wright, J., & Mustaine, E. (2005). *The experience of violence in the lives of homeless women: a research report.* Orlando: University of Central Florida.

Jasinski, J. L., Wesely, J., Wright, J., & Mustaine, E. (2010). *Hard lives, mean streets: violence in the lives of homeless women.* Boston, MA: Northeastern University Press.

Jelinek, G. A., Jiwa, M., Gibson, N. P., & Lynch, A.-M. (2008). Frequent attenders at emergency departments: a linked-data population study of adult patients. *The Medical Journal of Australia*, *189*(10), 552–556. doi:10.5694/j.1326–5377.2008.tb02177.x

Johnson, C. A. (2018, December 20). 'It's not always better than living on the street': couch surfing young adults part of a Chicago homeless population with unique struggles. *Chicago Tribune*. Retrieved from www.chicagotribune.com/lifestyles/ct-life-johnny-rivers-childserv-homeless-1210-story.html

Joint Center for Housing Studies of Harvard University. (2014). *Housing America's older adults: meeting the needs of an aging population: key facts.* Boston, MA: Harvard University. Retrieved from www.jchs.harvard.edu/sites/jchs.harvard.edu/files/jchs_housing_americas_older_adults_2014_key_facts.pdf

Kaup, M., Gonyea, J., & Melekis, K. (2019). *Older persons experiencing homelessness: their perceptions and needs influencing supportive interior design and architecture.* Tallahassee, FL: Design Resources for Homelessness. Retrieved from http://designresourcesforhomelessness.org/people-1/education/

Kidd, S. A. (2004). The walls were closing in, and we were trapped: a qualitative analysis of street youth suicide. *Youth and Society*, *30*(1), 30–55.

Kitchell, D., & Hearn, V. (2019). *Adolescents experiencing homelessness: their perceptions and needs influencing supportive interior design and architecture*. Tallahassee, FL: Design Resources for Homelessness. Retrieved from http://designresourcesfor homelessness.org/people-1/education/

Kushel, M., Evans, J., Perry, S., & Robertson, M. (2003). No door to lock: victimization among homeless and marginally housed persons. *Archives of Internal Medicine*, *163*(10), 2492–2499.

Larsen, L. (2007). Leonard's story. *Visions Journal*, *4*(1 "Housing and Homelessness"), 23. Retrieved from www.heretohelp.bc.ca/visions/housing-and-homelessness-vol4

Lee, C. T., Guzman, D., Ponath, C., Tieu, L., Riley, E., & Kushel, M. (2016). Residential patterns in older homeless adults: results of a cluster analysis. *Social Science & Medicine*, *153*, 131–140. doi:10.1016/j.socscimed.2016.02.004

Memmott, P. (2015). Differing relations to tradition amongst Australian Indigenous homeless people. *Traditional Dwellings and Settlements Review*, *26*(2), 58–72.

Memmott, P., Birdsall-Jones, C., & Greenop, K. (2012). *Australian Indigenous house crowding*. Melbourne, Australia: Australian Housing and Urban Research Institute Limited. Retrieved from www.ahuri.edu.au/research/final-reports/194

Memmott, P., Long, S., Chambers, C., & Spring, F. (2003). *Categories of Indigenous "homeless" people and good practice responses to their needs*. Melbourne, Australia: Australian Housing and Urban Research Institute, Queensland Research Centre. Retrieved from www.ahuri.edu.au/research/final-reports/49

Metraux, S., Clegg, L., Daigh, J., Culhane, D., & Kane, V. (2013). Risk factors for becoming homeless among a cohort of veterans who served in the era of the Iraq and Afghanistan conflicts. *American Journal of Public Health*, *103*(Suppl. 2), S255–S261. doi:http://dx.doi.org/10.2105/

Metraux, S., Cusack, M., Byrne, T., Hunt-Johnson, N., & True, G. (2017). Pathways into homelessness among post-9/11-era veterans. *Psychological Services*, *14*(2), 229–237. doi:http://dx.doi.org/10.1037/ser0000136

Milton, J. T. (2007). From rags to riches in happiness. *Visions Journal*, *4*(1). Retrieved from www. heretohelp.bc.ca/visions/housing-and-homelessness-vol4/from-rags-to-riches-in-happiness

National Alliance to End Homelessness. (2019). *Veterans*. Retrieved from https://endhomelessness.org/homelessness-in-america/who-experiences-homelessness/veterans/

National Coalition for the Homeless. (2009a). *Homelessness among elderly persons*. Washington, DC: Author. Retrieved from https://nationalhomeless.org/issues/elderly/

National Coalition for the Homeless. (2009b). *Substance abuse and homelessness*. Washington, DCL Author. Retrieved from https://nationalhomeless.org/references/publications/

National Coalition for the Homeless. (2017). *LGBTQ homelessness*. Washington, DC: Author. Retrieved from www.nationalhomeless.org

National Institute of Mental Health. (2017). *Statistics*. Bethesda, MD: Author. Retrieved from www.nimh.nih.gov/health/statistics/mental-illness.shtml

National Leadership Initiative to End Elder Homelessness. (2011). *Ending homelessness among older adults and elders through permanent supportive housing*. Revised Policy Paper. Retrieved from www.csh.org/resources-search/?s=Ending+homelessness+a mong+older+adults&s=

Navarro, M. (2013, September 18). In New York, having a job, or 2, doesn't mean having a home [Metropolitan Desk]. *The New York Times*.

New Zealand Parliament. (2014, July 17). Homelessness in New Zealand. Retrieved from www.parliament.nz/en/pb/research-papers/document/00PLEcoRP14021/homelessness-in-new-zealand#RelatedAnchor

Noack, M. (2018, July 20). Young, homeless and sick. *Mountain View Voice*. Retrieved from www.mv-voice.com/news/2018/07/20/young-homeless-and-sick

Nooe, R. M., & Patterson, D. A. (2010). The ecology of homelessness. *Journal of Human Behavior in the Social Environment, 20*(2), 105–152. doi:10.1080/10911350903269757

O'Carroll, A., & Wainwright, D. (2019). Making sense of street chaos: an ethnographic exploration of homeless people's health service utilization. *International Journal for Equity in Health, 18*(113). doi:https://doi.org/10.1186/s12939-019-1002-6

O'Connell, M. J., Kasprow, W., & Rosenheck, R. (2008). Rates and risk factors for homelessness after successful housing in a sample of formerly homeless veterans. *Psychiatric Services*, (59), 268–275. doi:http://dx.doi.org/10.1176/ps.2008.59.3.268

Patrick, C. (2014). *Aboriginal homelessness in Canada: a literature review*. Toronto: Canadian Homelessness Research Network Press. Retrieved from www.documentcloud.org/documents/1098160-aboriginalliteraturereview.html#document/p1

Pavao, J., Turchik, J. A., Hyun, J. K., Karpenko, J., Saweikis, M., McCutcheon, S., … Kimerling, R. (2013). Military sexual trauma among homeless veterans. *Journal of General Internal Medicine, 28*(2), 536–541. doi:10.1007/s11606-013-2341-4

Perlman, S., Willard, J., Herbers, J. E., Cutuli, J. J., & Eyrich Garg, K. M. (2014). Youth homelessness: prevalence and mental health correlates. *Journal of the Society for Social Work & Research, 5*(3), 361–377. doi:10.1086/677757

Peters, E., & Christensen, J. (. (2016). *Indigenous Homelessness: perspectives from Canada, Australia, and New Zealand*. Manitoba, Canada: University of Manitoba Press.

Pindus, N., Thomas, K., Biess, J., Levy, D., Simington, J., Hayes, C., & Urban Institute. (2017). Housing needs of American Indians and Alaska Natives in tribal areas: a report from the assessment of American Indian, Alaska Native, and Native Hawaiian housing needs. U.S. Department of Housing and Urban Development, Office of Policy Development and Research. Retrieved from www.huduser.gov/portal/publications/HNAIHousingNeeds.html

Potter, L., Sacks, J., Kresnow, M., & Mercy, J. (1999). Nonfatal physical violence, United States, 1994. *Public Health Reports, 14*(4), 343–352.

Ranasinghe, P. (2017). *Helter-shelter: security, legality, and an ethic of care in an emergency shelter*. Toronto, Buffalo, London: University of Toronto Press.

Ray, N. (2010). Lesbian, gay, bisexual and transgender youth: an epidemic of homelessness. In S. Lowrey & J. Burke, *Kicked out* (pp. 180–200). Ypsilanti, MI: Homofactus Press.

Reich, R., & Siegel, L. (1978). The emergence of the Bowery as a psychiatric dumping ground. *The Psychiatric Quarterly, 50*(3), 191–201.

Rosenthal, D., Mallett, S., & Myers, P. (2006). Why do homeless young people leave home? *Australian and New Zealand Journal of Public Health, 30*(3), 281–285.

Ruggiero, K., Smith, D., Hanson, R., Resnick, H., & Saunders, B. (2004). Is disclosure of childhood rape associated with mental health outcome? Results from the National Women's Study. *Child Maltreatment, 9*(1), 62–77. doi:10.1177/1077559503260309

Rutledge, K. (2019a). *Families and the built environment: their perceptions and needs when experiencing homelessness*. Tallahassee, FL: Design Resources for Homelessness. Retrieved from http://designresourcesforhomelessness.org/people-1/education/

Rutledge, K. (2019b). *Victims of domestic violence experiencing homelessness: their perspectives and needs influencing architectural support*. Tallahassee, FL: Design Resources for Homelessness. Retrieved from http://designresourcesforhomelessness.org/people-1/education/

Samuels, G. M., Cerven, C., Curry, S., Robinson, S., & Patel, S. (2019). *Missed opportunities in youth pathways through homelessness*. Chicago, IL: Chapin Hall at the University of Chicago. Retrieved from http://voicesofyouthcount.org/brief/missed-opportunities-youth-pathways-through-homelessness-in-america/#endnotes

Sapien, J., & Jennings, T. (2018, December 6). "I want to live like a human being": where N.Y. fails its mentally ill. *The New York Times*.

Schanzer, B., Dominquez, B., Shrout, P., & Caton, C. (2007). Homelessness, health status and health care use. *American Journal of Public Health, 97*(3), 464–465.

Sharma, A. (2019, April 25). A senior on the streets, with little chance of a home. Retrieved from KPBS: www.kpbs.org/news/2019/apr/25/senior-streets-little-chance-home/

Siciliano, C. (2015, December 21). Three LGBT youths describe being homeless in NYC. *Advocate*. Retrieved from www.advocate.com/commentary/2015/12/21/three-lgbt-youths-describe-being-homeless-nyc

Sottile, L. (2015, January 7). Homeless and hoarding. *The Atlantic*. Retrieved from www.theatlantic.com/health/archive/2015/01/homeless-and-hoarding/384036/

Stafford, A., & Wood, L. (2017). Tackling health disparities for people who are homeless? Start with social determinants. *International Journal of Environmental Research and Public Health, 14*(12), 1535. doi:10.3390/ijerph14121535

Stark, L. R. (1985). Strangers in a strange land: the chronically mentally ill homeless. *International Journal of Mental Health*, 95–11. Retrieved from www.tandfonline.com/toc/mimh20/14/4?nav=tocList

Statistics Canada. (2013). Aboriginal peoples in Canada: First Nations people, Métis and Inuit. National household survey, 2011. Ottawa: Minister of Industry. Retrieved from www12.statcan.gc.ca/nhs-enm/2011/as-sa/99–011-

Substance Abuse and Mental Health Services Administration. (2015). *TIP 55: behavioral health services for people who are homeless*. Rockville, MD: SAMHSA. Retrieved from https://store.samhsa.gov/product/TIP-55-Behavioral-Health-Services-for-People-Who-Are-Homeless/SMA15-4734

Sullivan, M. (2016, May 9). Leading homeless veterans back into the mainstream of life. UCLA. Los Angeles, CA. Retrieved from www.universityofcalifornia.edu/news/leading-homeless-veterans-back-mainstream-life

Tenzin. (2010). Dumpster diving, gay skinheads, boredom and violence: pestilential adventures on the streets of California. In S. Lowrey & J. Burke, *Kicked out* (pp. 19–25). Ypsilanti, MI: Homofactus Press.

Thistle, J. A. (2017). *Indigenous definition of homelessness in Canada*. Toronto, CA: Canadian Observatory on Homelessness Press. Retrieved from www.homelesshub.ca/IndigenousHomelessness

Thompson, M., Kingree, J., & Desai, S. (2004). Gender differences in long-term health consequences of physical abuse of children: data from a nationally representative survey. *American Journal of Public Health, 94*(4), 599–604.

Tobias, M. (2018, January 10). "So many of us come back broken": homeless veterans talk about why this happens. NET (Nebraska's PBS and NPR Station). Retrieved from http://netnebraska.org/article/news/1111067/so-many-us-come-back-broken-homeless-veterans-talk-about-why-happens

Torrey, E. F. (n.d.). 250,000 mentally ill are homeless. 140,000 seriously mentally ill are homeless. Retrieved from Mental Illness Policy Org.: https://mentalillnesspolicy.org/consequences/homeless-mentally-ill.html

Treatment Advocacy Center. (2016, September). Serious mental illness and homelessness. Retrieved from Treatment Advocacy Center: Evidence and Research: www.treatmentadvocacycenter.org/evidence-and-research/learn-more-about/3629-serious-mental-illness-and-homelessness

Tsai, J., Hoff, R., & Harpaz-Rotem, I. (2017). One-year incidence and predictors of homelessness among 300,000 U.S. veterans seen in specialty mental health care. *Psychological Services, 14*(2), 203–207. doi:http://dx.doi.org/10.1037/ser0000083

Tutty, L. M., Ogden, C., Giurgiu, B., & Weaver-Dunlop, G. (2013). I built my house of hope: abused women and pathways into homelessness. *Violence Against Women, 19*(12), 1498–1517. doi:10.1177/1077801213517514

United States Conference of Mayors. (2008). Hunger and homelessness survey: a status report on hunger and homelessness in America's cities. United States Conference of Mayors.

United States Conference of Mayors. (2016). Report on hunger and homelessness. United States Conference of Mayors.

United States Interagency Council on Homelessness. (2018). *Homelessness in America: focus on unaccompanied youth*. Washington DC: Author. Retrieved from www.usich. gov/tools-for-action/homelessness-in-america-focus-on-youth

Washington, D. L., Yano, E. M., McGuire, J., Hines, V., Lee, M., & Gelberg, L. (2010). Risk factors for homelessness among women veterans. *Journal of Health Care for the Poor and Underserved, 21*(1), 82–91. doi:10.1353/hpu.0.0237

Wise, C., & Phillips, K. (2013). Hearing the silent voices: narratives of health care and homelessness. *Issues in Mental Health Nursing, 34*(5), 359–367. doi:10.3109/01612840.2 012.757402

Woolley, E. (2016, July 15). How many people experiencing homelessness are employed? Retrieved from Homeless Hub: www.homelesshub.ca/blog/how-many-people-experiencing-homelessness-are-employed

Wright, J. D. (1989). *Address unknown: the homeless in America*. New York: Aldine de Gruyter.

Wright, J., Rubin, B., & Devine, J. (1998). *Beside the golden door: policy, politics and the homeless*. Hawthorne, NY: Aldine de Gruyter.

Youth Catalytics. (2015). Homeless youth estimation project in Connecticut. Retrieved from Homeless Youth Estimation Project: www.youthcatalytics.org/tools/homeless_and_transient_youth_counting/summary/

TEACHING MATERIALS

Lauren Trujillo

Key Terms

Generationally homeless

Situationally homeless

Couch-homeless

Agoraphobia

Self-neglect

Compulsive accumulation/hoarding

Working homeless

Rootedness

Written Exercises

1.   Review 7.3, "Considerations and priorities for project programming for select user groups," located in Chapter 7, Design Considerations. For each space listed on the table, determine if it is *high* priority (must be included), *medium* priority (nice to include), or *low* priority (ideal to include but not necessary) in an environment serving those experiencing homelessness. Compare your determinations with those made by your colleagues. Did you agree on the priority level of each space? Why or why not?

     a.   To help you with determining what spaces are of higher and lower priority, read Chapter 5 on theories that inform design solutions for vulnerable populations. Re-evaluate your determinations based on this additional information. Have you made any changes? If yes, what affected your decision? If not, why? Discuss with colleagues again.

     b.   Now, imagine you are a member of the team designing an environment serving those experiencing homelessness. What implications would this agreement or disagreement have on the design of the space? How might you convince your colleagues to agree with your determinations of priority?

2.   Review 7.3, "Considerations and priorities for project programming for select user groups," located in Chapter 7, Design Considerations. Based on this list, which user types could share a facility? Why? What are the potential benefits or risks to putting these user types together? Which user types could not share a facility? Why?

4 Perspectives

Jill Pable

Designing places to house or serve people who are without homes is complex, in part because projects such as shelters, day centers, and supportive housing are shaped by varying points of view held by their various stakeholders. People holding differing perspectives influence architectural choices on these projects, including on-site staff members, sponsoring organization administrators, donors, facilities managers, clients, policy makers, and the public. This chapter discusses these multiple voices, and especially those of the groups often most influential on project outcomes such as administrators and staff. Clients' perspectives are primarily addressed in Chapter 3 because of their importance and complexity.

Diverse priorities and influences acting on a project are also common with complex commercial architectural projects such as offices, hotels, and clinics. In some design project sectors, these disparities have led to new paradigms in thinking. For example, hospital administrators have taken extra efforts in recent years to explore and understand 'patient-centered care' in order to more successfully attract patients. This has led the health care design movement to build more empathetically and provide amenities that patients really care about. Similarly, mental and behavioral health center design (and we might view homelessness facilities in this light for the moment) is being impacted by emergent trauma-informed design principles that are reconsidering how best to help people in crisis (see Chapter 6 for further details on this framework). It is arguable that designing for homelessness situations may be marked by the particularly striking differences in life perceptions and experiences between housed and unhoused stakeholders that may eclipse such stakeholder variations in school, office, or hospitality projects. For this reason, we suggest that the day-to-day perceptions of operational staff members and people experiencing homelessness hold the potential to vary even more significantly than those of such groups on these other project types, and for the emotional qualities of an interior environment to matter more to clients who are in a heightened state of crisis when they access these buildings.

For example, staff, donors, and administrators may be accustomed to middle socioeconomic comforts that are absent of the desperation and unceasing anxiety that can accompany clients' low socioeconomic experience of life. Similarly, middle and low SE groups may have different familiarities with cultural customs and, owing to family and/or parent difficulties, life skills such as cleaning up after oneself or how one should inhabit and take care of a home or work environment (e.g., one should not peel paint from or deface walls or remove furnishings that are not permanently affixed). The differences are such that, despite exposure to the cultural problem of homelessness, the donors and especially the public who are removed from the 'front lines' of care may not understand the people they deeply wish to serve.[1]

The contrasts in design priorities that exist for residents, directors, facilities managers, and donors that are engaged with a homelessness-related project were explored in a small empirical study conducted by one of us (Jill Pable) with researcher Kenan Fishburne (Pable & Fishburne, 2015). In this study, the researchers interviewed 22 shelter residents, case managers, and shelter directors, examining the differences between 'user' and 'operational' preferences for a hypothetical bedroom space in a transitional family shelter; they also visited five shelters in the southeast U.S., observing and taking photographs of the facilities. The findings suggest that fundamental contrasts in preferences exist between prospective clients and support organization leaders. Users more highly valued experiential factors such as privacy, temperature control, and acoustic comfort, plus daily amenities such as mirrors and seating options, than the operational interviewees. Those in operations were more concerned with security, cleanability, potential for theft, and cost. The groups' cognitive schemes of priorities, needs, and values diverged so much, in fact, that the authors concluded that multiple post-occupancy evaluations (POEs) were probably necessary to determine the success of a given project, with one POE gathering users' points of view, and another those of operations stakeholders (Pable & Fishburne, 2015).

In our experience as designers and researchers who have examined supportive housing, shelters, and similar facilities, such disparate viewpoints about buildings make more complex new project questions of 'how should we build'? For example, as this chapter will discuss, facilities managers often, and understandably, prioritize furnishings and finishes that are easy to clean, resist breakage, and are cost-effective to make a building function more easily. Residents, on the other hand, typically prefer spaces that offer a welcoming atmosphere and have acoustical control to reduce echoes, finishes with tactile interest, and residential-like lighting solutions. A facilities director's choice of commercial-style LED ceiling-based lighting and hard flooring that is easy to clean can appear glary and forbidding to a prospective client.[2] Such programmatic tensions can be difficult to manage and complicate architectural programming. Yet, the stakes can be high – an environment that appears too sterile may dissuade needy clients from committing to services, whereas a building that moves too far toward a pleasant but fragile aesthetic can be problematic to maintain.

We join other voices in asserting that a design solution that effectively accommodates the needs of multiple stakeholders relies on a thorough understanding of the problem at hand, including the needs, expectations, and capabilities of *all* those involved. Pena and Parshall's seminal architectural programming book *Problem Seeking* advocates for thorough idea-gathering long before an architectural solution is crafted:

> Experienced, creative designers withhold judgment and resist preconceived solutions and the pressure to synthesize until all the information is in. They refuse to make sketches until they know the client's problem. They believe in thorough analysis before synthesis. They know that programming is the prelude to good design – although it does not guarantee it.
>
> (Pena & Parshall, 2001, p. 21)

For projects such as shelters, supportive housing, and day centers, we firmly believe that clients, owners, facilities managers, staff members – all need to be present on the design team, or at least thoroughly consulted, from early in a project. The positive outcomes of collaborative decision-making are also promoted, and in fact recommended by various building certification systems including Leadership in Energy and Environmental Design (LEED) and the WELL building certification systems that mandate collaborative participation.[3]

The inability to listen and react to varying points of view may lie at the heart of the failure of shelters and similar facilities to attract and engage with people experiencing homelessness. Places perceived as dirty or scary are directly related to a client's perceptions of dignity (Miller & Keys, 2001), and prospective clients may shun them for this and other related reasons.[4] We suspect that much top–down thinking is happening that ignores the perspective of users and, thus, has led in part to the emergence of 'homeless encampments' that are shaped by users' priorities and needs outside of the organized system of care (Neild & Rose, 2018; Donley & Wright, 2012). It is far better for a new or renovation building project that decision-makers realize and actually buy into the notion that "together we can do a better job than we can separately" (Pena & Parshall, 2001, p. 51).

A common design project question for shelters we have encountered from the public is "will the facility be 'too nice', and encourage people to stay longer than they should?" Seemingly embedded in this question is the notion that making it too easy on a person in need of these services would preclude them from working hard to exit their destitute state. Interviews with staff members at various shelters do suggest that, for some clients (especially those who have been homeless a long time), finding daily refuge in a place that offers a positive experience makes it a tempting place to linger. However, we point out that shelters hold the cards, so to speak, on the length of time a client may stay. Second, for most clients, perhaps this is the wrong question to ask, as it is an approach that ignores the relationship of shelter to well-being. If the objective instead is assisting someone to become physically, psychologically, and emotionally stable in a temporary place of support, then effective lighting is a way to provide a sense of calm so that full attention can be paid to one's exit plan, and a window view provides a needed sense of security from the dangers of the street so that someone can stop worrying for a moment to figure out their next steps.

Choosing building project objectives that place the emphasis on a design that provides fundamental humane conditions such as acoustics control, quality lighting, supportive color, and durable (and yes, visually pleasant) furnishings and finishes offers other research-supported benefits as well to the multiple stakeholder groups involved:

- Well-designed and cared for environments can exude a sense of respect and can send a signal for clients to not damage them.[5]
- A capable, thoughtfully designed building shows the public and donors that the organization is capable of executing its mission effectively and, by extension, helping its clients achieve success.[6]
- Shelter directors remark that a calming environment can reduce the incidence of altercations between clients and staff (personal communication, Jacob Reiter; personal communication, Jonathan Farrell).
- There are other applicable benefits outlined by Shepley and Pasha in their review of behavioral and mental health design research (Shepley & Pasha, 2013), such as spatial designs that can encourage socializing and reductions in isolated passive behaviors (Holahan & Saegert, 1973) and the ability of well-designed environments to boost the morale of both clients and staff within behavioral health wards (Stahler, Frazer, & Rappaport, 1984).

The balance of this chapter offers a case study of an actual shelter project in the design phase as of the time of this writing. One of us, Jill Pable, serves as an interior design client experience consultant for the project and had the opportunity to learn and observe various stakeholder priorities and how these differences led to contrasts, tradeoffs, and compromises during its development.

RESTORATION HOUSE

- Support organization client: Atlanta Mission, a Christian faith-based organization
- Location: Atlanta, Georgia
- Architecture and interior design: Nelson
- Programming consultant: Barbara Clark
- Interior consultant for client experience: Jill Pable, Design Resources for Homelessness
- Shelter type: low-barrier (admitting clients who may have mental illness, engage in substance abuse, or other conditions)
- Clients: single women and women with children
- Square footage: 45,000
- Number of floors: two
- Type of construction: new
- Approximate budget: $15,000,000.

BRIEF CONTEXT

The new shelter acts as the primary low-barrier women's shelter for Atlanta, fulfilling a specific, neglected need in the network of facilities in the city. The existing building on the site is used only as a day shelter for women and was repurposed from former office use. The existing building will be demolished, and the new project will greatly expand the facility's purpose, goals, and square footage, extending to two stories and approximately 45,000 square feet.

The program of services includes these primary functions:

- Education and work preparation
- Clinic
- Dining
- Sleeping for single women, women with children, and women with special needs
- "Clothing closet" providing donated items to clients and receipt of these donations
- Laundry
- Day lounge
- Counseling and therapy
- Children's services
- Volunteer support
- Administration offices
- Luggage storage and pest eradication.

The design team met multiple times over the course of a year and included the chief executive officer, representative of the organization's board, the chief operating officer, the facilities director, vice presidents of women and children's services and also client support, the project's campus administrator, and numerous other staff who provided suggestions about their areas of expertise. An external architectural programming consultant offered extensive comment on the space plan and its function. The project architect/interior design firm, landscape, and MEP (mechanical, electrical, and plumbing) practitioners offered their services without charge.

STAKEHOLDER PRIORITIES IN BRIEF

As introduced above, groups involved and invested in the design outcome of this project each held their own priorities for its function and visual qualities that sprang from the responsibilities of their role and/or their physical, psychological, and emotional needs. These points of view, summarized below, were expressed in multiple design team meetings that discussed the project's space plan and other aspects during conceptual design and design development phases.

Clients

One of us (Jill Pable) and social work researcher Tomi Gomory conducted a study that queried approximately 20 clients at the existing Atlanta Mission shelter, confirming these general human qualities that shape the intangible sense of well-being they most desired (unpublished raw data):

- Dignity and self-esteem
- Empowerment and personal control
- Security, privacy, and personal space
- Ability to cope and manage stress
- Feeling a sense of community and acknowledgement
- Being in the presence of beauty, interest, and meaning.

Staff confirmed that the clients may arrive in a state of high emotion, and the new facility should take active steps to manage this with clear policies emphasizing fairness and information transparency that let a client know if they are admitted for the night. Logical wayfinding is necessary because clients, most of whom are new to the building, will be highly distracted, with shortened patience.

Children's presence in the Ethel Street facility prompted further needs including durability of finishes and the ability to manage emotional outbursts. Mothers of children would be very concerned about safety, which makes open sightlines, positive distractions, and privacy from outsiders important qualities. Children's fear about their precarious living situation prompted goals about the apparent friendliness of interior spaces in general, as well as circumstance-specific needs such as traveling to a distant bathroom safely at night. Further, children of various ages would have differing priorities, with young children needing outlets for positive mental and especially physical activity, while older children require space for homework and for building their identities in positive ways with new friends. See Chapter 3 for further expanded information on clients' perspectives and architectural needs.

Staff

Fulfilling one's responsibilities as a staff member in a shelter is often stressful, as heightened client emotions, inappropriate behaviors, and near-constant neediness can be a draining experience. Work of this kind can place staff at risk of 'secondary traumatic stress' by virtue of listening to others' first-hand traumatic experiences. Burnout is a known problem and can create a negative feedback loop that intensifies feelings in remaining employees (Menschner & Maul, 2016). The average salary for a child and family social worker in 2017 was $44,380, but can be as low as $35,070 (U.S. News and World Report, 2017). In our experience, physical facilities too seldom consider the needs of staff.

Staff criteria included providing staff retreat spaces for solitude and managing noise better. Staff felt too available to others and were 'always on'. While they were enthusiastic advocates for clients' experience, staff also preferred client amenities that would be easy for them to manage, such as device charging stations to avoid arguments over electrical outlets, and easy wayfinding that would reduce client requests for directions. At times, the constant stress of working with crisis clients became clear in design meetings. For example, staff had no enthusiasm for replacing a broken piano with a new one, as it would just become broken again with client misuse. Staff also sought ways to minimize client-to-client disputes that take their time and concentration to solve, and office placement in the space plan that would offer effective observation points so that they would not have to move from their desks as much.

Facilities Manager

Ribbon-cutting day presents an architectural project in its most positive light. All the lighting shines brightly, the floors are beautiful expanses of well-kept surface, and wall corners are untouched by dents or dirt. However, the long-term viability of a project's finishes, furnishings, and other elements that are on the front lines of durability challenges each day flavors the priorities of the facilities manager. Designers would do well to gather this person's perspective when specifying products and working through space plan decisions, for they offer a necessary functional perspective that can simplify long-term upkeep for high-use places such as shelters, day centers, and supportive housing. For example, facilities managers prefer low-maintenance systems and features such as graffiti-resistant exterior surfaces and window fenestration that resists window breakage. Limiting the list of lighting fixture types can reduce the complexity and numbers of replacement fixtures and lamps, and high-abuse furnishings such as chairs should be easily repairable in the field and cleanable in the face of inevitable fluid accidents. The Restoration House project's space plan was also significantly influenced by the necessary placement of a loading entrance and service corridor for food and clothing donations, and a service elevator that permitted efficient off-site laundering of linens from the second-floor sleeping areas. Electrical and plumbing services were separated to reduce the chance of flooding of these areas.

Upper Leadership and Donors

Faced with the realities of fundraising for their work, support organizations exist at the crossroads of their portfolio of services, their mission orientation, and the need to foster public good will. The Atlanta Mission's chief executive officer sought to create a space that is welcoming to clients (offering the 'wow' factor at entry, for example) and provides a sense of safe refuge and a building that blends into its city neighborhood context effectively. It was determined the facility should reflect the Atlanta Mission's Christian mission and reflect capable stewardship through its operational efficiency and durability. The project was supported by public donations and, therefore, needed to be suitably attractive in its function and appearance to these donors.

The multiple perspectives discussed above coupled with the building's goals coalesce to produce a series of tensions. Collectively, the design team confronted questions that brought individual stakeholders' stances into discussion to solve a number of challenges:

- How can the site provide a welcoming campus yet send the message of safety and security from stalkers?
- How can the building project a long-term, positive image that can attract donors to support the mission of the organization?
- How can the building help women of differing capabilities in this low-barrier context while also attending to children's needs?

- How can the building provide a durable, maintainable space that looks clean while still offering a friendly, warm place of refuge?
- How can the building provide volunteers a place they perceive as safe to work while also admitting low-barrier clients who are susceptible to acting out?
- How can staff maintain a sense of order and fairness through rules and policies while helping clients resist 'shelterization', defined as a reduction in a sense of client autonomy and self-empowerment (Gounis, 1992; Grunberg & Eagle, 1990)?
- How can the building's design cease the long-standing habit of women camping in tents steps away from the entrance and instead convince those women to accept its sleeping accommodations and services?
- How can staff, services and the building itself convince clients to quit street living permanently, even when their sense of community with others they find outside is highly valued?
- How can the residential quarters help minimize disruptions such as bullying, body odors, and noise while still helping as many clients as possible?

The collection of images in 4.1–4.10 provide a glimpse of the discussions and choices that emerged over the course of the design team's discussions.

CONCLUSION

This chapter explored how stakeholder groups' perceptions about the design priorities of support facilities can vary. Their choices and preferences embody their various personal stances on how services are best offered. In our view, maintaining a human well-being orientation to goal-making for a building project can occasionally offer win–win potential across involved stakeholder groups, even in the face of the significant complexity that a large project presents. In the end, moving a project forward

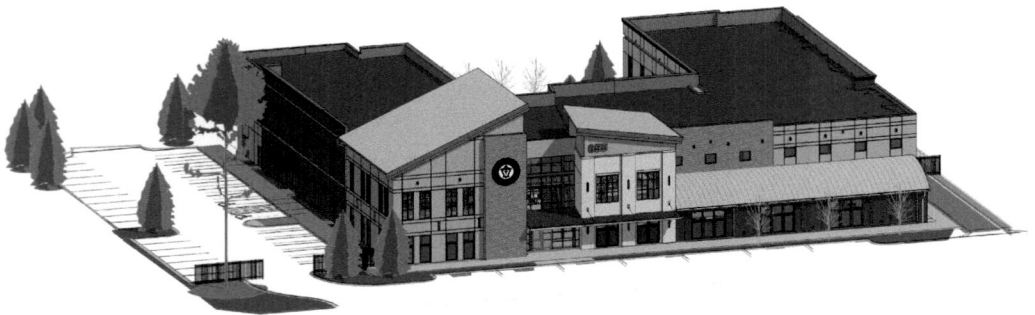

4.1
The exterior of the Ethel Street shelter was influenced by the materials and forms of neighboring buildings of the Georgia Institute of Technology campus, and particularly a mixed-use development in the area designed by the Nelson architectural firm. The design team emphasized clarity so that clients can intuitively locate the main entrance, and residential cues such as pitched roofs lend a sense of approachability. Window fenestration was initially street-level on the first floor to maximize natural light penetration, but this was later changed to permit views only from clerestory windows to prioritize safety and privacy. Exterior façade imagery is important for positively influencing the public who might support fundraising efforts and be comforted by the appearance of this social services building in a prominent part of the city.

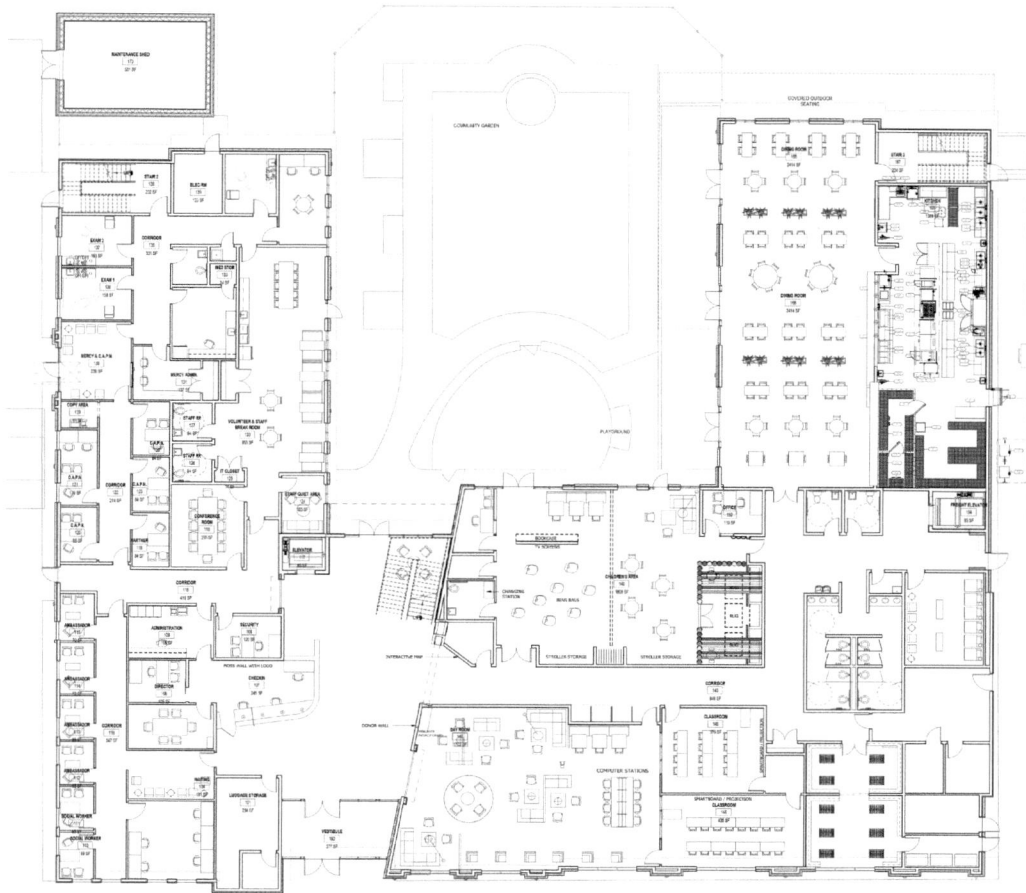

4.2

The first floor of the shelter hosts the most public of zones, including the reception and counseling areas in the lower left quadrant, clinic and volunteer areas in the upper left, day lounge, classrooms, and children's play spaces in the lower right, and dining in the upper right quadrant. The U-shape footprint hugs a multipurpose courtyard with green space, children's playground, and exterior dining. Earlier versions of the plan placed the volunteer suite in the right back quadrant, but this was moved to the upper left to better group client services together.

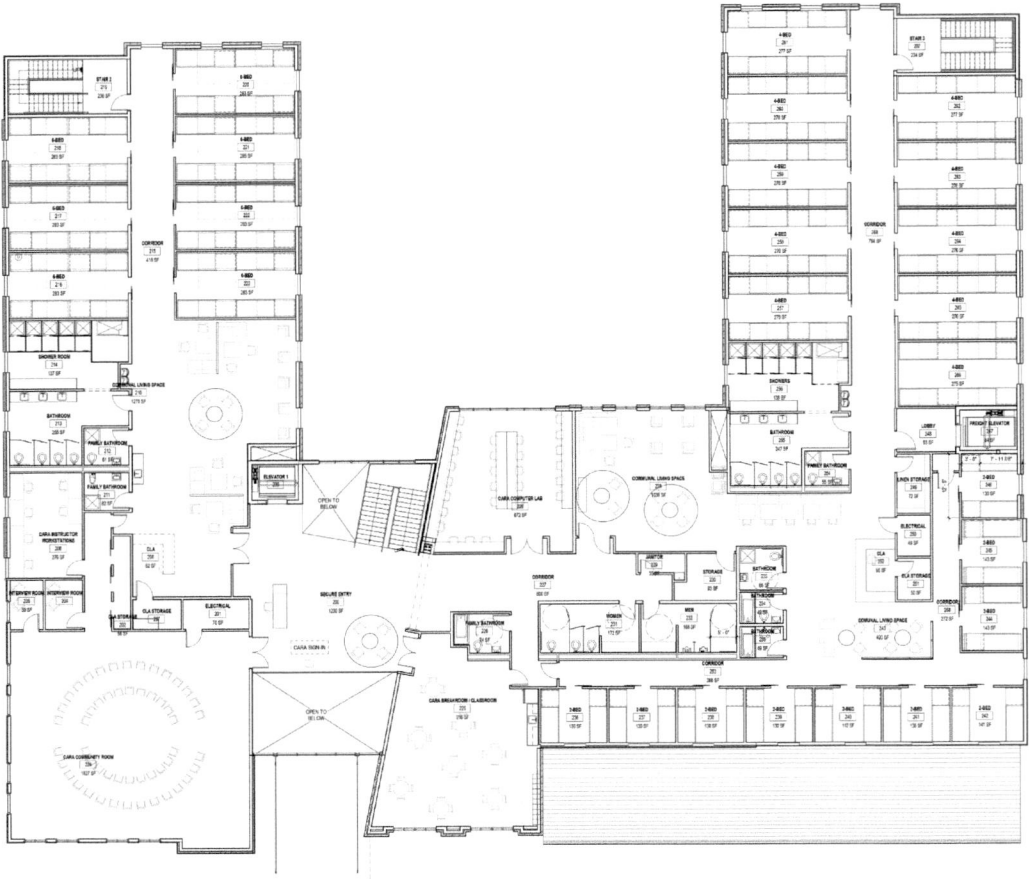

4.3
The second floor of the shelter houses job training suites and three 'neighborhoods' of sleeping suites, each with a separate 'living room' for residents.

4.4

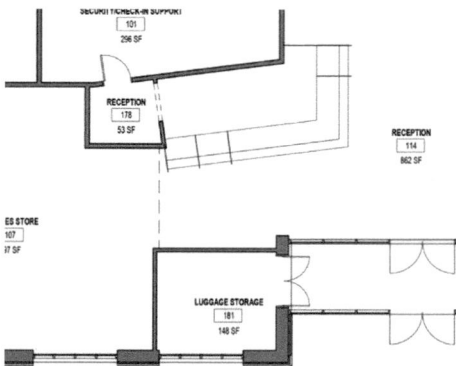

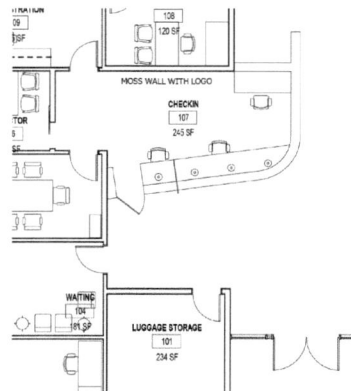

The design team worked through multiple iterations of the initial view of the reception area and desk. Friendly materials such as wood and projected lighting effects were early choices that have remained consistent. At first the desk matched the building's angular nature (upper view and lower left), but then transformed to a curved design to be a more welcoming, approachable element (bottom right). Separate desk zones at the left and back right permit confidential conversations.

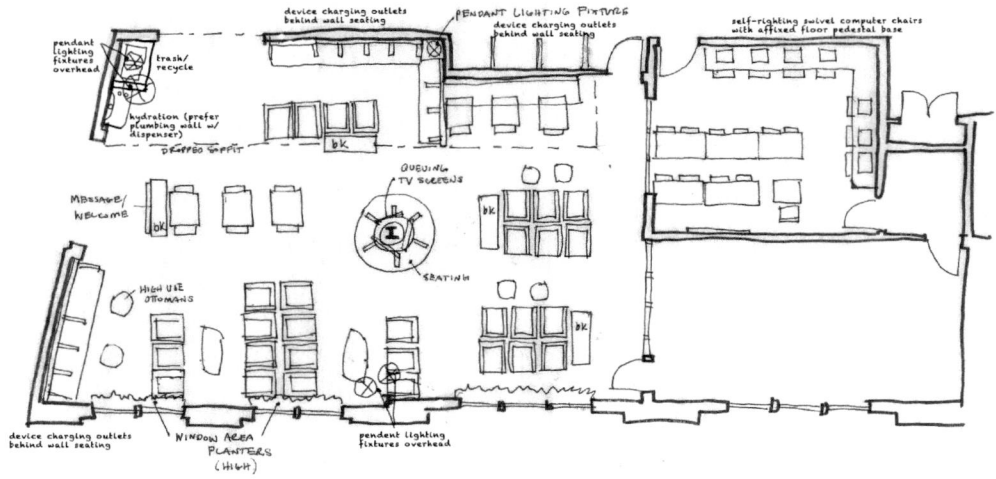

4.5

Early in the design phase, the team considered combining the day lounge and dining rooms to use space in the shelter more efficiently throughout the day. This idea was abandoned owing to concerns about cleanability. Early versions of the day lounge seated 40 clients, but the realities of client population size prompted denser layouts to serve 60 instead, shown here. A variety of seating types accommodate clients of various body sizes as well as task and lounge postures that provide a 'protected back' orientation where feasible. An early conceptual perspective shows priority placed on elements that would provide acoustic qualities. Television screens indicate that a client has been accepted for sleeping accommodation that night.

4.6

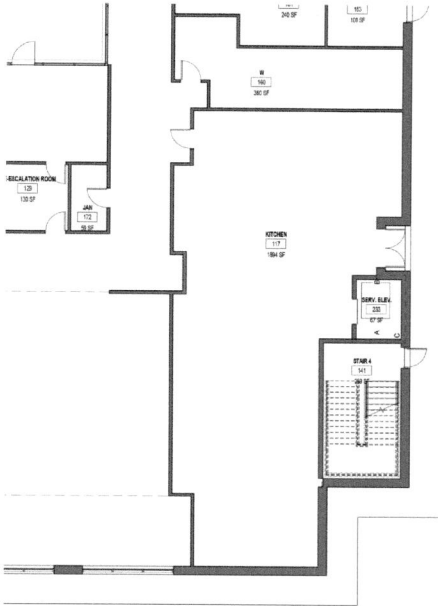

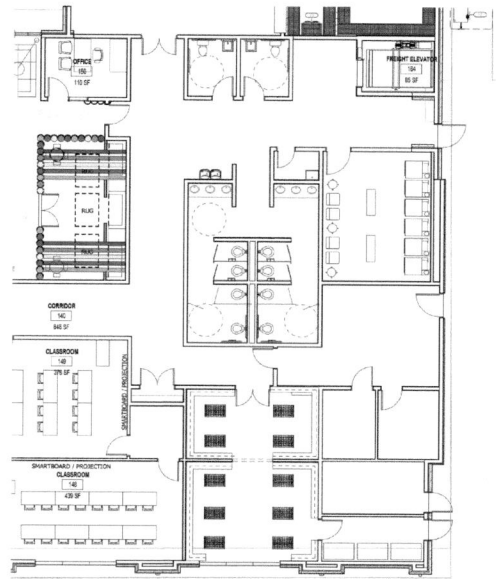

An early space plan on the left shows a direct entrance and service elevator's placement in the kitchen on the first floor. Further discussion by the design team and especially the facilities manager expanded this area into two corridors accommodating clothing donations and the electrical and services rooms at the bottom of the right image, and the laundry pickup and drop-off and kitchen deliveries at the upper entrance point. Location of these entrances in relation to the alley was a key consideration.

4.7

The second-floor residential neighborhood housing women with children evolved from the plan on the left to the one on the right. To accommodate safety concerns, the supervising staff desk was established in the plan and strategically placed to permit a sightline both to the general corridor and also to the newly located client 'living room'. A hydration station and bottle preparation area are also provided in this area.

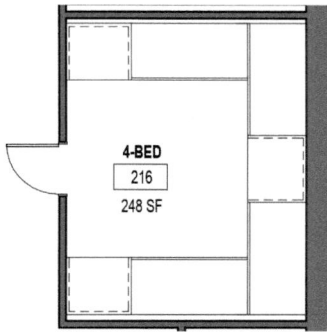

A

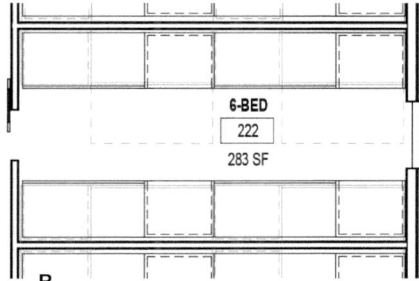

B

C

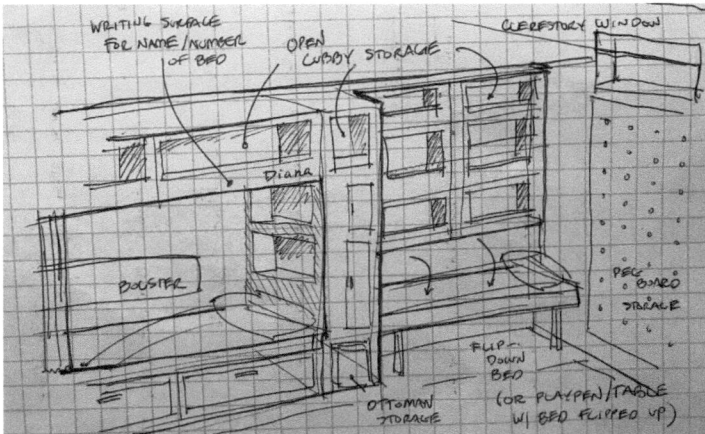

D

4.8

The design team gave considerable thought to the residential area space plan, as this is the most personal and private of zones for clients. From early on, small pods for four to six persons were created to help clients feel more at ease and build community, plus manage acoustics more effectively. Early four-person rooms were designed to provide a sense of enclosure for the head area of beds (see A); however, this was soon abandoned as potentially problematic for clients with psychological concerns. Later plans that were more linear (B and C) were adopted. Upper bunk beds were eliminated because of their difficult access, and flip-down and trundle beds were added instead to accommodate large families and times of high occupancy (D). To address concerns that clients would resist progressing on their personal plan to exit the shelter because the accommodations are too 'nice', storage is provided with open cubby holes, sending a message of temporary living quarters.

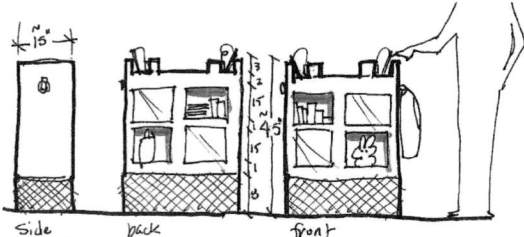

"HOME BASE" CASE FURNITURE
DAY LOUNGE • ETHEL STREET SHELTER
11-9-19   DRH   N.T.S.   FOR DISCUSSION ONLY

These small double-sided furniture peices help define seating clusters and provide a safe zone for keeping belongings close by, charging devices, and providing access to books, games and kid's toys.

Side tall style
back
front

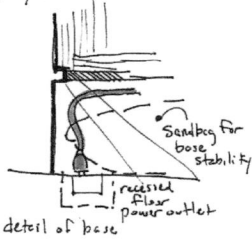

device charging (2) duplex outlets each end
impervious surface (solid surface or laminate)
book bag/purse hook
baltic birch plywood w/ protective finish or phenolic panels
example day pack
stainless steel box w/ sandbag weighting
(2) duplex electrical outlets

Sandbag for base stability
recessed floor power outlet
detail of base
open at back

short style
~28"

protected charging area

tall style used as a zone-defining element

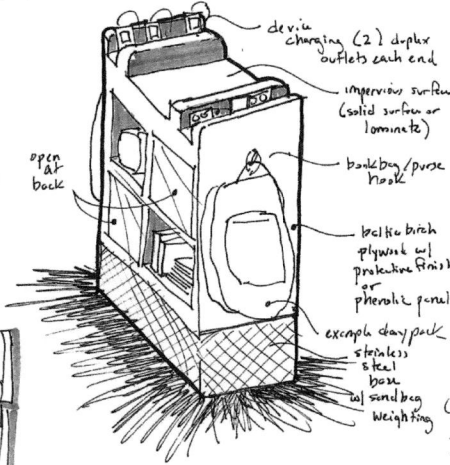

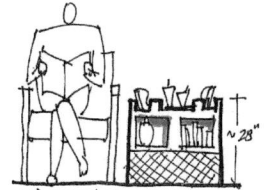

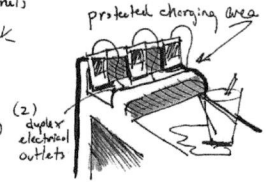

detail of charging area

4.9
Staff noted in the existing shelter that clients often argue over seating in the day lounge that provides easy, protected access to an outlet to charge devices. This combination charging station/belongings 'home base' case piece was developed to lessen these tensions and provide clients more options near their seat. Internal sandbag weights lessen the chance the piece will be knocked over.

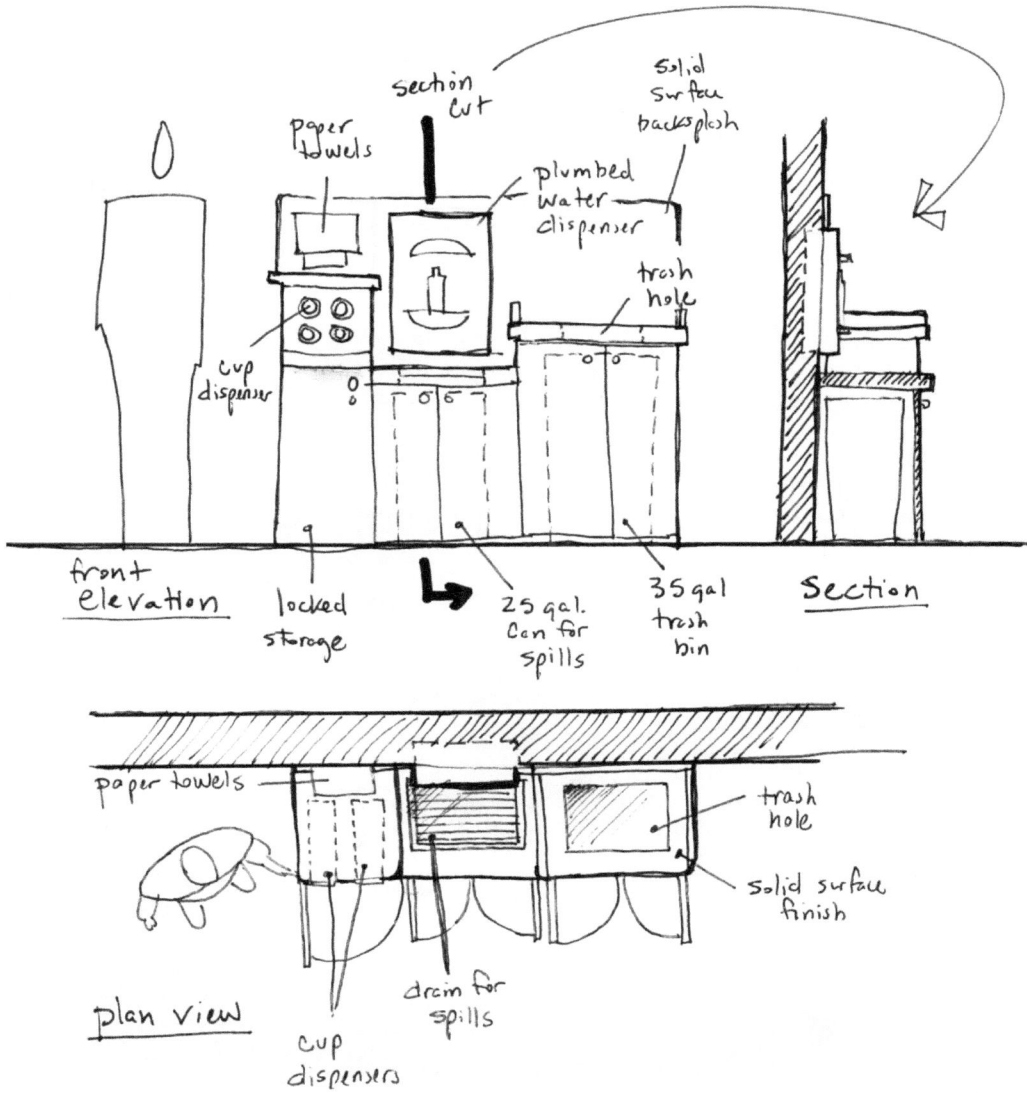

section cut

paper towels

Solid surface backsplash

plumbed water dispenser

trash hole

cup dispenser

front elevation

locked storage

25 gal. Can for spills

35 gal trash bin

Section

paper towels

trash hole

solid surface finish

plan view

drain for spills

cup dispensers

4.10
Staff noted that clients often do not drink enough fluids, and those with water bottles struggle to fill them from drinking fountains. This custom millwork provides a hydration station with built-in water dispenser, cups, paper towels, and trash can enclosure. These hydration stations will be placed in the day lounge and the residential neighborhood living rooms where space permits. Such small gestures can support dignity and help make clients feel that Atlanta Mission understands their situation.

requires willingness to compromise on the part of the design team members, for some tensions and preferences stand at polar opposites to each other. On the up side, as Pena and Parshall note, however, "creativity thrives when the limits of a problem are known" (Pena & Parshall, 2001, p. 19). The design team meetings for the Restoration House project offered moments of laughter and epiphany while they also gave rise to disagreements, yet prompted helpful information-sharing. A by-product of the design of the facility was the opportunity to understand others' points of view and, as a result, grow as people in understanding and empathy.

NOTES

1. We observe that most laypersons assume that people without homes wish to have a place to live that conforms to traditional visions of what a 'home' means. However, attitudes toward physical homes vary widely among people who do not have them, especially between persons who are only recently homeless and some who have been without a home for long periods of time. For example, when researcher and archaeologist Larry Zimmerman shared his findings about encampments with a group of homeless men in Vancouver, Canada, he recounts that, "within minutes of starting my talk and using the phrase 'hardcore homeless' several times, a man near the front interrupted me, saying, 'Some of us like this life. We aren't homeless. We are home free. No mortgage. No rules. All I have to do is find a warm place to sleep and food'" (Zimmerman, Singleton, & Welch, 2010, p. 453).
2. Sometimes, the contrasts in priorities can produce striking outcomes within a living environment. In his book *Helter Shelter*, Prashan Ranasinghe describes one shelter he visited that prioritized the placement of garbage cans over the quality of the space for its occupants (Ranasinghe, 2017, p. 122).
3. Though, interestingly, both do not currently require the inclusion of users.
4. Descriptions of a Canadian emergency center in Ranasinghe's 2017 book *Helter Shelter* are particularly disturbing.
5. Called the 'broken windows' theory, this idea has received examination also at the cityscape level, and large cities, including New York, have had success in applying it. Specifically, by improving neighborhoods through window repair, removing graffiti, removing abandoned cars, and planting flowers, crime was also modestly reduced. Although these effects were later overstated, there is still likely a connection between a well-cared-for building and positive behavior of users. In the words of researcher George Kelling, "strangers have to feel comfortable moving through communities for those communities to thrive. Order is an end in itself" (Vedantam et al., 2016, para. 34).
6. In his book *Defensible Space*, Oscar Newman noted that a neighborhood that ignores broken windows tacitly accepts this disorder, which displays to others vulnerability and a lack of defense. Thus, a well-kept building could be seen as a manifestation of a well-ordered organization whose apparent confidence discourages defacement (Newman, 1973). This theory is not without its skeptics, but was also the subject of positive discussion in more recent works such as *The Tipping Point* (Gladwell, 2002) and a 2018 National Academies panel about "Broken Windows Policing II" that declared the value of "place-based, problem-solving practices to reduce social disorder" (Medicine, 2018, n.p.).

BIBLIOGRAPHY

Donley, A., & Wright, J. (2012). Safer outside: a qualitative exploration of homeless people's resistance to homeless shelters. *Journal of Forensic Psychology Practice*, *12*, 288–306.

Gladwell, M. (2002). *The tipping point: how little things can make a big difference*. New York: Back Bay Books.

Gounis, K. (1992). The manufacture of dependency: Shelterization revisited. *The New England Journal of Public Policy*, *8*(1), 685–693.

Grunberg, J., & Eagle, P. (1990). Shelterization: how the homeless adapt to shelter living. *Hospital and Community Psychiatry*, *41*, 521–525.

Holahan, C., & Saegert, S. (1973). Behavioral and attitudinal effects of large-scale variation in the physical environment of psychiatric wards. *Journal of Abnormal Psychology*, 454–462.

Medicine, T. N. (2018). *Proactive policing*. Retrieved from The National Academies Press: www.nap.edu/catalog/24928/proactive-policing-effects-on-crime-and-communities

Menschner, C., & Maul, A. (2016). *Key ingredients for successful trauma-informed care implementation*. Center for Health Care Strategies, Robert Wood Johnson Foundation.

Miller, A., & Keys, C. (2001). Understanding dignity in the lives of homeless persons. *American Journal of Community Psychology*, *29*(2), 331–354.

Neild, M., & Rose, J. (2018). An exploration of unsheltered homelessness management on an urban riparian corridor. *People, Place and Policy*, *12*(2), 84–98.

Newman, O. (1973). *Defensible space*. New York: MacMillan.

Pable, J., & Fishburne, K. (2015). A case study in support of multiple post mortem assessments. *Journal of Systemics, Cybernetics and Informatics*, *1*(13); www.iiisci.org/journal/sci/FullText.asp?var=&id=JR527FM15.

Pena, W., & Parshall, S. (2001). *Problem seeking* (4th ed.). New York: John Wiley.

Ranasinghe, P. (2017). *Helter-Shelter: security, legality and an ethic of care in an emergency shelter*. Toronto: University of Toronto Press.

Shepley, M., & Pasha, S. (2013). *Design research and behavioral health facilities*. Concord, CA: Center for Health Design.

Stahler, G., Frazer, D., & Rappaport, H. (1984). The evaluation of an environmental remodeling program on a psychiatric geriatric ward. *The Journal of Social Psychology*, *123*, 101–113.

U.S. News and World Report. (2017). How much does a child and family social worker make? Retrieved from Child and family social worker: https://money.usnews.com/careers/best-jobs/child-and-family-social-worker/salary

Vedantam, S., Benderev, C., Boye, T., Klahr, R., Penman, M., & Schmidt, J. (2016, November 1). How a theory of crime and policing was born, and went terribly wrong. Retrieved from National Public Radio: www.npr.org/2016/11/01/500104506/broken-windows-policing-and-the-origins-of-stop-and-frisk-and-how-it-went-wrong

Zimmerman, L. (2016). Homeless, home-making, and archaeology: "To be at home where I find myself." In M. Bille & T. Flohr (eds), *Elements of architecture: assembling archaeology, atmosphere and the performance of building spaces* (pp. 256–272). Philadelphia, PA: Routledge.

Zimmerman, L., Singleton, C., & Welch, J. (2010). Activism and creating a translational archaeology of homelessness. *World Archaeology*, *42*(3), 443–454.

TEACHING MATERIALS

Lauren Trujillo

Key Terms

Socioeconomic (SE)
Experiential factors
Post-occupancy evaluation (POE)

Secondary traumatic stress
Shelterization

Discussion Questions

1. Imagine being a member of a team that is designing a new homeless shelter. What might be the benefits of having a diversity of voices at the table – clients, owners, facilities managers, staff members – during the early stages of a project? What might be the challenges?

2. Difficult as it may be, imagine you are a person experiencing homelessness. Would you prefer to conform your habits and preferences to the requirements of a shelter (or similar) system, such as eating and turning the lights out for bed at a particular time? Or would you prefer to live like the member of a homeless encampment described [as being] "home free. No mortgage. No rules. All I have to do is find a warm place to sleep and food"? What do you see as the benefits and challenges of each approach?

3. This chapter draws a connection between shelter and well-being. Reflect on your procedure for waking up this morning, including getting out of bed, having breakfast, and preparing yourself physically for your day. How has the space or physical environment positively or negatively impacted your well-being through these tasks?

4. After reading the chapter, you should have a better understanding of the goals of each stakeholder in the design of environments serving those experiencing homelessness. However, stakeholders can help each other meet their individual goals. In the next section, review the summary of each stakeholder's goals. Then answer the following questions about how the other members of the design team may be helpful in achieving these goals through compromise.

    a. *Public and donors*

        This group needs to see a building that is suitably attractive in its function and appearance and that blends into its city neighborhood context effectively. In addition, this group needs to see a facility that provides a sense of safety, reflects its mission, and offers capable stewardship through its operational efficiency and durability. How can the residents, facility manager, staff, and shelter director help the public and donors meet these goals?

    b. *Shelter directors*

        This group needs a calming environment that can both reduce the incidence of altercations and boost the morale for clients and staff. How can the residents, facility manager, public, donors, and staff help the shelter director meet these goals?

c. *Staff*

This group needs retreat spaces for solitude and rejuvenation as well as client amenities that would be easy to manage and wayfinding that would reduce client requests for directions. Staff also needs ways to minimize client-to-client disputes that take their time and concentration to solve. How can the residents, facility manager, public, donors, and shelter director help the staff meet these goals?

d. *Facilities Managers*

This group prefers furnishings and finishes that are easy to clean (i.e., resist stains and graffiti), resist breakage (such as durable windows and furniture), and are cost-effective to maintain (by fixing on site) and replace (by reducing the type and cost of replacement parts). Space planning should support easy delivery of donations and off-site laundering and reduce the impact of accidental flooding or wet areas. How can the residents, public, donors, staff, and shelter director help the facility manager meet these goals?

e. *Clients*

This group needs a space that can offer comfort in times of stress by providing clear policies that emphasize fairness and information transparency, as well as logical wayfinding, a welcoming atmosphere that has acoustical control to reduce echoes, finishes with tactile interest, and residential-like lighting solutions. How can the facility manager, public, donors, staff, and shelter director help the residents attain these needs?

5 Theory

Jill Pable

This book seeks to provide readers with the ideas and tools that can assist them in designing, researching, or establishing policy for buildings that assist persons experiencing homelessness. A chapter dedicated to theory may seem out of place and perhaps unnecessary to this goal. However, the ideas introduced here are intended to drill down to fundamental concepts that help us get to the 'whys' of homelessness in a "reflective effort to see beneath the surface" (Eaton, 1921, p. 683). A grasp of these underpinnings can help a designer make well-informed choices in designing built environments that can help their users, a researcher form the right research question, or a policy maker understand the implications of a potential course of action for a building's use.

The word *theory* comes from Greek, meaning "to look within as well as outside oneself," asking "why is something happening?" By definition, a theory is a plausible principle offered to explain a phenomenon (Malnar & Vodvarka, 1991). Theory can help us make sense of what can seem a chaotic world, but also offers other benefits if the objective is to create something that responds to an issue, such as a building's design. Understanding a theory can also significantly alter someone's perception of place or object and its design. For example, affordance theory states that we understand the world not just by perceiving physical objects and their spatial arrangements, but also by the possibilities of using an object to take action and have a human experience as a result (Gibson, 1966). In this way of thinking, a sofa is not just a sofa. It is a setting (an *affordance*) for human experience and cognitive activity. Therefore, the texture of the upholstery, comfort of the sitting posture, the placement of other seating and tables around the sofa, and the nature of lighting all hinder or help someone have a meaningful conversation while sitting there.

Theory can also help designers to 'keep their eye on the ball' of what matters the most. That is, just because we do not notice an effect of a room or building, does not mean it is not going on.[1] Theory can raise awareness and punch through the numbness of the everyday, helping people to reconnect with things and choices that can really matter for a building's users. The length of time it takes to design a building project, plus the naturally dominant visual qualities of spaces, can act to reduce the emphasis on social context or sense of safety to a side note (Perolini, 2011). It is easy to lose sight of what we are trying to solve, and touching base periodically with theory can help one stay grounded.

Designing for persons experiencing homelessness is a complex task, in part because designers themselves are rarely homeless and cannot fully empathize with this precarious situation. Being homeless represents a significantly different living experience. As such, theory can also help a designer or researcher understand why people perceive and act the way they do. For example, scarcity theory, discussed below, will reveal the potential 'whys' behind the unhealthy choices persons in crisis sometimes make, showing these decisions to be unproductive ones, yet still *rational* choices that are an understandable reaction to an extreme situation (Mullinaithan & Shafir, 2013). Keeping theory in mind can build a sense of empathy and a focus on helping people overcome hurdles so they can put homelessness behind them.

THEORY AND FRAMEWORKS

This book will treat theory as distinct from 'frameworks'. Frameworks are ways of thinking that are closely tied to action. For example, Chapter 6 will discuss trauma-informed care as a framework approach to treatment that offers persons in crisis choice in their therapies, with ramifications for the built environments where these therapies take place.

Theories are different in that they are more explanatory about an idea. Many theories can be tapped to understand fundamental ideas about homelessness and how to design in a way that supports people. The sections below introduce only a small number of these, selected for their potential to deepen understanding about how to design spaces for persons in crisis, or to conduct a research project from a position of knowledge. First are theories about '*why*': why attitudes, resources, and our cultural way of thinking and doing things are the way they are regarding homelessness. Theories about '*how*' then bring to bear ideas about how built spaces might be considered as a positive intervention.

THEORIES ABOUT 'WHY'

Writing in 1921, Ralph Eaton explained that a key value of theory is "to provide satisfaction to the 'independent hunger of the mind', which is curiosity" (Eaton, 1921, p. 683). One hundred years after Eaton, 'why' questions about homelessness seem only to have increased. On this topic, many questions arise: 'why are unhoused persons often stigmatized by the public?', 'what motivations most drive persons when they are homeless?', and 'what hurdles stand in the way of people accessing services?'.

This section introduces five theoretical systems, social distress theory, marginalization theory, terror management theory, scarcity theory, and threshold fear, drawn from the fields of criminal justice, social psychology, behavioral economics, and, curiously, museum studies (which is concerned with civility, public space, and inclusion). As a set, they represent only a small collection of explanations that confront the current situation of things and yet, in their breadth, introduce the potential of theory to inform architectural action.

Social Distress Theory and Marginalization Theory

People can react to quickly changing societal norms by exhibiting denial, help-lessness, frustration, or other responses. In 1992, Robert Rieber, editor of the journal *Social Distress and the Homelessness* and professor of criminal justice, introduced social distress theory, which examines the perceptions and attitudes of both persons experiencing homelessness and the general housed population about impoverishment and, by extension, homelessness. It discusses distur-bances in a society's functioning in the context of value conflicts that may arise as a result of rapid social change (Rieber, 1992) and examines why people some-times feel hostile towards those experiencing homelessness.

Rieber and others (Saltzman, 1994) maintain that *all* persons, housed or unhoused, experience social distress. Housed persons can feel both discomfort and guilt that can contribute to anger and, at times, direct blame toward unhoused people. The act of blaming others shields housed people from "knowledge that the world may not be as just as we would like to believe" (Saltzman, 1994, p. 104) and helps people feel in control of their world. Disassociating oneself from unhoused persons is a coping mechanism that leads to a compassionless "numbing" (Saltzman, 1994, p. 104). This situation of psychological separation from oneself, Rieber believed, also makes people more primed to follow the direction of cultural leaders and, consequently, brings larger political and ideological systems into the equation, such as capitalism (1992). In western capitalist cultures, the principles of market forces tell people they are not responsible for the plight of homelessness.

Social distress theory also explains that unhoused persons may disassociate from larger society and, thus, remove themselves to encampments under bridges or in abandoned buildings where they feel safe and valued. They may see housed persons as both exploitative and oppressive (Saltzman, 1994).

The four principles of social distress theory reveal a fascinating, if tragic, play of events that revolves around rapid societal change. The table in 5.1 describes these steps with indicators that are observable in western cultures. Social distress theory offers insights for designers and researchers of built environments. First, it is use-ful to recognize that proposing interventions that help address homelessness may be up against a societal process that entrenches people in their ways of thinking, and that participants think and act in ways conditioned by exterior forces that move people towards disassociation from resolving the situation. For example, should a shelter reception desk have safety glass for security, which may also reinforce the notion of hierarchical separation between staff and residents? Could the glass be removed to reduce this hierarchical atmosphere? Second, design programming will need to acknowledge both the subtle and overt messages of safety, respect, and care that can address and perhaps slowly soften these tendencies.

Like social distress theory, marginalization theory takes a sobering look at the origins of homelessness and grounds it in the naturally exclusionary and hierarchical tendencies of human nature (Melnitzer, 2007). These ideas arise from the critical theory tradition that seeks to confront cultural power sources that set up systems of repression. Marginalization theory identifies that social institutions operate to control less powerful groups such as persons experiencing homelessness and act to normalize the situation so that these institutions can continue to perpetuate this

5.1
Four principles
of social distress
theory.

Step	Examples of societal change indicators
1. Rapid and unplanned social change generates a shift in values	Deinstitutionalization of mental patients Gentrification Deindustrialization Changing gender expectations New family forms Discussion of rights versus responsibilities
2. A conflict between former and new values comes to light	
3. Social institutions, having no recourse, reassemble using both sets of values which reinforces the conflict and simultaneously complicates their ability to function well	Hospitals attend to both destitute patients and those that fully pay Police both protect victims and protect rights Housing or healthcare is viewed as a basic need but also a commodity sold in the market for profit
4. Social distress results	Evictions Elimination of housing Confusion and fear about the role of police Reactions: frustration, irritability, helplessness, violence, denial or disassociation, destructive coping mechanisms

control.[2] Those in power rationalize their actions through arguments such as the need for public safety. Physical manifestations of this process are ghettos, food deserts, and walled subdivisions that reinforce class distinctions. Discriminatory housing policies put in place by government administrators and advocated by concerned homeowners also fit this description, a phenomenon that is a significant hindrance to the necessary construction of low-income housing (Thomas, 2019; Wilson, 2019).

This hierarchical structure of insiders and outsiders affects its impoverished members in other ways too, such as exclusion from health insurance and job networks (Atkinson & Blandy, 2016). Restrictive rules imposed by those in control promote institutionalization and a sense of helplessness, further entrenching the system's workings by compelling a dependence on the forces that are suppressing them. Proponents of marginalization theory view architectural responses such as shelters as a strategy to merely treat the symptoms of homelessness rather than the cause, enabling the public to maintain a mood of complacency and effectively distance themselves from the situation (Melnitzer, 2007).

Terror Management Theory

Social distress theory, discussed above, describes that people can react to quickly changing societal norms by exhibiting denial, helplessness, frustration, or other responses. Terror management theory examines these responses further, tracing them to a fundamental, ongoing need for people to maintain their personal self-esteem. Such an idea is well supported historically; Alfred Adler, the founder of individual psychology, assessed self-esteem as perhaps the most important human motivating force (Salzman, 2001, p. 341). Embodied in this idea is that we are deeply grounded in and influenced by others' assessment of us. One example is a person who suffers from anorexia, enduring great pain through hunger in pursuit of a culturally described standard of beauty established by other people.

At the heart of terror management theory lies the notion that people are highly motivated to avoid feeling anxious (Leary, Barnes, & Griebel, 1986), a state that can lead to unsettling self-perceptions such as feeling worthless. In an effort to avoid this uncomfortable state of anxiety, people are motivated to maintain their sense of self-esteem in order to bolster their internal sense of importance and value. This can be seen, for example, in a person who places great stock in their professional achievements, enjoying amenities such as a home and car that their income makes possible. Their anxiety can be well managed through the accumulation of possessions and the respect paid to them by others that reflects back to them an image of prosperity and success.

However, the outcomes of terror management theory may be far different for a person of few means who has not conformed with societal expectations, either through their own actions or the unforgiving nature of the situation. A man who is homeless may experience the same anxiety about his self-esteem but lack the external, reassuring cues of others' approval. In an effort to maintain his self-esteem, he might take a number of actions. He might tie his self-esteem to an action he can control, such as describing himself as the most talented forager in town, or pride himself on the sturdy construction of a self-made home of tarps and reclaimed building materials. He might also, however, engage in maladaptive behaviors[3] such as misusing alcohol or drugs to avoid thinking about his situation, or violently abuse another person in an effort to increase his apparent dominion and power. He may fabricate a false history that paints himself in a positive light. He may adopt the opinion that the system is corrupt or join an extremist group that tells him he is worthy.

This active decision to prop up self-esteem by 'exiting the system' of standard behaviors may be why people sometimes choose to live in the woods, in their car, or in makeshift encampments, even though shelter spaces may be available. Terror management theory assesses that such a person has not perceived sufficient support for their self-esteem within a shelter's procedures and policies, and, therefore, the person makes the active choice to 'go it alone', even though they must endure great suffering from rain, heat, and cold, as well as potential dangers to their safety to do so.

Terror management theory's focus on self-esteem as a primary motivator of human choices can make apparently irrational choices, such as living outside, seem a logical, if mistaken and maladaptive, effort to boost self-esteem and manage existential terror. The principles of this theory suggest that built environments such as shelters and supportive housing should prioritize the maintenance of users' self-esteem so that these facilities will actually be accessed by those that arguably need their services the most (Chapter 7 examines applied techniques for supporting self-esteem within shelters and housing). Thought leaders in the fields of psychology and social work have reached this same conclusion and focus on people's self-esteem in their therapies outlined in the new principles of trauma-informed design (discussed in Chapter 6). If, as one writer states, it is a function of cultures to provide meaning that protects self-esteem that in turn provides an anxiety-buffering function (Becker, 1971), designing spaces that prioritize self-worth may be one such way to serve this end.

Scarcity

The field of economics seems an unusual source for a theory that would be helpful to understand homelessness and how to design effective places. However, examining the real experience of homelessness shows it to be very much a matter of resources and how people respond to the presence or absence of them. As authors Mullinaithan and Shafir outline in their book *Scarcity: Why Having So Little Means So Much*, both real and perceived scarcity of resources such as food, shelter, and money to pay bills may greatly influence people's behavior and attitudes and describe why people in crisis seemingly make poor choices in their lives.

Being without the necessities of life can affect people's *fluid intelligence*, meaning their ability to make decisions, which operates on top of other characteristics such as intelligence and personality. For example, being preoccupied by critically important, near-term problems, such as where you will sleep safely tonight without being assaulted, crowds out a person's ability to think long term and to make appropriate decisions that can help their future. Being in a situation of scarcity can also explain why people in crisis may sometimes have emotional outbursts, erupting in anger and frustration that seem odd and out of proportion to other people. A preoccupied state of mind where one is always in a defensive crouch or putting out the latest fire can make being pleasant extra difficult. Also, the stress of the unknown can affect impulse control, compelling people to latch on to the first opportunity for relief from the situation that presents itself – often in the form of drugs or alcohol.

Mullinaithan and Shafir suggest that the significant power of distraction a life crisis such as homelessness can create may deeply compromise a person's ability to function, regardless of their socioeconomic status, intelligence, or similar characteristics. That is, it is less about 'talent' or 'personality' and more about available 'cognitive bandwidth'. The person who struggles to fill out an intake form at a shelter may be smart, but also deeply distracted and, therefore, compromised in their ability to carry out a straightforward procedure.

We could probably safely assume that most users of shelters, supportive housing, and day centers will have their ability to make decisions compromised by their perceptions about scarcity. They will be distracted, potentially emotional, and have a restricted ability to perceive signals of where to go and how to act in new and unfamiliar environments. Designers armed with this knowledge can craft spaces with particular attendance to crafting a building's layout so that it is understandable at an intuitive level for people. For example, cues of where to check in, where to wait, and what to do should be clear without the need for excessive signs and rules. Off-limits areas should be out of users' sightlines, and wayfinding should be easy to navigate in order to minimize the impact on their reduced cognitive load capacity. In sum, the experience of a building should meet people where they are, empathetically offering them agency to do what they must using the capacity of their current mindset.

Threshold Fear

Elaine Gurian is a writer who examines the use and perceptions of museums by the public and, specifically, the thought processes a person takes in deciding whether to enter (Gurian, 2015). Her work starts with the simple premise that to enter a structure is a different experience than being somewhere outside where one is free of its influences. Although this may seem obvious, the simple choice whether to access the services of a shelter can mean the difference between acquiring the knowledge and skills to exit homelessness and not doing so. Museums would seemingly not relate to the issue of homelessness and built environments; however, the decision process of visiting a museum has some similarities to committing to the use of a shelter or housing. For example, most visitors to both building types are newcomers, and the exact nature of the activities and processes inside the buildings is essentially unknown. In both instances, to enter is to succumb to being changed. For people who have been abused, to enter a structure may be a fearful act because it reminds them of trauma that may have occurred there in the past. Fear of the home, or 'domophobia', may bring with it reminders of restriction, danger, or repression (Atkinson & Blandy, 2016).

What may work to increase museum visitor numbers may also be informative for the architectural design of shelters, day centers, and supportive housing spaces: the goal becomes to create the perception and reality of a 'neutral ground' place that is approachable and emotionally manageable by the clientele. One technique is to recognize that people by nature like to 'lurk', observing how a process works before submitting themselves to it. Therefore, creating spaces that encourage building users who are already comfortable there to hang out in the entrance space, signaling that it is safe to stay there, may be a useful strategy. Shopping malls with their balance of easily accessible public areas and stores are an example. Visitors want to 'see evidence' of safety, and cues such as positive interactions, music, and children playing are ways to convey this. Adding elements that promote trust such as acceptance of pets, presence of food, aquariums, and surfaces that invite touch are further ideas, as are staff whose behavior can be observed by prospective clients in a low-stakes way. A protected intake patio that is busy with positive interaction and offers seating, weather protection, and positive staff presence comes to mind. By attending to people's natural caution about commitment through architectural strategy, a sense of comfort and safety might successfully overcome suspicion.

THEORIES ABOUT 'HOW'

The previous section introduced a selection of theories that focus on why people's perceptions and actions about homelessness may be the way they are. This section builds on the first and moves on to examine how we might think about homelessness in relationship to designing built environments such as day centers, shelters, supportive housing, and similar places. How might design positively intervene to improve people's experiences, best supporting their goal to regroup and rejoin the workforce? How can a building best fit its users? What specific theories of space, light, and form can accommodate needful users who are experiencing crisis? Like the previous section, such theories are too numerous to capture within this chapter's constraints. However, the selections below discuss those theories we find to be particularly contributive to both crafting a productive mindset that is well-oriented to the design task and applying pragmatic theories to architectural decision-making that can result in meaningful, effective design solutions.

Perhaps the first question that confronts the designer is, "does thoughtful architectural design really matter in the bigger context of necessary therapies and supports for persons in the throes of homelessness?" One way to answer this question is to consider that homelessness and the co-occurring issues that often accompany it, such as poverty and substance abuse, are measurable and tangible threats to human health. For example, a person who experiences chronic homelessness is three to six times more likely to become ill than a housed person and will die on average 12 years sooner than the general U.S. population (National Health Care for the Homeless Council, 2019). The U.S. Department of Health and Human Services identifies that buildings are *determinants of health* (Office of Disease Prevention and Health Promotion, 2019). This agency's Healthy People 2020 initiative defines science-based factors that contribute to positive health that are controlled by four condition categories: personal, economic, social, and environmental. Notably, built environments are present in both the social and environmental categories. If we consider that buildings literally set the scene for human experiences, it is perhaps not so surprising that buildings are important for health, just as healthy food and living wages are. Architecture as a 'determinant of health' offers support agencies and designers a useful starting place when justifying the importance of quality design projects to human health objectives. As the National Health Care for the Homeless Council describes, there is little distinction between architecture and human health, because no amount of health care can substitute for stable housing. As they put it, "housing *is* health care" (National Health Care for the Homeless Council, 2019, p. 2).

The three theories discussed below broadly echo the determinants of health's inclusion of built environments while directly connecting spaces to human perceptions. Like the determinants of health, these theories offer a useful way to think about the ways architecture supports persons in crisis, and also a justifiable defense when presenting a design idea to a client.

Environment–Person Theory

As the name implies, this psychological theory proposes that people and environment do not operate apart from each other, but, rather, their reciprocal 'fit' to each other controls the level of stress a person may experience (Edwards, Caplan, & Harrison, 1998). With its focus on stress, this theory may be particularly relevant to designing for persons in crisis, as homelessness and its co-occurring issues such as poverty, mental incapacity, substance dependencies, and abuse are frequent sources of tension. Stress matters. As Chapter 6 explores in further detail, stress can be debilitating for a person trying to exit homelessness because it exacerbates insomnia, can elevate blood pressure, and over time can lead to heart disease and depression.

Environment–person theory describes several ways that a 'misfit' can occur between people and places. First, a building or room may not provide adequate features or tools to meet a person's needs. A dark parking lot with inadequate lighting may be terrifying for a victim of past violence. Second, a misfit may occur when a person's abilities fall short of being able to meet the demands that the environment requires. This might occur when a person who is unable to read well is confronted by a list of rules at a shelter reception desk, and the waiting line behind them makes them feel rushed. A key point in understanding environment–person theory is that a person's 'fit' to their environment has a subjective aspect. Put another way, a person must *perceive* that an environment is supporting them for lower stress to result. A person may in fact be able to read quickly, but they are so upset by having to wait for access in the rain and cold owing to the shelter's entrance design that they cannot work past their emotions to use their reading skills effectively.

The consequences of poor person–environment fit can result in a user changing themselves to 'fit' the environment, changing the environment to better suit themselves, or enlisting a variety of defense strategies to explain away the incongruence. Sometimes, the poor fit may lead the user to reject the use of a building altogether.[4] Environment–person theory identifies several coping responses that may result from reacting to the elevated stress levels, explained in 2.2.

In cases of such poor environment–person fit that a user withdraws from the setting altogether, a vicious circle aspect can also come into play: when the building's attendant social supports are withdrawn, now the user has even fewer options for resolving the environment misfit, leaving them only with their own defensive responses to rely on (Valentiner, Holahan, & Moos, 1994). For example, a man rejects a shelter because he resents being told where to sleep. When he returns to sleeping in the woods, he justifies the choice telling himself that shelters are only for weak people, thus lessening the chance that he will engage with support services in the future.

Response to Poor Environment–Person Fit	Example Outcome
Coping by changing themselves: user attempts to improve the fit by adapting themselves to it	A person counts the number of beds in a congregate sleeping room to find their own when no identification system is present
Coping by changing the environment	A person places a sign on their bed with their name to remind themselves which one is theirs
Defense through cognitive distortion of the subjective person or environment, such as repression, projection, or denial, without making objective, concrete changes	A person blames someone else for their inability to clean up their kitchen mess because the rules are too complicated to understand
	A person in a new housing-first apartment goes hungry because they cannot imagine eating by themselves without the community they developed while living on the street

5.2 Person–environment fit theory styles of responses with architectural example outcomes

Supportive Design Theory

Like environment–person theory, supportive design theory focuses its attention on the reduction of stress through built environment intervention. Unlike environment–person fit theory, however, Ulrich (1997) offers specific, practical intervention strategies that built environments can use to reduce the tensions associated with stress. Built environments should: (1) provide people a sense of personal control over their surroundings; (2) provide people access to social supports; and (3) provide access to positive distractions that increase positive feelings, hold people's interest, reduce worrisome thoughts, and potentially reduce blood pressure. It is perhaps this third factor that is the most ignored in the design of many shelters (see 5.3). A series of applied recommendations Ulrich offers to achieve these three goals are shown in 5.4.

Reducing stress through thoughtful architectural design may also be helpful to shelter staff, because lower stress levels may reduce time-consuming engagements with clients because they are less disruptive. Also, stress reduction can elevate users' level of alertness, which might reduce the number of policy, rules, and wayfinding questions staff must attend to.

Self-Actualization Theory

Ulrich's theory is unusual in that it includes applied recommendations for designing interiors and architecture. More often, theories do not prescribe specific design responses, but instead serve as a handy source material from which designers can derive applied strategies. Abraham Maslow's humanistic personality concept of self-actualization is one such theory. More commonly known as Maslow's hierarchy of needs, this pyramid identifies that we require physiological needs such as air, water, and food first, and then safety, love, and self-esteem. Less known is that the top of this pyramid describes the ultimate self-fulfillment goal called self-actualization, or the desire to become the best that one can be in a state of complete psychological health. These characteristics bring to mind qualities that might be used to describe a good friend. A self-actualized person is realistically oriented, is accepting of themself and others, is focused on problems outside themself, and believes in the basic good of life. Such a person also approaches people without stereotype, possesses a non-hostile sense of humor, and maintains a personal moral code (Maslow, 1968). Few people have likely reached a state of full actualization, but, given the many hurdles that homelessness presents to people, it is even less likely that self-actualization is within easy reach for them. Thus, this idea presents itself as a potential identifiable (if lofty) goal with the benefit of specific objectives for psychological health that might be addressed by including strategic architecture and interior design elements.

Using this premise, one of us undertook a study that supposed Maslow's concepts could be interpreted and supported through architectural form and applied to facilities that serve persons in crisis (Pable, 2007). The study posed the question, "How might personality theory serve as a framework for the user-centered design of a homeless shelter?"

By itself, Maslow's directives such as "a person holds an accurate sense of reality" are difficult to translate into architectural design recommendations.

5.3
Although shelters differ significantly in their appearance, the frequent low project budgets, desire to assist as many people as possible, and significant cleanability requirements can drive environments to a low level of visual interest.

5.4 Supportive design theory factors that reduce stress and potential architectural intervention strategies that might activate these factors.	Factors that Reduce Stress in Healthcare Environments for Patients	Architectural Strategies Applicable to Facilities that Attend to Homelessness
	1. Provide personal control over the environment	Reduce poor wayfinding, lack of privacy, uncontrolled noise, forced view of glare Increase privacy, dimmers, easy wayfinding, access to spaces such as gardens
	2. Provide people access to social supports	Reduce isolation, complicated pathways to reach people Increase comfortable waiting areas, autonomous cooking options, garden seating
	3. Provide access to positive distractions	Increase access to nature Promote laughter and comedy Make opportunities for interacting with caring, smiling people Include music Include art, especially natural scenes that are calm and open

For this reason, this study referenced two other thinking systems more closely allied to architectural design elements that could serve to help bridge the gap and provide ideas. The first were concepts from *A Pattern Language* that are an extension of the holistic theories of Christopher Alexander and his colleagues (Alexander et al., 1977) and offer broad recommendations for making architecture more human. The second were ideas drawn from CPTED (crime prevention through environmental design), applied architectural design strategies that can act to reduce a person's likelihood to commit a crime (Poyner, 1983). From these knowledge sources, a thinking tool called a *theory-to-practice grid* was created that yielded a series of practical strategies addressing each of Maslow's self-actualization characteristics. An excerpt from this grid that attended to one of Maslow's criteria is shown in 5.5. A homeless shelter intake patio area design that resulted from the theory to action grid analysis is shown in 5.6.

Built Environment Theories

Theories such as environment–person, supportive design, and self-actualization broadly lend guidance for thinking about built environments and are useful as a way to get oriented to architecture's potential. However, applicable theories in environmental psychology and other areas can help explain more specifically how people perceive and are affected by built environments. This section presents two such ideas that commonly confront designers and organizations that provide built environments for people in crisis: crowding and privacy.

Crowding
The number of people in need of shelter often exceeds the normal capacity of shelters, day centers, and other facilities owing to budget realities and related

5.5

This table shows an excerpt from Maslow's Theory-to-Practice Grid that informed these design programming choices calling for 'an accurate perception of reality'. The characteristic is interpreted as a call for provision for order and clarity in the applied design.

Self-Actualization Characteristic	Explanation of the Characteristic	Antithesis of this Characteristic	Patterns Response (with Sketches Showing Application to the Intake Area)	CEPTD/Proxemics Response	Patio Design Criteria
An accurate perception of reality	Self-actualizers are free of pessimism and defensive distortions. Can judge real from phony in people, events, and ideas	Pessimistic, defensive. May be unable to make accurate judgments concerning truth and fiction in others' intent or events	Patterns that relate to clarity in spatial experience and procedure: #120: *Paths and Goals.* Place goals at natural points of architectural interest #126 *Something roughly in the middle.* Design space to draw people towards a natural center 	Provide clear definition of controlled space so that people recognize differences between public/private An organization should stake claim to a space by creating a well-defined border and edges that imply ownership and control	Create a design that emphasizes clarity and legitimacy: Patio should send cues of separation from the problems of the street and a sense of security, stability, and refuge. Forms and textures that evoke an enduring presence will be used. Overhead forms will appear to be well supported, and overtly unsettling assemblies will be avoided Provide up-to-date, accurate information on digital boards and bulletin boards. Provide a way to queue up for check-in that is fair and efficient

5.6
This rendering shows an example of a homeless shelter intake patio project from the street. The proposed solution attends to clarity through its literal, physical outreach to the homeless from the existing building, clear site lines, unambiguous overhead support structures, and multiple entrances.

reasons. The degree of need can also vary for shelters over months or years, making it difficult to keep pace with demand.[5] The goal of assisting as many people as possible with emergency shelter can lead to places that are, or feel, crowded, often exceeding the commonly accepted measure of one person per room for western dwellings (Baldassare, 1979). It is not unusual for a family of four to be housed in a sleeping room 9 feet by 12 feet for 9–12 months. Shelters routinely use congregate sleeping rooms with 60 or more beds, where the only 'private' spaces are at the bedside where one stands up.

Because crowding occurs so often in shelters, it is easy to overlook its impact on human health. It is, however, well established that a sense of crowding negatively affects tolerance for frustration (Sherrod & Cohen, 1979) and disrupts the normally socially supportive relationships that exist within groups of cohabiting people. Crowding can also increase interpersonal hostility and decrease a person's positive frame of mind, even among family members (Chapin, 1951), a point that may be quite important for persons already dealing with the psychological crisis of losing their home. Shelter staff may bear the brunt of emotional outbursts made worse by people being on edge. Crowding also has physical health implications. It is easier to spread communicable diseases such as tuberculosis, flu, the COVID-19 virus, and hepatitis when people are in close proximity (National Healthcare for the Homeless Council, 2019).

The perception of crowding may also depend to some degree on a person's mindset. A person who does not feel they can control the outcomes of their life (a form of helplessness that often afflicts people who encounter adversity) may be apt to feel more crowded in a room compared with a person who has this sense of personal control (Shopler & Walton, 1974). Persons who feel they are a part of a cohesive group will tolerate more crowding than someone who senses that they are alone and not part of a collective (Baum & Valins, 1977). Given that social isolation is a common problem among people experiencing homelessness, the tolerance for crowding may be low.

The sense of crowding may also be affected by a space's purpose. That is, rooms can have different perceived functions associated with expected actions that take place there. A bedroom is regarded as a highly intimate place, whereas a living room has a more public function. A sense of crowding is more likely in a single-purpose room such as a single resident occupancy apartment that must operate as both a place to entertain visitors and as a personal bedroom. If such a room is occupied by multiple residents, these persons may perceive the actions of their roommates to be both invasive and committed intentionally, and the residents may be more apt to defend themselves against real or perceived attempts to thwart activities they are engaged in. Such a situation is likely to create strain for everyone, and perhaps even promote violence (Stokols, 1976).

Being aware that perceptions of crowding matter to people can affect the design of a variety of places. It may be a good idea to provide most seats in a day center lounge with charging ports for phones and computers to avoid arguments over seats. Because people experiencing homelessness may be particularly sensitive about their belongings, providing ample room for luggage in public spaces may help reduce anxiety. Steps can also be taken to reduce a potential perception of crowding, even if square footages cannot be altered. An emphasis on the diagonal in spaces can seemingly extend spaces further, and color can be used to visually expand apparent dimensions of rooms. Elements such as divided Dutch doors in sleeping rooms can lend a sense of expansion of the room into the corridor, an effect observed in a study involving the renovation of a transitional shelter room (Pable, 2007). The degree of perceived privacy can also serve as a hedge against perceptions of crowding (Evans, Schroeder, & Lepore, 1996). Privacy is discussed at further length next.

Privacy
In a shelter environment, privacy, defined as being free from being observed or disturbed by others, may be among the most elusive of built environment qualities. In our experience observing and working with shelters, oftentimes the need for staff to monitor people as they occupy beds in communal sleeping rooms (to prevent illicit behavior) is placed at higher priority than providing privacy curtains around beds. Discussions with residents, however, showed that privacy is one of the strongest and most frequently expressed needs in communal spaces, especially with intimate spaces such as bedroom areas and bathrooms, and the lack of privacy represents a significant source of stress for people. Similarly, locks on doors were a frequent point of discussion in a study of two families in a transitional shelter, especially with the presence of children.[6] Privacy may be more than just an expressed need, but the lack of it may also contribute to a larger problematic situation. Psychologist Shawn Burn's work in shelters led her to conclude that lack of privacy is one of the strongest predictors of a person developing a sense of helplessness about their situation. This matters, because feeling helpless can also interfere with a person's capacity to summon the resolve to take control of their predicament. Such resolve is necessary, says Burn, to secure a job and permanent place to live (1992).

Specific knowledge about privacy can assist an organization or its designer to anticipate users' perceptions of privacy. For example, the knowledge of roommates' schedules can help reduce the sense of privacy invasion, as a person can anticipate when they may be able to be alone. Also, if a person believes that a situation is temporary and leads to longer-term positive outcomes, they may be able to tolerate privacy invasions more easily (Baldassare, 1979). Interestingly, just providing a person the *opportunity* to have privacy, even if they do not exercise it, can reduce a perception of a lack of privacy (Sherrod & Cohen, 1979).

Spaces that support the need for privacy recognize that shielding a person from observation by others can occur in various ways. Acoustic privacy and visual privacy are two aspects that deserve attention. Both may be needed at a day center reception desk where clients are asked to share the reasons for their visit. Visual privacy may be especially key in a shared bedroom situation to have the ability to step away from roommates and "have some me-time" (Pable, 2007). See Figure 3.

Situated/Embodied Cognition Theory

From cognitive neuroscience, cognitive neuropsychology, ecological psychology, and similar fields has arisen the broad theory called situated cognition. Put simply, this theory sets forth that our physical bodies and their sensations influence how we see the world, as well as how we take action and why. Although this may seem obvious, this theory counters the previous general understanding in psychology before the 1990s that the brain essentially exists apart from the body, making exclusively internal decisions independent of physical influences. The theory represents a broadening of the role of perception and an acknowledgement that a person's thinking (or cognition) is influenced by tools and artifacts (including built environments) and also by their social interactions with others (Cobb, 2001). Much of this likely goes on at the subliminal level of cognition.

Situated cognition holds much promise for entirely rethinking the potential impact of built environment on what people think about their world, other people, and even themselves (Goldhagen, 2017). Situated cognition requires an understanding that people comprehend their world by building a mental 'schema', a scenario of sorts that includes sights, sounds, smells, and other inputs. For example, good conversation over a cup of coffee with your partner, sitting at the dining table with sunlight streaming in through a nearby window, all contribute ingredients to a collective memory of this moment. Cognitively speaking, we process that moment (or schema) as a combination of inputs, to the point that seeing that cup the next day might recall that happy occasion. Further, this schema can prompt us to act in certain ways, such as laughing out loud when we remember a shared joke from that conversation. This schema now prompts you to associate certain objects in your experience, like that coffee mug with this past experience. The coffee cup is now a trigger, or a 'prime' that prompts a great memory.

All schemata, however, do not necessarily recall happy moments. Imagine that you have recently been incarcerated, and one of your strongest memories of the experience is the feeling of entrapment and isolation prompted by your cell. Just looking at black tubular bars can now recall a cavalcade of negative experiences of

sight, sound, and touch. Now that you have been released from jail, you move into an emergency shelter. To your dismay, you discover that your sleeping space is the lower half of a black metal bunk bed, forcing you to be surrounded by the bars of the bunk bed's supports. This, plus loud arguing, music, and the smell of body sweat remind you of the unwanted memory of jail. You find it difficult to concentrate and get rid of these primed associations, and over time your mood suffers as a result. You are on edge, but you do not know why, and you fall into an argument with your neighbor because you feel so tense.

Situated cognition studies also hold the promise of understanding how certain architectural features may prompt particular ways of thinking. A striking example can be interpreted from a study conducted by two Yale researchers, Laurence Williams and John Bargh, to see how primed cues of distance might affect people's emotional connections (Williams & Bargh, 2008). Two separate participant groups were asked to plot two given points on an x–y graph that were far apart. Another, separate group plotted two points that were close together. Both groups' members were then asked about the strength of their emotional attachments to their family members. Controlling for other variables, the study found that the group primed with the idea of distance reported weaker emotional attachments to their family members than the group that plotted the close-together points. Results were the same with a series of other tests such as how detached the person felt from feeling embarrassed for a person in a difficult situation and

5.7
A transitional shelter mother uses a bed's privacy curtains to have some alone time away from her children in the room.

112 □

feeling empathy for a victim of violence. Generally, the group primed with the distant points were bothered less and felt more detached from the situations. The takeaway from the study suggested that people's sense of closeness or personal engagement in a situation could be altered if they were compelled to think about distance or closeness beforehand.

Might there be lessons here for architectural spaces? Williams and Bargh did not offer conjecture on the point; however, if their finding is true, might people feel less empathetic towards each other if they are experiencing a high-ceiling space versus a space where the ceiling is low? Although this premise has not been tested, other situated cognition studies show that "locations themselves can serve as contextual primes that influence specific attitudes and behaviors" (Pryor, 2016, Primed for Votes section, para. 3). For example, people attribute more power to elements that are placed higher in a room (think about a platform on which the courtroom judge sits; Schubert, 2005). Six different studies have also confirmed that polling locations sited in a church can prime people to more often vote in a way that supports a religious principle (Pryor, 2016).

It is becoming increasingly apparent that people's perceptions of their world are governed to a certain degree by previously unrecognized, primed associations, and some of these may arise from architectural cues. If so, there is a significant lesson here for design of the spaces that serve as the setting for lived experiences: we need to deeply understand the past experiences of a space's most likely users to avoid presenting them with unwanted likely associations. Conversely, the priming potential of architectural spaces offers promise of forming new, health-affirming associations people can rely on to help them evolve toward a better future. (Think about the positivity well-chosen color and patterns can impart.) This topic deserves further research to confirm its application to architectural design, as well as studies that identify commonly occurring associations either to be avoided or embraced in design projects.

On the Near Horizon: Epigenetics

Situated cognition describes potential influences of the built environment on people's perceptions, potentially connecting the dots of physical surroundings to human action. In contrast, epigenetics studies how the environment we inhabit (and other things) may also exert control over *our inherent genetic traits*. This intriguing new theory proposes that external influences, such as lighting, air quality, or other physical conditions, hold the power to turn on or off or otherwise alter genes' expressions within our DNA, which are read by our body's cells and control how our cells produce proteins. The impacts may be great – cancers and degenerative conditions are related to epigenetic errors (United States National Library of Medicine, 2019).

The built environment's potential influence on this series of events is illustrated in a study that examined the effects of sleep loss (Cedernaes et al., 2018), a condition we all have probably experienced that can be caused by poor acoustic conditions, a lumpy pillow, or other built environment influences. All these conditions, incidentally, also frequently occur within shelters. The study showed that lack of sleep can trigger bodily responses such as metabolic changes and DNA changes within fat tissue. Inflammation of fat and skeletal muscle tissues was also observed, all of which can contribute to weight gain. Memory was also impaired.

What might this mean for the design of environments for persons experiencing homelessness? Writers are already musing about its implications for the design of places (Franks, 2013), exploring the notion that the places we inhabit may affect our current bodily systems in ways that we don't fully appreciate. Clearly, a lot of research lies between our current understanding and putting these findings to actual use as we build. Once we get further along, however, we may find that conditions such as daylighting, carbon dioxide levels in indoor air, or the quality and comfort of bedding may prompt measurable changes in our bodies' DNA expressions that support or harm human health – and the possession of this knowledge may lead us to design in ways that harness these outcomes to positive effect.

CONCLUSION

Theories offer a way to make sense of complex situations and people's reactions to them. As such, they can provide a sense of grounded orientation concerning the complicated issue of homelessness, helping to fundamentally inform the goals that guide the design of a shelter, public square, day center, or supportive housing. Although theories are broad, they can still help inform specific choices in a building's design program. For example, theory could lead a designer to prioritize the support of self-esteem in a shelter project based on terror management theory or design a day lounge space plan that includes opportunities for positive distraction advocated in supportive design theory. It falls to the support organization, designer, researcher, and policy maker to make these connections, harnessing the potential of knowledge to craft spaces that stand the best chance of offering effective places that support people in crisis.

NOTES

1. Designers and laypersons may also have different levels of sensitivity to the pitfalls and potentials of a given space. Laypersons that notice how a wall allows them to eat lunch in the sun have discovered an 'affordance' (Goldhagen, 2017; Altman & Rogoff, 1987). Designers would do well to consider the orientation of the wall to the sun and wind patterns for optimal user comfort before it is built.
2. An interesting read on this topic is Craig Wilse's book *The Value of Homelessness: Managing Surplus Life in the United States.*
3. Salzman notes that, "our prisons are bursting with people compensating maladaptively for the failure to achieve a positive, stable source of self-esteem that is derived from the cultural drama and meaning system" (Salzman, 2001, p. 342).
4. It is interesting to consider the person–environment fit of a shelter that goes unused, with potential residents preferring to sleep in a tent even in bad weather. All too often, a real or perceived lack of safety, personal control, and/or autonomy of a shelter can make the 'fit' seem sufficiently poor to the user such that they would prefer to endure the physical pain and potential injury of being cold and wet.
5. The Austin Resource Center for Homelessness, for example, was built in 2004 to provide 400 people with day services and emergency shelter. By 2016, it was called to offer these

services for 830 people, making necessary mats for people to sleep in the conference rooms, cafeteria, and other spaces (Pable, 2016). The existing building has maxed out its site, and its design does not lend itself easily to expansion.

6. The stress that children place on parents when the family is living in a shelter deserves more research attention, in our view. Parents not only need privacy for their children and themselves when changing clothes, for example, but parents also need space and time away from others to maintain both their relationship and authority over their children (Pable, 2007).

BIBLIOGRAPHY

Alexander, C., Ishikawa, S., Silverstein, M., Jacobson, M., Fiksdahl-King, I., & Angel, S. (1977). *A pattern language: towns, buildings, construction*. Oxford: Oxford University Press.

Altman, I., & Rogoff, B. (1987). World views in psychology: trait, interactionist, organismic, and transactional approaches. In D. Stokols & I. Altman (eds), *Handbook of environmental psychology* (Vol. 1; pp. 7–40). New York: John Wiley.

Andrade, C., & Devlin, A. (2015). Stress reduction in the hospital room: applying Ulrich's theory of supportive design. *Journal of Environmental Psychology, 41*, 125–134.

Atkinson, R., & Blandy, S. (2016). A shell for the body and mind. In R. Atkinson & S. Blandy, *Domestic fortress: fear and the new home front* (45–65). Manchester, UK: Manchester University Press.

Baldassare, M. (1979). *Residential crowding in urban America*. Berkeley, CA: University of California Press.

Baum, A., & Valins, S. (1977). *Architecture and social behavior: psychological studies of social density*. Hillsdale, NJ: Erlbaum.

Becker, E. (1971). *The birth and death of meaning*. New York: Free Press.

Belk, R. (1988, September). Possessions and the extended self. *Journal of Consumer Research, 15*(2), 139–168.

Burn, S. (1992). Loss of control, attributions and helplessness in the homeless. *Journal of Applied Social Psychology, 22*(15), 1161–1174.

Cedernaes, J., Schonke, M., Westholm, J., Mi, J., Chibalin, A., Voisin, S., … Benedict, C. (2018). Acute sleep loss results in tissue-specific alterations in genome-wide DNA methylation state and metabolic fuel utilization in humans. *Science Advances, 4*(8), 1–14.

Chapin, F. (1951). Some housing factors related to mental hygiene. *Journal of Social Issues, 7*(1,2), 164–171.

Cobb, P. (2001). Situated cognition: origins. In N. J. Smelser & P. B. Baltes, *International encyclopedia of the social & behavioral sciences* (14126–14129). Oxford: Pergamon.

Eaton, R. (1921). The value of theories. *The Journal of Philosophy, 18*(25), 682–690.

Edwards, J., Caplan, R., & Harrison, R. (1998). Person–Environment fit theory: conceptual foundations, empirical evidence, and directions for future research. In C. Cooper, *Theories of organizational stress* (28–67). Oxford: Oxford University Press.

Evans, G., Schroeder, A., & Lepore, S. (1996). The role of interior design elements in human responses to crowding. *Journal of Personality and Social Psychology, 70*(1), 41–46.

Franks, S. (2013). What is epigenetics? And what's it got to do with architecture? Retrieved from https://issuu.com/stuartfranks/docs/pamphlet

Gibson, J. (1966). *The senses considered as perceptual systems*. Oxford: Houghton Mifflin.

Goldhagen, J. (2017). *Welcome to your world: how the built environment shapes our lives*. New York: Harper Collins.

Gurian, E. (2015). Threshold fear. Retrieved from www.egurian.com/omnium-gatherum/museum-issues/community/accessibility/threshold-fear

Leary, M., Barnes, B., & Griebel, C. (1986). Cognitive, affective and attributional effects of potential threats to self-esteem. *Journal of Social and Clinical Psychology, 4*(4), 461–474.

Malnar, J., & Vodvarka, F. (1991). *The interior dimension: a theoretical approach to enclosed space*. New York: Wiley.

Maslow, A. (1968). *Toward a psychology of being*. New York: Wiley.

Melnitzer, S. (2007). Marginalization and the homeless: a prescriptive analysis. *Journal of Social Distress and the Homeless, 16*(3), 193–220.

Mullinaithan, S., & Shafir, E. (2013). *Scarcity: why having too little means so much*. New York: Henry Holt.

National Health Care for the Homeless Council. (2019). Homelessness & health: what's the connection? In National Healthcare for the Homeless Council (Fact Sheets). Retrieved from https://nhchc.org/understanding-homelessness/fact-sheets/

Office of Disease Prevention and Health Promotion. (2019). Determinants of health. Foundation Health Measures Archive. Retrieved from www.healthypeople.gov/2020/about/foundation-health-measures/Determinants-of-Health

Pable, J. (2016). Austin Resource Center for the Homeless. Design Resources for Homelessness. Retrieved from http://designresourcesforhomelessness.org/foundation-information/

Pable, J. (2007). Homeless shelter design: a psychologically recuperative approach. *Journal of Interior Design, 32*(3), 93–99.

Perolini, P. (2011). Interior spaces and the layers of meaning. *Design Principles and Practices: An International Journal, 5*(6), 1833–1874.

Poyner, B. (1983). *Design against crime: beyond defensible space*. London: Butterworths.

Pryor, B. (2016, February 16). How different polling locations subconsciously influence voters. *Scientific American*. Retrieved from www.scientificamerican.com/article/how-different-polling-locations-subconsciously-influence-voters/

Rieber, R. (1992). Introductory statement. *Journal of Societal Distress and Homelessness, 1*(1), 3–6.

Saltzman, A. (1994). Social distress theory and teaching about homelessness: a retrospective analysis. *Journal of Social Distress and the Homeless, 3*(2), 99–133.

Salzman, M. (2001). Globalization, culture, and anxiety: perspectives and predictions from terror management theory. *Journal of Social Distress and the Homeless, 10*(4), 337–352.

Schubert, T. (2005). Your highness: vertical positions as perceptual symbols of power. *Journal of Personality and Social Psychology, 89*(1), 1–21.

Sherrod, D., & Cohen, S. (1979). Density, personal control, and design. In J. Baum, *Residential crowding and design* (217–227). New York: Plenum Press.

Shopler, J., & Walton, M. (1974). *The effects of structure, expected enjoyment, and participants' internality–externality upon feelings of being crowded*. (Unpublished manuscript). University of North Carolina, Chapel Hill, NC.

Stokols, D. (1976). The experience of crowding in primary and secondary environments. *Environment and Behavior, 6*, 49–86.

Thomas, J. (2019, May 22). Separated by design: how some of America's richest towns fight affordable housing. *ProPublica*. www.propublica.org/article/how-some-of-americas-richest-towns-fight-affordable-housing

Ulrich, R. (1997). Pre-symposium workshop: a theory of supportive design for healthcare facilities. *Ninth Symposium on Healthcare Design*. Martinez, CA: Journal of Healthcare Design.

United States National Library of Medicine. (2019, May 14). What is epigenetics? *Genetics Home Reference*. Retrieved from https://ghr.nlm.nih.gov/primer/howgeneswork/epigenome

Valentiner, D., Holahan, C., & Moos, R. (1994). Social support, appraisals of event controllability, and coping: an integrative model. *Journal of Personality and Social Psychology, 66*(6), 1094–1102.

Vandewalle, G., Maquet, P., & Dijk, D.-J. (2009). Light as a modulator of cognitive brain function. *Trends in Cognitive Sciences, 13*, 428–438.

Williams, L., & Bargh, J. (2008). Keeping one's distance: the influence of spatial distance cues on affect and evaluation. *Psychological Science*, 302–308.

Wilse, C. (2015). *The value of homelessness: managing surplus life in the United States*. Minneapolis: University of Minnesota Press.

Wilson, S. (2019, May 24). Berkeley loves its sanctuary label, but a housing crisis is testing its liberal values. *Washington Post*. Retrieved from www.washngtonpost.com

TEACHING MATERIALS

Lauren Trujillo

Key Terms

Affordance
Determinants of health
Domophobia
Environment–person theory
Epigenetics
Fluid intelligence
Maladaptive behaviors
Marginalization theory
Primed associations
Scarcity theory

Schema
Self-actualization theory
Situated cognition
Social distress theory
Supportive design theory
Terror management theory
Threshold fear theory
Trauma-informed care
Trauma-informed design

Discussion 1

Choose one theory that you find either agrees with or refutes your own experience or beliefs about people who are homeless. In a paragraph or more, explain your reasons for holding the belief that you do.

Discussion 2

There are many people or groups involved in the design of a shelter serving the unhoused population (see Chapter 4 Perspectives). Some are listed in the table below. Using this table, identify and write the name of a theory you find they might reference for their decisions, then give an example why. Which theories most directly relate to *their* role in serving this population. How or why? For each group, discuss what actions relate to that theory that you believe they could take the next time they are involved in a project to better serve this population.

Project team member	Theory	Example
Architect	Person–environment fit	Would lead them to design a place that …
Interior designer		
Staff member		
Director		
Custodial, operations, and maintenance staff		
Donor		
Policy maker		
Housing organization		

Discussion 3

Reread the section on marginalization theory. Why might an architect who has agreed to design an emergency shelter probably *not* be adherent to this way of thinking? In two or more sentences, explain why this would be so.

6 Frameworks

Jill Pable

Architectural and interior designers can find it difficult to design shelters and supportive housing that help clients and staff make progress toward ending homelessness. One reason for this is that it is difficult to fully empathize with what it feels like to be without a home with its sense of desperation, urgency, and vulnerability. It is a person's perceptions of the experience – the people encountered, feelings felt, and places visited – that arguably lie at the heart of how successfully a person can exit homelessness quickly and effectively. Interviews from a study of 17 homeless men and women living in shelters in Toronto (Wen, Hudak, & Hwang, 2007) speak to this perceptual quality, capturing these persons' reactions to a receptionist at a health care clinic:

> She snubbed me when I went up to ask her, you know, how long it's going to be? It will be as long as it takes, was her reply. It's just the way she moved her body, you know. I was sitting there and she was sitting here, and she sort of turned her back on me, and I said, excuse me, and she just looked over and kept pointing over there and kept turning away, so I finally gave up on this one and went back inside and waited.
>
> Yep, I felt like she was processing a piece of meat … Let's just do this guy out and get him into the waiting room.
>
> I got treated like that the first time over there, and I'm not going to get treated like that, I'm not going through that again. I'd rather sit here and f____n' die on a bench than go over there.

For these clients, the receptionists' perceived responses were powerfully negative, probably compelling the clients to avoid future encounters like this and with them, the benefit of necessary health care. Embedded in these scenarios are perceived power and authority imbalances that have the effect of inhibiting interaction and suppressing positive progress.

There are also other hurdles for people seeking help that the system of care presents that stem from the complexity of homelessness and its aspects. For example, oftentimes the variety of services a person needs, such as health care, job training, housing services, family courts, and juvenile justice, are not talking to each other or sharing information, creating a fractured support system that is frustrating and ineffectual for people. A person is faced with numerous forms that all require the same 'name and contact information' and they must repeat the (often painful) details of their situation to multiple social support staff in different locations. A missed signature on a form creates a return to a long queue line across town that keeps someone from going to work (which is pretty much impossible to get to anyway with the lack of a car). This silo approach is not only frustrating, but can also inflict harm on people. In their article "A Secret to Better Healthcare," authors Rubin and Davis describe an instance of policy/built environment communication failure that could have resulted in significant injury (Rubin & Davis, 2019) para. 6:

> Days after an elderly patient was treated for heart failure at Mount Sinai Hospital and returned home, the elevator in his apartment building broke down. Lacking the ability to climb stairs, he became a prisoner in his own home, unable to go out for a walk, shop for fresh food and visit his doctors for follow-up care. A social service worker took up his case, and the elevator was repaired. His substandard housing was literally a threat to his health; the intervention of the social worker may have saved his life – and certainly saved him from a possible relapse and expensive hospital care.

This fractured approach to care can also mean that well-intended policies developed in isolation without a full sense of people's situations oftentimes make it more difficult for people to exit homelessness and can influence fundamental decisions for people facing homelessness, such as where they live. For example, Josiah, Tricia, and their son moved from Alaska to Seattle because they secured new jobs there. Before moving, they were led to believe that affordable housing would be available for them. When they were unable to find an apartment there, they sought help from city shelters, with the plan to find their feet for the first few months with a roof over their heads. However, family shelters were not available, and those shelters that could accept them presented problems for their situation. The shelter curfews conflicted with their work schedules, and also they were deeply concerned about their son's safety there. Worst of all, shelter policies would require the family to split up, separating Josiah from Tricia and their son. Altogether, the family found they were not "homeless, disabled or addicted enough" to qualify for support. In the end, the family moved into Tent City 3, a city-sanctioned encampment in Seattle, living alongside 70 other people. Despite living in the rain and cold in a tent, Tricia is happy her son has other children to play with and has made her peace with her security concerns because residents patrol the perimeter 24 hours a day (Invisible People, n.d.).

The stories show the difficulties that fractured social policy thinking can create and how subpar outcomes can result from built environment decisions. However, findings from researchers and multiple government and advocacy organizations have begun to shape and reconsider these approaches at a fundamental level. This new thinking is valuing the power of personal perceptions anew, harnessing their potential power to help usher in change for a person in crisis. This chapter will discuss some of the details and assessments of this new thinking, here called frameworks of care, and how these ideas are beginning to shape a new generation of architectural spatial responses.

DEFINING A FRAMEWORK

Chapter 5 describes a collection of theories that provide insights about the 'whys' of homelessness and design, such as why people think about homelessness the way they often do, and *how* interior and architectural designers are responding to these ideas. This chapter introduces a related knowledge idea called frameworks.[1] For the purposes of this book, frameworks are ways of thinking that are often more closely tied to action strategies than theories are, and are typically more specific and, some would say, practical. Most arise from the fields of psychology and social work. Some directly arise from empirical research (see Felitti et al., 1998), and others are an amalgamation of conclusions reached through clinical or similar observations (such as the work of Levy & Johnson, 2017). Some describe ideas that are larger than a single theory. Regarding homelessness, the sections below will describe a series of frameworks of care that are each concerned with understanding an issue and prescribing action to improve a situation, such as staff–client power differentials and the sense of helplessness persons in crisis can experience. In our view, frameworks of care matter to interior and architectural designers and organizations that are building housing and facilities, because they can offer rich ground from which to derive actionable architectural approaches and physical attributes of shelters, day centers, supportive housing, and similar structures.

There are many frameworks that exist that might apply to the design of spaces that help people in crisis, and this chapter can only discuss a few within the bounds of space limitations. However, the ones noted here each exemplify a new fundamental attitude shift currently taking shape within the psychology, social work, and allied fields toward a more person-centered approach.

THE ASCENDANCE OF HEALTH AND WELL-BEING

Frameworks of care describe ways to think about the needs of people experiencing crisis. They can also describe approaches to assisting persons who are experiencing homelessness that can include psychological therapies, work training, health care, and family and child services assistance. Two broad frameworks are introduced below, called trauma-informed care and psychologically informed environments. Both have in common a substantially reconsidered way in which to think about people and to offer them support services from previously prevailing approaches, and both focus on health betterment as a central goal. Some of the broad changes these frameworks are advocating concerning the relationship between support services staff and their clients are shown in 6.1.

These new approaches are seeking to place new value and priority on clients' perceptions of their service experience. The benefit to this is that people in need will want to seek care more than before and can feel they are an empowered partner in their own success.[2]

From an Attitude of	To One of
Top–down problem solving	Bottom–up solution seeking
Solving problems in a fractured, prescribed sequence of steps	Finding solutions from holistic, integrated thinking that crosses former boundaries
Silo isolationist thinking	Shared decision-making and responsibility
Mandating change with consequences for failure	Coaxing change with forgiveness for failure
Issuing edicts	Offering guidance
Hierarchical policy-making	Shared governance (to the degree that is feasible and effective)
Belittlement	Empowerment
Health care as a reactive response	Proactive well-being achievement and maintenance

6.1
Observations on the evolution of social programmatic thinking and action in services for persons experiencing homelessness.

This chapter began by describing some negative experiences people had with a health care clinic receptionist that were in keeping with previous attitudes and approaches. In contrast, trauma-informed care and psychologically informed environment approaches aspire to lead to clients' perceptions such as these:

- "They're open and receptive and they don't stereotype me"
- "They ask you how you are feeling and you talk about what is wrong with you. Some places are better at doing that" (Wen et al., 2007 p. 1013).

Before discussing the two primary and emerging frameworks of care called trauma-informed care and psychologically informed environments, it is helpful to provide a brief introduction to research and related endeavors associated with new awareness about well-being, and also discuss objections and cautions to well-being approaches applied to homelessness support.

NEW FINDINGS THAT LEND FOCUS AROUND HOLISTIC HUMAN WELL-BEING

ACE Study

One contribution to the new support systems approach has come from empirical studies exploring the circumstances of human health. In 1998, the Adverse Child Experiences study (ACE) was released; it concluded that childhood exposures to adverse experiences among the general population are correlated with (but do not necessarily cause) adult health risk behaviors. For example, child experiences such as physical or psychological abuse or living with someone who commits violence or uses drugs are associated with heightened frequency of suicide attempts, smoking, and alcoholism. In turn, these behaviors are associated with a higher risk of adult diseases such as cancer, heart disease, and depression.

The ACE study findings may directly relate to homelessness as well. In a later study that examined the adverse childhood experience backgrounds and frequencies of homelessness of 2 million American residents, researchers found that higher levels of child adversity also increased the likelihood of adult homelessness (Cutuli, Montgomery, Evans-Chase, & Culhane, 2013). Specifically, of the persons who reported no incidents of childhood adversity, 1.3% had experienced adult homelessness, and 33.5% of persons who experienced eight or more adverse childhood experiences also experienced adult homelessness. Such results support the ACE researchers' conclusions that the impact of adverse child experiences may be "strong and cumulative" (Felitti et al., 1998, p. 251).

The ACE study raises an interesting issue – it seems clear that childhood experiences over which a person has no control are linked to the likelihood of a person making injurious choices that compromise their later health. These choices, such as smoking, overeating, substance abuse, and sexual engagement, may be coping mechanisms that seemingly offer immediate relief to feelings of anxiety, fear, and depression. Considering the findings from these studies brings new light to questions of 'nature versus nurture' when thinking about why people may make the choices that they do.

Determinants of Health

Another framework shares similarities with the ACE study (and, in fact, embraces the ACE study in its findings) and is useful to design practitioners and support organizations seeking to make a connection between thoughtfully designed environments and human well-being. The United States government's Healthy People 2020 initiative (healthypeople.gov) has consulted a range of research studies to assemble a list of personal, social, economic, and environmental factors that affect human health either positively or negatively. Notably, the physical built environment is directly included or indirectly referenced in both the social and environmental categories. For example, effective buildings can provide physical assistance to people, such as eliminating barriers that bodily disabilities create, providing quality lighting conditions and benches, and preserving trees. Buildings also directly affect the quality of social well-being, with safe housing and quality schools influencing the quality of social support and interactions (Office of Disease Prevention and Health Promotion, 2019). Determinants of health connections such as these link architectural choices to wellness, bringing important grounding that can anchor a potential defense for the design of thoughtful projects.

Behavioral Influence Stairway Model

Wellness can seem an elusive goal for people who have lost their homes, especially those who have lived a homeless lifestyle for an extended period of time. Such persons often sleep in the woods, the forest, or their car and have been conditioned by hardship. They can be 'service-resistant', and an estimated 70% suffer from mental health issues (Rafailovitc, 2018). As they perceive they cannot, or actually cannot, resolve the matter, people in a state of chronic crisis can resort to coping mechanisms to receive immediate relief.[3] Having reached a state of mind of both helplessness and hopelessness, they may not want help, even as they live in situations rife with pain that can shorten their lives. In such situations, the person him/herself is the hostage, overcome with a long-standing crisis that is both external and internal in origin and effect.

Dr. Edward Rafailovitc is a social scientist who oversees the Crisis Intervention Team and Homeless Outreach Team in south Florida. His experiences as a police officer working with chronically unhoused persons have led him to realize the value of the behavioral influence stairway model (BISM) as a framework for his outreach (Rafailovitc, 2018). Developed by the Bureau of Federal Investigation's Crisis Negotiation Unit, BISM is a systematic, multistep process with the goal of peaceful, non-lethal resolution of critical incidents such as hostage situations (Vecchi, Van Hasselt, & Romano, 2005). This model's ideas and approach may have lessons for effective outreach to people experiencing chronic homelessness, including potential goals for built environments where supportive services can be provided.

BISM acknowledges that the objective is to lower the level of a person's emotional response by reducing the tension she or he is feeling. Once emotional barriers are managed, a rational state of mind can emerge that can eventually influence behavior in a positive way. Physiologically, a reduction in tension can trigger endorphin release that can increase a person's ability to think logically, which in turn can make them more receptive to offers of assistance (Rafailovitc, 2018). Establishing trust through positive relationships is critical to this process, as is working toward establishing a state of homeostasis in a person's hormone levels.[4] BISM references five steps that can lead to positive behavioral change, listed in 6.2.

Might the built environment itself serve as an intercessor for reducing tension and increasing receptivity to services? It is tempting to examine if built space design for day centers and shelters, for example, might itself exude a sense of active listening and empathy and help build rapport. Indeed, our interview with Dr. Rafailovitc suggests that designers should see places as 'situational environments' that can offer a change of culture from hopelessness to one that advocates for positive progress. If people can see that others are being effectively supported, this can be a powerful motivator for change. We suggest there are signals that a day center might send – for example, through a respectful and discreet street interface

6.2
The behavioral influence stairway model.

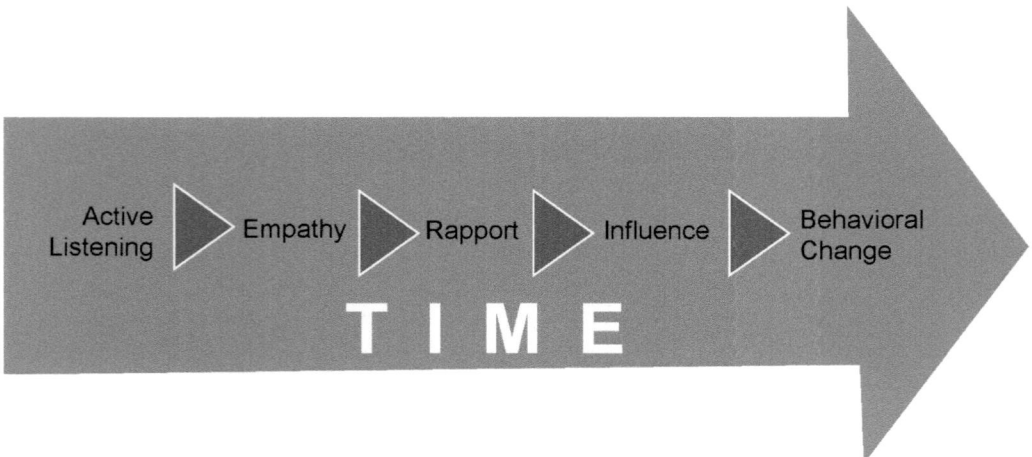

Active Listening ▷ Empathy ▷ Rapport ▷ Influence ▷ Behavioral Change

TIME

that allows people to wait for check-in in a place removed from the street. An emergency shelter's sleeping spaces might provide lighting that supports melatonin release for good sleep, and supportive housing apartments could employ color and interior finishes that prompt a sense of calm. The reduction of tension that BISM prioritizes may be a tangible approach that can support well-being that is worth considering as an architectural goal.

OBJECTIONS TO THE WELL-BEING MOVEMENT AND ITS LANGUAGE

The notion of well-being is grounded in the movement known as positive psychology, which holds as its goal examining those factors that contribute to a well-lived and meaningful life. This approach focuses on promoting self-esteem as a means to a person's full actualization (Mruk, 2008). Cognitive behavioral therapy is a therapeutic treatment approach for persons in crisis in keeping with positive psychology.[5]

Up to this point in this chapter, we have made the assumption that well-being is an appropriate perspective from which to consider how to create support systems for people experiencing homelessness, including how to build environments that house these systems. It bears discussing that some informed voices question this notion. Considering their argument also brings up a necessary conversation about the use of certain terms when referring to helping people who are experiencing homelessness. Support organizations, policy makers, and designers would be well advised to be aware of these issues, summarized here.

The positive psychology approach (and its accompanying cognitive behavioral therapy treatment technique) is by definition optimistic, and this outlook tacitly assumes that well-being embodies happiness. According to authors Scanlon and Adlam (2010) and also Turner, Lovell, and Brooker (2011), this ignores the culturally systemic origins of underlying problems such as joblessness, lack of housing, poverty, and crime, tacitly ascribing these problems to the person him/herself. Thereby, the terms 'recovery', 'well-being', and 'positive psychology' are being "cynically deployed to address profoundly damaging processes of social traumatization" and exacerbating an 'us' versus 'them' societal tendency (Scanlon & Adlam, 2010, p. 100). These authors suggest that 'being unwell' is a way to shove the responsibility for this condition onto the sufferer – so that when they do not 'recover', it is their failure and not the system's. For example, positive psychology "argues that unhappy individuals could, if they put their mind to it, change and be made happier" (Scanlon & Adlam, 2010, p. 103). In this way, the system defines the legitimacy of the sufferer. The underlying implication is that "under-employment and worklessness (i.e. worth-lessness) [are] related to individuals' unapplied cognitive abilities or failure to act" (Scanlon & Adlam, 2010, p. 104).

Scanlon and Adlam (2010) add that this blame displacement also occurs at the scale of a country's policies. Speaking of their own country, these authors state that, "the 'wellness' movement is at times colluding with anti-social aspects of political movements that have beset the UK – and simultaneously reduced the provision of social services" (Scanlon & Adlam, 2010, p. 3). In this way wellness becomes a convenient story that paves over system inadequacies such that, "the recovery approach is in grave danger of becoming a professionally governed fig-leaf to cover up the political failing and consequent limitations of our chronically under-funded mental health system" (Scanlon & Adlam, 2010, p. 102).

The comments from these outlier voices are worthwhile because they make clear how market and other prevailing societal forces can back movements that piggyback on a system's assumptions. For example, the 'American dream' of being successful through one's own efforts also intertangles with wellness in subtle ways. The United States is an inherently optimistic country that has embraced positive psychology. As Scanlon and Adlam uncomfortably note, however, the common American myth that says that "anybody can be somebody" (likely meaning healthy, well known, and monetarily comfortable) ignores the underappreciated fact that everybody is already somebody (Scanlon & Adlam, 2010, p. 16).

EMERGING TRAUMA-SPECIFIC FRAMEWORKS

Oftentimes, people experience homelessness as a co-occurring problem alongside poverty, substance abuse, mental illness, or violence. The nature of people's needs drives much of the effective interior design/architecture program response that sets the scene for supportive treatments to occur. Psychology and social work practitioners and other experts in both the United States and the United Kingdom have developed frameworks of care that describe systemic-comprehensive approaches to supportive treatment for persons who are in crisis, both within the last 10 years. They offer much guidance to interior designers and architects.

Trauma has emerged as a centerpiece of care approaches in both the United States and the United Kingdom, in part owing to the new appreciation for the influence and impacts of pain and suffering on people's self-esteem, perceptions, and associated choices and actions. In the United States, it is estimated that 61% of men and 51% of women have been exposed to at least one lifetime traumatic event, and 90% of persons in public behavioral health care settings have experienced trauma as well (Administration, n.d.). The ACE study discussed previously has had a significant impact on this new direction, which draws direct links not only to personal coping responses, but also to likely contributing societal problems including poverty, housing discrimination, crime, and mental illness.[6] Trauma is also an objective approach that avoids blame assignment and focuses its attention on helping people overcome adversity, whatever its source.

Trauma-Informed Care, United States

Although no universally adopted definition of trauma has yet emerged, the Substance Abuse and Mental Health Services Administration (SAMHSA), a U.S. government agency, describes that trauma results from "an event, series of events, or set of circumstances experienced by an individual as physically or emotionally harmful or life-threatening with lasting adverse effects on the individual's functioning and mental, physical, social, emotional, or spiritual well-being" (Center for Health Care Strategies, Inc., 2017, p. 9). Echoing the discussion above about the ACE study, these events include those often experienced by someone who has lost their home, such as being subjected to or observing abuse, enduring child neglect, having a family member with a mental or substance abuse issue, or experiencing forced displacement, poverty, or discrimination. Also of particular note is the concept of toxic stress, defined as "strong, frequent, and/ or prolonged adversity that stimulates the body's natural protections against stress and can have a long-term negative impact on neurobiology, psychology, and physical health" (Center for Health Care Strategies, Inc., 2017, p. 10). Pertinent to built environment projects such as supportive housing that provide long-term dwellings, toxic stress identifies that a person who has experienced trauma may continue to exhibit a defensive response such as depression or emotional out-bursts, even in situations (and places) that are no longer threatening (Trauma and Justice Strategic Initiative, 2014).

Trauma-informed care is a philosophy of support that has arisen in response to these new realizations about trauma's importance, and research thus far that examines what happens when a trauma-informed service system is put in place suggests that improved outcomes such as decreased mental health, trauma-related, and substance abuse symptoms and behaviors can result (Hopper, Bassuk, & Olivet, 2010). Although early outcomes seem promising, no single definition of trauma-informed care has yet emerged. However, one group of researchers has produced a meta-analysis (a study that examines groups of studies) that defines trauma-informed care as:

> a strengths-based framework that is grounded in an understanding of and respon-siveness to the impact of trauma, that emphasizes physical, psychological, and emotional safety for both providers and survivors, and that creates opportunities for survivors to rebuild a sense of control and empowerment.
>
> (Hopper et al., 2010, p. 82)

Notably, these researchers recommend that trauma-informed services should be supported by trauma-informed physical environments that attend to "issues of physical space, triggering materials, privacy/confidentiality, and structure/predict-ability" (Hopper et al., p. 94).

Enabling Environments/Psychologically Informed Environments, United Kingdom

In 2015, the Royal College of Psychiatrists in the United Kingdom released a list of essential human values applicable to people in general, called enabling envi-ronments (with 'environments' defined broadly to include therapies and human relations as well as built space; Levy & Johnson, 2017). These qualities support people's social, psychological, and community needs for health and well-being. Soon thereafter, another group of social work and psychology professionals further developed its recommendations for support of persons in crisis by developing the psychologically informed environments (PIE) framework (Johnson & Moore, 2019). This expanded set of directives explicitly identifies the physical environment as a means of support.

PIE researchers state that the purpose of a psychologically informed environ-ment is to enable people to make positive changes in their lives (Keats, Maguire, Johnson, & Cockersell, 2012). In this way, such places are emotionally aware and prioritize human perceptions (Johnson, 2019). For example, an open reception desk in a shelter, without bank-style safety glass, offers a more welcoming first impression to clients and encourages unhindered interactions with staff. In keeping with the principles of positive psychology, the goal is to assist clients to understand their behavior, take responsibility for it, and then to work to change/evolve their thinking and action patterns to ones that will help them end their crisis as soon as possible. The PIE system identifies that a supportive systemic experience (or what Levy & Johnson call a "wraparound recovery environment"; Levy & Johnson, 2017)) can result from considering the physical environment alongside staff training, relationship management, and a humanistic psychology therapy approach, plus evaluating outcomes for continual improvement.

TRAUMA-INFORMED DESIGN

At the time of this writing and as discussed above, trauma frameworks of care are only starting to gel within the psychology and social work fields. Similarly, there is no current consensus on what content or guidelines might constitute an architectural response to trauma, although various voices (including ours) are starting to reference the term 'trauma-informed design' (Bennington-Davis, 2014; Farrell & Weeks, 2019; Pable, 2019; Richardson & Rosenberg, 2018).

Perhaps owing to their field experiences, support organizations, advocacy groups, and medical experts have been among the first to advocate for built environment consideration as a tool alongside therapies and other supports. Shelter director Jonathan Farrell of the Committee on Temporary Shelter in Burlington, Vermont, has noted that, "the physical environment is the program as much as routines, goals, and staff are" (Farrell & Weeks, 2019). Several advocates have identified three fundamental reasons that place matters, offering these broad directives for organizations that build housing and other support facilities (Bennington-Davis, 2014; Farrell & Weeks, 2019):

1. Realize that physical environment affects an individual's sense of identity, worth, dignity, and empowerment
2. Recognize that physical environment has an impact on attitude, mood, and behavior. There is a strong link between our physiological state, our emotional state, and our physical environment.
3. Respond by designing and maintaining supportive and healing environments for trauma-experienced residents or clients to resist re-traumatization.

Various writers and advocates for trauma-informed approaches are now identifying a series of goals for physical place design that support their trauma-informed missions, and this chapter concludes with a series of summaries, perspectives, and examples. Trauma-informed design goals from the findings of multiple authors are summarized in 6.3. The WELL Building Standard also supports well-being that is a foundation for trauma-informed design action and thus offers support for interior designers, architects, and support organizations seeking guidance on how to build for human health. It is highlighted below in the *Perspective* section.

The goals of trauma-informed design are as follows:

- Reinforce the individual's sense of personal identity and sense of ownership;
- Provide an environment that is safe while also inviting;
- Promote opportunity for choice while balancing program needs and the safety/ comfort of the majority;
- Engage the individual actively in a dynamic, multisensory environment;
- Reduce/remove known adverse stimuli and triggers;
- Reduce/remove environmental stressors such as noise and crowding;
- Provide ways for the individual to exhibit their self-reliance (ability to do things for him/herself);
- Provide the means for privacy and confidentiality;
- Reinforce the sense of stable and consistent policy support for individuals that is worthy of their trust;
- Provide/promote connectedness to the natural world;
- Promote a sense of community and collaboration;
- Separate an individual from others who may be in distress.

PERSPECTIVE: THE WELL BUILDING STANDARD

This is a building standard that supports trauma-informed design principles.

Rose Winer

Community Concept Lead, Standard Development

International WELL Building Institute™

The WELL Building Standard (WELL™), created by the International WELL Building Institute (IWBI™), is a global tool for catalyzing built spaces as mechanisms to support human health and well-being. Grounded in public health research, WELL has a holistic view of health: not just as a state free of illness, but also the ability to enjoy a fulfilled life. WELL's ten concepts – air, water, nourishment, light, movement, thermal comfort, sound, materials, mind, and community – promote physical, mental, and social health, offering human-centered design strategies intended to create welcoming, comfortable, healing environments.

The WELL design strategies offered in mind, community, and movement specifically encourage inviting and restorative spaces that promote mental well-being and community-building and may be applicable to housing and facilities for people experiencing homelessness. For example, providing a restorative space, such as a prayer or healing room with calming colors, dimmable lighting, and sound masking, can promote calm and improve mental well-being (Kant, 2003). Similarly, designating a public use space can encourage greater social interaction and feelings of ownership, reducing stress and depression, and a designated eating area, by encouraging individuals to share a meal, can be a powerful tool to promote community connectivity (Heroux, Rube, & Nadimi, 2016; Robinson et al., 2013). Bathrooms designed to serve diverse populations, including families, people with disabilities, and individuals with diverse gender identities, are crucial to supporting the privacy and comfort of all occupants, and private personal storage can reinforce those feelings of privacy and ownership (Anthony & Dufresne, 2007; Vischer, 2007).

Incorporating beauty into these and other shared areas, such as hallways or staircases, or even into private spaces such as bedrooms, can foster a shared sense of safety and community, encourage physical activity, and improve emotional wellness (Boutelle, Jeffery, Murray, & Schmitz, 2001; Ipsos Mori, 2010). In particular, incorporating nature directly (e.g., plants), indirectly (e.g., nature views), or representationally (e.g., photographs) can relieve stress and bolster psychological well-being (Kant, 2003; Lottrup, Grahn, & Stigsdotter, 2013; Larsen, Adams, Deal, Kweon, & Tyler, 1998). Supplementing beauty and nature elements with natural daylight, mitigation of background noise levels, and increased acoustic separation between common and private areas can help reduce stress and depression, support sleep quality, and improve rates of healing (LeGates, Fernandez & Hattar, 2014; Edwards & Torcellini, 2002; World Health Organization Europe, 2018).

Ultimately, WELL offers a toolkit that can be considered by practitioners designing shelters and supportive housing for people experiencing homelessness to help create inviting, calming spaces that effectively promote holistic well-being for clients, staff, and visitors.

Trauma-informed design principles were applied to the design of the Waystation day center in Burlington, Vermont. The *Spotlight* section below describes this project and its choices.

SPOTLIGHT: THE WAYSTATION

The Waystation is a day center renovated with trauma-informed design strategies in mind.

Committee on Temporary Shelter (COTS)

Burlington, Vermont, United States

Jonathan Farrell (JF), Facilities Director, COTS, and Bob Duncan (BD), Duncan•Wisniewski Architecture

JF: The Committee on Temporary Shelter's Waystation Shelter for single adults has been in continuous operation since 1982. For 365 nights a year, it offers shelter to 40 adults. First impressions of the Waystation were less than relaxing. The breeze from the door opening in winter caused the tattered lists of rules and expectations that were hanging on the wall to flutter in the breeze. The bright yellow walls, art, old notices taped to the wall, and the open shelves of haphazardly stacked guest supplies in the adjoining office did little to add to the welcome. Guests were stopped almost as soon as they set foot in the entry behind a counter, and actually had to stand in line behind the recycling bin to check in for the evening.

We knew the space could be better, and we tried to get at how the spaces were used, and what routines were most important to guests. We looked at questions about everything from storage to room arrangement, to programmatic questions about how the space supported the work of the staff. It turns out that the answers to an overwhelming number of those questions like "Why are the walls painted bright yellow?" and "Why is there a storage cupboard in the window?" were similar – "it was that way when I got here."

Based on what we have learned from working with architects on more recent housing projects, we knew that we wanted a more welcoming feel, that lighting needed to be updated, that the colors had to be changed, and that the layout and flow of space was awkward. We wanted this to be more than someone's opinion or gut feeling. We wanted to talk to staff about the reasons that these changes should be made, how these changes would benefit the people whom we serve, and that these changes would help support the hard work that they do day in and day out with our guests. We accessed research information on aesthetics, art, color, furnishings, lighting and daylight, plants, spatial layout, and visual interest. Importantly, the discussions and suggestions that we were making about the space were research-backed, and not simply opinion.[7]

We applied the core principles of trauma-informed design throughout the facility and were able to transform the space with a limited budget. Key design components that worked well for us were color, quality of lighting, furniture, spatial layout, and understanding the difference between visual interest and visual complexity. In addition to helping us to provide the 'why' behind the need for changes within the space, the very language of trauma-informed design has helped our agency. COTS was already steeped in the language of trauma-informed care, a lens through which we view our work with those who are experiencing homelessness. The language of trauma-informed design has quickly become part of our everyday lexicon. The more staff understand and appreciate the concepts, the more they begin to think about, and care about, the ways in which program spaces and offices impact those we are striving to serve.

BD: Long before the concept of "trauma informed design" ever became part of the lexicon or even my vocabulary, I would have to say that much of what I believe about designing spaces for people who have experienced trauma or any other hardship(s) in life – and for that matter, people who are blessed to not have experienced such difficulties – are an extension of what I learned in Sunday School and kindergarten: treat others as you would like to be treated.

Harmony is a characteristic that we strive to achieve, and that's much more nuanced. Some design principles like centering a table in a space, or on a window, or a long axis through a series of spaces can bring a sense of order and calm to an interior, and that acts more subtly on a person's experience of the space, such that why it feels comfortable may not even be apparent, but it just is. At the personal scale of dwelling, sleeping spaces can be calming and welcoming. And then there's just plain old proportion – I have a book called *The Old Way of Seeing*, and not unlike *The Pattern Language*, there are myriad ways and techniques of how scale and proportion can be thought about and applied so they feel "just right". I don't mean that to be trite or simplistic, but for me, spaces that are warm, maximize or at least introduce natural materials, have a comfortable scale, certainly have natural light – preferably some direct sunlight, all contribute to feeling comfortable and respectful (see 6.3 and 6.4).

6.3
Before renovation and after renovation photos of the COTS Waystation shelter reception area. The entry at the Waystation, brightly painted with best intentions to 'lighten up the place', used colors that can have negative effects on those who are experiencing trauma. The redesigned entry at the Waystation achieves a sense of calm with color, updated warm lighting, natural daylight, organized supplies and information systems, and plants.

6.4
Before renovation and after renovation photo of the COTS Waystation shelter living room. The former living room space, left, was transformed into an open, relaxing space for families to enjoy while they transition from shelter into permanent housing in the image on the right. A reduction in visual clutter was an important strategy.

CONCLUSION

By necessity, a support organization that operates a shelter, day center, or support-ive housing location will adopt a philosophy that guides its choices of therapies and support services for people experiencing homelessness. Among these choices, a trauma-informed care approach is becoming more common.

Understanding the organization's philosophy of care is central to designing the physical setting that lets these therapies assist people effectively. In this way, an organization's care philosophy is the guiding wind that drives architectural design response. Frameworks such as psychologically informed environments and trauma-informed care offer interior designers and architects user-centered guidance that focuses on human experience based on which they might make decisions such as room design, adjacencies, and furniture/finish/equipment choices. As this chapter describes, these two frameworks are only starting to be described in detail, and how these ideas can be activated within physical spaces represents an area ripe for design exploration (Shepley & Pasha, 2013). The principles of trauma-informed design will be a consistent undercurrent in certain chapters of this book, perme-ating for example Chapter 3, which discusses user needs in further detail, and Chapter 7, which describes interior design and architectural design strategies.

NOTES

1. There appears to be little consensus on the meaning of 'theory' and 'framework', and the divisions are muddied further when there are references to a 'conceptual framework' or a 'theoretical framework'. Academic fields tend to select their own adoptions of the terms to serve their purposes, and some feel that frameworks, once well considered and tested, can lead to theory (Khoso, 2015).
2. For example, treatment models associated with trauma-informed care principles have been reviewed and endorsed by organizations including the World Health Organization, the California Evidence-Based Clearinghouse, and the American Psychological Association (see Menschner & Maul, 2016, p. 8).
3. These situations can lead to behaviors that seem illogical, but on closer inspection are entirely rational. For example, the question "how many beers are necessary to sleep on a hard floor?" shows the connection of coping mechanism to the realities of street life. In the same way, a person who stops taking a bath may do so because they know it will repel other people, which suits the person's desire for isolation just fine (Rafailovitc, 2018).
4. Persons suffering from mental illness are often plagued by unbalanced hormone states. Although this may not be the entirety of their problem, taking steps through calm, persis-tent communication tactics, built environment design, or other means can help support a return to homeostasis – a balanced state of hormone levels that can positively affect their perceptions and actions, such as epinephrin/norepinephrine levels (fight or flight, with increased heart rate), serotonin levels (mood), and cortisol levels (regulation of metabo-lism and immune system; Rafailovitc, 2018).
5. Cognitive behavioral therapy techniques are among the most researched of psychother-apy options (Kazantzis, Luong, & Usatoff, 2018; Butler, Chapman, Forman, & Beck, 2005). Various meta-analyses of existing research suggest it is highly effective for conditions that persons experience who are homeless such as depression, anxiety, panic disorder, social phobia, and post-traumatic and childhood depressive and anxiety disorders.
6. As Chapter 2 notes, treatment strategies for mental illness changed in the middle 20th century in the United States, causing many persons previously institutionalized to be released to the streets, many with no place to go. In this way, mental illness became a

problem that society chose to not deal with – but ended up dealing with it anyway through increased homelessness, emergency room visits, and police interventions.

7. Among the resources they accessed, Farrell and his colleagues used the Review of Research report, available at http://designresourcesforhomelessness.org/people-1/education/ (Berens, 2016)

BIBLIOGRAPHY

Center of Excellence for Integrated Health Solutions (n.d.). *Trauma*. Retrieved from SAMHSA Center of Excellence for Integrated Health Solutions: www.integration.samhsa.gov/clinical-practice/trauma

Anthony, H. K. & Dufresne, M. (2007). Potty parity in perspective: gender and family issues in planning and designing public restrooms. *Journal of Planning Literature*, *21*(3), 267–294. doi:10.1177/0885412206295846

Bennington-Davis, M. (2014). Trauma informed environments. Retrieved from Oregon Society of Physician Assistants: www.oregonpa.org/resources/2014CME/Speaker%20Presentations/Trauma%20Informed%20Care%20-%20Bennington-Davis%20-%20Largest.pdf

Berens, M. (2016). Orientation reports. Retrieved from Design Resources for Homelessness: http://designresourcesforhomelessness.org/people-1/education/

Boutelle, K. N., Jeffery R. W., Murray, D. M., & Schmitz, M. K. H. (2001). Using signs, artwork, and music to promote stair use in a public building. *American Journal of Public Health*, *91*(12), 2004–2006. doi:10.2105/AJPH.91.12.2004

Butler, A., Chapman, J., Forman, E., & Beck, A. (2005). The empirical status of cognitive-behavioral therapy: a review of meta-analyses. *Clinical Psychology Review*, *26*, 17–31.

Card, A., Taylor, E., & Piatkowski, M. (2018). *Design for behavioral and mental health: more than just safety*. Concord, CA: Center for Health Design.

Center for Health Care Strategies, Inc. (2017). Understanding the effects of trauma on health. Retrieved from www.chcs.org/resource/understanding-effects-trauma-health/

Center for Health Design. (2018). *Lessons learned about behavioral and mental health*. Retrieved from The Center for Health Design: https://www.healthdesign.org/insights-solutions/lessons-learned-about-behavioral-and-mental-health

Cutuli, J., Montgomery, A., Evans-Chase, M., & Culhane, D. (2013, June 1). Factors associated with adult homelessness in Washington State: a secondary analysis of behavioral risk factor surveillance system data (final report). Retrieved from Building Changes: https://buildingchanges.org/library-type/evaluation-results/item/635-factors-associated-with-adult-homelessness-in-washington-state-a-secondary-analysis-of-behavioral-risk-factor-surveillance-system-data-final-report---is

Edwards, L., & Torcellini, P. A. (2002). A literature review of the effects of natural light on building occupants. Contract. doi:10.2172/15000841

Farrell, J., & Weeks, R. (2019). Trauma-informed spaces & places. Retrieved from https://cotsonline.org/wp-content/uploads/2018/04/Trauma-Informed-Design.BOD_.pdf

Felitti, V., Anda, R., Nordenberg, D., Williamson, D., Spitz, A., Edwards, V., … Marks, J. (1998). Relationship of childhood abuse and household dysfunction to many of the leading causes of death in adults. *American Journal of Preventive Medicine*, *14*(4), 245–258.

Heroux, J., Rube, K., & Nadimi, V. (2016). The case for healthy places. Retrieved from https://daks2k3a4ib2z.cloudfront.net/5810e16fbe876cec6bcbd86e/5a626855e27c0000017efc24_Healthy-Places-PPS.pdf

Hopper, E., Bassuk, E., & Olivet, J. (2010). Shelter from the storm: trauma-informed care in homelessness services settings. *The Open Health Services and Policy Journal*, *3*, 80–100.

Invisible People. (n.d.). Seattle homeless family finds support in Tent City 3. Retrieved from Invisible People: https://invisiblepeople.tv/videos/josiah-and-tricia-seattle-homeless-family/

Ipsos Mori. (2010). People and places: public attitudes to beauty. Retrieved from www.design council.org.uk/sites/default/files/asset/document/people-and-places.pdf

Johnson, R. (2019). Welcome to the PIELink. Retrieved from PIE link Net: http://pielink.net/

Johnson, R., & Moore, X. (2019). The PIES/EES grid approach. Retrieved from PIElink: http://pielink.net/

Kant, I. (2003). An epidemiological approach to study fatigue in the working population: the Maastricht Cohort Study. *Occupational and Environmental Medicine, 60*, i32–i39. doi:10.1136/oem.60.suppl_1.i32. Retrieved from www.ncbi.nlm.nih.gov/pubmed/12782745

Kazantzis, N., Luong, H. K., Usatoff, A. S., Impala, T., Yew, R. Y., & Hofmann, S. G. (2018). The processes of cognitive behavioral therapy: a review of meta-analyses. *Cognitive Therapy and Research, 42*(4), 349–357. https://doi.org/10.1007/s10608-018-9920-y

Keats, H., Maguire, N., Johnson, R., & Cockersell, P. (2012). Psychologically informed services for homeless people good practice guide. Retrieved from Eprints: https://eprints.soton.ac.uk/340022/1/Good%2520practice%2520guide%2520-%2520%2520Psychologically%2520informed%2520services%2520for%2520homeless%2520people%2520.pdf

Khoso, P. A. (2015, January 6). What are the differences between conceptual framework and theoretical framework. Retrieved from Researchgate: www.researchgate.net/post/What_are_the_differences_between_conceptual_framework_and_theoretical_framework

Larsen, L., Adams, J., Deal, B., Kweon, B.-S., & Tyler, E. (1998). Plants in the workplace: the effects of plant density on productivity, attitudes, and perceptions. *Environment and Behavior, 30*(3), 261–281. https://doi.org/10.1177/001391659803000301

LeGates, T. A., Fernandez, D. C., & Hattar, S. (2014). Light as a central modulator of circadian rhythms, sleep and affect. *Nature Reviews Neuroscience, 15*(7): 443–454. doi:10.1038/nrn3743

Levy, J., & Johnson, R. (2017). *Cross-cultural dialogues on homelessness.* Ann Arbor, MI: Loving Healing Press.

Lottrup, L., Grahn, P., & Stigsdotter, U. K. (2013). Workplace greenery and perceived level of stress: benefits of access to a green outdoor environment at the workplace. *Landscape and Urban Planning, 110*(1), 5–11. doi:10.1016/j.landurbplan.2012.09.002

Menschner, C., & Maul, A. (2016, April). Key ingredients for successful trauma-informed care implementation. Retrieved from Center for Health Care Strategies Inc.: www.chcs.org/media/ATC_whitepaper_040616.pdf

Mruk, C. (2008). The psychology of self-esteem: a potential common ground for humanistic positive psychology and positivistic psychology. *The Humanistic Psychologist, 36*(2), 143–158.

Office of Disease Prevention and Health Promotion. (2019, April 12). HealthyPeople.gov. Retrieved from Determinants of Health: www.healthypeople.gov/2020/about/foundation-health-measures/Determinants-of-Health

Pable, J. (2019). Homelessness: supporting dignity through design. Retrieved from Tedx Talks: www.youtube.com/watch?v=2NufuRg6qyY&feature=youtu.be

Rafailovitc, E. (2018, January). Collaborating homeless outreach in Broward County: a law enforcement and social services engagement. Dissertation, Nova Southeastern University College of Arts, Humanities and Social Sciences. NSUWorks.

Richardson, J., & Rosenberg, L. (2018). Recommendations for trauma-informed design. Retrieved from National Council for Behavioral Health: www.nationalcouncildocs.net/wp-content/uploads/2018/10/Trauma-Informed-Design-Summary.pdf

Robinson, E., Aveyard, P., Daley, A., Jolly, K., Lewis, A., Lycett, D., & Higgs, S. (2013). Eating attentively: a systematic review and meta-analysis of the effect of food intake memory and awareness on eating. *The American Journal of Clinical Nutrition, 97*(4), 728–742. doi:10.3945/ajcn.112.045245

Rubin, R., & Davis, K. (2019, May 27). A secret to better health care. *New York Times.*

Scanlon, C., & Adlam, J. (2010). The recovery model or the modelling of a cover-up? On the creeping privatisation and individualisation of dis-ease and being-unwell-ness. *Groupwork, 20*(3), 100–114.

Shepley, M., & Pasha, S. (2013). Design research and behavioral health facilities. Retrieved from The Center for Health Design: www.healthdesign.org/system/files/chd428_ researchreport_behavioralhealth_1013-_final_0.pdf

Trauma and Justice Strategic Initiative. (2014). *SAMHSA's concept of trauma and guidance for a trauma-informed approach.* Washington, DC: Substance Abuse and Mental Health Services Administration.

Turner, K., Lovell, K., & Brooker, A. (2011). '… and they all lived happily ever after': 'recovery' or discovery of the self in personality disorder? *Psychodynamic Practice, 17*(3), 341–346.

Vecchi, G., Van Hasselt, V., & Romano, S. (2005). Crisis (hostage) negotiation: current strategies and issues in high-risk conflict resolution. *Aggression and Violent Behavior, 10*, 533–551.

Vischer, J. C. (2007). The effects of the physical environment on job performance: towards a theoretical model of workspace stress. *Stress and Health, 23*(3), 175–184. doi:10.1002/ smi.1134. Retrieved from https://onlinelibrary.wiley.com/doi/abs/10.1002/smi.1134

Wen, C., Hudak, P., & Hwang, S. (2007). Homeless people's perceptions of welcomeness and unwelcomeness in healthcare encounters. *Journal of General Internal Medicine, 22*, 1011–1017.

World Health Organization Europe. (2018). Environmental noise guidelines for the European region. Retrieved from www.euro.who.int/en/health-topics/environment-and-health/ noise/publications/2018/environmental-noise-guidelines-for-the-european-region-2018

TEACHING MATERIALS

Lauren Trujillo

Key Terms

Behavioral influence stairway model	Service-resistant
Cognitive behavioral therapy	Situational environments
Determinants of health	Supportive systemic experience
Enabling Environments	Toxic stress
Framework	Trauma
Positive psychology	Trauma-informed care
Psychologically informed environments	Trauma-informed environments

Written Exercises

Experiential narrative

According to this chapter, frameworks are defined as "ways of thinking that are often more closely tied to action strategies than theories are, and are typically more specific, and some would say practical." Reread the sections on each framework listed below, paying close attention to the examples provided by the author of how they might be applied to one's experience of engaging in an environment that serves people experiencing homelessness:

- Psychologically informed environments
- Trauma-informed design

Then, write an experiential narrative for each framework in which you describe in at least three paragraphs how these frameworks might shape a user experience. Answer the following questions:

- Describe the physical approach to this building from the street to the interior. How do the sidewalk, path to the building, outdoor space, porch, and front door feel?
- What does the reception desk look like? Can you see the people who will be helping you? Do you see their workspaces? What do they look like?
- How do the employees treat you as you approach and fill out the required paperwork?
- Describe the waiting area. What do you see, hear, feel, smell, and taste as you are waiting to be brought to your sleeping area? What might you need while you are waiting? How might the staff provide what you need most effectively?
- Describe your sleeping area. What might you need in this area to relax and feel comfortable and safe enough to get a few hours of sleep?

Comparing Frameworks

Now that you have described how a framework might shape a user experience, compare and contrast these frameworks.

- How is the user experience shaped by trauma-informed design different from that of a psychologically informed environment?
- How is the user experience the same?
- Which user groups might be best served by an environment designed using the principles of trauma-informed design? Why?
- Which user groups might be best served by a psychologically informed environment? Why?

7   Design Considerations

Jill Pable & Yelena McLane

As previous chapters have described, the design of buildings that assist people experiencing homelessness is not as straightforward as it might seem. Users who have endured trauma vary in their background and needs significantly (Chapter 3), and there are many externalities that influence choices in these building projects (Chapter 4). Therefore, it is challenging to present specific design strategies or recommendations that accommodate all users. Further, the needs of shelters differ from supportive housing and also from day centers.

These issues have led us to conceptualize this chapter along two lines, both addressing universal considerations at a fundamental level. First, it will discuss holistic needs present on all such projects. These are general considerations of site, the basics of building shell, and the interior. There are certain issues to be mindful of that make these projects different from those of healthcare, mental and behavioral facilities, and other project types, but they are also of a collective, sufficiently unified purpose that some fundamentals bear discussion.

Second, this chapter places at center stage the notion that designers must first understand what people need the most before they can design the environments that they will inhabit. This user-centered design prioritizes the *perceptions* of people that access these buildings.[1] That goal was the impetus behind the creation of a framework developed by one of us in collaboration with another researcher that addresses those bedrock human needs for people experiencing trauma. This research is now being prepared for publication (Pable & Gomory, unpublished data, 2020), and this chapter offers a brief explanation of these elements. Not coincidentally, these tenets are in line with the goals of trauma-informed care and, in our way of thinking, form the menu of human perceptions to which trauma-informed design must respond (for more information on trauma-informed care and trauma-informed design, see Chapter 6). These human needs that we have determined are so important to people are, in no particular order:

1. Dignity and self esteem
2. Empowerment and personal control
3. Security, privacy, and personal space
4. Stress management and coping
5. Sense of community
6. Beauty and meaning.

A perusal of this list reveals our philosophic stance and hopes for future trauma building projects. Broadly speaking, places should offer an experiential setting that supports healing from trauma and an effective exit from homelessness as swiftly as possible.[2] Several actionable objectives that support this intent are (1) affirm, shape, and reshape social structures and hierarchies between people; (2) as necessary, positively alter the socially constructed meanings of people who experience the space; and (3) countermand the effects of trauma to open up a mental space for rethinking and regrouping. In short, placemaking for people experiencing the trauma of homelessness is about laying a foundation of stability for progress toward well-being.

Such a goal exists in great contrast to what designers (including us!) have encountered from some members of the public – that efforts to improve shelters or supportive housing are about making things 'pretty' or 'just making it too easy' such that people will languish there, delaying their progress out of homelessness.[3] Such attitudes, honestly, are an insult to the hardships that homelessness imposes on people and invoke a counterproductive sense of punishment as a means to a solution. It also disavows the potential of intentionally designed places to positively impact the well-being of both the users of services and staff – a notion, interestingly, that has achieved general acceptance in healthcare design (Commission for Architecture and the Built Environment, 2004; Payne, Potter, & Cain, 2014; Devlin & Arneill, 2003).

This chapter commences with a discussion of the broad aspects of site selection and neighborhood context for a day center, supportive housing, or shelter and then progresses the discussion toward more detailed concerns including building form, size, capacity, and graphic identity.

SITE SELECTION

Choosing the location for a day center, supportive housing, or shelter is an exercise fraught with complexity within most Western societies, and in our experience is particularly difficult in the United States. The high-stakes property values homeowners and business owners contend with naturally lead to often significant 'not in my back yard' or 'NIMBY' conflicts between developers or support organizations and potential neighborhood property owners.[4] The difficulties with solving a shelter's siting is a pointed, vivid example of the exclusionary zoning that has formed the fabric of some cities' policies for extended periods of time (Manjoo, 2019; Thomas, 2019). As the significant quantities of literature and commentary on the sociological and political forces in play in the societal rejection of people in need show, many forces of money, influence, bias, and racial discrimination complicate the availability of sites. This section will instead summarize characteristics and issues that an organization, developer, or other entity should consider as it embarks on the process of considering various sites, even despite these hurdles.

The book *Homeless Shelter Design: Considerations for Shaping Shelters and the Public Realm* (Graham, Walsh, & Sandalack, 2008) examines shelter design from a community economic development, social work, and urban design point of view. Social work researchers John Graham and Christine Walsh and urban design researcher Beverly Sandalack analyzed 63 shelters in 16 cities in Canada, 2 in the United Kingdom, and 7 cities in the United States, including Montreal, Toronto, Vancouver, London, Atlanta, New York, and San Francisco. The goal was to gather case study insights to identify the most salient issues and ways that environmental design impacts the shelters' social support goals. Given the broad nature of some of their points and the commonalities of user types, we also suggest that this shelter commentary may have lessons to offer for supportive housing and other building types too. We recount some of these authors' points below, coupled with other literature information and our own observations. As noted above, this chapter intentionally prioritizes user perceptions so that architectural place can most successfully assist human experience as a pathway out of trauma.

Graham, Walsh, and Sandalack describe that a building project stands the best chance for success if it is designed to recognize the integral relationships between the delivery of its services to users, its relationship to the broader community, and its physical architectural form. The quality of its community relationship emerges from its site location, which in turn is heavily dependent on factors such as zoning, funding, and public attitudes toward homelessness.[5] For user satisfaction and a sense of belonging, the authors found that neighborhoods of small, locally owned businesses offered a better neighborhood context than one filled with big box stores or high-rise office towers. The 60-plus case studies the authors reviewed led them to conclude that there is no ideal zoning district per se, but that residential or mixed residential–commercial districts were most successful. No project sited in a heavy industrial zone was found to be satisfactory, nor those near waste management centers or utilities centers. A primary consideration is the reasonable walking distances or public transit access to social and other services, necessary to aid the limited mobility of many clients.

Physical site selection greatly shapes the integration of the building with its nearby community. A priority for positive client perceptions is to reduce or eliminate the sense of themselves as 'us' separate from the rest of the public as 'them'. Three factors that may affect a positive sense of community are: (1) the degree of alienation that people feel; (2) their perceived quality of life in the community; and (3) the level of care the person wishes to provide to the community or the people that live in it (Hughey & Bardo, 1984). It should, therefore, be the goal of the sponsoring organization to provide for a sense of safety and normalcy and, in particular with supportive housing, prompt people to personally invest and bond with the place to improve their sense of psychological health.

Neighborhoods that are visibly busy with people walking and riding bicycles, dining options, and parks are desirable, as they contribute to clients' perceptions of living in a 'normal' place, where their presence would be less scrutinized. Positive activity can also reduce fear among clients and potentially reduce the likelihood of feeling targeted for violence (Graham et al., 2008, p. 81). One new innovative solution is to place supportive housing next to libraries, with the benefit that area residents and businesses may view the new mixed-use project as a positive addition to their community (Kimmelman, 2019).

Neighborhood character and its cues of activity and vibrancy can support a sense of belonging for residents of a shelter, day center, or supportive housing

7.1
The Booth Centre
supportive housing
in Southampton,
United Kingdom.

development. The Booth Centre in Southampton, United Kingdom (7.1), occupies the building in which sailors stayed before setting sail aboard the ill-fated Titanic ocean liner. Its location in a historic district (see arrow), with lively retail and restaurant establishments, enhances its acceptability to clients.

The way a building looks can also contribute to a community's impression of a program. Several case studies in subsequent chapters illustrate how investing in non-institutional forms can lead to more effective integration into the local culture. Quality buildings may also contribute to the economy by transforming rundown or unused sites, which enhances the value of adjacent properties. The Six and the MLK 1101 supportive housing projects in Los Angeles (Chapter 10) and the Ozanam House in Melbourne, Australia (Chapter 11), are two such examples.

GENERAL BUILDING DESIGN

Despite the many forces acting on the design of buildings to assist people in crisis (budget, zoning, politics, and public sentiment all quickly come to mind), we suggest that a building's highest and most important calling is the accommodation it successfully renders to its users – the calmness it imparts, the psychological 'breathing space' it facilitates so that a person can develop a plan for the future, and the efficiency it lends to the organization's client-focused activities. The building's general design contributes greatly to its success or failure in these matters, and we suggest that much can be gained or lost by thinking carefully about the subjective (and sometimes highly individualistic) perceptions that the building creates, as many social housing problems are linked to such impressions (Dean & Hastings, 2000). Other authors agree that such socially constructed meanings are lasting and impactful (Hastings, 2000; Lefebvre, 2000). For example, for supportive housing, day centers, and shelters alike, there are significant perceptual differences between what might be called 'house services', such as food and basic shelter, and 'home services', which implies an emotionally welcoming environment (Friedman, 1994).

One example that stands out as welcoming and emotionally supportive is the London-based program Shelter from the Storm. The building is located in a well-established neighborhood where it serves as an attractive community café in the daytime and a home-evocative emergency shelter for unhoused men and women at night. Designers converted an existing glazed shopfront into the café entrance (7.2). Reinventing the space as a popular café has helped the public to overcome some of their concerns about a shelter moving into their neighborhood. Impressions of shelters as foreboding places diminished as café patrons and shelter guests saw more of one another and spent time eating and drinking in a common space.

Making the space feel like a true home was the guiding approach to design. The architects started by thinking, "when you have lost everything, what is familiar to you?" or "When you come home, what is it that makes you feel like you are in a safe, warm place?" These are concepts rooted in familiarity, comfort, and intimacy. The architects thought at length about scale within spaces, layout, finish materials, and lighting. In our time, all homes, however modest, generally have a sofa on which to relax and a kitchen in which to prepare meals. The kitchen often serves as the heart – and the hearth – of the home. At Shelter from the Storm, activities (both for café patrons and shelter guests) revolve around kitchens, and all are welcome to join in a conversation at the table. Chapter 8 presents more details about the Shelter from the Storm project.

7.2
The entrance to the café reflects the degree to which design and charity efforts have been directed towards a public space that is available for community enjoyment.

DESIGN CHARACTERISTICS: SIZE AND CAPACITY

Project decisions of number of persons served, the program of services, as well as choices of building form are important considerations influenced by the support organization's goals, extent of need in a community, funding availability, and site selection. The variety of these influences has given rise to great diversity in building size, style, and architectural program in existing shelters, day centers, and supportive housing.[6] Five in-depth case studies of supportive housing and shelter projects can be downloaded from Design Resources for Homelessness (2016). A select list of projects across the United States and designers and architects engaged in this work are also available.

In building projects that assist people experiencing trauma, we sense that decisions of project size (20 apartments or 200?), capacity (50 beds or 800?), and similar matters affect users' perceptions of the experience in these spaces – both staff and clients. In our travels, for example, we have seen shelters that serve 20 individuals in a small wing of apartments and high-rises that house 800 in congregate sleeping rooms of 60 or more persons.

Questions about size and style are also occurring about buildings that provide healthcare. In their extensive review of such projects, Verderber and Fine (2000) have observed a number of tensions in the ongoing evolution of healthcare buildings and services. These include: (1) bigness versus smallness; (2) compactness versus linearity; (3) low-rise versus mid- or high-rise design; and (4) centralized versus decentralized approaches (Devlin, 2010; Verderber & Fine, 2000). In the sector of trauma services for people experiencing homelessness, these choices of how to build occur as well, but in a way more often characterized by crisis management for a community faced with an exploding homeless population, rather than having the opportunity to consider the issue in a measured, preparatory fashion. Behind these physical environment choices, of course, are diverse decisions about keeping service offerings efficient, and the often under-reported positive intentions of offering quality care by staff and administrators. The assessment of performance outcomes through metrics also exerts an increasing influence over building decisions. One assessment system in use in Europe and Australia, for example, measures the degree of recidivism for drug and alcohol misuse and clients' degree of motivation and acceptance of personal responsibility (Johnson & Please, 2016).[7]

With the above caveats now offered, and again bringing our discussion back to a focus on positive human experience, we wish to point out the potential benefits for smaller sizes in trauma-supportive projects, and especially shelters. Note Walsh, Graham, and Sandalack, in their review of 63 shelters in the U.S., Canada, and the United Kingdom, "large, monolithic shelters may not be appropriate in contrast with smaller scale approaches to service delivery" (Graham et al., 2008, p. 72), although they allow that large shelters can be successful within urban settings. In our experiences visiting shelters, interviewing staff and clients, and observing the buildings' abilities to meet programmatic needs, we have observed that larger shelters are primarily an American phenomenon, with some housing upwards of 800–1000 people. Architecture arises out of its situational context, and the American economic and values system brings to bear a combination of NIMBY siting pressures, the frequent desire to centralize (and therefore optimize) services, and the difficulty of acquiring parcels of land in mixed-use districts. With their smaller unhoused populations, the approaches of Canada, the United Kingdom, and other countries have somewhat naturally led to smaller facilities that house and/or provide services to 20–60 persons.

Admittedly, our advocacy for smaller buildings serving more modest numbers of persons may be influenced by the kinder, gentler treatment of people we have witnessed in places other than the United States. One particularly dramatic contrast was our experience at a 400-bed Texas shelter where the situation required a metal-detector system at the entry used in concert with an attendant-serviced check-in system for clients' weapons, including machetes, guns, and knives. In contrast, a staff member would greet new clients at the entrance from an open desk area and then bring them a cup of hot tea at a supportive housing development for 75 clients in the United Kingdom. Although it would be an oversimplification to assume these experiential differences exist thanks only to large-capacity architectural choices (the larger neighborhood context in Texas probably requires weapons policies, for example), it still begs the question – if you have been traumatized and have nowhere to sleep tonight (and knowing that sleeping is about the most vulnerable act someone can engage in), at which of these facilities would you rather seek shelter?

There are three primary reasons why we suggest smaller building projects servicing or housing up to 30 persons may be advantageous:

1. It is almost inevitable that a large facility will exude a sense of intimidation and the sense of a client being an anonymous cog in a very big and intimidating process. Wayfinding becomes more complicated, and numbers on rooms and beds become necessary. Larger spaces have louder echoes. The larger scales and numbers of users makes them harder to clean, so they often use high-gloss, easy-maintenance finishes that exude a shopping mall or hospital feeling. Although perceptions of welcome or alienation, or privacy or crowdedness, may be intangible, their effects may be very real on persons experiencing trauma.[8]
2. The act of grouping large numbers of people who are all in crisis can tend to breed and spread negative emotions and coping responses, potentially producing a lowest common denominator attitude of helplessness. The term 'shelterization' describes a person's loss of empowerment under the rigorous rules enforced in shelters (Stark, 1994), and these rules often expand as the numbers of persons served rise.
3. At the time of this writing, the COVID-19 communicable virus is a significant problem in the United States, the United Kingdom, and other countries. The virus is spreading through close-contact places quickly, including prisons and shelters (Balsamo, 2020; Stewart, 2020). The United States Centers for Disease Control and Prevention guidelines currently identify the need for 6-foot social distancing in public gathering areas (Centers for Disease Control and Prevention, 2020, April 25), including day rooms, dining rooms, and sleeping

areas. Other sources are suggesting that, in some circumstances, greater distances are needed (Bromage, 2020). This greatly complicates the management protocols in all facilities, and especially high-density developments. Virus transmittance discoveries are beginning to bring scrutiny to building ventilation systems, the degree of openness/accessibility to rooms, and open versus closed floor plans. Large spaces, including those of apartment buildings, require more stairwells, elevators, and corridors, where increased numbers of people can potentially infect each other (Centers for Disease Control and Prevention, 2020, April 25). Although small development projects are not immune to viral transmittance and must be cleaned to the same extent as large ones, the number of people is reduced in small projects, therefore statistically reducing chance of infection.

Large spaces, simply put, are more likely to inhibit the emotional tone that can support well-being and also present more procedural, maintenance, and potential health problems than smaller ones. Of course, a plethora of smaller buildings will bring a different requirement for staffing than large, concentrated facilities might.

Architect Michael Maltzan has worked on a number of projects and has engaged with the specific needs and situation of Los Angeles. His experience has shown how multiple variables impact choices of apartment project size in California.

EXPERT OPINION: MICHAEL MALTZAN ON PROGRAM SIZES

Los Angeles-based architect Michael Maltzan has completed four housing projects* for the Skid Row Housing Trust, a nonprofit dedicated to providing permanent supportive housing to people in the greater Los Angeles area. Maltzan describes medium-size projects as "the sweet spot" for such projects, effectively combining scale economics, ready construction methods and materials, and delivery of services, to support the individual and group needs of residents.

The majority of these buildings have been built by a group of nonprofit developers. They tend to be a smaller scale, in the 70- to 200-unit range. There is a practical side to this. They are large enough to have a meaningful effect while also making the economics work. The economics are very challenging for these nonprofit corporations, as the requirements for fundraising and "packaging" the financing for these projects are constantly changing. There are also useful connections between this type of construction, local codes, and regulations. Larger buildings almost invariably lead to increased time, efforts, and cost during the permitting process – so there is a kind of a sweet spot there.

I think there is a programmatic side to this as well. Buildings that are much larger in scale are harder to program and may be tougher to manage. A 1000-person building is going to tend to silo these communities in ways that disconnect and distance them from the community around them. It will be much harder to provide clients with different types of spaces, and it will be a challenge to engender relationships or a sense of common purpose.

Finding larger-scale building sites at reasonable purchase prices is much harder. This generally leads to such buildings being pushed out to the periphery of the city. This is exactly the challenge that we saw in the United States after World War II with a lot of the larger government-sponsored affordable housing developments, what we called "projects." Early on, many of the goals for those buildings were extremely altruistic. They were coming from a model or idea of the "garden apartment" (a point tower surrounded by a garden landscape). Despite this optimistic vision, there were many factors that led to their demise, their vast and inhumane size among them.

We have been trying to work against these larger-scale apartments. Developers defaulted to efficiency versus generosity. They balkanized socioeconomic groups away from a fuller, more real, more humane mix of economic types, social statuses, and ethnic backgrounds in the city. That isolation certainly has had negative effects, and it continues to have such effects on those types of projects. Clients were separated from social services and from the services that a person needs in their daily life – the market across the street, the schools. They were very unnatural places.

We have completed four buildings for the Housing Trust, which amounts to around 350 units. What we have completed is a drop in the bucket towards satisfying the overwhelming demand for affordable housing. The scale of the response needs to be increased dramatically. There is still a real debate about whether the focus should be on developing many 100-unit buildings or instead creating fewer, but much larger, developments with thousands of people in them. Certainly, if we simply scale up the size of the buildings without carefully considering how to create a diverse mix of programs, not just units, we will be reintroducing some of the same challenges that led to less successful outcomes in the past.

* Crest Apartments (2016), Star Apartments (2014), New Carver Apartments (2009), and Rainbow Apartments (2006).

DESIGN CHARACTERISTICS: DETAILED CONSIDERATIONS FOR VARIOUS GROUPS

Given the great variety of persons experiencing homelessness, programming criteria for developments vary widely to reflect the needs of likely clients as well as staff and volunteers. Nonetheless, there are certain commonalities that may apply to multiple project types that can accommodate physical, psychological, and emotional needs. Some of these are summarized in 7.3 and prioritized by client type.

7.3
Considerations and priorities for project programming for select user groups.

	Design Considerations	Families	Youth and LGBTQ Youth	Women	Veterans	Elderly
Safety and Security	Quiet, concealed entrance façade	X	X	X	X	O
	Limited street access windows	X	X	X	X	
	Limited access for non-residents	X	X	X	X	
	Visitation spaces for family and friends	O			X	X
	Easy wayfinding	X	X	X	X	X
	Secure access to personal spaces and possessions inside facility	X	X	X	X	X
	Safe furnishings and fixtures to prevent injury and suicide and/or to accommodate disabilities	O	O	O	X	X
	Clear visibility for staff supervision and security cameras		X		X	X
Privacy and Personalization	Personal spaces that support good rest	X	X	X	X	O
	Sleeping areas for children and parents that are separate but connected	X				
	Semi-private bathrooms		X			
	Bathrooms in each room/unit	X		X	X	X
	Opportunities for personalization (decoration or display of personal possessions)	X	X	X	X	X
	Separate spaces for breastfeeding	X				
	Housing with similar age groups		X			X
	Small or private resident rooms				O	X
Physical and Mental Health Needs and Social Support	Physical and mental healthcare facilities	X	X	X	X	X
	Childcare	X		X		
	Playroom for children with opportunity for parent(s) to play with or watch children	X		X		
	Variety of semi-private, semi-public, and communal spaces that support diverse educational, therapy, socialization, and recreation activities	X	X	X	X	X
	Quiet study room/library with access to computer and Wi-Fi	X	X	O	X	O
	Increased mobility spaces (gyms, rock walls, bowling alleys)		X			
	Counselling/support spaces for children and parents	X	X			
	Music/art/physical therapy rooms	X	X	X	X	O
	Vocational training facilities	O	X	X	X	
	Quiet study room/library for school age children who are unable to attend school or for summer educational programs	X	X			
	Connection to the outdoors (internal yards, gardens, balconies, skylights, etc.)	X	X	X	X	X
	Pet accommodations	X	X	X	X	X

7.3
(Continued)

	Design Considerations	Families	Youth and LGBTQ Youth	Women	Veterans	Elderly
	Control for sensory overload and injuries: noise control, glare avoidance, presence of handrails and scald guards	O	O	O	X	X
	Incorporate and provide for control of relaxing ambient sounds; increased lighting levels and visual contrasts, including color	O			O	X
	Aesthetically pleasing materials and finishes	X	X	X	X	X
Minimizing Restrictions and Regulations	Open access to meals, laundry facilities, and other amenities	X	X	X	X	X
	Separation of noisy/communal areas from quiet/private areas	X	O	O	X	O
	Designing for multiple users and activities that increase a sense of self-worth and reliance	X	X	X	X	X
	Flexible furniture that can be rearranged easily	X	X	X	X	X
	Smoking area			X	X	X

Legend: X – primary priority; O – secondary priority; no mark – tertiary priority

A FRAMEWORK THAT SHAPES DESIGN ACTION: ELEMENTS OF ONTOLOGICAL SECURITY

With a discussion of siting, exterior, and fundamental form elements behind us, this next section examines connections between human perception and the local scale details of built space. We suggest that examining the issue of how to build through the lens of what people want and need the most is a useful construct, and a way to get at what may matter the most to people and their health. This sense of healthy human 'being' is what the academic area of *ontology* addresses. A variety of researchers and writers have examined those fundamental innate needs people possess, such as dignity, and linked them to how they see themselves and engage with the world. These needs make up what a person needs to feel 'ontologically secure', meaning those qualities that must be present for a person to feel a sense of confidence and trust in the world as it appears (Dupuis & Thorns, 1998).[9] We might think of ontological security as a feeling that everything is alright or will be, or that there is a sense of order and continuity in one's experiences (Giddens, 1991).

Feeling at peace with oneself and the surrounding world may be particularly elusive for people experiencing homelessness, as ontological security involves holding a positive view of oneself, the world, and the future. Losing one's home often throws a person into a situation where others treat them as deficient or even repulsive. This, coupled with an internal sense of failure over becoming homeless to begin with, can alter a person's internal sense of worth. Thus, the objective of therapies, in concert with the built environment, is to maintain or help rebuild the internal structure of positive self-regard.

Our discussion here is particularly concerned with wellness and how buildings can best support people to become their best selves. As such, an ontological security framework might similarly serve as a list of goals that architecture could address. Opinions vary, but the consensus of those authors that have examined such needs of people in crisis[10] is that these goals include:

1. Dignity and self esteem
2. Empowerment and personal control
3. Security, privacy, and personal space
4. Stress management and coping
5. Sense of community
6. Beauty, meaning, and order.

Each is further defined and discussed in the sections below.

RESEARCH THAT IDENTIFIES HOW ARCHITECTURAL DESIGN CAN ASSIST

Other research exists as well that could be brought to bear on how architectural space might effectively lend support to people in crisis. Empirical research that provides guidance on the design of shelters and supportive housing is sparse at the current time (Shepley & Pasha, 2013),[11] as is architectural research concerning mental and behavioral health facilities that represent a close (but not entirely identical) analog. Nonetheless, some findings classified as 'emerging evidence' for mental and behavioral health facilities that lend details on how to build in a general sense are summarized in 7.4. The links of these findings to the ontological security framework are listed on the right.

7.4
Emerging evidence from mental and behavioral health research that lends guidance to architectural design.

Recommendation for Architectural Design	Link to Ontological Framework
Provide home-like cues	Beauty, meaning, and order
Support patient autonomy and spontaneity	Empowerment and personal control; stress management and coping
Provide order and organization	Beauty, meaning, and order
Provide high-quality maintenance, furniture, and landscaping	Beauty, meaning, and order; dignity and self-esteem
Choose furnishings that resist damage and are easily replaced or repaired	Beauty, meaning, and order; dignity and self-esteem
Provide private, lower-density sleeping rooms	Empowerment and personal control; stress management and coping; security, privacy, and personal space
Provide common areas that encourage social interaction and promote community	Stress management and coping; security, sense of community
Facilitate staff observation of community spaces from a nearby station	Stress management and coping; security, privacy, and personal space

Recommendation for Architectural Design	Link to Ontological Framework
Plan a mix of seating arrangements that support social interaction	Empowerment and personal control; sense of community
Include spaces for staff mental health support	Stress management and coping
Maximize use of daylight	Stress management and coping; beauty, meaning, and order
Provide both indoor and outdoor spaces for activities	Stress management and coping; security, privacy, and personal space
Provide visual or physical access to nature	Beauty, meaning, and order
Enhance staff safety and security	Stress management and coping; security, privacy, and personal space
Accentuate functional uses and humanistic values through color and graphics	Beauty, meaning, and order
Provide spaces with clear territorial designations	Empowerment and personal control
Avoid ambiguity in design cues	Beauty, meaning, and order
Provide good temperature control and acoustic privacy	Empowerment and personal control; stress management and coping
Create a welcoming reception area	Beauty, meaning, and order; stress management and coping

7.4
(Continued)

IDEAS AND EXAMPLES OF ARCHITECTURAL SPACES THAT SUPPORT ONTOLOGICAL WELLNESS

Design Resources for Homelessness is a collection of references created by one of us on how architectural spaces can support human health, and this resource has used the ontological needs framework as a guide for crafting case studies of supportive housing and homeless shelter projects. You can view these at designresourcesforhomelessness.org to see how various organizations have shaped their environments to suit their users' perceptions and needs.

The information in the research summaries, reports, and project case studies of Design Resources for Homelessness have revealed further links between research or organizations' recommendations and how architectural space could be formed and detailed to support the six user needs outlined in the ontological framework above. The sections below define each element in the framework and reference external research or recommendations to support a specific design feature. Although not all of these research recommendations and architectural responses would rise to the level of rigorous empirical research confirmation, we argue that the need for design guidance exists now and cannot wait. Photos of the application of some of these within built shelter or supportive housing projects are also provided.

Dignity and Self-Esteem

Inner worth lies at the heart of the notion of dignity and is a fundamental aspect of being human (Gewirth, 1992). Self-esteem is closely allied to dignity; if a person has self-esteem, they are confident in their own worth or abilities. According to Seltser and Miller and based on their interviews with 100 adult heads of households,

Indicator	Brief Definition	Architectural Ideas
Promote individual identity, and avoid person identification only by number (Miller & Keys, 2001)	People like to be treated as and recognized as individual people	Provide opportunities for proclaiming ownership and expressing one's name and/or identity to others by an entrance door or a bed. Do not mandate sharing an identity as some persons will be uneasy to do so.

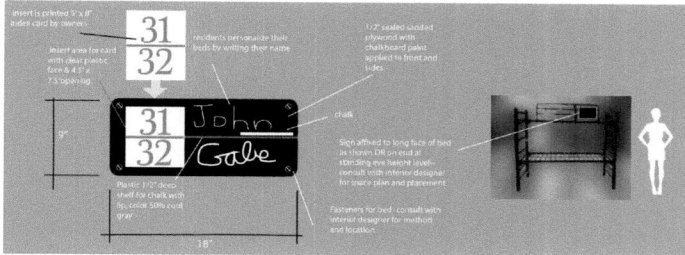

7.5
A changeable sign for identifying one's name on a bed in a shelter.

Indicator	Brief Definition	Architectural Ideas
Built environment's design should neutralizes power differentials (American Association of Children's, 2010)	People can be sensitive to feeling dominated or overpowered.	Space can invite or discourage an 'us' versus 'them' approach through vertical design. For example, higher floor levels are often associated with authority, while same-level space is seen as more equal.

7.6
Careful selection of chair styles and reception desk millwork can mean that staff and clients communicate at the same height.

"being homeless threatens the essential dignity of human beings, undermining or often destroying their ability to be seen, and to see themselves as worthwhile persons" (Seltser & Miller, 1993, p. 93). That is, having one's dignity recognized by others is also at play with how a person perceives themselves as worthy of respect.

In our view, dignity and self-esteem are among the most fundamental human needs and, perhaps consequentially, among the most difficult for a person to repair. Improving the sense of dignity and/or self-esteem likely takes time, and, thus, the impact of a single physical environment's design may be minimal. Nonetheless, we feel a space's design should provide opportunities that support this slow evolution, as do the tenets of trauma-informed care.

Indicator	Brief Definition	Architectural Ideas
Avoid triggering negative associations and memories (Hopper, 2010)	People who experience trauma often have negative memories of abuse, scarcity, desperation or pain. Surroundings can trigger memories of these which can affect peace of mind and self-esteem.	While every person is different, some physical associations with materials or shapes are universal. For example, black painted metal, when used in certain ways, can evoke prison bars.

7.7
Beds do not have to be beige or black. Custom metal colors are often available that can blunt negative associations without sacrificing durability and cleanability. Norix.com bed showing custom metal powder coat color.

Indicator	Brief Definition	Architectural Ideas
Communicate positive messages (Hopper, 2010)	People experiencing trauma benefit from positive gestures in their surroundings. Ideas like acceptance, invitation, and joy support well-being.	Color, texture, and objects (for example, flowers) carry with them positive messages. Spaces that give priority to these ideas can convey optimism.

7.8
A view to an exterior courtyard with flowers provides clients in this shelter a protected, safe view of nature.

Empowerment and Personal Control

The situation of scarce resources, homelessness, and trauma often means that people must depend on government services, nonprofit organizations, or other people for their health and survival. This can produce feelings of helplessness that can reduce a person's ability to exit homelessness and significantly interfere with self-esteem (Berens, 2016). This can produce a state of 'learned helplessness' that

	Indicator	Brief Definition	Architectural Ideas
	Provide users the opportunity to alter the environment where possible (Burn, 1992)	People like feeling they have control over their surroundings because it supports self-determination.	Operable windows, dimmable lighting, and acoustic controls support personal control. The ability to inhabit a choice of rooms can offset a sense of crowding.

7.9
A shelter bed provides residents with controllable lighting to read by, a ventilation fan, a clock radio with earbuds, and an electrical outlet to charge their devices.

	Indicator	Brief Definition	Architectural Ideas
	Allow users to choose the degree to which they socially engage others	People like having the ability to participate with others when they want, or withdraw to be alone, or be nearby to listen but not engage.	A physical built environment can give permission for a person to fully engage with others or not through physical cues. Window and door options can send these signals, or even walls that vary in open or closed configurations are ideas.

7.10
This bar-style counter facing outside within a larger shelter dining room provides clients the option to eat alone if they wish. Their proximity to others nearby gives them the control to engage with others if they wish.

reduces a person to someone who feels nothing is within their ability to change. Built environments such as shelters that provide no opportunity to adjust to suit a person's needs have rightly been called out as factors in the promulgation of learned helplessness (Burn, 1992). In our experience, even modest opportunities to change a space's qualities such as ventilation, light level, and noise contribute to lowered stress levels.

Security, Privacy, and Personal Space

Closely related to a sense of personal control, security and its related concepts are among the most primal and highest priority for persons in crisis that we have interviewed. The fear of being vulnerable is well founded for persons who live on the streets or in otherwise compromised places. A 2016 survey by a charity in England identified that almost half of respondents had been intimated or threatened with violence while 'sleeping rough', and 33% had been deliberately hit, kicked, or otherwise attacked while homeless (Foster, 2016). These concerns are particularly significant for parents with children, which speaks to the reasons people live in their cars, or often band together in encampments for protection. In our experience, privacy is a top desire for persons staying in shelters that economize on space by providing large, congregate sleeping rooms. Being able to change clothes without others watching (or to have one's children do so) is understandably a large concern. Staff observe residents using sheets on bunk beds to create privacy, but also report that illicit activities are easier and more likely to take place when these privacy modifications are permitted to occur. This dilemma is a significant and widespread

7.11
This planter provides the seating area a sense of 'protected back' that enhances a feeling of perceived security for people and their belongings as they wait for entry to a day center.

Indicator	Brief Definition	Architectural Ideas
Provide cues that lead users to feel safe (Hopper, Bassuk, & Olivet, 2010)	People with past crises can be sensitive to mental or even physical attacks by others. This can elevate stress levels.	Persons with Post Traumatic Stress Disorder or are victims of domestic violence may be sensitive to being able to see their entire environments from one vantage point. They also appreciate space plans that do not allow them to be approached from a direction they cannot see. Having a 'defensive back' layout can help.

Indicator	Brief Definition	Architectural Ideas
Provide visual privacy and thoughtful sight lines within congregate living projects (Stewart-Pollack & Menconi, 2005)	Sight is a powerful influence on state of mind. Most people appreciate views while also having the ability to feel visually private while in their homes.	Flexibility in architectural layout that permits both distant views (especially if in a very small space) and also privacy when necessary is helpful.

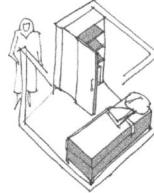

7.12
These single-occupancy sleeping units are surrounded by 52-inch-tall partition walls, providing women who were previous victims of violence a positive sense of others around them while their immediate privacy is protected.

Indicator	Brief Definition	Architectural Ideas
Design with sense of personal space and sensitivities to crowding in mind (Evans, Schroeder, & Lepore, 2010)	A sense of overcrowding is stressful to people. Western standards for a sense of crowding is approximately one room (8' x 10') for one person).	If a space must accommodate many items or functions or more than one person, take extra steps to minimize sense of crowding. Techniques include windows to visually expand space, Dutch doors to flexibly extend space outward, and diagonal space plans to make the most of a small squarish footprint.

7.13
This shelter bedroom for families houses four persons in a 10-foot by 10-foot room (plus bathroom) for 3–12 months. A Dutch door helps expand the perception of space to the hallway and lets the family easily interact with passersby on their terms.

Indicator	Brief Definition	Architectural Ideas
Design applicable spaces with a calming ambience in mind (American Association of Children's Residential Centers, 2010)	While desired moods vary, people generally prefer an environment that can be calm when the moment calls for it.	Color, spatial layout, and surface materials are a few design tactics that can promote calmness. Lighting quality and ability to dim lighting can affect sense of atmosphere.

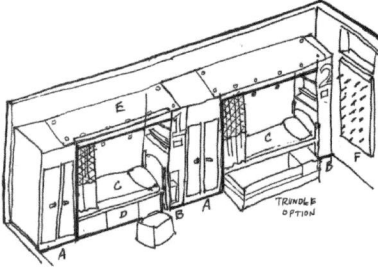

tension in shelters. Security also extends to the perception that one's belongings are safe as well.

Stress Management and Coping

On a daily basis, persons experiencing trauma must contend with a heightened sense of stress stemming from lack of shelter, food, water, or other life requirements. Such stress can increase fatigue and heighten an inability to solve problems (Pacione, 1990). This can result from threats to security, procedures that cause a sense of defeat, noise, pollutants in the environment, crowding, or many other stressors. For some people in a state of crisis for years at a time, long-term 'toxic stress' manifests that can interfere with socialization (Turner, 1981), cause both psychiatric and physical illness (Kearns, Smith, & Abbott, 2007), and shorten one's life span. Coping responses range from productive reactions such as behavior modification to negative ones such as anger or denial (for more details on the effects of scarcity on stress and coping, see Chapter 5). In a study of a family's experience in a shelter, the stress a mother felt over her children's well-being was a significant factor in her overall sense of well-being (Pable, 2012). Although a built environment cannot eradicate perceptions of stress, thoughtfully designed places can serve as a temporary refuge to provide 'space to breathe' so that a person can relax for the moment to think and plan more efficiently.

Sense of Community

The shock of a traumatic life crisis can cause a person to push others away out of a sense of shame or guilt. If one becomes homeless, a new stigma can also enter that can cause a person to sever ties to former social networks. Negative coping mechanisms such as substance abuse can also alienate others and cause

7.14
This concept for a women's emergency shelter sleeping area prioritizes a layout that allows a resident to withdraw to their bed with privacy curtains (with translucent panel to permit bed checks), residential-referenced materials such as wood effects, and personal lighting controls.

7.15
Further architectural response strategies for reducing stress

Indicator	Brief Definition	Architectural Ideas	Example
Provide sufficient storage opportunities for both housing possessions and also categorizing them for long-term situations	People identify with and are assisted by their possessions, and so they are deeply aware of how safe these items are from theft and destruction. Jewelry, photos, clothes, technology are just a few things people often protect	Barriers and locks provide physical protection and also peace of mind. Concealment is also a strategy to discourage theft	Custom beds in an emergency shelter with storage accessible from beneath a mattress with a changeable combination lock
Establish clear spatial boundaries so people can perceive procedures with minimal conscious effort (Hopper, Bassuk, & Olivet, 2010)	People naturally establish and protect their personal physical territory as a way of maintaining their identity	Built spaces can send messages of 'this is mine' through figurative or literal lines, boundaries, changes of material, shape, or height. The raised porch is a classic example	A system of changeable 'stop' and 'go' signs that a resident can change at the entrance to their sleeping area that indicates how willing they are to speak with others at any given time
Create built environments that are interesting but also have an element of predictability for a sense of stability (Hopper et al., 2010)	People, especially those who have seen crisis in their past, generally prefer environments that offer comfort, solace, and reliability	Forms and assemblies that seem off-balance or top heavy or unstable are not usually loved. Although creativity in an environment can be positive, being too experimental can interfere with a sense of comfort	Create building designs that offer clearly marked entrances. Avoid extreme cantilevered overhangs and other visually unbalanced assemblies
Provide users the ability to retreat to perceived safety (American Society of Interior Designers, 2016)	Giving the ability to control one's engagement in a place or group can provide a comforting 'out' to persons who may be wary of situations	Provide intentional 'away spaces' that permit engagement with others and a space on a person's own terms, especially in large rooms. Keep enclosures permeable with apparent exits for psychological comfort	Provide seating alcoves with walls, moveable elements, or other tactic within large gathering spaces. Place seating so user can observe others approaching them
Provide acoustic privacy (Stewart-Pollack & Menconi, 2005)	To live life is to experience noise, and to also create it. Noises can be triggers for negative memories and affect concentration and stress levels	Acoustic wall qualities and soft materials are but two methods to dampen sound transmission	Acoustic felt-clad baffles or lighting fixtures offer ways to bring in sound dampening materials in high-abuse areas

Indicator	Brief Definition	Architectural Ideas
Provide access to nature or natural elements (Penndorf, 2016)	People have an affinity for engaging with the natural environment, either seeing it, being in it, or both, as it provides stimulation and builds connections to the greater world for a sense of groundedness.	Window views, door access, daylight, and/or bringing natural elements inside are techniques to create engagement with nature.

7.16
In the heart of Los Angeles, this permanent supportive housing project by Skid Row Housing Trust prioritizes an atrium that residents see as they enter and leave the project.

Indicator	Brief Definition	Architectural Ideas
Create positive distraction within architectural spaces (Shepley & Pasha, 2013; Ulrich, 1996)	As a means to change the subject and provide positive input, provide architectural features that move focus toward positive elements.	Art with restorative image content such as nature, well-chosen music. views from key locations, or comfortable seating for reading or activities support simply thinking about something else besides one's worries.

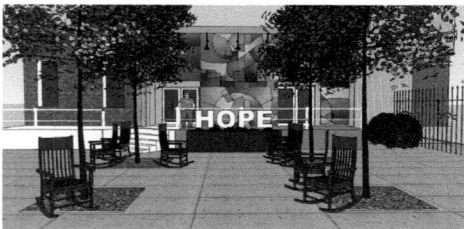

7.17
This simple strategy of providing rocking chairs in a courtyard waiting area can provide means to conversations as well as a way to use motion to dissipate stress.

Indicator	Brief Definition	Architectural Ideas
Provide opportunities in built environments for camaraderie and also collaboration (American Association of Children's Residential Centers, 2010)	Working toward a shared goal or participating in activities that others also enjoy can build relationships and is nourishing to most people—and provides a shared experience.	Charity activities, gardening and other group events can purpose persons toward collective goals.

7.18

At a transitional shelter in the United Kingdom, residents participated in an art project that asked them to describe their state of mind and how it would affect the design of a box. Art rooms stocked with materials make such therapy projects possible and allow the resident to begin to reckon with their current situation.

Indicator	Brief Definition	Architectural Ideas
Design environments that provide opportunities for users to feel they are part of a group (Miller & Keys, 2001).	A sense of being a part of something greater is a healthy human attribute and is associated with spiritual health.	Built space can serve as the setting for activities that engage multiple people, such as discussions, parties, cookouts, and worship services.

7.19

A community room at New Genesis Apartments in Los Angeles hosts resident group cooking events, workshops, and impromptu gatherings. Its location in this permanent supportive housing project, visible along the path from the entrance to the apartments, may positively affect its use.

a person to become isolated. Loneliness is a frequent partner with homelessness and is a serious concern – the presence of social relationships increases a person's odds of extended mortality by 50%, making loneliness a major risk factor for length of life (Holt-Lunstad, Smith, & Layton, 2010). For this reason, built environments should proactively promote socialization in a way that its users can positively interact with.

Beauty, Meaning, and Order

Of the six human needs described here, the quality of beauty, meaning, and order is probably least publicly accepted, as aesthetics are sometimes viewed as an expendable asset that should be included only if funds permit. However, new discussions are now suggesting that beauty and meaning are cognitively nourishing stimuli for people's brains. Organizations such as the Johns Hopkins Foundation have created a NeuroAesthetics initiative to understand how brain science can support the design of built spaces (International arts + mind lab, 2020). Similarly, building organizations such as the International WELL Building Institute and its WELL Building Standards call for the inclusion of aesthetic elements such as plants, art, and water features within and around spaces (International WELL Building Institute, 2020). Specific to trauma, art therapy programs have long been present in shelters and day centers. More recently, research discussion is also turning to the neurological effects of visually chaotic environments and the potential for such places to negatively impact a person's sense of self. Such information suggests that places that intentionally include elements of beauty and wonder may support well-being.

7.20
This new design concept for men's transitional housing apartments provides residents with the opportunity to organize their belongings. In order to provide a subtle reminder that this is not their final stop, bins for possessions do not have concealing doors and yet allow for the sorting and categorizing of belongings.

Indicator	Brief Definition	Architectural Ideas
Provide the means for users to organize their belongings and create a living place that can be visually ordered (Orth & Wirtz, 2014)	Living in a situation of visual chaos is mentally exhausting. Some people start to associate their inability to organize and store their belongings with personal failings, affecting self-esteem.	People appreciate the opportunity to not only store belongings, but to categorize them for easy retrieval. Giving someone the ability to maintain a place to live where things have their dedicated 'home' is comforting and supports a sense of calm.

Indicator	Brief Definition	Architectural Ideas
Conduct programming for a project that includes an understanding of meaning for intended users. Where possible, reference these meaningful elements in new built spaces.	A feeling of being oneself, comfortable and surrounded by familiarity provide a sense of grounding and community for people.	People in trauma out of necessity band together and build meaning together. Spaces that send signals of respecting and acknowledging these meanings can build bridges to assist their future well-being.

7.21
Bakhita Gardens, a supportive housing project in Seattle, Washington, works with female clients who have experienced domestic violence. Female empowerment is conveyed through the inclusion of art throughout the space that references women in a positive light.

ARCHITECTURAL DESIGN CONSIDERATIONS FOR INDIGENOUS POPULATIONS

Unhoused Indigenous persons often share similar experiences with non-indigenous populations, including poverty, substance abuse issues, and trauma. Some design strategies for homeless populations may be applicable for Indigenous populations living under similar conditions. It is also important, however, for designers and stakeholders to work with members of Indigenous communities to plan spaces and environments that are culturally appropriate and accommodating to the interpersonal relationships and spiritual and cultural practices of the people. In Chapter 3, we briefly discussed the traditional Indigenous construct of home as closely associated with the campsite. Architectural typologies and scales should aspire to reflect such concepts. Having identified common attributes of Indigenous spatial arrangements and structure, planning for ample outdoor spaces for spiritual practices; areas for community gathering, preparing, and sharing food; and traditional healing gardens becomes obvious. Designers and stakeholders must avoid designing environments that reinforce white colonial practices, such as smaller nuclear family-based approaches, social isolation (often couched as 'privacy'), individual ownership of supplies and equipment that could instead be communal, and social hierarchies (Greenop & Memmott, 2016).

Other important design considerations may include:

- Indigenous-led design, governance, and management processes;
- Cross-cultural recognitions of space:
  - Orientations and layouts responding to natural landscapes and scenic vistas;

- Orientations and layouts considerate of cultural and spiritual practices;
- Integration of outdoor food preparation and sharing areas;
- Integration of medicinal plants, traditional food gardens, and healing spaces;
- Use of regional Indigenous building practices, including forms, spatial arrangements, and construction techniques and materials (i.e., cross ventilation, natural lighting and heating, water collection, and wind protection); one example is the Synapse (Supported Accommodation Innovation Fund) SAIF project (Cairns, Australia). Here, architects Shaneen Fantin and Belinda Allwood recognized Aboriginal beliefs that malevolent ancestral spirits may rest in 90-degree corners between walls, walls and ceilings, and walls and floors. They eliminated straight corners and used gentle "bull-nosed" curves instead (Memmott & Keys, 2016, p. 13);
- Organization of spaces and buildings to support kinship well-being and visual surveillance while providing culturally appropriate personal spaces; for example, with respect to avoidance practices within extended family members;
- Incorporation of Indigenous creative features and elements of artistic practice into the landscape and interior and exterior spaces, including soundscapes, stone or wood carvings, weavings, and decorative patterns (Auckland Council & mana whenua, 2020).

When combined with the six principles of trauma-informed care, such design considerations can help to design safe, predictable, stress-mitigating, and culturally appropriate residential settings that support normative Indigenous kinship well-being and mobilize individual and community agency in assisting with exiting homelessness.

CONCLUSION

A discussion of design choices for permanent supportive housing, shelters, day centers, and other buildings assisting people experiencing trauma is marked by its diversity, as every project must attend to the specific needs of its targeted users. As this chapter's discussion of site selection, building design, and choice of size and capacity shows, one size (or style) definitely does not fit all. A useful gauge for making decisions lies in what clients, staff, and other users will perceive about a space – its unstated, often implicit messages of welcome (or hostility), its function in meeting clients where they currently are, and effective support of the policies and procedures of the organization's therapies are all at play in the architectural programming endeavor and, as a system, lie at the heart of human well-being. We suggest that the sum of a place's attendance to well-being lies not in an individual element such as windows or color, but rather in the amalgamation of many influences that together can summon a sense of optimism, support, and positive distraction – or not. The saying "Housing Is Healthcare" (Lozier, 2019) was never more salient than now, at a time when the style of housing and other assistive centers can be a positive setting that enables a person to take necessary, positive steps in a safe place that supports dignity and relationships with others. Alternately, in its worst iteration, a place can exacerbate human need and act as a hurdle to treatments, heightening stress levels, and, in this age of pandemic illness, even creating a deadly health situation. Architectural programming that empathetically takes human experience into account can positively influence this critically important outcome.

NOTES

1. Concentrating one's design efforts around user perceptions is not a new idea. For all intents and purposes, people's perceptions are their reality and acknowledge the link between psychology and place, for better or worse. Some experts feel that, in fact, a wide array of social problems are tied to how people feel about their neighborhoods and the neighborhoods of others (Dean & Hastings, 2000; Graham et al., 2008).
2. Acknowledging, of course, that the reasons many persons experience homelessness has little to do with themselves, their behaviors, or character, and instead is a reflection of deeply systemic problems that their societies have presented them with such as lack of housing, lack of job training, and little or no healthcare support.
3. Given the often-decrepit state of housing and support for people in need, it is entirely logical that a person would want to cling to a humane space in which to live temporarily, especially if they see no better option in their future.
4. Robert Rosenberger's *Callous Objects: Designs against the Homeless* chronicles some particularly blatant examples of streetscape city features designed to repel people who are unhoused (Rosenberger, 2017).
5. This varies more than one would think by culture. For example, we have seen a homeless shelter in a historically notable building exist in harmony steps away from a vibrant dining district in the United Kingdom. We have also seen a shelter sequestered to a repurposed windowless warehouse in a concrete-clad industrial food desert district underneath an interstate exchange in the United States.
6. Some would argue that current apartment architecture suffers from stylistic monotony. A fascinating discussion of why many apartment buildings have the same massing, limited menu of materials, and window fenestration patterns can be found in the article "Why Do All Apartment Buildings Look the Same" (Sisson, 2018).
7. The successful ability of a support organization to effectively vet its clients for suitability to its housing and services can be a critically important measure, as this has direct bearing on the success rate for those clients that access and are counted within the organization's system (personal communication, Mike Alvidrez, Skid Row Housing Trust).
8. Owing to the COVID-19 viral pandemic, one emergency shelter in Florida moved all of its 370 clients to nearby motel rooms. Unexpectedly, those with mental health diagnoses experienced significant changes for the better with their new privacy and less crowded experiences. Staff reported a "180-degree turn" in attitude and sense of calmness. The chair of the board of directors noted that "now that we see the importance of moving all in-house people into safe, isolated housing, we question first if we will ever move them back into a congregate living center such as the Kearney Center" (Schneider, 2020, para 9).
9. Elements of this list are also corroborated in a number of other frameworks that examine a variety of user groups such as Housing First participants (Bird, Rhoades, Lahey, Cederbaum, & Wenzel, 2017), shelter residents (Rivlin, 1990), newly resettled people who were formerly homeless (Rivlin & Moore, 2001), and people generally (Despres, 1991).
10. A research study is currently underway to confirm the validity of this list by people who have experienced trauma (Pable & Gomory, 2020). Data and statistical tests to date suggests that the list indeed forms the primary needs of these users.

11. Of the 115 studies Shepley & Pasha reviewed, approximately 10 were sufficiently rigorous to merit drawing of conclusions (Shepley & Pasha, 2013).

BIBLIOGRAPHY

American Association of Children's Residential Centers. (2010). *Redefining residential: trauma-informed care in residential treatment.* American Association of Children's Residential Centers.

American Society of Interior Designers. (2016). Healthcare design sector brief. Washington, DC: American Society of Interior Designers.

Auckland Council & mana whenua. (2020). Auckland design Manual. Retrieved from www.aucklanddesignmanual.co.nz/design-subjects/maori-design/te_aranga_principles#/design-subjects/maori-design/te_aranga_principles/guidance/about

Balsamo, M. (2020, April 29). Over 70% of tested inmates in federal prisons have COVID-19. Associated Press. Retrieved from https://apnews.com/fb43e3ebc447355a4f71e3563dbdca4f

Berens, M. (2016). A review of research: designing the built environment for recovery from homelessness. Design Resources for Homelessness. Retrieved from http://designresourcesforhomelessness.org/wp-content/uploads/2015/11/FINAL1_8_2017.pdf

Bird, M., Rhoades, H., Lahey, J., Cederbaum, J., & Wenzel, S. (2017). Life goals and gender differences among chronically homeless individuals entering permanent supportive housing. *Journal of Social Distress and the Homeless*, *26*(1), 9–15.

Bromage, E. (2020, May 6). The risks - know them - avoid them. Retrieved from Erin Bromage blog: www.erinbromage.com/post/the-risks-know-them-avoid-them

Burn, S. (1992). Loss of control, attributions, and helplessness in the homeless. *Journal of Applied Social Psychology*, *22*(15), 1161–1174.

Centers for Disease Control and Prevention. (2020, April 25). COVID-19 Guidance for Shared or Congregate Housing. Retrieved from Coronavirus Disease 2019 (COVID-19): www.cdc.gov/coronavirus/2019-ncov/community/shared-congregate-house/guidance-shared-congregate-housing.html

Centers for Disease Control and Prevention. (2020, April 21). Interim guidance for homeless service providers to plan and respond to coronavirus disease 2019 (COVID-19). Retrieved from Centers for Disease Control and Prevention: www.cdc.gov/coronavirus/2019-ncov/downloads/COVID19_Homeless-H.pdf

Commission for Architecture and the Built Environment. (2004). *The role of hospital design in the recruitment, retention and performance of NHS nurses in England.* Belfast: Price WaterHouse Coopers.

Dean, J., & Hastings, A. (2000). *Challenging images: housing estates, stigma and regeneration.* York: Policy Press.

Design Resources for Homelessness. (2016). Case studies. Retrieved from: http://designresourcesforhomelessness.org/foundation-information/

Despres, C. (1991). The meaning of home: literature review and directions for future research and theoretical development. *The Journal of Architectural Planning and Research*, *8*(2), 96–115.

Devlin, A. (2010). *What Americans build and why: psychological perspectives.* Cambridge: Cambridge University Press.

Devlin, A., & Arneill, A. (2003). Health care environments and patient outcomes: a review of literature. *Environment and Behavior*, *35*(5), 665–694.

Dupuis, A., & Thorns, D. (1998). Home, home ownership and the search for ontological security. *Sociological Review*, *46*, 24–47.

Evans, G., Schroeder, A., & Lepore, S. (2010). The role of interior design elements in human responses to crowding. *The Open Health Services and Policy Journal*, *70*(1), 41–46.

Foster, D. (2016, December 22). Crisis report reveals shocking dangers of being homeless. *The Guardian*. Retrieved from www.theguardian.com/housing-network/2016/dec/23/homeless-crisis-report-attack-violence-sleeping-rough

Friedman, B. (1994). No place like home: a study of two homeless shelters. *Journal of Social Distress and the Homeless*, *3*(4), 321–339.

Gewirth, A. (1992). Human dignity as the basis of rights. In M. Meyer, & W. Parent, *The Constitution of Rights: Human Dignity and American Values* (pp. 10–28). Ithaca NY: Cornell University Press.

Giddens, A. (1991). *Modernity and self-identity*. New York: Wiley Blackwell.

Graham, J., Walsh, C., & Sandalack, B. (2008). *Homeless shelter design: considerations for shaping shelters and the public realm*. Calgary, Alberta: Detselig Enterprises.

Greenop, K., & Memmott, P. (2016). *"We are good-hearted people, we like to share": definitional dilemmas of crowding and homelessness in urban Indigenous Australia*. Winnipeg, Canada: University of Manitoba Press.

Hastings, A. (2000). Discourse analysis: what does it offer housing studies? *Housing Theory and Society*, *17*, 131–139.

Holt-Lunstad, J., Smith, T., & Layton, J. (2010, July 27). Social relationships and mortality risk: a meta-analytic review. *PLOS Medicine*. Retrieved from https://doi.org/10.1371/journal.pmed.1000316

Hopper, E., Bassuk, E., & Olivet, J. (2010). Shelter from the storm: trauma-informed care in homelessness service settings. *The Open Health Services and Policy Journal*, *3*, pp. 80–100.

Hughey, J., & Bardo, J. (1984). The structure of community satisfaction in a southeastern American city. *Journal of Social Psychology*, *123*, 91–99.

International arts + mind lab. (2020). The biology of beauty. Retrieved from Brain Science Institute Johns Hopkins Medicine: www.artsandmindlab.org/the-biology-of-beauty/

International WELL Building Institute. (2020). *WELL*. Retrieved from Better buildings to help people thrive: www.wellcertified.com/certification/v2/

Johnson, G., & Please, N. (2016, June). How do we measure success in homelessness services? Critically assessing the rise of the homelessness outcomes star. *European Journal of Homelessness*, *10*(1), 31–51.

Kearns, R., Smith, C., & Abbott, M. (2007). The stress of incipient homelessness. *Housing Studies*, *7*(4), 280–298.

Kimmelman, M. (2019, May 15). Chicago finds a way to improve public housing: libraries. *New York Times*. Retrieved from https://nyti.ms/2WMn4V9

Lefebvre, H. (2000). *The production of space*. Oxford: Blackwell.

Lozier, J. (2019). Housing is health care. Retrieved from National Health Care for the Homeless Council: https://nhchc.org/wp-content/uploads/2019/08/Housing-is-Health-Care.pdf

Manjoo, F. (2019, May 22). America's cities are unlivable. Blame wealthy liberals. *New York Times*.

Memmott, P., & Keys, C. (2016). The emergence of an architectural anthropology in Aboriginal Australia: the work of the Aboriginal Environments Research Centre. *Architectural Theory Review*, *21*(2), 218–236. doi:https://doi.org/10.1080/13264826.2017.1316752

Miller, A., & Keys, C. (2001). Understanding dignity in the lives of homeless persons. *American Journal of Community Psychology*, *29*(2), 331–354.

Orth, U., & Wirtz, J. (2014). Consumer processing of interior service environments: the interplay among visual complexity, processing fluency, and attractiveness. *Journal of Service Research*, *17*(3), 269–309.

Pable, J. (2012). The homeless shelter family experience: examining the influence of physical living conditions on perceptions of internal control, crowding, privacy and related issues. *Journal of Interior Design*, *37*(4), 9–37.

Pable, J., & Gomory, T. (2020, June). Unpublished data.

Pacione, M. (1990). Urban liveability: a review. *Urban Geography*, *11*, 1–30.

Payne, S., Potter, R., & Cain, R. (2014). Linking the physical design of health-care environments to wellbeing indicators. In C. L. Cooper (Ed.), *Wellbeing and Buildings Volume. Wellbeing: A Complete Reference Guide*. Retrieved from https://onlinelibrary.wiley.com/doi/abs/10.1002/9781118539415.wbwell069

Penndorf, J. (2016, July 25). How design mitigates environmental stressors. Building Design + Construction. Retrieved from www.bdcnetwork.com/blog/how-design-mitigates-environmental-stressors.

Rivlin, L. (1990). The significance of home and homelessness. *Marriage & Family Review*, *15*(1–2), 39–56.

Rivlin, L., & Moore, J. (2001). Home-making: supports and barriers to the process of home. *Journal of Social Distress and the Homeless*, *10*(4), 323–336.

Rosenberger, R. (2017). *Callous objects: designs against the homeless*. Minneapolis: University of Minnesota Press.

Schneider, T. (2020, May 20). "A smile on their faces": Some Kearney Center residents thriving in motels, apartments. *Tallahassee Democrat*. Retrieved from www.tallahassee.com/story/news/2020/05/20/a-smile-their-faces-some-kearney-center-residents-thriving-motels-apartments/5221935002/

Seltser, B., & Miller, D. (1993). *Homeless families: the struggle for dignity*. Urbana IL: University of Illinois Press.

Shepley, M., & Pasha, S. (2013). Design research and behavioral health facilities. Center for Health Design. Retrieved from www.healthdesign.org/system/files/chd428_researchreport_behavioralhealth_1013-_final_0.pdf

Sisson, P. (2018, December 4). Why do all new apartment buildings look the same? Retrieved May 2020, from Curbed: www.curbed.com/2018/12/4/18125536/real-estate-modern-apartment-architecture

Stark, L. (1994). The shelter as "total institution." *American Behavioral Scientist*, *37*, 553–562.

Stewart, N. (2020, April 13). "It's a time bomb": 23 die as virus hits packed homeless shelters. *New York Times*. Retrieved from https://nyti.ms/2RAhrZy

Stewart-Pollack, J., & Menconi, R. (2005). *Designing for privacy and related needs*. New York: Fairchild.

Thomas, J. (2019, May 22). Separated by design: how some of America's richest towns fight affordable housing. *ProPublica*. Retrieved from www.propublica.org/article/how-some-of-americas-richest-towns-fight-affordable-housing

Turner, R. (1981). Social support as a contingency in psychological wellbeing. *Journal of Health and Social Behaviour*, *22*(4), 357–367.

Ulrich, R. (1996). Pre-symposium workshop: a theory of supportive design for healthcare facilities. *Proceedings from the Ninth Symposium on Healthcare Design* (pp. 3–7). *Journal of Healthcare Design*.

Verderber, S., & Fine, D. (2000). *Healthcare architecture in an era of radical transformation*. New Haven CT: Yale University Press.

TEACHING MATERIALS

Lauren Trujillo

Key Terms

Away spaces
Crowding
Defensive/protected back layout
Dignity and self-worth
Empowerment
Learned helplessness
Negative association triggers
NIMBY (Not-in-my-backyard)
Ontology

Ontologically secure
Personal control of one's environment
Power differentials
Shelterization
Site selection
Social engagement
Toxic stress
Wayfinding

Discussion Questions

1. Review the section on site selection. What qualifications of a neighborhood might make it an ideal location for a facility serving those experiencing homelessness? Describe a site in your neighborhood or community that would meet these qualifications. If so, describe the ways in which the site might help people experiencing homelessness. Or, discuss a site in your neighborhood that would be problematic for potential users' perceptions such as safety, acceptance, or other impression. In either case, what physical cues, specifically, are sending these 'signals' to users?

2. Early in the chapter, one author refers to differences between what might be called 'house services' such as food and basic shelter and 'home services', which implies an emotionally welcoming environment. Review the list of potential services discussed in Chapter 11 Multi-service Complexes. From your point of view, what services would you most likely associate with 'home services'? With 'house services'? Finally, what other services do you think such spaces should offer to increase the sense of 'home'?

3. In the section titled "Design Characteristics: Size and Capacity," the author compares large-capacity buildings with smaller ones. Which type is common in your community? Why?

4. In the section titled "Ideas and Examples of Architectural Spaces that Support Ontological Wellness," the author shows examples of indicators and architectural ideas. Think of places where you enjoy spending time. Answer one or more of these related questions:

   a. Which of the indicators are present in these places?
   b. How does the presence of these indicators contribute to your sense of social engagement, privacy, and identity?
   c. How might your experience in these spaces be different if these indicators were not present?
   d. What other indicators not listed here form a part of your positive perception of this place?

8 Shelters

Yelena McLane

Shelters, alternately called homeless shelters or emergency shelters, are places designed to help unhoused persons get off the street to avoid danger or harm (Hurtubise, Babin, & Grimard, 2009). Shelters range widely in the number of beds that they offer (from a few to several hundred) and they generally provide their clients with access to per-night accommodations with daily readmissions. Services common to most shelters include showers and laundry facilities, hot meals, medical triage care, counseling, and sleeping quarters, and, increasingly, shelters provide limited computer and internet access.

Shelters may accept both women and men, segregated by sex into separate areas of the facility, youths, elderly persons, domestic violence victims, and families. Admissions policies may differ from open to all on a first-come-first-served basis to restricted only to clients who arrive with references from other support organizations. Some shelters are located in preexisting buildings retrofitted for shelter services, whereas others are specifically designed as new buildings or subunits of larger complexes for the purpose of serving homeless populations. Some shelters offer more comfort and support to their guests, responding to their needs and offering vocational training and help with finding employment. Others, with fewer resources, offer little in the way of comforts and provide minimal services.

Not all unhoused individuals use shelters, and those who do are not a homogeneous group. For example, youths are less likely to use shelters and prefer couch surfing or sleeping rough (Brooks et al., 2004), whereas families tend to rely more on public support in the form of shelters or other surrogate housing. In Canada, indigenous persons and immigrants have been found to use shelters less compared with the overall homeless population (Distasio, Sylvestre, & Mulligan, 2005). In the United States, black and Hispanic persons are disproportionately represented among shelter users (Hurtubise et al., 2009).

There are a number of reasons why homeless persons tend to avoid using shelters: concern for their personal safety and security of their possessions; perceptions of disrespectful or humiliating treatment by shelter personnel and other clients (Wasserman & Clair, 2009); fear of aggression or abuse perpetrated by older clients against younger clients; distrust of staff and case managers; and an overall perception that shelters are too restrictive on clients' behaviors and activities

(Hurtubise et al., 2009). For many, going to the shelter means accepting that they are in fact homeless, making it an option of the very last resort.

CASE STUDIES

In this chapter, we discuss three homeless shelters – Hope of the Valley's NoHo Bridge Housing Shelter, an adaptive reuse facility in Los Angeles, California; the Kearney Center, a new construction facility located in Tallahassee, Florida; and Shelter from the Storm, an adaptive reuse emergency shelter in London, United Kingdom. The footprints for these three buildings are shown in 8.1. We analyze each through the perspective of trauma-informed design, assessing the extent to which architectural features and amenities may be conducive or detrimental to the well-being of their clients. We examine their overall spatial program and layouts, visibility and accessibility, and the levels of control exerted over clients and staff, together with other aspects, including access to outdoor areas, multifunctionality, flexibility, and aesthetics, to determine the degrees to which they may reflect human-centered approaches to design.

Hope of the Valley's NoHo Bridge Housing Shelter, Adaptive Reuse Facility in Los Angeles, California, USA (2020)

- Design: DNA Architecture + Design, Los Angeles, California
- Type: overnight shelter
- Capacity: 85 beds
- Guests: 60 men and 25 women, with companion animal accommodations

8.1
Building footprints of the three shelters. Sizes are relative to actual dimensions.

Hope of the Valley's NoHo Bridge Housing Shelter is located at the end of an industrial road inside a North Hollywood warehouse, within walking distance of a bus stop connecting the shelter to other Los Angeles Metro areas (Chou, 2020). The building needed to be economically and expediently renovated, reflect

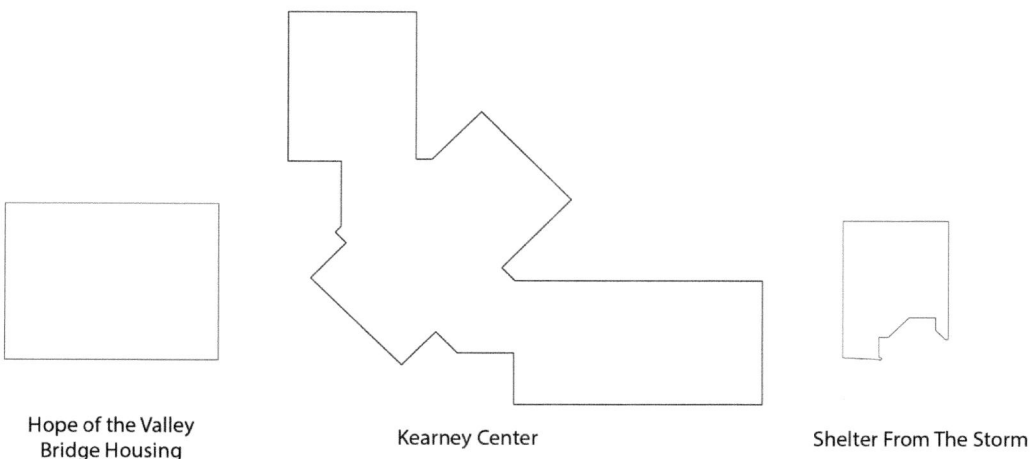

Hope of the Valley
Bridge Housing

Kearney Center

Shelter From The Storm

8.2
Hope of the Valley
Shelter entrance,
dining/community
room, dorm,
and sleeping
accommodation.

well-established approaches to emergency service provision, and operate efficiently to accommodate unhoused persons' essential needs. The overall plan of the shelter is streamlined, with allocation of spaces to the most essential services: personal hygiene and medical triage, overnight resting (men and women share one large space divided by a nine-foot-tall partition), eating, internet access, and support services (mental health, intensive case management, substance abuse, veterans services, job training and placement, and permanent supportive housing assistance; see 8.2; Hope of the Valley, 2020).

The architects made a special effort for the building to feel airy and uplifting. Daylight enlivens the community dining room, spilling onto the women's sleeping area. The walls throughout the building are painted in light blue and white. The ceiling design incorporates irregular patterns of fluorescent strips on dropped down shapes called "clouds," softening the appearance of the previously industrial spaces (Hope of the Valley, 2020).

The designers were considerate of individual clients' privacy and enclosed beds with six-foot partitions on three sides, although there are also open, multi-bed accommodations. Each bed comes with securable storage for personal possessions, which helps to put the unhoused person's mind at ease. Individual bedside tables and lights and outlets for charging cell phones or other electronic devices are also a small but considerate, homey touch. The design includes accommodations for clients with pets. These seemingly small details may reduce stress among clients and allow them to focus on attending to their physical and mental health or searching for or retaining employment. We do note, however, that the rather small entry size and limited seating options in the "recreation" spaces located along the dormitory corridors may lead to crowding or underuse of these important areas. In light of the intensity of homelessness in Los Angeles and California, NoHo offers an effective housing solution for persons who would otherwise lack safe and supportive places to eat and sleep.

The Kearney Center, a New Construction Facility in Tallahassee, Florida, USA (2015)

- Design: Clemons, Rutheford & Associates, Tallahassee, Florida
- Type: overnight shelter
- Capacity: 220 beds
- Guests: single men and women

The Kearney Center provides emergency accommodations and medical services to individuals experiencing homelessness in the North Florida region. This shelter also serves as a point of entry into assistance by offering case counseling and responding to the immediate needs of single individuals and families until appropriate permanent housing can be arranged. The interiors are bright and clean, with vibrant walls and artworks contributing to the support of users' senses of dignity and self-esteem. From the reception and service areas at the front of the building, down the corridors leading to the dormitory, the building feels more office-like than institutional. Playful color schemes, lighting, and artwork define those spaces (see 8.3). The cafeteria and dormitory wings are less so, with standardized furniture and bunk beds arranged in rows.

8.3
Kearney Center reception area, cafeteria, women's wing corridor, and men's wing community room.

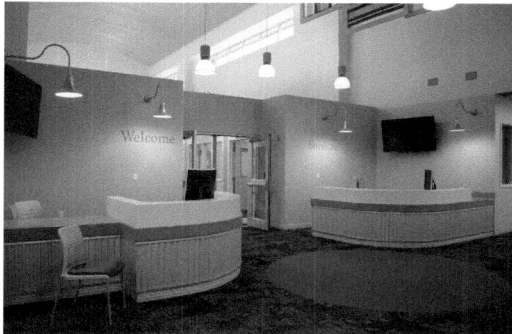

Safety is addressed through a combination of spatial layout and security features, including a metal detector in the reception area and swipe-card access to exterior porches. The men's and women's wings are at opposite ends of the building, with each sleeping area segregated by the degree to which clients have exhibited behaviors that might be disturbing to others. Once they have entered the building, users are generally subject to observation by staff, whether in generously sized corridors, in the cafeteria, or in the sleeping quarters. This lack of privacy may contribute to higher stress levels among certain guests, whereas others may enjoy a heightened sense of protection from perceived threats. Without semipublic zones, users are generally in positions of visual co-awareness. Opportunities for socializing and engagement with service staff are available in each space, but the degree of visual exposure may discourage shyer persons from engaging in community building or expressing their needs. Overall, the Kearney Center offers its guests an uplifting interior environment, access to daylight, and finish details that de-emphasize the institutional aspects of the facility while also providing for security and efficient delivery of services.

Shelter from the Storm, Emergency Shelter, Adaptive Reuse, London, UK (2019)

- Design: Holland Harvey Architects, London, UK
- Type: emergency/transitional housing (28 days, often longer); doubles as a café during daytime
- Capacity: 44 beds (24 men and 16 women)
- Guests: single men and women

Shelter from the Storm serves unhoused women and men from the London area. Admissions are by referrals only. The shelter provides a bed, freshly cooked dinner and breakfast, and assistance with healthcare needs, job searches and training, counseling, English classes, and support in obtaining public benefits. When appropriate, some services are delivered by volunteers who were previously unhoused themselves but able to exit homelessness. According to the project architect, the design is meant to respond to misconceptions about homelessness through a range of "transparencies" – transparency of the shelter's operations (during daytime, the shelter's community dining area serves as a café open to the public), transparency of its glass frontage, and the openness of its community interior spaces (see 8.4). To empower the shelter's guests and instill a sense of domesticity and ownership of the place, the designers aimed to treat the space as a private residence, not an institution.

From the homey red door of the unmarked entrance, the building is intended to be private, personal, and familiar. The lack of signage or public identification addresses in a subtle way issues of safety and security. Clients are residents and are not perceived by their neighbors as homeless persons with the range of associated stigmas. The lobby area is small and domestic in scale, with an adjacent private room if guests need to compose themselves before entering the shelter. Guests check in one at a time in a manner similar to an urban hotel. The activity areas are configured to support choice. Guests may spend time in the dining and community

8.4
Shelter from the
Storm café/dining
area, community
area, bathroom,
and shelter guest
entrance.

area sitting by themselves or with others, read or study in a small quiet room next door, play pool, watch TV in the living room, or spend time in an enclosed yard at the back of the building.

The bathrooms incorporate a number of residential design elements, including separate sinks to provide guests with individual washing space within a communal bathroom. The showers and toilet cubicles are sealed from top to bottom (both to address safety and to preserve privacy in a unisex facility). Access to daylight and plants, combined with a warm color palette of pinks, teals, and creams, floral patterns, and natural materials, adds to the sense of hominess. The program emphasizes shared activities during communal meal times centered, "hearth-like," around the kitchen and café areas (Anderson, 2019). By comparison, the sleeping quarters are more typical in their regimentation, with bunk beds and securable storage lockers assigned to each guest, and these shared spaces lack opportunities for real privacy. Overall, however, Shelter from the Storm stands as an example of the effective blending of homey, community-focused interiors and efficient provision of sleeping arrangements, and social services.

SPATIAL ANALYSIS

The spatial program for each of these three shelters includes the entrance and reception space, community areas, cafeterias, laundry facilities, sleeping room(s), bathroom facilities, and case managers' offices. The percentage distribution between uses for each shelter are shown in 8.5.

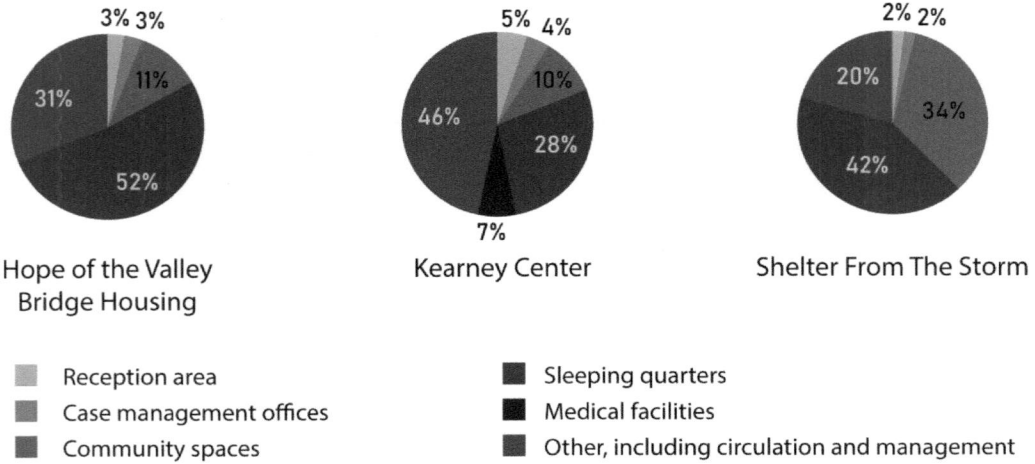

Hope of the Valley Bridge Housing
3% 3% · 11% · 31% · 52%

Kearney Center
5% 4% · 10% · 28% · 7% · 46%

Shelter From The Storm
2% 2% · 20% · 34% · 42%

- Reception area
- Case management offices
- Community spaces
- Sleeping quarters
- Medical facilities
- Other, including circulation and management

Although the quantity of space allocated to guests' accommodations and services appears to support the main purpose of the shelters – varying from 54% (Kearney Center) to 80% (Shelter from the Storm) – the percentage distribution of sleeping and social spaces may be viewed as more telling about the focus of each shelter. The design of NoHo Bridge Housing Shelter supports the provision of sleeping accommodations (52%), with less emphasis on support services and medical help (4.5%) or recreational and socializing opportunities (11%). Space planning in Shelter from the Storm, at the other end of the spatial spectrum, emphasizes supportive recreation and community building not only through closer to equal distribution of sleeping quarters to community and support spaces (with 42% and 36%, respectively), but also in the programmatic diversity and multifunctionality of public zone spaces (discussed further below). This illustrates an approach that focuses on interpersonal connections, mutual support, and community building in addition to providing for the most acute needs.

Let us now look more closely at how spaces are arranged and interconnected in each of the case-study shelters. We use space syntax methods to analyze how spaces in these buildings are interrelated visually and in terms of physical access. Space syntax is an approach to analysis of architectural environments based on the premise that urban, neighborhood, or individual buildings reflect social norms, hierarchies, and policies of society as a whole, its groups, or institutions. The theory and methods were developed by Bill Hillier and Julienne Hanson in their seminal 1984 book titled *The Social Logic of Space*. The methods include visual representations of relationships between spaces based on visual and physical access. This information is useful as it may reveal topologically how spaces may be perceived and used by their users, thus affecting – liberating or restricting – movement, legibility, communication, interaction, and information exchange patterns within spatial configurations (Hillier, 2010; Hillier & Hanson, 1984).

The relationships between spaces indicate how much choice and freedom guests have in these buildings, revealing the potential for agency and individual

8.5
Space allocation of functional areas.

control over privacy, movement, and encounters. This information will also provide us with data on how much control – visual and physical – the staff may potentially have over clients' movements, encounters, and activities. The spatial arrangements in the three buildings are presented in justified graphs shown in 8.6. Each circle, or node, represents a space or a room within a building. Two spaces that are connected (i.e., that allow for walking from one space into another) are represented by a line linking the two nodes. Each time a user has to walk through a space to get to the next space, or each time a user has to turn a corner, the subsequent space is depicted one level up from the starting point. This is one of the methods of space syntax analysis used to visualize the spatial layout of a building from the perspectives of distance and depth.

The more levels, the *deeper* the configuration, which means that visitors have to go through many spaces (corridors or rooms) or turn many corners in order to arrive at the most removed spaces in the building. Deeper structures have greater potential for imposing movement control and access restrictions. In the context of shelters, security measures and the need to maintain order may dictate the need for deeper spatial structures. Typologically, traditional workhouses, as with more modern shelter buildings, are most often buildings in which entrances, corridors, and other public spaces are controlled by supervisors, managers, or other authoritative personnel, and spaces for tenants, clients, or guests are located further away from the entrances or the fronts of the buildings (Hillier & Hanson, 1984; Markus, 1993). Hillier and Hanson (1984) call this a "reversed" building. The two characteristics of this type of building pertinent to our discussion are segregation of guest spaces, with the consequence that interactions and relations between users are reduced or eliminated, and the loss of individuality and agency among users, who are often perceived as a homogeneous group. Consequences include a reduced sense of control, increased stress, lower self-esteem, and disempowerment, common both to workhouses and some shelters.

The justified graphs in 8.6 show that the two larger shelters – NoHo Bridge Housing Shelter and the Kearney Center – have deep configurations of five and seven levels, respectively. Not surprisingly, the reception areas, case managers' offices, and health facilities are located closer to the front of the buildings (levels 1–3), whereas dormitories, dining, and social spaces are placed closer to the back (levels 4–7). However, this removed location from the entrance adds to the sense of privacy there (to the extent that it can be achieved in a large room containing multiple rows of bunk beds).

8.6
Justified graphs for each of the three shelters. The entrances into each building (typically a reception or intake area) are depicted by a node marked with the letter "R." Guest-focused areas are indicated through the use of grayed-out nodes identified by corresponding letters.

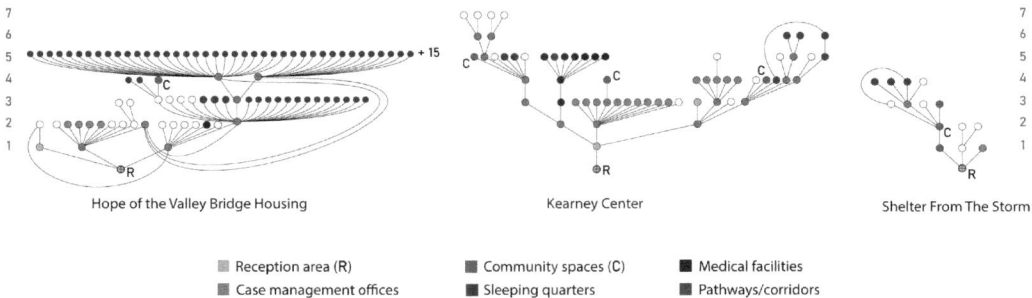

Hope of the Valley Bridge Housing

Kearney Center

Shelter From The Storm

■ Reception area (R)   ■ Community spaces (C)   ■ Medical facilities
■ Case management offices   ■ Sleeping quarters   ■ Pathways/corridors

The idea of privacy as "the state or condition of being alone, undisturbed, ... free from interference or intrusion" (*Oxford English Dictionary*, 2019) is applicable to the conditions found in homeless shelters only marginally, if at all, because almost everything that guests do in shelters, including eating, resting, or sleeping, sometimes including performing most private bodily functions, are done together with others (see, for example, Ranasinghe, 2017). The two most private things that guests may do there are meetings with case managers and using a bathroom. Thus, the concept or private/public space does not often apply when it comes to traditional space planning distinctions between public and private spaces. The fact that dormitories may be located far from the entrance does not mean that they are de facto the most private spaces. It is an illusion of privacy. Rather, their location is dictated by security concerns and institutionalized attitudes toward homeless persons. This spatial practice reflects a structure of a typical community where the main street appears to be clean and orderly (represented by nicer reception desks for non-guest visitors, shelter administration and case manager offices), while the undesirable elements lurk somewhere in the alleys and on the outskirts of communities. This is, of course, not the case in all shelters, many of which are run by compassionate administrators, but it does occur as an "inequality genotype" (Hillier, 2010, p. 196), or spatial pattern that manifests itself within many shelter buildings.

Navigation throughout the two buildings is for the most part linear and offers little choice and thus supports little agency among shelter users. If there are choices, most often they are limited to two (turn to the dining area or dorms). In the case of Shelter from the Storm, this prescriptive circulation arrangement is successfully mitigated by the fact that it is a shallow building, and that the main community area is centrally located (the light gray node marked with the letter "C" on level 3 in 8.6). It becomes a functional activity hub, akin to a living room, offering more choices to the shelter's guests (going to the dorms, to the dining area, to the outside garden area, or to the washroom).

Another important aspect of spatial layout is visibility, which describes the potential for users to perceive a building as "legible" and "navigable." Visibility measures represent the number of other spaces that an observer can see from the center of each space (Hillier & Hanson, 1984; Hillier, 2010). The highest levels of visibility are often related to frequency of visits and higher numbers of users, and these areas often function as junctures within the building. Integration is one of the visibility measures that reveals how intelligible, accessible (open, central), or inaccessible (enclosed, peripheral) spaces can be (Hillier, 2010). For shelter clients, this means that, if the building is open and well integrated, guests may be able to read the building layout and amenities and make informed decisions on where they need to go and how to get there.

Another important aspect of visually accessible and well-integrated spaces is that the guests may be able to assess occupancy and activities in different spaces, which would give them control over the level of social engagement they would like to have with other guests. This clarity in its turn may help reduce the stress of navigating through the building and the fear of being in awkward social situations or undesired or unsafe encounters. In general, safety for both staff and guests within the building increases with increased visual access to public spaces in the building. There must be established a careful balance, however, between absolute surveillance (in the manner of the panopticon), a configuration that has been used historically as a tool for visual control, and respectful opening of boundaries, which is associated with buildings and organizations that de-emphasize hierarchies (Hillier & Hanson, 1984; Hillier, 2010).

A visibility analysis is shown in 8.7. NoHo Bridge Housing Shelter is revealed to be an efficient, highly controlled environment, in which guests' movements are directed through corridors with low visual integration. The building offers little room in its operations for guest or staff autonomy, which enhances security. The three most visually integrated spaces are the corridors, whereas dormitory space and staff offices have the lowest levels of visual integration. On the one hand, this somewhat addresses the lack of privacy in a large open dormitory room (see 8.2). On the other, safety and security risks are heightened, especially towards the very back of the room, and particularly when combined with its location as the deepest space in the building. By comparison, the Kearney Center has considerably higher levels of visual integration throughout the building, with unimpeded paths of movement and sight lines extending from the lobby into each wing, which may reduce degrees of antisocial behavior and thus reduce guests' stress levels. Overall, however, the rather more traditional building design of the NoHo Bridge Housing Shelter and Kearney Center is rooted in the workhouse model, in which residents share large spaces and move in and out along systematic, clearly delineated paths.

8.7
Visual integration graphs (VGA) show the number of other spaces that a moving observer can see from the center of each space. Areas highlighted in light gray are the most visually connected in the building; dark gray areas are the least visually accessible.

Although the total footprint, common areas, and sleeping quarters at Shelter from the Storm are significantly smaller relative to the other two buildings, the proximity to the front entrance of all space types and the generously proportioned dining and community area present users with a clear nexus of community and convenience and may enhance the overall perception of safety.

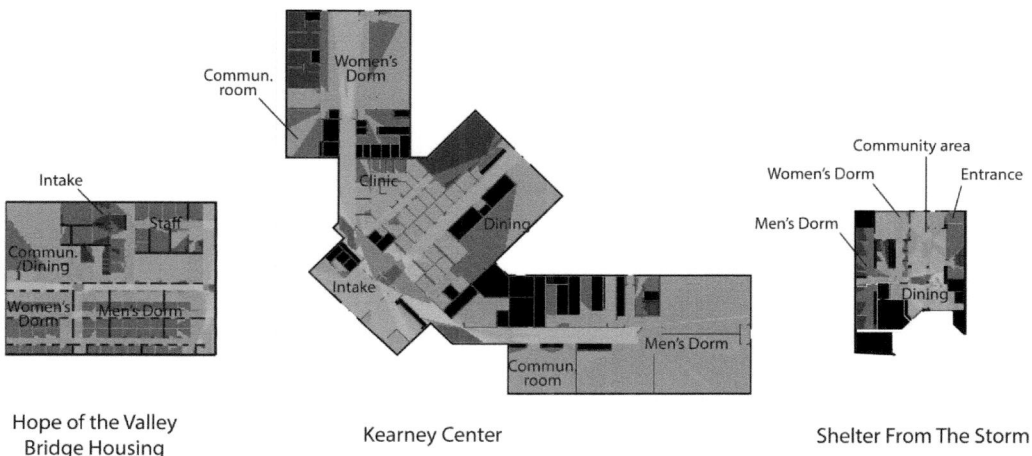

Hope of the Valley
Bridge Housing

Kearney Center

Shelter From The Storm

CONCLUSION

These three case studies begin to suggest the diverse ways in which design considerations and spatial arrangements may contribute to the well-being of guests and staff in matters of security, stress management, and personal control within community spaces, semiprivate spaces, and private spaces. Thoughtfully selected surface treatments, integration of artworks, pleasing color palettes, and common areas with domestic attributes such as patterned cloth, assorted furniture, plants, and windows that let in natural light may combine to reduce the extent to which a building feels institutional. The degree to which layouts reinforce qualitative aspects of the care services for which these buildings are intended is measurable, in part, through visual integration and navigability characteristics. Space planning may support or suppress individual agency, enhance or reduce regimentation attributes associated with "shelterization," and regulate or empower guests by extending control over their environments.

Enabling choice is key to trauma-informed care and its associated development of self-identity, personal wellness, and a confident adaptability to life's circumstances. Consideration of users' need for choice in their surroundings can be expressed in a number of design attributes, including: offering space users alternative navigation pathways through the building; increasing the visibility of social and auxiliary spaces; allocating larger floor area to social and recreational life apart from dining or dormitory spaces; integrating "living rooms" or "city squares" as activity and navigational hubs; placing dining areas closer to the front of the building; and providing for secluded, semiprivate areas, other than the clients' beds. In the words of one of the architects for Shelter from the Storm, it is "about giving people ownership of the space, and ownership of their own personal needs and care" (Anderson, 2019).

BIBLIOGRAPHY

Anderson, C. (2019, December 12). Interview conducted by Y. McLane.

Bollo, C., & Donofrio, A. (2019). From trauma informed care to trauma informed design: the integration of research and design for permanent supportive housing. Presentation at the annual meeting of the Environmental Design Research Association. New York. Retrieved from https://edra.confex.com/edra/EDRA50/meetingapp.cgi/Session/2646

Brooks, R. A., Milburn, N., Rotheram, M., & Witkin, A. (2004). The system-of-care for homeless youth: perceptions of service providers. *Evaluations and Program Planning, 27*(4), 443–451.

Chou, E. (2020, July 6). North Hollywood "bridge" beds help turn the tide on sheltering LA's homeless, officials say. *Los Angeles Daily News.* Retrieved from www.dailynews. com/2020/07/06/north-hollywood-bridge-beds-help-turn-the-tide-on-sheltering-las-homeless-officials-say/

Dilani, A. (2009). Psychosocially supportive design: a salutogenic approach to the design of the physical environment. *1st International Conference on Sustainable Healthy Buildings* (pp. 55–65). Seoul, Korea. Retrieved from www.researchgate.net/publication/265349464_Psychosocially_Supportive_Design_A_Salutogenic_Approach_to_the_Design_of_the_Physical_Environment

Distasio, J., Sylvestre, G., & Mulligan, S. (2005). *Home is where the heart is and right now that is nowhere: an examination of hidden homelessness among aboriginal.* Winnipeg, MB: University of Winnipeg, Institute of Urban Studies.

Hillier, B. (2010). *Space is the machine.* London: University College London.

Hillier, B., & Hanson, J. (1984). *The social logic of space.* Cambridge: Cambridge University Press.

Hope of the Valley. (2020). 85-bed NoHo Bridge Housing Shelter. Retrieved from www.hopeofthevalley.org/nohoshelter/

Hopper, E. K., Bassuk, E., & Olivet, J. (2010). Shelter from the storm: trauma-informed care in homelessness services settings. *The Open Health Services and Policy Journal, 3,* 80–100. doi:10.2174/1874924001003010080

Hurtubise, R., Babin, P.-O., & Grimard, C. (2009). Shelters for the homeless: learning from research. In J. D. Hulchanski, P. Campsie, S. Chau, & S. W. Hwang, *Finding home: policy options for addressing homelessness in Canada* (Chapter 1.2). Toronto: Cities Centre, University of Toronto. Retrieved from www.homelesshub.ca/FindingHome

Markus, T. A. (1993). Re-formation. In *Buildings and power: freedom and control in the origin of modern building types* (pp. 95–145). London & New York: Routledge.

Oxford English Dictionary. (2019). Privacy. Retrieved from www-oed-com.proxy.lib.fsu.edu/view/Entry/151596?redirectedFrom=privacy#eid

Pable, J., & Gomory, T. (2020, June). Unpublished data.

Ranasinghe, P. (2017). *Helter-shelter: security, legality, and an ethic of care in an emergency shelter.* Toronto, Buffalo: University of Toronto Press.

SAMHSA's Trauma and Justice Strategic Initiative. (2014, October). SAMHSA's concept of trauma and guidance for a trauma-informed approach. Retrieved from Substance Abuse and Mental Health Services Administration: https://store.samhsa.gov/product/SAMHSA-s-Concept-of-Trauma-and-Guidance-for-a-Trauma-Informed-Approach/SMA14-4884.html

Wasserman, J. A., & Clair, J. M. (2009). *At home on the street: people, poverty, and a hidden culture of homelessness.* Boulder, CO: Lynne Rienner.

TEACHING MATERIALS

Lauren Trujillo

Key Terms

Human-centered approach to design
Privacy
Sense of domesticity and ownership
Shelterization
Space syntax
Deep or shallow configuration

Prescriptive circulation arrangement
Spatial integration
Visibility
Visual co-awareness
Visual access

Discussion Questions

1. The author states at the beginning of the chapter that there are many reasons why people may avoid shelters. Review these reasons. Would you avoid using a shelter in a moment of need because of these reasons? Why or why not? How could a shelter be designed or operated differently to eliminate the reasons that people in need avoid using them?

2. There is a large continuum of support services offered to clients of a shelter, from minimal to extensive. Which support services do you think should be mandatory at all shelters? What are the benefits and challenges of offering a consistent menu of support services at all shelters?

3. Shelter from the Storm, the third case study, instills a sense of domesticity, community-building, and ownership in its clientele. Do you think that this treatment of guests has long-range benefits? If so, who benefits, and how do they benefit?

4. In this chapter, the author introduces a space syntax analysis method, which links spatial configuration to a user's agency. Do you think that agency is important for clients at a homeless shelter? Why or why not? What short- and long-term benefits does individual agency offer to those experiencing or recovering from trauma?

9 Day Centers

Yelena McLane

Day centers, which may also be referred to as day shelters or drop-in shelters, offer protection from the elements, access to basic facilities (bathrooms, showers, laundry, telephones or power stations, and computers), and meals to unhoused or vulnerable populations in non-judgmental settings with low barriers to entrance (Bowpitt, Dwyer, Sundin, & Weinstein, 2014; Petrovich, Murphy, Hardin, & Koch, 2017; Tucker, Pedersen, Parast, & Klein, 2018). Unlike emergency shelters, day centers are generally only open during business hours, and they do not offer overnight accommodations. Although a smaller portion of clients use day centers, mainly owing to limited program availability relative to overnight emergency shelters (Burt et al., 1999), they play several important functions: providing for material needs, opportunities to socialize, welfare support, and rehabilitation (Crane, Fu, Foley, & Warnes, 2005). Better-resourced facilities may offer a wider range of services, including health and dental care, mental health therapists, case management, vocational and life skills training, employment assistance, pet accommodations, and bicycle rentals and storage, all of which aim to help clients cope with trauma while gaining independence.

Day centers are most often used by persons who cannot get assistance elsewhere, including the chronically homeless, persons suffering from substance abuse or mental disabilities, or undocumented immigrants (Burt et al., 1999; Homeless Link, 2016). Clients can view these programs as a "physical lifeline" (Bowpitt et al., 2014), offering shelter and safety, with readily available food, personal hygiene facilities, and laundry access, all with low barriers to entry. In a study conducted by Grella (1994), a woman from an upper-class background in her 60s was a regular visitor at a day center, but she refused to enter any overnight shelter, characterizing her 3 years of homelessness as "only temporary." The day center provided her with meals and place to rest among friends. It was a stable "home base" for her and other vulnerable women – homeless, seeking respite from hostile home environments, or on the cusp of losing their homes. According to Grella, many guests "improved over the course of coming to the day center, appearing less dirty and disheveled and better able to interact with others, some even forming close friendships" (p. 15).

Studies in the United States and the United Kingdom have revealed, however, that male guests are more likely to use day centers than women, elderly people, or youths, and only marginal percentages of persons from the LGBTQ community use them (Burt et al., 1999; Homeless Link, 2016; Shillington, Bousman, & Clapp, 2011). It is important to consider factors that may inhibit these groups from using day centers. Tucker et al. (2018) have described four such factors that shape use habits among unhoused youths: (1) safety and comfort; (2) availability of fun and engaging recreational opportunities; (3) availability of confidential support services; and (4) convenience of location and operation hours (see similar findings in Bantchevska, et al., 2011; Shillington et al., 2011). Petrovich et al. (2017) reemphasized that safety and security, dignity, and health and well-being were critical considerations when planning and designing day centers. The researchers also noted how low visibility areas, such as enclosed courtyards, introduced safety concerns that may disincentivize use, while observing that design features that reduce unnecessary wait time and allow for efficient service administration (meals, mail storage and distribution) positively affect guests' perceptions of self-esteem and dignity.

Waters (1992) distinguished three models of day centers based upon their sponsoring organizations and missions (see also Bowpitt et al., 2014). The most prevalent type embraces a "spiritual or missionary" approach, often associated with religion-affiliated organizations, with the purpose of providing sanctuary and support to all in need and imposing minimal expectations for service recipients. The second model exhibits a social services approach. It aims to rehabilitate clients by challenging them to alter their behaviors, habits, and choices that may lead to improvements in their lives. These centers offer social casework and other support to help clients navigate through their traumas and challenges. The third model uses a community work approach to encourage clients to engage more fully with the support community by pursuing professional training or skills development, followed by employment in joint work or business enterprises, such as on-site cafés or bicycle shops.

Low barrier to entrance is the first step in creating a positive therapeutic environment. By focusing on physical and emotional safety, shared rules of behaviors and interaction practices, and freedom to engage or avoid encounters and services and by introducing ways to accept responsibility in a non-judgmental and low-stress environment, day center programs can assist clients in managing the physical and emotional traumas associated with homelessness. It is important, however, to mention that there is growing evidence that, to reach as high a number of clients as possible, day center services should be tailored to particular demographics within the larger population of people experiencing homelessness (Burt et al., 1999; Madsen et al., 2003; Shillington et al., 2011).

CASE STUDIES

True Worth Place, Fort Worth, TX, New Construction, 2017
- Design: HKS, Fort Worth, TX
- Client: Forth Worth Foundation
- Management: Presbyterian Night Shelter
- Type: Day shelter and resources center for single men and women[1]
- Operation hours: Seven days a week, from 7:00 a.m. to 3:00 p.m.

The True Worth Place day shelter and services center was conceived in 2009 as part of a 10-year plan adopted by the mayor and city council to address homelessness in Fort Worth. The site selected for the building was in east Fort Worth, the area with the highest concentration of people experiencing homelessness and services for vulnerable populations.[2]

The day shelter was conceived as a place to provide "respite shelter, access to basic services, and function as a 'front door' to housing, case management, medical, dental, and behavioral health care, and other services" (Petrovich et al., 2017, p. 65). The stakeholders and the designers from HKS teamed up to create a facility that would offer a "positive experience for clients, staff, and volunteers" while also fostering "engagement and positive service outcomes" (Petrovich et al., 2017, p. 66). The facility opened in 2017, at which point ownership and management were transferred to Presbyterian Night Shelter, a charitable organization that manages overnight shelter and housing-focused programs nearby.

The day shelter looks sleek and modern, not at all like a building typically associated with serving disadvantaged populations (see 9.1). The design team and stakeholders made a special effort to avoid an institutional feel by selecting a "refined industrial" aesthetic. The building appears clean, spacious, and sophisticated, not unlike an upscale hotel. At the same time, the designers wanted to ensure that the appearance would not be off-putting to guests. According to the lead interior designer Jamie Castillo, "These people are very used to living in warehouses, in abandoned spaces, and so they are coming into the facility for help," and so the designers asked, what would elevate unhoused persons' dignity while keeping them comfortable. "Refined industrial" seemed a right fit for the space

9.1
Exterior and interior lobby views of the True Worth Place day shelter and resource center in Fort Worth, Texas.

considering the security and heavy maintenance requirements (Castillo, 2020). The atmosphere was achieved by opening the space up, exposing structural elements (posts, staircase, and ceiling ductwork), and specifying glass, polished concrete flooring, and metal fixtures. The upscale hospitality elements – warm woodgrain veneers, natural stone cladding the fireplace and two-story hearth, lounge furniture, and light fixtures – soften the edges. Before the restrictions dictated by the 2020 pandemic, the main lobby, or "day room," as staff also call it, could accommodate around 300 people.[3]

The ground floor area is open to all guests and houses amenities – restrooms, showers, laundry facilities, meals, lockable storage, mail boxes, charging stations, and computers. The medical center is also located on the first floor. Staff offices and spaces for specialized services and support programs are located on the upper level. These include case management, obtaining paperwork services, and educational, employment, and enrichment programs (cooking classes, Bible studies, yoga, and voter registration).

The project designers emphasized connecting to the outdoors as a special stress coping and releasing tool. The working fireplace is a literal hearth around which clients can gather for warmth. The abundance of windows and daylight throughout the building contributes to the psychological and emotional well-being of guests and staff: "If we did not have windows and if we had cinderblock walls, that would contribute to what often feels like a hopeless situation" (Mayer, 2020). Overall, the building's connection with the outdoors is three-tiered. First, there is a carefully planned and landscaped community courtyard in front of the building. Second, extensive use of glass for the exterior and for interior partitions introduces natural light that brightens and dims with the weather. Third, an outdoor terrace on the roof deck provides a space that is secure, while still being outside. In addition to visual access, glazing reiterates the dual senses of openness and safety for guests and staff. Transparency as a deterrent of antisocial behavior also fosters trust between guests and staff, a key concept behind the design.

Throughout the building, guests have a variety of seating options, allowing them to choose open individual or small group lounge seating to armchairs in enclosed areas, such as at one end of the building past the staircase. Clients seeking time to be by themselves often sit and use mobile devices, read, or look out the window. Staff use the dayroom seating areas to check up on regular guests and meet with first-time users to familiarize them with center services.

Art therapy programs are one way that True Worth Place helps guests address their traumatic experiences. Art making (from painting to clay work) has become an important part of the educational and enrichment program, supported through a generous arts room on the second floor (Castillo, 2020). Artworks made by program participants are displayed on a rotating basis throughout the facility, fostering pride and empowerment through the discovery of new talents.

Guests and staff enjoy the building and feel that it instills a sense of respect, from the visual cues in the design to more functional features and layout. As Erin Mayer, the program manager, observed, "In terms of design, this building respects the dignity and inherent worth of people, regardless of their station in life" (Mayer, 2020, n.p.).

First Base Day Centre, Adaptive Reuse and Conservation, Brighton, UK, 2011

- Design: Camillin Denny Architects
- Client: Brighton Housing Trust (BNT)

First Base is an example of adaptive reuse – a historic building redesigned for an entirely new purpose. What was once a royal retreat is now a day center for vulnerable populations in Brighton and Hove, one of the most popular seaside vacation destinations in the United Kingdom. The initial 1766 assembly room designed by John Crunden was a large, high-ceiling space accentuated by neoclassical pilasters, free-standing columns, and cornices decorated in the fashionable style of the architect Robert Adam[4] (Robson, n/d). In 1822, King George IV purchased the structure and converted it into a private chapel, adding it to the Royal Pavilion Estate. After Queen Victoria sold the complex back to the town, the building was moved to its current location in Montpelier Place and embellished with a new and somewhat austere classical façade (Robson, n/d; see 9.2). It continued to serve as St. Stephen's Church until 1939. For a while, the building was neglected, then repurposed as a center for the deaf and blind, and, in 1984, it became First Base, a shelter and service program for homeless and insecurely housed city residents (Brighton Housing Trust, 2020). In 2008–10, BHT received funding to preserve and renovate the building with the aim of updating the space while protecting the historic features of the original Georgian interior. The scheme had to accommodate a wide range of services and activities, including social support, healthcare, vocational and work assistance programs, fitness and arts spaces, a training kitchen,

9.2
Exterior and interior views of the First Base Day Centre in Brighton, England.

toilets, showers and laundry facilities, staff offices, medical examination rooms, and consultation rooms. As envisioned by project architect Chloe Hobden, First Base was to be a "fully functional new center that combines the attributes of the original Adam-style interior with high-quality contemporary features" (Brighton Housing Trust, 2020).

First Base adopted the *psychologically informed services* approach originally developed by Robin Johnson and Rex Haigh (2010) as a model for meeting the needs of people with so-called "challenging" or "antisocial" behaviors. It emphasizes the circumstances under which these behaviors originate to enable more creative and constructive work with clients (Breedvelt, 2016; Keats et al., 2012). This approach is widely known in the United Kingdom and is a rough equivalent to the trauma-informed care approach in the United States.

The psychologically informed services model includes five key delivery methods. The first four focus on meaningful engagement with clients at different stages of their recovery. These include developing a psychological framework, training and support for staff, managing relationships between staff and clients, and dedicated follow-up and evaluation of outcomes. The fifth focuses on the qualities of physical environments that have been proven to be instrumental in facilitating successful outcomes. Special importance is placed on a mix of larger and smaller spaces, with open seating plans adaptable to various uses and allowance for clients to determine their own levels of engagement according individuals' needs or preferences (Breedvelt, 2016; Keats et al., 2012). In addition, noise, light, color, art, and surface decoration have likely effects on the psychological state of clients already experiencing elevated stress levels. The design approaches at First Base are attuned to these considerations, particularly in light of the stately associations with the original Georgian structure. The project team was purposeful in recognizing the various (at times competing) signals that physical structures communicate to clients. "Whether a building is redeveloped or redecorated, it can signal that there is a changed approach to the service, which is the key message for staff and clients" (Keats et al., 2012, p. 17).

The design strategy was based around a respectful incorporation of two free-standing pods placed close to the two ends of the interior, leaving the central area open (9.2). One of these pods is a gently curving, glazed, two-level structure that incorporates a secure entrance and exit into the building and meeting spaces on the upper level. The second accommodates a training kitchen and food-serving counter. Detaching the two pods from the building's envelope created a generous circulation pathway with a number of smaller spaces throughout the interior. The spaces are of different sizes and afford varying degrees of privacy. This layout, combined with the open central area, allows for free circulation around the space and diverse sitting options, meaning that guests can enjoy the historic interior decoration in its entirety (Robson, n/d). Combined with educational and community outreach programs, the unhoused guests have an opportunity to use the space as they need and engage in spontaneous or planned, private or shared activities.

The Adams-style light blue walls accentuate the exquisitely detailed white architectural detailing of the interior – order capitals, friezes, and cornices. Under the clean outlines of the white and glass pods, all flooded with natural light, the interior appears clean and elegant. Although this palette may present some maintenance challenges, the space communicates trust and invites shared responsibility for the center staff and guests to take care of the space.

This creative solution was hailed not only for providing a very effective ways to address the *First Base* needs, but for allowing the renovation "to be experienced in all its glory." The project was awarded a Sussex Heritage Trust award in 2012 (Brighton Housing Trust, 2020).

SPATIAL ANALYSIS

Physical openness reflects the goals of transparency and fairness inherent to the programs at True Worth Place and First Base Day Centre. The visibility graph analysis (VGA) in 9.3 shows that the majority of publicly accessible spaces in both locations are well integrated and perceptually provide a view of the community spaces as a whole. This allows guests to quickly orient in the building, navigate, and use spaces with ease and confidence.

As Hillier (2010) observed, an integrated and accessible visual field, when combined with low-barrier access policies and services, may draw users into the spaces and create a condition of co-awareness, conviviality, a sense of environmental belonging, and place attachment. At True Worth Place, the openness of public areas emphasizes informality while lessening the pressure of social hierarchies, although access to the second floor is restricted to guests with appointments or who have registered for classes. At First Base Day Centre, there is little hidden from sight, as clients can observe what is going on virtually anywhere in the building. Even in the elevated offices, glass partitions enhance transparency and a sense of sharing space with peers. By the same token, safety and security are reinforced as guests are much less likely to behave in antisocial ways when they can be observed. At True Worth Place, high levels of visual integration are achieved not only by the absence of closed spaces but through the open central staircase and perforated metal and mesh "industrial" railings along the upper walkway facing the lobby. In both facilities, the less visually integrated spaces are reserved for limited-access functions where privacy is needed, including restrooms, staff offices, and clinical service rooms.

9.3
Visibility integration graphs (VGA) of True Worth Place (first and second floor) and First Base Day Centre. The diagram shows well-integrated areas in light gray and poorly integrated spaces in dark gray. Areas not part of the analysis (staff service areas) are marked as black.

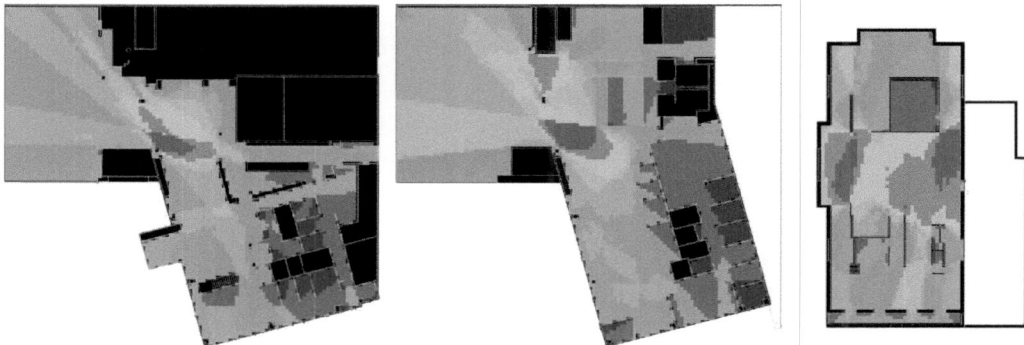

CONCLUSION

The case studies discussed in this chapter represent very different approaches to designing for disadvantaged populations. The first exemplifies a thoughtful contemporary design planned specifically to serve the needs of guests experiencing homelessness. The second illustrates how respectful treatment of cultural heritage structures may be adapted to diverse, and at times challenging, new functions. These approaches intersect in their emphasis on user-focused design, supporting users' autonomy through accommodating navigation and spatial options (open or enclosed, individual or group), which enables users to choose for themselves whether to socialize, remain quiet observers, or withdraw, and supports a sense of well-being through day-lit interiors and secure outdoor spaces. Both facilities exhibit high levels of interior visual integration and ease of navigability, which can contribute to comfort and satisfaction among space users. These design features must be accompanied by comparably client-focused policies and low-barrier access to support services to be truly successful, a consideration that will be explored more fully in the next chapter, which focuses on multiservice complexes.

NOTES

1. Demographics as of Fall 2019: 65% male, 35% female; 15% ages 25–35, 45% ages 36–55, 16% ages 56–60, and 15% were 61 and older (Mayer, 2020).
2. According to the most recent 2019 count, there were 2,028 homeless individuals in Fort Worth area (Tarrant County Homeless Coalition, 2019).
3. In the midst of the pandemic in April–May of 2020, only 80 people were allowed to be in the center at one time (Mayer, 2020).
4. Robert Adam (1728–92) was one of the most important British architects working in the Neoclassical style – an 18th-century movement in architecture and the decorative and visual arts that drew inspiration from the 'classical' art of Ancient Greece and Rome. Adam's interiors were light and elegant, decorated with delicate, small-scale architectural ornaments and detailing (Victoria and Albert Museum, 2020).

BIBLIOGRAPHY

Bantchevska, D., Erdem, G., Patton, R., Linley, J., Letcher, A., Bonomi, A., & Slesnick, N. (2011). Predictors of drop-in center attendance among substance-abusing homeless adolescents. *Social Work Research*, *35*(1), 58–63.

Bowpitt, G., Dwyer, P., Sundin, E., & Weinstein, M. (2014). Places of sanctuary for 'the undeserving'? Homeless people's day centres and the problem of conditionality. *The British Journal of Social Work*, *44*(5), 1251–1267. doi:doi.org/10.1093/bjsw/bcs196

Breedvelt, J. F. (2016). *Psychologically informed environments: a literature review.* London: Mental Health. Retrieved from www.mentalhealth.org.uk/publications/psychologically-informed-environments-literature-review

Brighton Housing Trust. (2020). BHT Heritage. Retrieved from About the Building and First Base: https://bht-heritage.org.uk/first-base/

Burt, M. R., Aron, L., Douglas, T., Valente, J., Lee, E., & Iwen, B. (1999). Homelessness: programs and the people they serve. Summary report. Urban Institute. Retrieved from www.urban.org/research/publication/homelessness-programs-and-people-they-serve-findings-national-survey-homeless-assistance-providers-and-clients/view/full_report

Castillo, J. E. (2020, June 2). Interview with Principal Senior Vice President and Director of Health Interiors Jamie Castillo, HKS Fort Worth, conducted by Y. McLane.

Crane, M., Fu, R., Foley, P., & Warnes, A. (2005). *The role of homeless sector day centres in supporting housed vulnerable people.* Sheffield, UK: Homeless Programme Team, Sheffield Institute for Studies on Ageing, University of Sheffield.

Grella, C. (1994). Contrasting a shelter and day center for homeless mentally ill women: four patterns of service use. *Community Mental Health Journal, 30*(1), 3–16.

Hillier, B. (2010). *Space is the machine.* London: University College London.

Homeless Link. (2016). *Support for single homeless people in England: annual review 2016.* London: Homeless Link. Retrieved from www.homeless.org.uk

Johnson, R., & Haigh, R. (2010). Social psychiatry and social policy for the 21st century – new concepts for new needs: the "psychologically informed environment." *Mental Health and Social Inclusion, 14*(4), 30–35. doi:10.5042/mhsi.2010.0620

Keats, H., Maguire, N., Johnson, R., & Cockersall, P. (2012). Psychologically informed services for homeless people (Good Practice Guide). Southampton, UK: Communities and Local Government. Retrieved from https://eprints.soton.ac.uk/340022/

Madsen, L. H., Blitz, L., McCorkle, D., & Panzer, P. (2003). Sanctuary in a domestic violence shelter: a team approach to healing. *Psychiatric Quarterly, 74*(2), 155–171. doi:10.1023/A:1021307811184

Mayer, E. (2020, June 2). Interview with True Worth Place Program Director Erin Mayer, conducted by Y. McLane.

Petrovich, J. C., Murphy, E. R., Hardin, L., & Koch, B. (2017). Creating safe spaces: designing day shelters for people experiencing homelessness. *Journal of Social Distress and the Homeless, 26*(1), 65–72. doi:10.1080/10530789.2016.1260879

Robson, D. (n.d.). Breathing new life into St Stephen's. Retrieved from Regency Society: https://regencysociety.org/our-heritage/breathing-new-life-into-st-stephens/

Shillington, A. M., Bousman, C., & Clapp, J. (2011). Characteristics of homeless youth attending two different youth drop-in centers. *Youth and Society, 43*(1), 28–43. doi:10.1177/0044118X09351277

Tarrant County Homeless Coalition. (2019). 2019 state of the homeless annual report. Fort Worth: Tarrant County Homeless Coalition. Retrieved from https://ahomewithhope.org/education/local-stats/

Tucker, J. S., Pedersen, E., Parast, L., & Klein, D. (2018). Factors associated with drop-in center utilization among unaccompanied youth experiencing homelessness. *Children and Youth Services Review, 91*, 347–354. doi:10.1016/j.childyouth.2018.06.027

Victoria and Albert Museum. (2020). Robert Adam: Neoclassical architect and designer. Retrieved from www.vam.ac.uk/articles/robert-adam-neoclassical-architect-and-designer

Waters, J. (1992). *Community or ghetto? An analysis of day centres for single homeless people.* London: CHAR.

TEACHING MATERIALS

Lauren Trujillo

Key Terms
Low-barrier entry
User-focused design
Psychologically informed services

Discussion Questions
1. Review the differences between the three models of day centers: spiritual or missionary approach, social services approach, and community work approach. What are the benefits or challenges of each?
2. Do you think that certain demographics of users might be better served by one model over another? Explain your answer.
3. Which day center model would be the best fit for your neighborhood and why?
4. Imagine you were a person in need of the services offered by a day center. Which model appeals to you most and why? Which model appeals to you least and why?
5. Both of the case studies make a strong unified statement with their architecture (an industrial warehouse aesthetic and a historic restoration) while incorporating flexible interior spaces. How does this unified yet flexible approach to design relate to the goals of psychologically informed services and trauma-informed care? Do you think that this relationship is perceptible to the users of the space?

10 Transitional and Permanent Supportive Housing

Yelena McLane

In Chapter 8, we discussed the design of emergency shelters, which often serve as a first step in assisting unhoused persons who would otherwise be living on the streets, in overcrowded "camps" or dilapidated structures, or in other substandard situations. A next step may include moving from the shelter, through which unhoused persons cycle daily, into transitional or permanent supportive housing. At present, many experts consider transitional housing, which is an intermediate step to permanent housing under the continuum of care model, to be outdated and ineffective, particularly when permanent supportive housing is available, as practiced under the Housing First or Rapid Re-Housing models.

As the name implies, permanent supportive housing is a stable, private, and secure home where subsidized rent-paying residents enjoy the same rights and responsibilities as other members of the community. Residents may have access to the support services and mental health care that they need or want (Substance Abuse and Mental Health Services Administration, 2010). In the United States, federal law prohibits any form of discrimination against tenants based on their substance abuse history, physical or mental health, psychiatric disability, or participation in or rejection of support services. Similar statutes govern service provision in Canada, the United Kingdom, and other Commonwealth countries. Permanent supportive housing, especially if paired with the Housing First model, has been found effective at solving a range of problems associated with homelessness (Pearson et al., 2007; Substance Abuse and Mental Health Services Administration, 2010). Permanent supportive housing contributes to longer-term housing stability, improved physical and behavioral health outcomes, and reduced use of crisis services such as shelters, emergency rooms, and jails. Recent studies indicate that service recipients consistently rate this model more positively than other housing models (Rog et al., 2014).

There are two main approaches to permanent supportive housing: *scattered-site housing*, in which residents live in various locations throughout the community in housing that may be privately owned or government owned and which is managed by an agency; and *single-site housing*, in which residents who receive support services live together in a single building or complex of buildings. The former is a form of *tenant-based assistance*. Individual residents receive vouchers that can be used to rent a unit of their choice if a landlord agrees to accept the voucher.

The latter is a form of *project-based assistance*. Housing subsidies are tied to a particular building or building units, and tenants living in those units pay reduced rents (Substance Abuse and Mental Health Services Administration, 2010). Further details of these approaches are given in 10.1.

10.1
Permanent supportive housing site and support models: advantages and disadvantages.

Approach	Advantages	Disadvantages	Examples
Scattered-site	Residents are integrated into the community and are not identifiable as having a disability or homeless background based on where they live	Finding quality affordable housing is difficult in many communities	HOM Inc., Phoenix, Arizona: operates Permanent Supportive Housing, Rapid Re-Housing, rental assistance, and other permanent housing programs (HOM, 2020)
		Logistics of providing mobile services in a scattered-site setting are more complicated	
	More choices are available with regard to neighborhoods, proximity to family, employment, or places of worship	Residents are more likely to be socially isolated and lonely	Homeward Trust, Edmonton, Alberta: focuses on moving people who experience homelessness into independent and permanent housing as quickly as possible, with no preconditions, and then providing them with access to supports and services (Homeward Trust Edmonton, 2020)
Tenant-based	Greater mobility: residents can move to locations that better meet their needs without losing their subsidies or support	Not always a long-term solution	
		Limited funding available for tenant-based rental assistance	
	Does not require the service organization to own or operate housing	Locations might be limited, as finding landlords who accept vouchers is difficult in some communities	
	Support and housing can start quickly		
Single-site	Convenience of having services and housing co-located	Not always integrated into the community; choices of location can be limited	The New Genesis Apartments, Los Angeles, California, USA (2012)
	Residents are not isolated and may develop a sense of community, especially if reinforced through building designs	Neighborhood resistance might be encountered	Crest Apartments, Van Nuys, California, USA (2016)
		Some programs restrict resident choice and freedom	The Six, Los Angeles, California, USA (2017)*
		Living in designated housing can be stigmatizing	MLK1101 housing, Los Angeles, California, USA (2019)*
Project-based	Ensures long-term availability and affordability	Development is a lengthy and complicated process	Westside Community, Tallahassee, Florida, USA;
	Landlord is aware of service needs of residents and may be more understanding if a crisis arises and less likely to pursue eviction if something goes wrong	Depending on market conditions, developing and building housing can be more expensive	The Booth Centre, Southampton, United Kingdom (2010);
			Brisbane Common Ground, Australia (2014)*.
			Ozanam House, Melbourne, Australia (2019)

Note: * indicates projects discussed in this chapter.

It is important to note, however, that, despite a high level of success in getting people of the street and offering them stable and affordable housing options (Padgett, Henwood & Tsemberis, 2016), this type of housing may not be the right fit for everyone. Access to permanent supportive housing works well for many unhoused individuals, especially for those who may have only recently found themselves without a permanent home or for those in a "couch-surfing" situation. Other groups, including the chronically homeless and those who need greater assistance moving into independence, may benefit from living in transitional housing for a period, especially when permanent housing options are not immediately available (Woolley, 2010). Those with severe mental or physical disabilities may find it difficult to live by themselves, and living alone may deepen senses of alienation and isolation (Pearson et al., 2007). The permanent supportive housing model has also been criticized for diverting already limited resources from emergency shelters and day centers serving homeless populations. In fact, some proponents thought variations of the Rapid Re-Housing or Housing First models would entirely replace shelters, but this has not occurred.

CASE STUDIES

In this chapter, we will discuss four single-site housing-based assistance projects – Eva's Phoenix, Toronto, Ontario, Canada; The Six, Los Angeles, California; MLK1101, Los Angeles, California; and Brisbane Common Ground, Brisbane, Queensland, Australia. Each of these features unique design solutions conceived and implemented with specific populations in mind. We will examine their spatial and design features as they relate to the principles of trauma-informed design, resident empowerment, and the general well-being of persons exiting homelessness. These case studies focus on facilities that were newly constructed or renovated within the last 10 years, representing the latest approaches to supportive housing design. We selected these projects for their differences in scope and size, space planning, target groups, and geographic location.

Eva's Phoenix, Adaptive Reuse, Toronto, Canada (2016)

- Client: Eva's Initiatives
- Design: LGA Architectural Partners, Toronto, Canada
- Residential units: ten (housing up to 50 youths for up to 1 year)
- Type: transitional housing

Eva's Phoenix is a transitional housing facility for young people aged 16–24. They may come directly from the street or from other precarious situations. It is one of three accommodations for homeless youth in downtown Toronto run by Eva's, a nonprofit initiative. Eva's Phoenix was a 1930s-era brick warehouse (see 10.2), which designers transformed into an enclosed neighborhood containing ten shared townhouse-style residential units, which front into a generously sized central "main street" (10.3 and 10.4). Each unit has a separate entrance and staircase to the upper level. Unit living rooms, kitchens, and bathrooms are generally shared by five unit residents and are located on the ground floor. Each resident receives an individual upper-level bedroom with key access.

10.2
Entrances to Eva's Phoenix (top left), The Six (top right), MLK1101002C (bottom left), and Brisbane Common Ground (bottom right).

10.3
Eva's Phoenix's central promenade, unit staircase with a balcony, and unit living room view.

The jagged geometry of the façade is a combination of more or less open or enclosed spaces, nooks, and porches formed by protruding upper-level apartments. The ground floor offers a variety of seating or activity options (television, football table) for individual use or two-person or small group socializing. The residents have control over their own privacy or exposure by the many partitions, columns, and large planters distributed throughout the space. Staircases have balconies, which

Eva's Phoenix   The Six   MLK 101

	Atrium / Courtyard		Community spaces
	Apartments		Offices / Management

Brisbane Common Ground

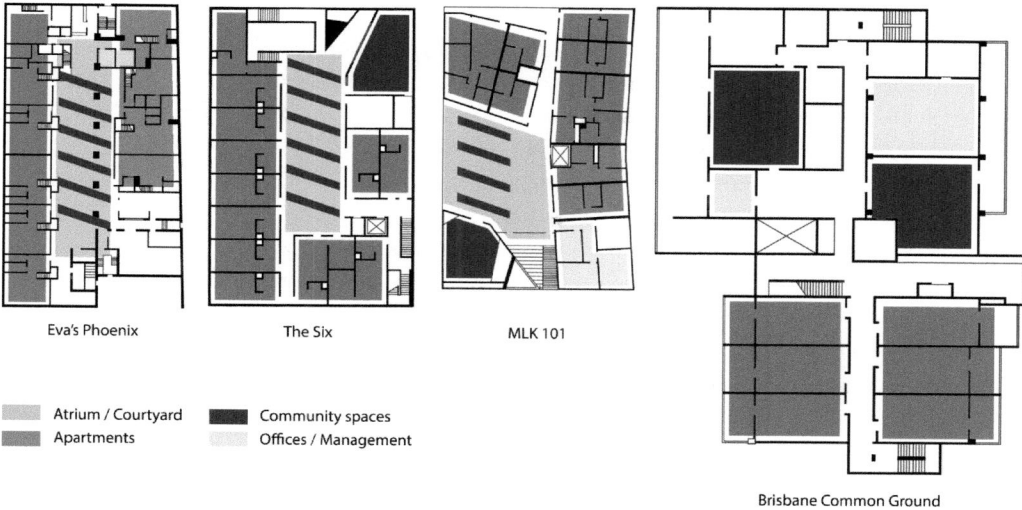

10.4
Floor layouts of
Eva's Phoenix, The
Six, MLK1101, and
Brisbane Common
Ground.

allow residents to see the promenade level and decide whether they want to join in public activities downstairs.

Building security is generally treated similarly to emergency shelters, with lockable doors and reception at the main entry point to control public access. Resident safety is also maintained through the dispersal of administrative and counseling offices. Staff circulate throughout the building, seeing and talking with the residents, which in its turn fosters a sense of connectivity and community.

Several design attributes of Eva's Phoenix reflect applied principles of trauma-informed design:

- *Empowerment and personal control* – the combination of public and semipublic areas, each of which is visibly accessible from any location in the building, provides residents a sense of control over their social encounters;
- *Passive stress management* – access to natural light and nature through the glazed roof allows the building to synchronize with day and night and seasonal light cycles;
- *Socializing and community building* – interacting with peers is particularly important for teenagers. The design supports small group socializing in unit living rooms and in the seating areas in the central promenade;
- *Aesthetics* – angular geometries throughout the interior, combined with clean white surfaces, bright color accents, and staggered volumes, add visual interest. The glazed roof and planters bring natural light and vitality. The space impresses upon visitors and residents a sense of respect, optimism, and cheer (especially on sunny days).

The next two case studies are from Los Angeles, California, a city with the largest homeless population in the United States. As of early 2020, there were over 58,000 people living in the streets (Los Angeles Homeless Services Authority, 2019). The municipal authorities, together with a range of nonprofit organizations, including the California Community Foundation, Skid Row Housing Trust, the Los Angeles Mission, and the Single Room Occupancy Housing Corporation, enter into partnerships to raise funds and develop affordable housing. These projects are often located in rundown or distressed areas and involve renovating existing buildings or new construction on vacant lots. Upon learning about a proposed homeless housing project, neighborhood councils often express concern. To rebuff this 'not in my back yard' reaction, project-sponsoring organizations and stakeholders strive to commission artful designs with the potential of becoming neighborhood landmarks that will restore pride in both the project residents and the wider community (O'Herlihy, 2020).

These projects aim from the earliest phases to treat prospective residents with dignity and to educate the community on the circumstances that often lead to homelessness. Designers of The Six and MLK 1101 sought to destigmatize the project and reinforce a sense of "normalcy." Lawrence Scarpa, the lead architect of The Six, observed that,

> there is very little difference between someone on the street and someone functioning normally … They may have their problems, but they want the same things that we do – they want access to natural light, they want their privacy, they want to be social … By and large, society treats them like aberrations. We try to make it feel as normal as possible.
>
> (Scarpa, 2020)

The Six, New Construction, Los Angeles, California (2016)

- Client: Skid Row Housing Trust
- Design: Brooks + Scarpa, Los Angeles, California, USA
- Residential units: 52 (18 allocated to veterans)
- Type: permanent supportive housing

The Six is located in the MacArthur Park area of Los Angeles. In the 1980s and 90s the area was largely controlled by gangs. Since then, the neighborhood has gradually been freed from violence through policing and increased residential and commercial development. It remains a majority immigrant community, with one of the highest population densities in the United States at more than 120,000 people in 2.72 square miles. The Six is a 52-unit affordable housing complex that offers support and rehabilitation services to veterans and other community members exiting homelessness (10.5).

Several design attributes of The Six reflect applied principles of trauma-informed design:

- *Security and privacy* – the courtyard is located on the second floor of the building but visually connected with the street by an open-front façade and sloping down green terraces. The apartments are towards the rear of the building. This arrangement allows for the courtyard, the communal spaces, and the vertical framing of the front corner to serve as a buffer between the street and the private areas, which enhances the sense of protection. This feature inspired

10.5
The Six central
courtyard,
community room,
apartment interior,
and rooftop
'sculpture' garden.

the name of the building. In military slang, "the six" means that your back is covered. All doors swing to the outside to prevent residents from barricading themselves in. Railings are 8 inches higher than standard to decrease the likelihood of risky behaviors such as climbing or jumping.

- *Personal control and empowerment* – generously allocated public spaces and distinct and separated semipublic and private areas within each unit give residents a sense of control over where they want to be.

- *Passive stress management* – throughout the complex, visitors have access to light, open air, and views of the courtyard and surrounding neighborhood, which promotes physical and emotional healing. Some of the residents may suffer from schizophrenia or other sensitivities to noise and ambient sounds, and many of the layouts, circulation pathways, and materials serve dual purposes as sound control.

- *Socializing and community building* – the design embraces the importance of staying connected as integral to the stress management and healing process. Life in the building is centered around the open courtyard and the adjacent community room. Residents may open doors to create one continuous common space. The community room is available for individual or group use (TV watching, computer games). The courtyard is large enough to accommodate simultaneous social events and more isolated sitting and observing. These design elements empower residents to take control of the form and level of their social activities. Single-loaded corridors, opening into the central courtyard, also facilitate a sense of community among the residents.

- *Aesthetics* – bold and dynamic geometry, clean lines, and an uncluttered modern look both in shared spaces and inside apartments convey respect for residents, reinforcing the idea that thoughtful design should be available to everyone. Light makes the interior spaces feel uplifting. Floor-to-ceiling operable windows are a particularly nice touch that adds a feel of sophistication to the apartments. Conversion of the roof into a sculptural feature integrating elements of green landscaping was an extra feature upon which the architects insisted. "Good design and being disadvantaged are not mutually exclusive," said Scarpa (2020). "To the extent that designers can provide it to disadvantaged people, they are part of the healing process."

MLK1101, New Construction, Los Angeles, California (2019)

- Client: Clifford Beers Housing
- Design: Lorcan O'Herlihy Architects, Los Angeles, California, USA
- Residential units: 26 (17 one-bedroom and 9 three-bedroom)
- Type: permanent supportive housing
- LEED Gold

This building at an intersection in an otherwise underdeveloped and distressed neighborhood in South Los Angeles is marked by its entranceway – a sloping, sharp-angled green triangle of grass with bright white trim. The MLK1101 is a supportive housing complex for formerly homeless veterans, chronically homeless persons, and low-income families (10.6). Given the alarming rates at which area families with children lose their homes, project planners included a real rarity among permanent supportive housing facilities: private units with three bedrooms.

10.6
MLK1101 exterior view, an apartment interior, the community garden, and the adjacent common room.

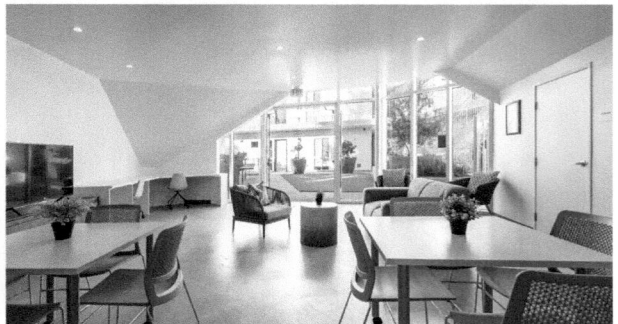

Several design attributes of MLK1101 reflect applied principles of trauma-informed design.

- *Socializing and community building* – one of the core concepts that drove the design of this project was the idea of reintegrating the persons trying to exit homelessness through their engagement with community – from other residents of the apartments to the broader neighborhood. The locations of offices, recreational rooms, and commons were intended to facilitate interpersonal encounters and socializing among residents. As at The Six, the heart of the layout is the neatly landscaped garden located on the upper level. The garden functions as an outdoor living area for the residents and their guests. An enclosed community room opens directly into the garden. Residents use the community room on a daily basis for games, cooking classes, and communal meals. More intimate socializing occurs in the generously sized circulation pathways on the upper levels. These not only provide access to apartments, but serve as balconies on which residents talk with one another while enjoying views of the neighborhood.
- *Security and privacy* – the architects had to raise the pedestal to accommodate required parking on the site. The resulting stoop was an attempt to connect people to the sidewalk, inviting guests to hang out and socialize in the courtyard. The L-shaped building allows residents to see out as much as others can see in – "eyes on the street" as opposed to turning their backs on the street, as in a traditional courtyard configuration. Although there is a gate at the top of the stoop for security purposes, the architects moved the fence back so that it was not visible from the street. The garden gate locks for the night (O'Herlihy, 2020).
- *Personal control and empowerment* – generously allocated public spaces, complemented by distinct and separated semipublic and private areas within each unit, provide residents with a sense of control over where they want to be. The gradual, tiered transition of enclosed and semipublic spaces into open public areas provides residents the opportunity to control the degree of privacy. Bicycles are a critical means of transportation among the homeless community, and MLK1101 residents enjoy access to a private bicycle storage and repair shop. Property managers offer bicycle rental services, while also partnering with a company that trains residents to repair and maintain their own bicycles. This innovative program has been lauded by the City of Los Angeles.
- *Passive stress management* – the design addresses stress management in two ways: ease of navigation within the building and, more importantly, being able to go outside and spend time in a safe and secure environment. Residents often use the garden to sit by themselves or engage in conversation. Large operable windows bring light into apartments and allow for airing of the space.

For Lorcan O'Herlihy Architects' founder and design principal, Lorcan O'Herlihy,

The importance of bringing good design to all socio-economic levels cannot be overstated. The project demonstrates how architecture has the ability to restore pride to marginalized people and to the neighborhoods in which they live. Our hope, too, is that we can shift people's perception about what homeless housing can be. (O'Herlihy, 2020)

Brisbane's Common Ground, New Construction, Brisbane, Australia (2012)

- Client: Queensland Government, Common Ground Queensland, Grocon Constructors, and Micah Projects
- Design: Nettleton Tribe Architects
- Residential Units: 146 (studio and one-bedroom apartments)
- Type: permanent supportive housing

Brisbane Common Ground is a 14-story midrise building with a large entry foyer and separate retail spaces at street level. It is a 10-minute walk from Brisbane city center. Historically, the neighborhood was mostly industrial, interspersed with a few residential buildings. This was the place where local homeless used to congregate in camps. A seafood warehouse formerly stood at this location. Brisbane Common Ground looks like a nice, new apartment building that would be very much at home in any modern city, and its conventional appearance aids in reducing stigma. The project follows the Rosanne Haggerty Common Ground model, which originated in New York City in 1990. Haggerty's approach combined affordable housing with supportive on-site services including health care, counselling, vocational training and job placement, and help with life skills, such as cooking and money management (Community Solutions, 2020). Residents consist of chronically homeless persons transitioning from street living, many of whom are Indigenous Australians.

10.7
Brisbane Common Ground main lobby, a library, a private apartment, and a roof garden.

Several design attributes of Brisbane Common Ground reflect applied principles of trauma-informed design.

- *Sense of community* – the designers of Brisbane Common Ground aimed to foster social inclusion and facilitate developing a sense of community among its residents. There are several common areas, which allow for varying degrees of engagement. Residential floors are subdivided into smaller 26-unit "neighborhoods" that span two floors interconnected by stairs. Vertical neighborhood residents may access two community seating areas overlooking the city. Each neighborhood features a unique art wall completed by residents. In addition to the neighborhood amenities, there is a community garden, art room, media library, computer room, and group work spaces on the first floor, and a lounge room, library, and rooftop garden on the top floor. Sonya Keep, chief executive officer of Brisbane Common Ground, observed that this project is unusual among Australia's social housing projects because of the variety and number of differently purposed community spaces available to residents (Keep, 2020). By placing community spaces throughout the building, designers encouraged residents to move around, see their neighbors, and get to know one another. Managers noted that, when a group of residents is genuinely interested in an activity, informal enthusiast groups will form. These groups meet regularly in common areas to cook, play games, discuss books, or share stories. Over time, others join in, which leads to developing friendships among residents.
- *Dignity and self-esteem* – Brisbane Common Ground does not look like typical social housing. On residential floors, a subtle but meaningful feature – recessed apartment entries – helps to reduce the institutional feel in the hallways. Not only do these recesses interrupt the monotony of the long corridor, they also introduce a discreet element of privacy. Public spaces and private units have art on the walls. New residents are welcomed into furnished apartments with clean sheets, towels, cooking supplies, and utensils. Generous use of glass in the foyer opens up the space and enhances lines of sight, creating opportunities for casual sitting and people-watching. It is a nice, sophisticated look that serves a dual purpose as a safety measure. Managers proudly report that all of the common interiors are well maintained by the residents, and the private apartments, when vacated, often show no signs of intentional damage.
- *Security and privacy* – 24/7 concierge front desk service is available to all residents. A CCTV system provides oversight in publicly accessible areas, and access to residential floors is limited.
- *Stress management* – operable windows and balconies in each apartment provide residents with generous amounts of daylight and fresh air. Vegetable and flower planting beds in the roof garden offer a productive means of recreating within the building. An art room and two libraries ensure that residents have access to digital media and books and supplies for creative crafts-based projects.

At Brisbane Common Ground, Indigenous persons make up about 20% of all residents. Managers have emphasized the importance of creating a comfortable environment for this important constituency. Indigenous residents generally stay the longest, and this housing model has proven very successful because many of these individuals come from this area of the country and they have family and other close relations nearby. Some residents maintain ties with people who are still in the street. At times, some residents will try to accommodate these friends and acquaintances in their apartments, sharing with these other homeless persons the graciousness that Brisbane Common Ground had extended to them. In the street, it is a constant struggle to control one's personal space, to look after possessions, and to feel agency in the world. Brisbane Common Ground seeks to give these people literal space, to help them to gain a sense of control. With unauthorized visitors, however, management must draw a line and say no for them, so that they do not lose their tenancies. Many residents report being happy with that.

SPATIAL ANALYSIS

Let us now consider how spatial layouts and design characteristics of the case-study locations relate to the principles of trauma-informed design and potentially facilitate the process of exiting homelessness. One starting point is to avoid singling out and alienating future tenants who may already feel set apart from the community. The site selection process must take into account connectivity and integration of housing into the community, with its infrastructure, public services, educational and employment opportunities, and cultural life, providing ready access to public transportation and safe roads for biking or walking. All four projects are located in existing and well-established neighborhoods in major urban areas – Toronto, Los Angeles, and Brisbane. Public perception of the facility is also key. Designing an understated entrance without signage or other markings allows labeling and stigmatization of the building and its residents to be avoided (see 10.2).

Each site offers a variety of community-shared public and semiprivate amenities. The common features are reception areas, central public courtyards or atria, and one or more community rooms (ranging from public to semiprivate). The majority of locations offer casework support, professional training opportunities, and outdoor courts or gardens. The summary of programmatic spaces and amenities for all locations is presented in 10.8.

In the chapter addressing emergency shelters, we used space syntax analytical methods, including layout, depth, navigation patterns, and visual integration, to identify the degree to which interior architecture may enable personal control, privacy, and the formation of a sense of community among residents. In Eva's Phoenix, The Six, and MLK1101, the main floor spaces center around a promenade or courtyard, which facilitates freedom of navigation and potentially liberates residents' use habits (see 10.4). Floor spaces at Brisbane Common Ground are arranged in a linear sequence as double-loaded corridors, making navigation more controlled. Both types of arrangements are "shallow" systems, in which residents have easily legible and accessible apartments or other spaces, but their varying degrees of visual accessibility make them distinct.

Not surprisingly, the central courtyards, reception areas, and resident services offices (located on the street level) are the most visually accessible. The visibility

10.8
Permanent supportive housing case studies – programmatic spaces and amenities.

Housing	Residents	Square footage: total (public spaces, incl. circulation/ residential units)	Community Spaces			Casework support	Vocational training spaces	Other amenities
			Reception or check-in office	Courtyard or atrium	Community room(s) (public to semiprivate)			
Eva's Phoenix	Youth	41,000 sq. ft. (15,300/15,000)	✓	✓	✓	✓	✓ (classrooms, teaching kitchen, print shop)	✓ (clothing bank, laundry)
The Six	Single individuals and disabled veterans	40,250 sq. ft. (20,000/20,000)	✓	✓	✓	✓		✓ (communal kitchenette, laundry, bicycle storage, green roof, large public patio and edible garden)
MLK1101	Chronically homeless persons, veterans, and families	34,000 sq. ft. (15,600/19,240)	✓	✓	✓		✓ (community room, retail spaces)	✓ (communal kitchenette, laundry, bicycle shop)
Brisbane Common Ground	Chronically homeless single, including Indigenous persons	145,000 sq. ft. (14,300/76,250)	✓	✓	✓	✓	✓ (computer room)	✓ (concierge service, communal kitchen, computer room, art studio, lounge, billiards room, vegetable garden, rooftop garden, free Wi-Fi)

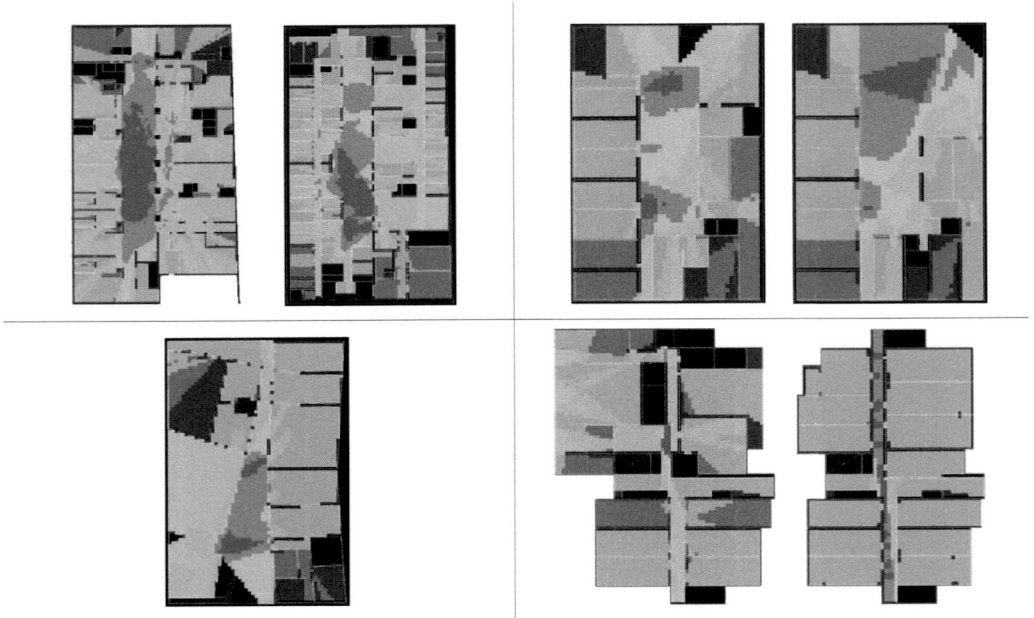

diagrams (VGA; see 10.9) show that the presence of a central courtyard or promenade opened to upper stories allows residents to "read" the building at a glance and create a mental image of the entire space. This helps eliminate confusion with navigation, enables free movement, and, when combined with multiple upper-story entry points, enhances the residents' ability to control interpersonal encounters, which contribute to an increased sense of safety.

CONCLUSION

Analyzing these four supportive housing buildings has helped us to identify how some aspects of space planning, including visual openness and the presence of public spaces, may help alleviate anxiety and increase the sense of individual agency and pride among residents. Three of the four designs clearly benefit from expansive central foyers with atria or elevated ceilings. The striking difference in visibility and visual integration translates to a general sense of openness and overall accessibility within the common areas and as the client navigates from entrance points to the doors into private residential units. This is not to say, however, that lowered visibility in a quantitative sense translates necessarily into diminishment of function or quality of life among residents. Within retrofitted buildings or new construction in denser urban environments, particularly multistory apartments, design choices may be limited. Space is at a premium, and comparably welcoming and navigable public spaces, resident-only spaces, and private quarters may be achieved through the integration of design elements conducive to the provision of trauma-informed care. These may include large windows, natural features such as plants and daylight, considerately appointed rooms, and spatial arrangements that

10.9
Visual integration graphs (VGA) of Eva's Phoenix, The Six, MLK1101, and Brisbane Common Ground. Images on the left are of the main building entrance floors. Images on the right are of one of the upper floors. Areas colored in light gray exhibit the highest levels of visual integration, with medium to darker gray reflecting areas with lower levels of visual integration and visual access into and through adjoining spaces. Persons standing in the light gray areas will have the most commanding perspective over the full range of spaces and movement options within the building.

encourage interaction between residents and staff, which are attributes of each of the four case studies presented in this chapter.

BIBLIOGRAPHY

Community Solutions. (2020). Retrieved from Our Story: https://community.solutions/about-us/our-history/

HOM. (2020). Retrieved from HOM: www.hominc.com/

Homeward Trust Edmonton. (2020). Housing and supports. Retrieved from Homeward Trust Edmonton: http://homewardtrust.ca/

Keep, S. (2020, February 2). Interview with Sonya Keep of Brisbane Common Ground conducted by Y. McLane.

Los Angeles Homeless Services Authority. (2019). 2019 Greater Los Angeles homeless count – data summary. Total point-in-time homeless population by geographic areas. Los Angeles: Los Angeles Homeless Services Authority. Retrieved from www.lahsa.org/documents?id=3467-2019-greater-los-angeles-homeless-count-total-point-in-time-homeless-population-by-geographic-areas.pdf

O'Herlihy, L. (2020, May 8). Interview with Lorcan O'Herlihy of MLK1101 Housing in Los Angeles conducted by Y. McLane.

Padgett, D. K., Henwood, B. F., & Tsemberis, S. J. (2016). *Housing First: ending homelessness, transforming systems, and changing lives.* Oxford and New York: Oxford University Press.

Pearson, C. L., Locke, G., Montgomery, A. E., & Buron, L. (2007). *The applicability of Housing First models to homeless persons with serious mental illness.* Washington, DC: U.S. Department of Housing and Urban Development, Office of Policy Development and Research.

Rog, D. J., Marshall, T., Dougherty, R. H., George, P., Daniels, A. S., Ghose, S., & Delphin-Rittmon, M. E. (2014). Permanent supportive housing: assessing the evidence. *Psychiatric Services*, *65*(3), 287–294.

Scarpa, L. (2020, 05 15). Interview with Lawrence Scarpa of The Six conducted by Y. McLane.

Substance Abuse and Mental Health Services Administration. (2010). *Permanent supportive housing: building your program*. HHS Pub. No. SMA-10–4509. Rockville, MD: Center for Mental Health Services, Substance Abuse and Mental Health Services Administration, U.S. Department of Health and Human Services.

Woolley, E. (2016, February 26). What are the limitations of Housing First? Retrieved from Homeless Hub: www.homelesshub.ca/blog/what-are-limitations-housing-first

TEACHING MATERIALS

Lauren Trujillo

Key Terms

Permanent supportive housing
Scattered-site housing
Single-site housing
Tenant-based assistance

Project-based assistance
Transitional housing
Trauma-informed design

Discussion Questions

1. Review the definitions for scattered-site housing versus single-site housing and tenant-based assistance versus project-based assistance. Which type of permanent supportive housing do you think would work best for your community? Why? Which do you think would not be successful in your community? Why?

2. Review the section discussing how a combination of visual integration and readability helps "eliminate confusion with navigation, enables free movement, and, when combined with multiple upper-story entry points, enhances the residents' ability to control interpersonal encounters, which contribute to an increased sense of safety." Describe a space that you are familiar with that offers greater visibility and readability. Do you have a similar response to this space?

3. Based on the examples you have seen, do you think that the design and architecture of a permanent supportive housing structure can add value to a neighborhood that might otherwise subscribe to the NIMBY (not in my backyard) response to constructing a building of this nature? If so, what exterior design features do you think add the most value to the fabric of these neighborhoods?

4. After reviewing some of the causes of homelessness in the introduction chapter and the responses that users have to unsuitable interventions, do you think that there would be user types that might have an adverse reaction to these spaces? What do you think these reactions would be? What might be the cause of these reactions?

11 Multi-service Complexes

Yelena McLane

Defining and measuring the extent of one's homelessness can be difficult, as it often results from a combination of personal, health, structural, economic, and social conditions. For some populations, such as those who may recently have lost access to housing and need a place to eat and sleep, the immediate aide of a shelter is the readiest option. For other, chronically homeless persons, longer-term housing solutions may be appropriate. Youths or persons addressing mental health-or substance abuse-related issues may benefit from middle-term, temporary transitional housing that paves the way to independent living. Recognition of this complexity leads to an understanding that programs and architectural responses must be tailored to the specific needs of groups and individuals – both to manage the delivery of resources and to prevent homelessness.

We question the wisdom of the prevailing approaches to assistance, which are often based on degrees of vulnerability[1] and desperation experienced by the client and which seldom rise to a fully integrated system of services and housing accessibility (Fowler, Hovmand, Marcal, & Das, 2019). When the complex and evolving nature of homelessness is understood and integrated at an organizational level, the urgency of providing 'one entry' access to flexible solutions that serve the needs of diverse populations becomes clear. One of the forms that this approach can take is multi-service complexes, the focus of this chapter. We present two case studies of this building type, together with analysis that examines thexir attendance to human wellness.

CASE STUDIES

Arroyo Village, Denver, Colorado, USA, New Construction, 2019
- Client: Rocky Mountain Communities and the Delores Project
- Design: Shopworks Architecture, Denver, Colorado
- Type: multi-service complex including an emergency shelter, permanent supportive and affordable housing

Arroyo Village was conceived and supported through a partnership between Rocky Mountain Communities, an affordable housing developer, and the Delores Project, a nonprofit organization dedicated to providing safe, comfortable shelters and personalized services for unaccompanied women and transgender individuals experiencing homelessness. The project site is located in the West Colfax neighboorhood, a historically transit-oriented Denver community established by Jewish immigrants in the late nineteenth century (Denver Public Library, n.d.). Today, this predominantly Hispanic and Caucasian community has a poverty rate of approximately 48%, with unemployment rates among the highest in the region (Shift Research Lab, n.d.). A light rail line and a main freeway connect the neighborhood to downtown Denver.[2]

Prior to redevelopment, the site hosted an emergency shelter and 'workforce' housing managed by different nonprofits. The facilities were outdated, and space for individual accommodations was very limited. The stakeholders expanded capacity and adapted an experimental approach of combining three types of housing programs, serving unhoused persons and individuals experiencing housing instability: a 60-bed overnight shelter; a 35-unit permanent supportive housing (PSH); and 95 one-, two-, and three-bedroom affordable 'workforce' housing units.[3] All three programs are managed within a continuum of care framework.

Each program occupies its own space within the building, with separate entrances and distinct appearances. The Delores Project homeless shelter serves women and transgender guests. The entrance is from the interior courtyard of the building, away from the street (see 11.1). For many individuals experiencing homelessness, safety is of the utmost concern, and providing privacy while they wait for the door to be open was of paramount importance to the staff and guests alike. This led the designers to locate the entrance discreetly, under an overhang. Guests call to reserve a bed in the shelter, and the shelter opens at five o'clock each evening. All guests are required to leave for the day each morning. Guests in the Emergency Shelter Program may stay in the shelter for up to a week at a time and can renew their stay beyond that by calling to reserve additional time. Program guests have access to a bed as long as they are moving towards stability, with an average stay of 3–6 months.

The designers intended to create shelter experiences similar to those of a home. After being admitted, the guests enter a 'living room' – a spacious area painted in calming sage green, accentuated with a natural wood dropped ceiling canopy and furnished with inviting midcentury modern-inspired furniture, including

11.1
Arroyo Village partial first-floor plan for shelter and affordable housing public spaces and first-floor plan visual integration graph (VGA). Areas shown in light gray have the highest levels of visual integration, with medium to dark gray reflecting areas with lower levels of visibility and integration. Persons standing in the light gray areas will have the most commanding perspective over the full range of spaces and movement options within the building. Areas shown in black were not included in this analysis.

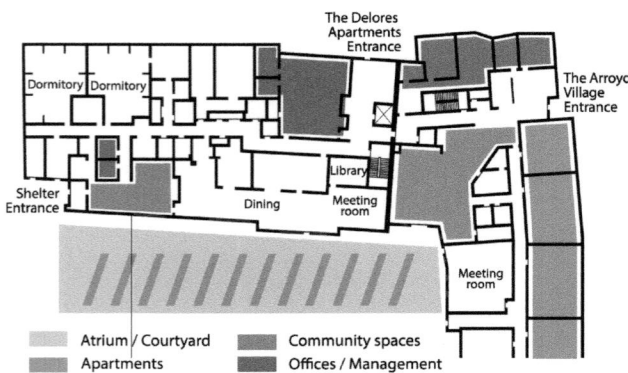

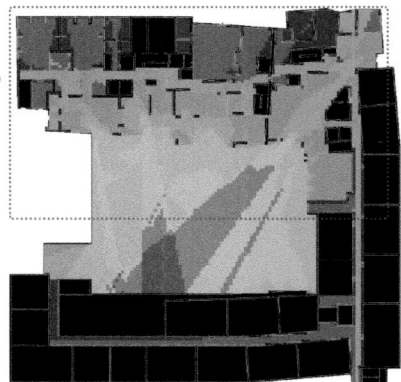

The Delores Apartments Entrance

The Arroyo Village Entrance

Dormitory | Dormitory

Library

Shelter Entrance

Dining

Meeting room

Meeting room

Atrium / Courtyard | Community spaces
Apartments | Offices / Management

11.2
The Delores Project shelter living room and dorm-style sleeping accommodations (above) and the Delores Apartments PSH program street entrance and lobby (below) provide different appearances and ambience to suit their respective clients.

rocking chairs meant to help guests self-soothe when stressed (11.2). Guests may leave their coats or other small items in secure cabinets, just as one would when arriving home. The shelter offers hot meals, showers and toiletries, a clean bed, laundry facility, and a phone for local calls. Guests may access a secure courtyard through the living or dining room.

The Delores Apartments, a PSH program, is located on the upper levels of the building (11.2). Unlike the entrance to the shelter, the entrance into the apartments faces a busy street. It has an attractive design consisting of a generous and brightly accentuated overhang, large lettering, contrasting dark tile, and glass doors. These features stand out, inspiring pride in those who live there. Amenities available to PSH residents include a community room, a laundry room on each floor, and small pet-friendly apartments with full kitchens, individual bathrooms, and small storage closets.

The third and largest part of the program is the affordable 'workforce' housing. It occupies a separate, L-shaped section of the building (see VGA, 11.1). Similar to the Delores Apartments, the entrance is designed with care and respect to residents (11.3). In addition to individual apartment conveniences, residents can access an open living room, multipurpose classroom, and community courtyard.

Trauma-Informed Design and the Three-Cs Framework
The creative team at Shopworks Architecture applied trauma-informed principles for planning and designing the three areas with the goal of creating an environment that would meet programming needs while supporting residents' well-being.

The architects partnered with Group 14 Engineering and the Center for Housing and Homelessness Research at the University of Denver to perform a study on how the built environment can help individuals recover from trauma (Shopworks Architecture, Group 14 Engineering, and University of Denver Center for Housing and Homelessness Research, 2020). Starting with the six principles of trauma-informed design referenced at designresourcesforhomelessness.org (Pable, n.d.; Berens, n.d.), the architects developed a practical model for applying these principles to complex building systems to address residents' health needs and social preferences. The model emphasizes user *choice*, *community*, and *comfort* (Shopworks Architecture et al., 2020, p. 13). Working within this 'three-Cs' framework, the architects designed an environment with a strong potential to empower residents to make positive changes in their lives and facilitate reintegration into the wider community (Rossbert, 2020).

11.3
The Arroyo Village affordable housing entrance, living room, and community courtyard shared by all three housing programs.

Safety
Persons who have to sleep on the streets or in makeshift tents have to be alert for their physical safety and the security of their possessions. Program staff at the Arroyo Village report that residents often remark on the sense of quiet and relaxation that comes with having their own private living space. As noted in previous chapters, people feel safe in visually connected areas with higher density and movement levels. The PSH program residents revealed that they felt safest in their apartments, but, next to that, their perception of safety increased in open spaces such as the entrance lobby, which is close to the welcome desk where

staff sit. Staff noted that they often prefer to work out in the lobby area rather than in their private offices, which are behind a door, so that residents see them and feel more comfortable asking questions and seeking assistance. The visibility diagram (11.1) shows that the PSH entrance lobby is the space with low visibility and integration levels, which may be why staff proximity was emphasized. In the shelter, the most visible spaces are the living and dining rooms, which face the shared courtyard.

Choice

The concept of choice relates to supporting individual agency and developing a sense of ownership by giving residents control over their level of engagement with spaces (Shopworks Architecture et al., 2020). Such engagement may be spatial, through choosing a navigational path throughout the building to socialize with friends, relax, or just be by oneself, or psychological, by incorporating personal items or aesthetic choices with residents' immediate environments. It should be noted that the double-loaded corridor-based layout offers little navigational control to guests and residents in any of the three programs. Movement unfolds linearly and offers limited width of interior or exterior visibility. However, the ground floor shelter and affordable housing community spaces are more open, both visually and in navigational terms. Each has multiple points of entry and offers a range of sitting options.

Being able to control where to be in a building is important for managing one's stress. Residents have access to several spaces conducive to relaxation, from the privacy of their apartments to the open-plan entrance lobby, community rooms, and courtyard. Cooking a meal for oneself also constitutes choice, something of which persons experiencing homelessness are often deprived.

Comfort

This aspect of the built environment moves beyond residents' basic needs (Maslow, 1987). In addition to food and safety, comfort takes the form of access to personal hygiene facilities, serene sleeping areas, and laundry amenities. Comfort also encompasses physical attributes of spaces that affect emotional and psychological well-being, including odors, acoustics, and access to daylight, street views, and natural landscapes. These elements affect cognitive processes and perceptions of self-esteem and may enhance residents' abilities to manage stress and heal. The name of the project – Arroyo Village – was inspired by a creek running through the nearby Lakewood Dry Gulch Park, where residents regularly bike or use walking trails. Sunlight is the most "celebrated" of nature's elements (Goldhagen, 2017, p. 145), and the designers incorporated generous access to daylight and views throughout the building. The housing team invested in spacious windows in all of the apartments to allow individuals a view of the mountains and daylight. The ground floor community spaces face the central courtyard. Each building corridor ends with a large window, and those in the PSH are dotted with whimsically positioned openings along the north wall. All apartments have operable windows, a feature that several residents noted as very important to their sense of control over their private living environment (Shopworks Architecture et al., 2019).

Aesthetic perceptions of spaces can be no less important for psychological and emotional comfort. Spaces that look beautiful, clean, and home-like "bring calm" and "spark joy" in residents (Shopworks Architecture et al., 2020, p. 13). The designers selected a soothing color palette of pastel greens and purples with splashes of lively lime greens and yellows to accentuate and energize interior spaces. Finishes included natural looking materials, polished concrete, and wood patterned flooring, creating an engaging interplay between textures and colors (11.2). Varying ceiling heights, the organic curves of furniture, and lively light fixture designs and positioning contribute to the overall sense of brightness and playfulness in the spaces. These elements combine to create an environment of "patterned complexity," which can stimulate users' senses and draw them to return to it repeatedly (Goldhagen, 2017, p. 236).

Community
The designers of the Arroyo Village incorporated public and semipublic spaces throughout the first floor. Many residents noted that they had formed friendships and enjoyed spending time in their friends' apartments (Shopworks Architecture et al., 2019). One of the most popular places where PSH residents like to socialize is the modestly sized front lobby of the apartments (11.2). This might suggest that the residents enjoy not only the uplifting environment and intimately grouped furniture layout, but proximity to staff who may help by facilitating interactions and activities among residents (Shopworks Architecture et al., 2019). The choice of the lobby as a preferred socializing spot could also reflect clients' desire to become aware of who their neighbors are and to meet them, visually or through brief interactions, in the safety of a liminal public space.

This project is one of very few in the nation in which the principles of trauma-informed care were implemented in a systematic way, from spatial layouts to architectural detailing and materials and finishes specifications. Being in a place that helps one feel good and that respects clients' needs and dignity can have a powerful effect on individual user experiences. As one resident shared, "I am happy at Arroyo Village, I have a beautiful apartment, and I feel safe."

Ozanam House Resource Centre, Melbourne, Australia, New Construction, 2019
- Client: VincentCare
- Design: MGS Architects, Melbourne, Australia
- Type: multi-service complex includes short-, medium-, and long-term supportive housing; day center; healthcare services; and dining

Every 2 years, the City of Melbourne recruits hundreds of volunteers to collect comprehensive information on unhoused persons in the area. According to the latest StreetCount (City of Melbourne, 2018), there were around 300 persons sleeping rough on the city streets. VincentCare, a nonprofit organization established by the Society of St. Vincent de Paul with the aim of supporting and advocating for disadvantaged and unhoused Victorians, tasked MGS Architects to design new facilities for Ozanam House, a service that the Society has been running for men experiencing homelessness since 1953 (VincentCare, 2020a). The project brief outlined the need to bring VincentCare's previously dispersed services "under one roof" to better meet the needs of Melbourne's most disadvantaged men and women, "particularly those sleeping rough and facing daily crises in their lives" (Wheeler & Buchanan, 2020). Ozanam House was one of the first schemes in Australia that embraced a systemic approach to assisting persons experiencing homelessness. Susan Buchanan, the interior designer for the project, observed that one of the important reasons of having everything on one site was that,

> when the services are in one location, when someone comes in, they only have to tell their story once. When you have services on multiple sites, people have to tell their story multiple times. In this situation, people did not feel respected and valued, and it becomes demeaning having to repeatedly explain why one needs these services.
>
> (Wheeler & Buchanan, 2020, n.p.)

11.4
Ozanam House main entrance, community courtyard shared by visitors, guests, and residents, street-facing café, and custom brick and tile exterior façade finish, and street-facing café.

The building is located in densely developed, residential North Melbourne, an inner-city area along a main arterial road to the north-west of the city that leads to Melbourne Airport. The 11-story structure rises high above the surrounding low-rise neighborhood buildings (11.4). The project architect, Joshua Wheeler, envisioned the building as a "beacon, opening early in the morning to offer social connection, access to a health clinic; or a warm meal and perhaps a shower" (Wheeler & Buchanan, 2020, n.p.).

The new facility programs offer day center services welcoming anyone who is hungry, needs a meal, a hot shower, medical help or counselling, or who to just wants a safe place to rest off the street. The building has dedicated spaces for three housing programs: 60 short-term crisis accommodations (4–12 weeks' stay), 48 medium-term apartments with individual addresses (16–24 weeks' stay), and 24 long-term apartments (primarily targeted at residents over the age of 50 with complex needs; VincentCare, 2019). Residents in all three of these programs have access to a range of communal areas, including a large centrally located courtyard, bike storage, laundry, and lounge room on every floor, with panoramic city views, abundant natural light, comfortable lounge furniture, and televisions. All feature attractive soft interior finishes (11.5). Apartments include separate bathrooms and storage closets, and medium- and long-term units are equipped with kitchenettes to allow for greater privacy and independence.

The design team focused on helping visitors and guests overcome stigma and the psychological barriers against asking for help. The entrance engages visitors directly through a generously sized canopy and seats built into the brick façade. The benches invite guests to rest and participate in the street activities from the safety of having a solid building behind one's back (11.4). Custom-designed and manufactured bricks provide both visual interest and a sense of tactility. "It is a building that suggests touch" (Wheeler & Buchanan, 2020). Large exterior glazing makes the interior social spaces visible when one approaches the entrance. This relationship between bricks and glass – the solidity, texture, and small variations juxtaposed with smooth tinted transparency – suggests that this is not an institutional building, but a welcoming building that will treat its guests with respect.

11.5
Ozanam House short-term accommodations' corridor and meeting room, lounge, and individual apartment.

Over many decades of working with vulnerable and homeless populations, VincentCare developed what it terms a homelessness recovery model (HRM; VincentCare, 2020b). The HRM begins with a recognition that trauma is often a precursor of and an accompaniment to being unhoused. It further acknowledges that service delivery design plays a crucial role in the degree to which individuals will accept services and thrive within assistance programs.[4] The model was operationalized in Homelessness to Recovery evidence-based practice principles that focus on supporting hope and optimism, healing from trauma, autonomy and self-determination, collaboration and community, and, ultimately, a reconnection with self, family, friends, and the community (VincentCare, 2020b). The designers anchored their solutions within the HRM, while also utilizing salutogenic principles that support well-being, including comprehensibility, manageability, and meaningfulness (Antonovsky, 1979, 1987; Golembiewski, 2010; Lindström & Eriksson, 2005; Mazuch, 2017; Mittelmark et al., 2017).[5] By incorporating biophilic design elements (Wilson, 1986) that reflect through the integration of natural elements the value placed on diverse clients' and staff's safety and physical needs, emotional and psychological well-being, and choice, the designers further stressed the important role that the building would play in cultivating social connections.

Comprehensibility and Manageability

Although the building is big, it is subdivided into manageable chunks that give it a more comfortable, residential feel. For people who may have mental or cognitive disabilities and who struggle with daily tasks, these subdivisions help them to orient, navigate, and feel secure. The ground floor spaces are separated into neighborhoods based on their function and the staff or residents granted access (11.6). The least restricted areas are the publicly accessible health clinic, café, courtyard, and restrooms. Spaces accessible only to staff and residents include the dining room, library, gym, laundry room, activity rooms, and courtyard.

The navigation pathway loops around the core area of the building. The designers carefully choreographed navigational experiences and plotted the most common

11.6
Ozanam House ground floor plan and visual integration graph (VGA).

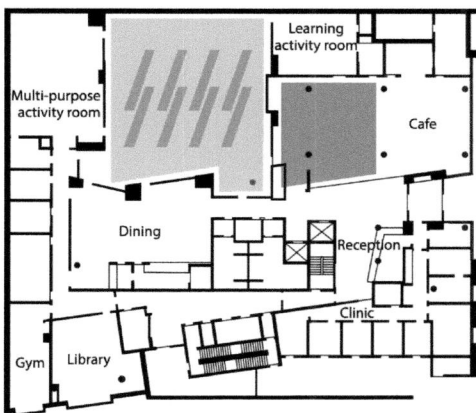

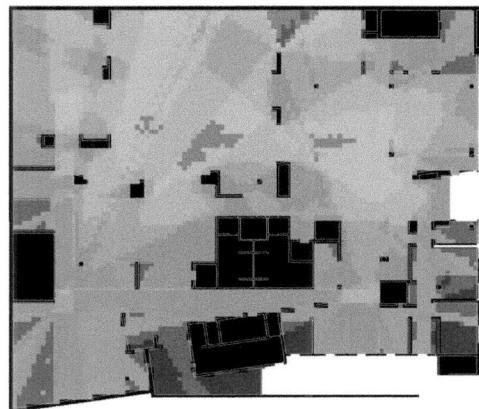

Atrium / Courtyard   Community spaces

routes of each user group. Non-resident visitors progress through the spaces linearly. The spaces branch out from the main 'street' in sequence towards the café, health clinic, and bathrooms, climaxing in the courtyard. Residents have access to all ground-floor facilities and thus may choose to navigate through the building as they prefer (11.6). The apartments on the upper stories are arranged along two short 'streets' on either side of a centrally placed elevator bank and resident lounge. The architects intended for this configuration to work as easily accessible and navigation-friendly neighborhoods. Breaking up large spaces into manageable districts illustrates the practical application of one of the overarching principles of salutogenic design – comprehensibility.

Comprehensibility is also manifested in a high level of visibility throughout the building. Visibility works well as an unimposing yet effective security feature, while also helping with navigation. Openness contributes to residents' ability to see what is happening in social public spaces and avoid the awkwardness of sudden or undesirable encounters which they did not have time to evaluate and prepare for (Hillier, 2010; McLane & Pable, 2020). Experiences become more orderly, structured, and predictable (Antonovsky, 1987), which aids in developing confidence after the relative chaos of living on the street.

Meaningfulness and Biophilia

The overall design, from space planning to furniture and finishes selection, embraces the idea that each person's recovery from homelessness is nonlinear and individualized. Choices of where to take meals, whether to be by oneself or with others, and where and to what degree to be involved in social scenarios empower residents to make decisions based on their individual needs and wants. At Ozanam House, public spaces are balanced with spaces for retreat, both internally and externally. Residents may choose to gather in large social groups, partake in one-on-one consultations, or seek solitude.

The designers' adherence to biophilic design strategies led them to enhance residents' access to daylight, fresh air, plants, and landscaped spaces throughout the building, with the central courtyard being the most prominent natural feature (11.4). Guests and residents may lounge, chat with friends, dine al fresco, or take a nap there. A 'green wall' creates a verdant backdrop. This vertical garden feature was added to the metal screen of the north façade to soften the summer light in the interior lounges, frame views, and mediate temperature differentials (Wheeler & Buchanan, 2020). Long-term accommodations include individual balconies, access to outdoor terraces, and a rooftop garden.

The building stands out, but it stands out in a positive way. It is one of the higher buildings in the neighborhood, but its design integrates the domestic scale and language of surrounding buildings, further emphasizing the degree to which a center for serving unhoused persons should look no different than any other quality building. Meaningfulness and respect towards residents are further manifested in the selection of natural materials and finishes – brick, timber, stone, and glass. Environmental graphics and soothing colors – combinations of greens, turquoise, blues, and purples – distinguish each of the residential floors. Thermal and acoustic control was also noted to be very important. Residents of the building frequently express their appreciation for the quiet acoustics of their apartments. This is aided, in part, by the specification of high-quality materials for interior finishes, quality unit partition construction, and double-pane windows. This sense of quiet also helps residents to feel safe, secure, and relaxed.

CONCLUSION

In this chapter, we examined two case studies that adapted somewhat different, but overlapping, approaches to designing housing and services for specific subsets of homeless and vulnerable populations. The foundational design principles for each of these projects were safety, rejection of institutionalizing facilities and services, and respect for human dignity. It is the indignity of the very situation that drives many people experiencing homelessness away from admitting that they are in fact homeless and deters them from seeking organized assistance. As a result, some may use shelter facilities only as a last resort. Designing buildings and environments that treat unhoused persons with respect, that address the needs of residents and guests, and that look genuinely attractive while doing so must be of the highest priority for both therapeutic and preventive reasons. People should not be made to feel stigmatized or embarrassed when they are in spaces designed and built specifically to help them. Thoughtful exterior design and building entranceways can put people at ease and reduce a singular barrier to service – a sense of unwelcome. Low levels of overt security, clearly navigable interior spaces, and good visibility are measures that communicate trust and respect. Green spaces, natural light, and clean, modern color schemes can be aids to relaxation. Ultimately, however, it is not only design, but a merging of design with sound social services philosophies and institutional policies that will lead to more successful outcomes – the movement of persons away from homelessness into permanent, stable housing.

NOTES

1. The Vulnerability Index Service Prioritization Decision Assistance Tool (VI SPDAT) is one of the "triage" tools used to determine whether a household or a person is really in a difficult situation, the severity of the situation compared with that of others experiencing similar problem at the same time, and the priority of homeless assistance (Jong, 2015).
2. The light rail system offers over 200 rides per day of affordable mass transit, which is essential in the fight against homelessness. Both guests of the Delores Project shelter and residents of the permanent supportive housing apartments receive free transit passes (Rossbert, 2020).
3. The term *workforce housing* is applied to indicate a program for households that earn too much to qualify for traditional affordable housing subsidies. Most often these households have incomes between 80 and 120% of area median income (Ford & Schuetz, 2019).
4. The model consists of four foundational elements – client engagement, client coordination, case management, and client participation – that offer clients wrap-around services within a continuum of care framework (VincentCare, 2020b).
5. As Lindström & Eriksson (2005) summarized, "Comprehensibility refers to the extent to which you perceive the stimuli that confront you, deriving from the internal and

external environments, as making cognitive sense as information that is ordered, consistent, structured, and clear. The person scoring high on the sense of comprehensibility expects that stimuli they encounter in the future will be predictable, ordered, and explicit. Manageability is the extent to which a person perceives that resources are at their disposal that are adequate to meet the demands posed by the stimuli that bombards them. 'At a person's disposal' refers to resources under the person's own control or to resources controlled by legitimate others. Meaningfulness refers to the extent to which a person feels that life makes sense emotionally, that problems and demands are worth investing energy in, are worthy of commitment and engagement, seen as challenges rather than burdens" (p. 441). See also Antonovsky, 1979, 1987.

BIBLIOGRAPHY

Antonovsky, A. (1979). *Health, stress and coping*. San Francisco, CA: Jossey-Bass.

Antonovsky, A. (1987). *Unraveling the mystery of health: how people manage stress*. San Francisco, CA: Jossey-Bass.

Berens, M. J. (n.d.). *Designing the built environment for recovery from homelessness: a review of research*. Tallahassee, FL: Design Resources for Homelessness. Retrieved from http://designresourcesforhomelessness.org/people-1/education/

City of Melbourne. (2018). StreetCount. Retrieved from Health and Support Services: www.melbourne.vic.gov.au/community/health-support-services/social-support/what-we-are-doing/Pages/streetcount.aspx

Denver Public Library. (n.d.). West Colfax neighborhood history. Retrieved from Denver Public Library: Genealogy, African-American & Western History Resources: https://history.denverlibrary.org/west-colfax-neighborhood-history

Ford, T., & Schuetz, J. (2019, October 29). Workforce housing and middle-income housing subsidies: a primer. Retrieved from the Brookings Institution: www.brookings.edu/blog/up-front/2019/10/29/workforce-housing-and-middle-income-housing-subsidies-a-primer/

Fowler, P. J., Hovmand, P., Marcal, K., & Das, S. (2019). Solving homelessness from a complex systems perspective: insights for prevention responses. *Annual Review of Public Health*, *40*, 465–486. doi:10.1146/annurev-publhealth-040617-013553

Goldhagen, S. W. (2017). *Welcome to your world*. New York: HarperCollins.

Golembiewski, J. A. (2010). Start making sense: applying a salutogenic model to architectural design for psychiatric care. *Facilities*, *28*(3/4), 100–117. doi:https://doi.org/10.1108/02632771011023096

Hillier, B. (2010). *Space is the machine*. London: University College London.

Jong, I. D. (2015, February 17). VI-SPDAT and Rapid Re-Housing recommendations. Retrieved from OrgCode Blog: www.orgcode.com/vi_spdat_and_rapid_re_housing_recommendations

Lindström, B., & Eriksson, M. (2005). Salutogenesis. *Journal of Epidemiology & Community Health*, *59*, 440–442.

Maslow, A. (1987). *Motivation and personality* (3rd ed.). New York: Addison Wesley Longman.

Mazuch, R. (2017). Salutogenic and biophilic design as therapeutic approaches to sustainable architecture. *Architectural Design*, *87*(2), 42–47. https://doi.org/10.1002/ad.2151

McLane, Y., & Pable, J. (2020). Architectural design characteristics, uses, and perceptions of community spaces in permanent supportive housing. *Journal of Interior Design*, *45*(1), 33–52. doi:https://doi.org/10.1111/joid.12165

Mittelmark, M. B., Sagy, S., Eriksson, M., Bauer, G., Pelikan, J., Lindström, B., & Espnes, G. (2017). *The handbook of salutogenesis*. Cham. Switzerland: Springer. Retrieved from www.ncbi.nlm.nih.gov/books/NBK435831/

Pable, J. (n.d.). Designing for human health and wellness. Design Resources for Homelessness. Retrieved from http://designresourcesforhomelessness.org/

Rossbert, L. (2020, June 8). Trauma-informed design approach in Arroyo Village project. Interview conducted by Y. McLane.

Shift Research Lab. (n.d.). West Colfax. Retrieved from Neighborhood Summaries: https://denvermetrodata.org/neighborhood/west-colfax

Shopworks Architecture, Group 14 Engineering, and University of Denver Center for Housing and Homelessness Research. (2019). Arroyo Village study summary. Personal communication.

Shopworks Architecture, Group 14 Engineering, and University of Denver Center for Housing and Homelessness Research. (2020). Designing for dignity & joy: promoting physical health, mental health, and well-being through trauma-informed design. Denver, CO. Retrieved from https://shopworksarc.com/wp-content/uploads/2020/06/Designing_Healing_Dignity.pdf

VincentCare. (2019, March 5). Living at Ozanam House: an insight into life and care. Retrieved from VincentCare: www.vincentcare.org.au/news/latest-news/ozanam-house-insight-into-life-care/

VincentCare. (2020a). Our history. Retrieved from VincentCare: https://vincentcare.org.au/about-us/history/

VincentCare. (2020b). Homelessness recovery model. Retrieved from VincentCare: www.vincentcare.org.au/our-services/homelessness-recovery-model/

Wheeler, J., & Buchanan, S. (2020, June 6). Ozanam House design: interview and personal communication. Interview conducted by Y. McLane.

Wilson, E. O. (1986). *Biophilia*. Cambridge, MA: Harvard University Press.

TEACHING MATERIALS

Lauren Trujillo

Key Terms

Biophilic design elements
Comprehensibility
Concept of choice
Continuum of care framework
Double-loaded corridor-based layout
High density levels
High/low visual integration levels
High movement levels
Homeless recovery model

Multi-service complex
Navigational control
Patterned complexity
Salutogenic principles
Service delivery design
Trauma-informed design
Three-Cs framework
Visually connected areas
Workforce housing

Discussion Questions

1. The Arroyo Village complex provides an overnight shelter, permanent supportive housing, and affordable housing units. What might be the benefit of offering spaces for multiple user needs? What might be the challenges?

2. The design of Arroyo Village was guided by the principles of the three-Cs framework: choice, comfort and community. Review the section called "Trauma-Informed Design and the Three-Cs Framework" in the chapter and consider the spaces in which you reside and/or choose to spend time. How do these spaces allow for choice, comfort, and community?

3. The design of the Ozanam House Resource Centre focuses on comprehensibility of a space to provide visibility, safety, easy navigation, and control. When you read this section, were you surprised by the far-reaching physical, social, and psychological benefits of a space's comprehensibility? Why or why not?

4. Think of places that you have visited for the first time during a state of mental or physical stress – for example, a hospital or friend's home. Did these spaces offer choice, comfort, community, and comprehensibility? If so, how did these spaces reduce your stress? If not, what did the spaces lack? How could they be improved?

12 Trends and Experiments

Jill Pable & Yelena McLane

As previous chapters in this book explain, many societal factors may drive people into a state of homelessness, and this situation is not a new one for the countries that are the subject of this book. By any measure, however, things are not going well at the present time. Discussions of racial disparities are at boiling point, poverty is worsening, and unemployment has reached heights not seen since the Great Depression. The current COVID-19 pandemic has dramatically and in quick fashion worsened these long-simmering social ills. Demand for quality shelter is staggering – it is estimated that the global urban population growth will require that a city for 1 million people must be built every week until 2030 (TEDGlobal 2014, 2014).

Arguably what lies at the heart of this broad situation of shelter is what people experience at the personal level in their everyday lives. Observes one United States writer, "the problem is the steady collapse of livability. The problems of affordable housing and homelessness have surpassed all superlatives – what was a crisis is now an emergency that feels like a dystopian showcase of American inequality" (Manjoo, 2019, para 2).

Money is often thrown at this problem,[1] but there is only slow movement in the systemic evolution that will be necessary for long-lasting change. Much of the resistance to solving homelessness lies within human nature – we seek to exclude what is not similar to us and what we do not understand. People often fear the unknown and, as a result, try to keep such dilemmas out of their lives by maintaining the status quo (Thomas, 2020). From this stance flows biased zoning laws set in place through local resident objections to 'others', exclusionary housing segregation, and cities' lack of agencies that create public housing (Thomas, 2020). In the United States, the problem transcends political party[2] (Manjoo, 2019) and extends its reach into disparate or collective attitudes about our obligations to each other, beliefs of shared destiny, and interpretations of the notion of freedom.

At this time, it is also distressing to see that the United States federal government's reasoning and policies are inflicting more pain on the situation and seemingly taking steps that are reversing progress. For example, the Council of Economic Advisers' 2019 report claims that substitutes for permanent housing have the effect of increasing homelessness, and that the good conditions of shelters invite people to enter into homelessness because it can be a better situation than their own housing. Alarmingly, this Council also views encouragement of persons experiencing crisis to be more self-sufficient as a viable way to reduce homelessness and discounts housing first approaches as an ineffective strategy (Council of Economic Advisers, 2019).

At the time of this writing, the COVID-19 virus pandemic has also greatly heightened societal stress and tension across the world. Its nature as a physical disease made deadly through the ease of its person-to-person transmission has quickly brought matters of built environment design to the forefront and has dramatically altered spatial priorities. Within mere months, questions of surface finish safety, widths of corridors, and presence of sneeze guards on millwork have become subjects of active discussion.

The dangers of COVID-19 are particularly salient for populations already compromised through poor health, poverty, or loss of jobs such as people experiencing homelessness. Shelters, in fact, have served as 'super spreader' venues for viral transmission. In New York City, the closure of soup kitchens and inmates being released from prisons, both owing to virus concerns, have driven more people to use shelters. Twenty-three people have died of COVID-19 in one New York City shelter (Stewart, 2020). Systemically, the COVID virus may also produce longer-lasting effects – some countries' governments will cease their moratoria on housing evictions in the coming months, which may throw more people into a homeless situation (Malson, Martin, Rogers, & Power, 2020; Valdez, 2020)

To combat COVID 19 infections, the United States Centers for Disease Control regulations directly reference numerous interior architecture programmatic decisions, such as position and spacing of beds in congregate sleeping quarters, disinfection of surfaces, and establishment of quarantine living spaces (Centers for Disease Control and Prevention, 2020, April 21, 2020, April 25). Such new requirements and the extra work they bring to shelters and similar places tax an already stretched system of support organizations seeking to assist people in crisis.

This broad review of current societal health, prosperity, and equality could only be described as grim, and it affects all of the countries this book addresses to varying degrees. All too frequently, the itch of former societal problems has now progressed to open wounds. Despite this avalanche of calamities and burdens, however, we would argue that this moment is a rare and particularly visible opportunity for architectural design to attend to its compact of usefulness to its public. Suddenly, interior design and architectural choices can be a matter of life and death. It is times of great duress that can give rise to change (and it is only looking at the situation in the rear-view mirror at a later time that this becomes clear). Several hints of coming adjustments are even now emerging:

1. Some governments in the United States are changing their zoning to effectively ban single-family-only areas, permitting congregate housing that would be more affordable to permeate into former strongholds of privilege. In Oregon, new laws permit the construction of duplexes, fourplexes, and 'cottage clusters' in most towns (Andrews, 2019).

2. In 2020, the United Nations approved a resolution calling on all governments and sectors to respond to homelessness, noting that 1.6 billion people live in inadequate housing, and 15 million are forcefully evicted every year. Young people are at highest risk of eviction (United Nations Department of Economic and Social Affairs, 2020, para 2).

The review of broad trends above makes clear that architectural response to homelessness is but a small component of a much larger and highly intricate dilemma. In reaction, designers must first realize their environmental design work itself will not solve this thorny problem (Lerner, 2019). (Much more important and effective, in fact, would be to craft societal supports that prevent people from losing their homes to begin with.) Even more importantly, however, it is essential to realize that deep knowledge of the complex phenomenon of homelessness – its causes, responses, and consequences for people – is vitally important for designers creating environments for work, rest, and play. Repeated and detailed talks with clients and staff, consulting literature, understanding local attitudes and hurdles – in essence, doing one's homework – best ensure that built space can be effectively inserted into the situation. Indeed, this is among the most primary objectives of this book.

With this overview of trends established, the next section turns specifically to architectural responses to homelessness for supportive housing. We concentrate primarily on this building type here, as shelters and day centers have seen less dramatic evolution in their architectural styles. See Chapters 8 and 9 for case studies about these building types.

EMERGENT ARCHITECTURE TYPOLOGIES: PERMANENT SUPPORTIVE HOUSING

The ingenuity of architects, interior designers, and residents themselves has given rise to a number of distinct types of temporary and permanent dwelling types for supportive housing that exist alongside typical apartment buildings or congregate living complexes. Here, we review the most predominant types and examine their qualities (both positive and negative) through the lens of habitability and experiential wellness. This list is by no means comprehensive, as solutions such as living in recreational vehicles (Lerner, 2019), 'squatting' in existing buildings, or residing in tents are all too often the choices that people make out of necessity. We will not consider here impermanent structures, as much as they form the location for many people in crisis right now.[3] However, the types discussed below will lend context to a discussion of forthcoming evolutions of some of these approaches in Chapter 13.

Tiny House Communities
As a means to resident autonomy and dignity, a tiny house (12.1 and 12.2) can lend a sense of identity and self-esteem through its stand-alone character. Some tiny house communities (also known as 'intentional co-housing communities') are

12.1
A tiny house.

Positives	Negatives	
Sense of autonomy for users	May not hold up over time and require upgrades and repairs (United States Interagency Council on Homelessness, 2018)	12.2 Positive and negative aspects of tiny houses.
Ability to form community with similar dwellings/users nearby	Require significant security (United States Interagency Council on Homelessness, 2018)	
Access to services, if nearby	Smells from cooking can permeate the entire dwelling and linger (Tempest, 2017)	
Enhanced privacy when compared with multi-family types	Things wear out more quickly because of frequency of use.	
	Must greatly limit possessions, groceries, etc.	
	Difficult to host guests	
	Access to services, if distant from these supports	
	Small space demands constant attention to visual order/keeping things picked up	

either created and governed by support organizations or residents govern themselves. As with many housing types that vary from societal traditions, zoning can be challenging for this housing type, especially if within the bounds of cities. These communities are also challenging conventional norms of property law (Alexander,

2019). Although charming, the challenges of reducing one's possessions to fit in a 200–500 square foot dwelling can be daunting, both physically and also psychologically.[4] Some believe that tiny houses should be for temporary use only (Lerner, 2019). Gene Tempest, tiny home dweller, notes that:

> life in our tiny home is characterized above all by shabbiness. Like the apartment's pervasive, undomesticateable dust bunnies, the threadbare feeling grows and grows simply because it already exists. No one warns you that everything is more concentrated in a tiny house, that the natural life cycle of objects accelerates.
>
> (Tempest, 2017, paras 12–13)

Similar approaches include:

- Sleeping pods (small one-bedroom units) that are added onto existing buildings' exterior walls or roofs (Framlab, n.d.; Mairs, 2015).

Half Houses and Other Modular Approaches

Supportive housing developments are often plagued with visual, overly simplistic monotony made necessary by low budgets (Zilliacus, 2016), and their unceasing similarity stands in contrast to people's innate desire for variety that supports their identity. Architect Alejandro Aravena has evolved a building strategy called 'half houses', with built-out interiors on one side and a second side left open and undeveloped, but under a finished roof for residents to complete on their own at a later time (12.3 and 12.4). One development in Chile was constructed for $7,500 each. Aravena was awarded the Pritzker Prize for his work in 2016.

Modular building approaches are also lending their economy to the construction of permanent supportive housing.

Similar approaches include:

- Modular multi-family units such as those by sLAB LI with the NYIT School of Architecture and Design and other partners (Architectural Research Centers Consortium, 2011; Dougherty, 2018).
- Prefab building companies are prevalent in Europe. United States companies include Blokable and Kasita. The architectural firm Gensler has proposed permanent supportive housing that leverages modular housing efficiencies (Handelman, 2016).

Accessory Dwelling Units (ADUs)

A primary dilemma of supportive housing projects is how they can support residents' dignity through providing a 'normal' living situation, and how such projects can achieve acceptance into neighborhoods of homeowners with a large financial stake in their properties.

Neighborhood-integrated small residential projects in the form of ADUs have long existed in the form of 'renting out the spare room' or mother-in-law cottages, but this movement is now being considered in a more systematized way (12.5 and 12.6). One local government is experimenting with incentivizing this

12.3
A half house-style supportive housing project in Chile by Alejandro Aravena of the architectural firm Elemental.

Positives	Negatives
Sense of autonomy and empowerment from users having a say in the home's design	Requires education sessions and instructional manuals for residents to complete the units
Economical to build and affordable to purchase	Residents may not complete the open side to the visual satisfaction of neighbors
Scarcity of skilled tradespersons can be mitigated	Ganged nature of homes can still exhibit monotony

12.4
Positive and negative aspects of half houses.

12.5
An accessory dwelling unit in an existing home's back yard.

12.6
Positive and
negative aspects of
Accessory Dwelling
Units.

Positives	Negatives
Sense of autonomy and empowerment from a feeling of normalcy	Requires governmental or other bodies' support to incentivize participation and to vet applicants
Provides residents an address to receive mail	May be isolating for some residents in need of mental health services
Reduces the need to concentrate people in crisis, which can exacerbate emotional and psychological issues	Some neighborhood residents may be difficult to convince

idea. The Los Angeles County Second Dwelling Unit Pilot Program (Los Angeles County Department of Regional Planning, 2017) provides homeowners a small fund to assist with construction of an ADU in their backyard in exchange for housing a person in need for a period of time. Seattle's BLOCK project is notable for its approach of one ADU per block in a back yard, which can ease NIMBY ('not in my back yard') concerns. See Chapter 13 for more discussion of the BLOCK project.

Similar approaches include the following:

- Grant-providing bodies can incentivize low-income apartment units within larger market rate apartment projects. One example is New Genesis Apartments in Los Angeles by Skid Row Housing Authority. It is better in such instances to spread the units evenly around the property than to group these units together, to reduce stigma (Aldinger, 2015).

Single Resident Occupancies and Micro-Apartments

Apartments of various designs have long been the refuge of people who have lost their homes because the former are relatively economical and convenient for services. Decades ago, single resident occupancy (SRO) rental apartments (with a shared bathroom down the hall) composed a large percentage of the housing choices for those with little economic means in cities such as New York, and the elimination of this housing type during mid-twentieth-century 'cleanup' efforts presaged a disastrous period of time for people confronted with homelessness and trying to stay off the streets (Sullivan & Burke, 2014). See Chapter 2 for further context and Chapter 13 for the potential future of this dwelling type.

Not all apartments are designed the same, and varying these designs can assist persons with specific needs. For example, open floors with partial-height wall enclosures within a larger building can create quasi-private single occupancy bedrooms with nearby bathrooms. This style has been successful for female victims of domestic violence and homelessness who are residents of Bakhita Gardens in Seattle (12.7 and 12.8).

12.7
Single resident residential pods for women in Bakhita Gardens, Seattle by Catholic Housing Services.

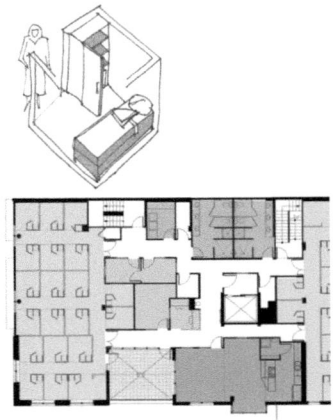

12.8
Positive and
negative aspects
of SROs or
micro-apartments.

Positives	Negatives
Support services can be nearby with proper planning	Apartments can be isolating for some with mental health challenges if support services are distant
SROs can be an economical choice for renters	Possessions can quickly overwhelm small square footages
Apartments can be a 'normal' choice that supports dignity	Acoustics can be distracting with close neighbors
Shared facilities such as community rooms and bathrooms in SROs can build relationships with neighbors	
Can provide a mailbox for connection to service and benefits	

OBSERVATIONS AND RECOMMENDATIONS

Through their great variety, the dwelling types above illustrate that finding workable, nurturing homes for people who have experienced homelessness is an exercise shaped by forces including user needs, community influences, and funding. We sense some of these ideas may not withstand the test of time, such as tiny homes. Others, such as SRO apartments, have long offered a solid, if not ideal, solution to a place and moment in someone's life.

In the totality of homelessness and architectural response, a review of litera-ture and our own design research in this area have led us to several observations on the state of things and ideas that sorely need further attention.

First, it is time to discard former limited perspectives on ways that one can dwell with dignity and to examine new designs, building technologies, and materi-als that address problems of construction costs and sterile environments. There may be better strategies suited to meeting current and future challenges that respond to informed priorities of user needs *and* those of community, which must exist in harmony with each other. The very ubiquity of homelessness in cities is forging experimental responses – some of them hostile to the problem, and others, such as those that acknowledge the tenets of trauma-informed care, supportive of people exiting homelessness for good. Chapter 13 will explore positive ideas that may be on the horizon.

Second, we observe that people most directly engage with *interior* architecture – it is in the interior that people touch things, are affected by lighting, odors, and the sense of spatiality within the spaces that they inhabit every day. The age of signature buildings that beguile on the outside and irritate on the inside is over. New attention must be paid to interior spaces informed by emerging find-ings from cognitive psychology and trauma-informed design (see Chapter 6) and the importance of cultural traditions that point to the need for the individuation of places (12.9).

If we are to effect change in people's attitudes toward support services so that they can receive the assistance they need, not only must staff and services

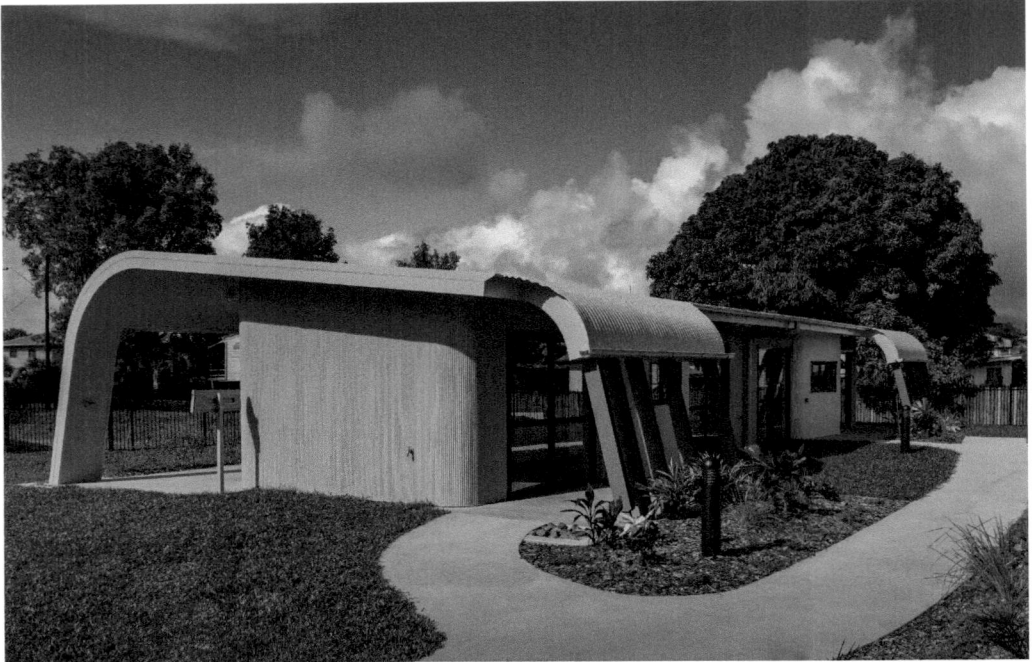

be aligned with trauma-informed care principles, but architecture, both inside and outside, must send the right cues of acceptance and organizational effectiveness, adjusting project budgets as necessary to better support intentional interior elements such as approachable furniture, dignity-supportive lighting, and spatial layouts that are intuitive to navigate. In essence, a building's design must acknowledge that people are deeply affected by place and internalize reactions that can positively or negatively affect their dignity. Relationships to space, connections to memory, and self-awareness of being in a place and belonging to a place matter (Sliwinska, 2019). Architects and designers, alongside their supportive organization clients, must commit to deep understanding of the psychological and physical factors that make up the ingredients of a conducive and supportive built environment.

12.9
The Synapse Supported Accommodation Facility in Cairns, Australia, provides dwellings for people with brain injuries. The form was influenced by cultural traditions of the Aboriginal and Torres Strait Islander people, referencing traditional rainforest dwellings.

NOTES

1. In 2020, for example, more than 25% of the United States' population of persons living homeless resided in California. Governor Gavin Newsom has sought US$1.4 billion from the California budget to build supportive housing and shelters and provide services for mental health and housing assistance (Allyn, 2020).
2. For example, both conservative residents in Westport, Connecticut, as well as liberal citizens of Berkeley, California, have exerted exclusionary controls through restrictions on zoning (Thomas, 2020) and people living in their recreational vehicles, respectively (Wilson, 2010).
3. In the words of Matthew Doherty, former executive director of the United States Interagency Council on Homelessness, "As we respond to the crisis of unsheltered homelessness, we must not repeat past mistakes of focusing only on where people will be

tonight. We must simultaneously be focused on where people can succeed in the long term – and we know that is permanent housing" (United States Interagency Council on Homelessness, 2018, p. 1).

4. Notes one author, "the downsizing isn't so much a lifestyle enhancement as it is a demotion" (Howard, 2018, p. 8).

BIBLIOGRAPHY

Aldinger, B. (2015). Florida Housing Finance Corporation. Interview conducted by J. Pable.

Alexander, L. (2019, March). Community in property: lessons from tiny homes villages. Retrieved from Law.nyu.edu: www.law.nyu.edu/sites/default/files/Community%20 in%20Property-Alexander-%20NYU%20Law.pdf

Allyn, B. (2020, January 8). Calfornia governor pushes $1.4 billion plan to tackle homelessness. Retrieved from National Public Radio: www.npr.org/2020/01/08/794687084/ california-governor-pushes-1-4-billion-plan-to-tackle-homelessness

Andrews, J. (2019, July 1). Oregon just effectively banned single-family zoning. Retrieved from Curbed: www.rbasf.com/single-post/2019/07/08/Oregon-just-effectively-banned-single-family-zoning

Architectural Research Centers Consortium. (2011). sLAB LI: sustainable affordable housing design-build for Long Island (New York Institute of Technology). Architectural Research Centers Consortium, *Newsletter*, Fall , 22–25.

Bay Area Economic Institute. (2019, April). Bay Area homelessness. Retrieved from A regional view of a regional crisis: www.bayareaeconomy.org/files/pdf/BayAreaHomelessness Report.pdf

Bernstein, F. (2005, February 6). In Santa Cruz, affordable housing without the sprawl. *New York Times*.

Centers for Disease Control and Prevention. (2020, April 21). Interim guidance for homeless service providers to plan and respond to coronavirus disease 2019 (COVID-19). Retrieved from Coronavirus Disease 2019 (COVID-19): www.cdc.gov/coronavirus/2019-ncov/community/homeless-shelters/plan-prepare-respond.html

Centers for Disease Control and Prevention. (2020, April 25). COVID-19 guidance for shared or congregate housing. Retrieved from Coronavirus Disease 2019 (COVID-19): www.cdc. gov/coronavirus/2019-ncov/community/shared-congregate-house/guidance-shared-congregate-housing.html

Corkery, M. (2018, June 13). A Macy's goes from mall mainstay to homeless shelter. *New York Times*.

Council of Economic Advisers. (2019). *The state of homelessness in America*. Washington, DC: Executive Office of the President of the United States.

Crites, J. (2018, May 22). 5 innovative homeless shelters from around the world. Retrieved from Housing Futures: https://housing-futures.org/2018/05/22/5-innovative-homeless-shelters-from-around-the-world/

Dougherty, C. (2018, June 7). Piece by piece, a factory-made answer for a housing squeeze. *New York Times*.

Dwyer, M. (2018, November 12). 2018 healthcare environment awards winner in social innovation. Retrieved from *Contract Magazine*: www.contractdesign.com/projects/ healthcare/2018-healthcare-environment-awards-winner-in-social-innovation/

Framlab. (n.d.). Shelter with dignity. Retrieved from Framlab: www.framlab.com/homed

Fuller, T. (2019, October 21). As homelessness surges in California, so does a backlash. *New York Times*.

Handelman, A. (2016). Designing innovative solutions for chronic homelessness. Retrieved from GensleronCities: www.gensleron.com/cities/2018/4/26/designing-innovative-solutions-for-chronic-homelessness.html

Hatch, J., & Hobbes, M. (2019, August 26). The 'incredibly dangerous' solution Sacramento has for homelessness. *Huffington Post*.

Howard, M. (2018, May 22). You can't just put homeless people in tiny houses. Retrieved from *The Outline*: https://theoutline.com/post/4639/tiny-house-affordable-housing-adu-boston-portland

Lerner, J. (2019, August). Home away from no home. *Landscape Architecture Magazine*, 69–75.

Los Angeles County Department of Regional Planning. (2017). Second dwelling unit (accessory dwelling unit) pilot program. Retrieved from Los Angeles County Department of Regional Planning: http://planning.lacounty.gov/secondunitpilot

Mairs, J. (2015, August 19). James Furzer to crowdfund parasitic sleeping pods for London's homeless. Retrieved from *Dezeen*: www.dezeen.com/2015/08/19/james-furzer-crowdfund-parasitic-sleeping-pods-london-homeless-indiegogo/

Malson, S., Martin, C., Rogers, D., & Power, E. (2020, March 22). Why housing evictions must be suspended to defend us against coronavirus. Retrieved from *The Conversation*: https://theconversation.com/why-housing-evictions-must-be-suspended-to-defend-us-against-coronavirus-134148

Manjoo, F. (2019, May 22). America's cities are unliveable. Blame wealthy liberals. *New York Times*.

Nguyen, T. (2019, July 2). Trump blames homelessness on 'liberals', threatens to 'intercede'. *Vanity Fair*.

Sliwinska, M. (2019, March). The spirit of public space: embodied through writing and movement. *Journal of Interior Design*, *44*(1), 13–27.

Smith, M. (2018, October 16). Why a private landowner is fighting to keep the homeless on his property. *New York Times*.

Stewart, N. (2020, April 13). It's a 'time bomb': 23 die as virus hits packed homeless shelters. *New York Times*.

Sullivan, B., & Burke, J. (2014, May 6). Single-room occupancy housing in New York City: the origins and dimensions of a crisis. *CUNY Law Review*, *17*(1), 901–931.

TEDGlobal 2014. (2014, October). My architectural philosophy? Bring the community into the process. Retrieved from TED: www.ted.com/talks/alejandro_aravena_my_architectural_philosophy_bring_the_community_into_the_process

Tempest, G. (2017, June 2). What no one ever tells you about tiny homes. *New York Times*.

Thomas, J. (2020, May 22). Separated by design: how some of America's richest towns fight affordable housing. Retrieved from ProPublica: Propublica.com

United Nations Department of Economic and Social Affairs. (2020, March 9). Social inclusion. Retrieved from First-ever United Nations Resolution on Homelessness: www.un.org/development/desa/dspd/

United States Interagency Council on Homelessness. (2018, May 25). Caution is needed when considering 'sanctioned encampments' or 'safe zones'. Retrieved from United States Interagency Council on Homelessness: www.usich.gov/tools-for-action/caution-is-needed-when-considering-sanctioned-encampments-or-safe-zones/#:~:text=Caution%20is%20Needed%20When%20Considering,Encampments%E2%80%9D%20or%20%E2%80%9CSafe%20Zones%E2%80%9D&text=Communities%20are%20working%

Valdez, R. (2020, April 1). COVID-19 and eviction: government action uneven across the country. Retrieved from Forbes: www.forbes.com/sites/rogervaldez/2020/04/01/covid-19-and-eviction-uneven-actions-across-the-country/#6ba4c3653d05

Wen, C., Hudak, P., & Hwang, S. (2007, July). Homeless people's perceptions of welcomeness and unwelcomeness in healthcare encounters. *Journal of General Internal Medicine*, *22*(7), 1011–1017.

Wilson, S. (2010, May 24). Berkeley loves its sanctuary label, but a housing crisis is testing its liberal values. *Washington Post*.

Zilliacus, A. (2016). Half a house builds a whole community: Elemental's controversial social housing. Retrieved from ArchDaily: www.archdaily.com/797779/half-a-house-builds-a-whole-community-elementals-controversial-social-housing

TEACHING MATERIALS

Lauren Trujillo

Key Terms

Accessory dwelling units (ADUs)
Half house style
Modular building/modular family units

Single resident occupancies/
   micro-apartments
Tiny house communities/intentional
   co-housing communities

Discussion Questions

1. In this chapter, the author states, "There may be better strategies suited to meeting current and future challenges that respond to informed priorities of user needs *and* those of community, which must exist in harmony with each other." Is there a housing solution described in this chapter that you feel would be most successful in meeting these needs and challenges in your community? If so, which solution would work best? If not, describe why these solutions would not work. Then, propose and describe an alternative solution.
2. Would you be willing to incorporate any of these housing solutions on your property where you live? On your block? On your street? If there are challenges to accepting these solutions for you, describe these challenges. What steps could you and your neighbors take to personally overcome these challenges? Do you think there would be a personal benefit in doing so?
3. At the end of the chapter, the author states, "In essence, a building's design must acknowledge that people are deeply affected by place and internalize reactions that can positively or negatively affect their dignity. Relationships to space, connections to memory, and self-awareness of being in a place and belonging to a place matter." Have you ever felt a deep connection to a place in the way that the author describes? Do you feel there is an intrinsic value to you (or to an individual not experiencing homelessness) to facilitate this connection for others?

13 Blue Sky Thinking

Yelena McLane & Jill Pable

This final chapter offers an opportunity for speculation, an activity seldom undertaken with regard to architectural choices for persons experiencing trauma. We might ask, "what elements would the perfect program or built environment for unhoused persons include, and what good might it do?" Drawn from the ideas and inspirations of stakeholders – including directors, case managers, designers, and unhoused persons themselves – a series of ideal, mind's eye portraits emerge in this chapter. Although budgets, politics, and stereotyped thinking will always be factors, taking a moment to muse about the possibilities unobstructed by these barriers may help us to realize, if only through a pastiche of texts and images, how the most thoughtful and ambitious projects might look. In turn, such blue sky thinking may be the starting point for more practical conversations that shift the terrain from "what can we do with what we have" to "what might the possibilities be?"

OBSERVATIONS ON PROBLEMS, NEEDS AND NEW PRIORITIES

Before examining inspirational ideas, however, we offer a series of brief but broad observations on architectural design for people experiencing crisis. This loosely holds together as a list of reactions to current programs, an acknowledgement of needs, and also recommendations for a reassessment of priorities for designing and building.

A Building's Messages Need to Be the Right Ones

First, we know that architecture has the power to embody and reinforce hierarchies that impede individuals' abilities to retain their dignity, and that poor design can exacerbate this problem (Holmes, 2020). We need a reassessment of how the perceptions people hold of one another perpetuate stereotypes, manifest mistaken assumptions, and stand in the way of progress. Such dynamics are often reflected in built environment choices. For example, 'shelters' have long been perceived (and often accurately so) as vast halls with bunk beds, overflowing with people, none of whom have any privacy. It is little wonder that many traumatized individuals use shelters only as a last resort, even risking their physical safety on the streets to avoid them. Design is difficult because it embodies emotional as well as rational, functional values (Holmes, 2020). What emotional value are designers and support organizations assigning when the psychological process of envisioning oneself moving into a shelter is itself a point of trauma? Designers can begin to create more successful spaces only if they are prepared to see the end user as the client, and to set as a primary, practical goal the preservation or rebuilding of dignity. Spotlighting thoughtful programs and practitioners that model creativity, innovation, and client-centeredness is one way to gather insights from which to proceed.

Better Contact Documentation Can Match Client to Shelter Type More Effectively

To better understand what types of housing and how much of them are needed, designers should ideally be equipped with a range of information, including *better real-time tracking* of unhoused persons to assess potential user demographics and service demand. One model of this data-centered approach is the Built for Zero national initiative to end homelessness, which developed through a partnership between a non-profit, Community Solutions (2020), and the Tableau Foundation, a philanthropic arm of Tableau Software (Peters, 2019). Whenever an unhoused person contacts a supportive services representative (at any time and for whatever need), individual information is gathered, and the system updates to reflect the client's current situation. Information is shared between providers, allowing them to coordinate interventions, including finding permanent housing. The goal is to help communities with reducing homelessness to zero and maintaining it at that (Bornstein, 2018).

Architecture Must Match, Support, and Serve Policies and Procedures Well

For projects to be successful, they should be *incorporated* into the existing fabric of the city and diverse in the ways in which they serve their clients, learn from their clients, and recognize and respond to both current necessities and enduring needs. Some of the best architectural details we have observed emerged from clients themselves. A thoughtful, client-centered service will go to the people and serve them where they are found. One such example is the City of Refuge Program in Atlanta, which states, "our process takes place under one roof in the most dangerous zip code in Atlanta. The needs are great, but when like-minded community members, organizations, and volunteers partner together, we are able to see amazing things happen" (City of Refuge, 2020). City of Refuge provides food, healthcare, vocational training, low-barrier bridge housing for families, childcare and child development services, and safe houses for women. Comprehensive solutions assembled under one roof can enhance safety and impart a spirit of support by reflecting the recognition that people have diverse needs and may require help with meeting those needs.

Thoughtful, Responsive Architecture and Cost-Effectiveness Are Not Mutually Exclusive

Buildings and programs cost money, and we know that we cannot afford all that we want. Are good design and cost-cutting contradictory goals?

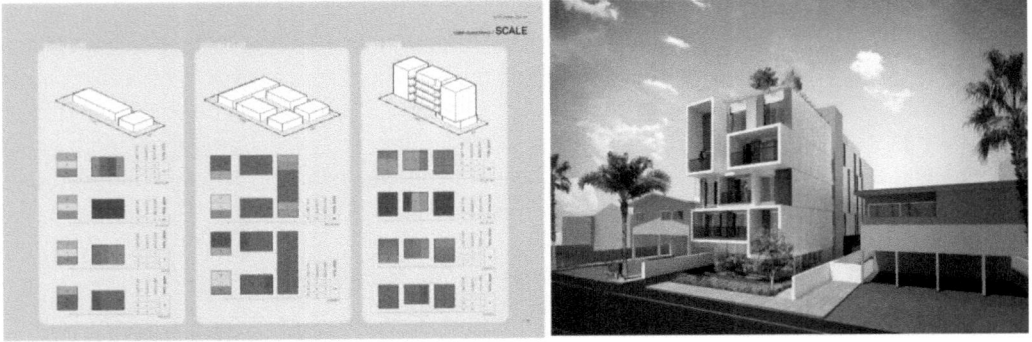

Good design thinking can help developers frame the problems they are solving, question their assumptions, and embolden them to try the new and unproven. It can also help policymakers create a regulatory environment that actually allows these ideas to scale. Families – particularly in low-income communities – shouldn't have to sacrifice good design for affordability.

(Swenson, 2018, para. 10)

13.1
Nest toolkit by
Brooks + Scarpa
(drawings by
Brooks + Scarpa).

One option is to build more compact and economical housing using newer technologies and construction methods. In 2019, in partnership with Community Corp.[1] and Plant Prefab's Design Studio,[2] Brooks + Scarpa developed Nest, a prefabricated module toolkit consisting of five rooms, a kitchen, bathrooms, and shared spaces. Nest modules can be assembled in a variety of configurations and sizes and stacked up to five stories high (Brooks + Scarpa, n.d., 13.1). Construction is quick and adaptable to both on- and off-grid settings. Modular buildings such as these also reflect an intention to locate housing solutions within existing communities to accelerate social reintegration and leverage existing service networks and support structures at lower costs.

Rapid advances in 3D printing robotics, software, and materials are introducing new, lower-cost options into the markets. Although only in pilot programs as of the date of this book, 3D printed homes of up to 2,000 square feet are popping up in communities such as Austin, Texas. In partnership with Mobile Loaves & Fishes, a construction technology company named ICON is creating 400-square-foot homes by using a large 3D on-site printer that forms walls with a viscous concrete solution. The homes, composed of one bedroom, one bath, a full kitchen, living room, and a large porch, will be constructed for formerly unhoused persons at the Community First! Village (ICON, 2020).

Homelessness Is Not Only an Urban Issue

Blue sky thinking must take into account the rising incidences of homelessness in rural communities. Among other leaders in the field, Andrew Freear, director of Auburn University's Rural Studio, has been leading the charge to disrupt the convention of city-based mass housing. The Rural Studio's $20K House Project is an endeavor to design and build a high-quality rural home for just $20,000 in hard costs (Bourdeau, 2018). Researchers derived this dollar figure from what a low-income family could readily afford in monthly payments over a 30-year mortgage. Through trial and error, Freear and his team have developed several strong design solutions that meet this criterion. In test projects, as is often the case, local construction firms chose to interpret the Rural Studio's detailed blueprints as a sort of helpful guide, which resulted in a near doubling of project costs (Swenson, 2018). To deliver the low-cost homes that it designed, the team is now at work solving the real problem: how to design a communication system that motivates builders to follow their plans.

Thoughtful Architecture Respects Cultural Traditions

Innovative designers are also attuned to the importance of applying the concepts of social space and architectural anthropology to their work (Grant, Greenop, Refiti, & Glenn, 2018). The *Indigenous behavior setting approach* articulated by Paul Memmott is one such example. This potentially therapeutic architectural practice "assists with transformation back into a form of normative Aboriginal lifestyle incorporating salient dimensions of traditional personhood" (Memmott, 2015, p. 71). Recognizing that behavior patterns emerge and are reinforced by spatially interrelated physical settings, and that traditional lifeways may be repressed by poor or inconsiderate design, the conscientious practitioner proceeds with the intent to reestablish a "synomorphic" relationship, or close "fit" between human behavior and the physical and temporal environment (Memmott, 2015; see also Memmott & Keys, 2017; Memmott, 2018)).

EXPERT OPINION: PAUL MEMMOTT ON APPROACHES TO DESIGNING HOUSING FOR ABORIGINAL POPULATIONS

Paul Memmott is a professor at the University of Queensland School of Architecture and Institute for Social Science Research and the director of the Aboriginal Environments Research Centre. Dr. Memmott is the author of over 300 publications on a range of topics related to Indigenous populations, including well-being, homelessness, community planning, and housing. He also has extensive experience in Aboriginal land rights claims, native title claims, and associated issues since 1980.

Aboriginal Homelessness

In Aboriginal Australia, the big three drivers of homelessness are *residential mobility*, *crowding*, and *family violence*. We must understand all three in detail before planning for emergency housing or permanent housing for members of these communities.

Residential Mobility

There is high residential mobility among Aboriginal people, when people move around regularly between residences, which demographers call "circular mobility" (Birdsall-Jones, Corunna, Turner, Smart, & Shaw, 2010; Taylor & Bell, 2004). Some people from more traditional communities choose to have outdoor or itinerant lifestyles because they maintain ancestral social and cultural practices. This itinerancy is not, as such, a manifestation of a problem (Memmott, Long, Chambers, & Spring, 2003). Another type of mobility, which is often termed "dysfunctional" mobility, is the result of personal problems (personal identity crises, alcohol or substance abuse), social instability, or a lack of personal safety or adequate emotional support in the home. Regardless of the causes, when persons go to a new residence, kinship rules come into play, such as avoidance behaviors, and new spatial requirements are activated. People now living together must reorganize their space uses to accommodate one another. If it is difficult or impossible for occupants to enact customary avoidance behaviors in a house or a building, the occupants may experience stress and trauma (Fantin, 2003; Reser, 1979).

Crowding

The problem with census and government assessment of crowding is that these entities use what we call "density models" (Australian Institute of Health and Welfare, n.d.). If there are more than 4.5 people per bedroom in a house, it is considered crowded. According to the social science definition of crowding, in addition to density characteristics, persons should experience notable stress (Gifford, 2007). That stress can come from violation of culture-based rules, such as Aboriginal avoidance rules – for example, avoidance behavior between a mother-in-law and a son-in-law. This relationship requires a social distance, such that they may not be able to be in the same room or car (Central Land Council, n.d.). We need to understand a different construct of crowding and a different construct of privacy – as *cultural* constructs. Memmott's research team conducted a survey in an outback town using Aboriginal researchers and found an average of 10 people per house, with some homes housing up to 30 individuals. Because the way the census data were gathered, they did not capture this dynamic transformation of movements of people and households.

Family or Domestic Violence

Rates of violence are disproportionately high among Indigenous communities. Family violence may be anything from spousal assault to alcohol-related violence, gang violence, suicide or self-injury, or sexual assault. It affects large numbers of Indigenous people, especially women, children, and youths. This in turn catalyzes 'dysfunctional' mobility. It is a major challenge to understand how institutional settings may be designed to help address related social problems.

Culturally Appropriate Design and Aboriginal-Led Design Process

When designing for Indigenous communities or populations, stakeholders and designers need to prioritize cross-cultural approaches and culturally appropriate design. It is difficult to produce a good design unless you work with the service delivery staff, and the idea here is to reform the style of service delivery together with design improvements. The process should begin with Indigenous thinking about program management and service methods, integrated with kinship rule systems and environmental and social spatial design practices within the community. The latter calls for understanding relationships between groups, between families, between related or unrelated individuals, and a real desire to understand customary behavior types or practices ranging from intimacy to respect, joking, avoidance, and how these might manifest in space. Knowledge of the cultural landscape is another important ingredient. There is great significance embedded in Aboriginal names, places, or regions. The principle of exteriority in design is also crucial – encompassing landscaping, climate, and bush food production – into which a seasonal calendar may be incorporated.

Structures

The structures in which Aboriginal persons live often look quite conventional, but there are often important differences. In the 1970s and 80s, the standard response to housing was to ask what a "normal" non-Aboriginal person would ask for, because there might have been shame or inferiority associated with something different. The challenge was to make it look like a conventional house that did not work like a conventional house. There was a lot of subtlety required in consultation and design. A western typology might have been used as the starting point, but the way it was put together reflected an Aboriginal way of thinking and behaving.

Example: Jimaylya Topsy Harry Centre

Jimaylya Topsy Harry Centre is a transitional accommodation center for Indigenous people in Mount Isa. The center is run by Aboriginal managers and offers culturally appropriate care.

There are several types of housing, each of which was designed to help Indigenous persons to find culturally and spatially appropriate accommodations, including a camping option – a tin shed with low partitions to simulate outdoor sleeping in a semi-enclosed environment. There are also emergency men's and women's dormitory accommodations. Residents may transition into house-like settings to learn or practice life management skills for a period, which may then lead to fast-tracking on the wait list for permanent rental housing in the area. The center also organizes training – cooking classes, budget classes, or basic life skills classes – subjects that that people often take for granted. There were not any capital "A" architects involved in the design. It was basically prefabricated accommodation units, incrementally installed over time.

In order to confront serious, widespread social problems such as alcoholism and binge drinking in a measured way, the organizers decided to allow people to come in and drink alcohol in a controlled environment. The drinking sessions are regulated, and, if people do not want to have their session closed down, they will control their behaviors and the behavior of others. This has actually led to moderation in drinking. So, it has led to a change in behavior, which works very well for both the residents and the management. This program is the first of its kind in Australia. People have to go through medical tests regularly, and, if any serious health conditions arise, they lose their liberty to drink.

To summarize, an Indigenous approach to management, kinship rules, and spatial arrangements are three key ingredients to creating a culturally appropriate environment in which interventions may potentially lead to beneficial behavior changes and a better quality of life and well-being.

Some Promising New Directions in Built Environment Design

At its root, designing for homelessness is creating the setting that assists people to end their state of trauma, maintain their dignity, and ultimately to secure permanent shelter. Effective programs and projects often exhibit like characteristics: acknowledging the individual's physical, psychological, and budgetary needs, and evincing a willingness to work with the surrounding neighborhood's concerns and limitations. Such projects recognize that affordability and accessibility are integral to overall client wellness. They move away from prior assumptions about facility sizes, concepts of "deserving" persons and disqualifying behaviors, and exclusionary zoning practices. They recognize the importance of meeting people where they are, psychologically speaking, with particular regard to the degree of their social alienation, their willingness to accept services, and their coping mechanisms, including substance abuse. They acknowledge the differences in clients' degrees of helplessness, their abilities to assist themselves, and the extent to which autonomy and freedom, even within the controlled environment of a shelter, day center, or multi-service complex, are key to their self-perception and health.

A number of novel housing types have emerged in recent years, each of which embody the principles that we have espoused throughout this book. The three types detailed below represent potentially positive directions for the future and reinforce how designing for unhoused persons can and should:

- Encourage persons who have been disenfranchised owing to crisis and trauma to view permanent shelter as a positive, workable solution for their circumstances;

- Support trauma-informed care principles and empower clients through buildings that manifest user choice and autonomy;
- Acknowledge that smaller group settings are better than large ones, and that habitation clusters reduce anonymity and help build a sense of community;
- Employ housing and building styles that support psychological cues of security and familiarity using forms, colors, and surface treatments to reduce the stigmas associated with bland "institutional" facilities;
- Seek and value harmony with neighbors, the natural environment, and the cultural conditions that affect the project;
- Acknowledge the great diversity of unhoused persons and their distinctive identities.

TRANSITION VILLAGES

Transition villages are a cluster of buildings grouped within a permeable walled enclosure offering outside–inside accommodations and support services including dining, bathrooms, social services, and mail.

- *Examples*: Homeless Transition Village (Luoni, 2019); Pinellas Hope Camp (Green, 2009).
- *Intended users*: Persons that avoid shelters, live on their own outside or in otherwise compromised places, and are cautious of traditional house forms, but who need services. Persons that have to relocate periodically owing to employment or family circumstances, or who prefer itinerancy for personal reasons. Persons who may fear for their personal safety or the safety of their children or pets. Families that want to stay together and persons who prize their autonomy but prefer communal living (Price, 2009).
- *Geographical location*: suburban or rural; possibly urban.
- *Alternative to*: informal encampments, street living, living in vehicles.
- *Description*: Transition villages are an affordable, shelter-first solution (Luoni, 2019). Open, sheltered areas or hard tents offer clients options for those cautious of traditional walled dwellings. Electrical, sewer, and water services are available, and a building with a community porch for safe cooking provides a covered dining hall and bathrooms. Services and managerial oversight are present. We suggest that maximum occupancy be limited to 20 people to reduce a sense of intimidation among newcomers. Transition villages may be suitable for specific identity groups, especially adolescents or members of the LGBTQ community who may face particular dangers and discrimination in traditional shelter settings.
- *Advantages and hurdles*: Transitional villages capture many of the most attractive qualities of tiny homes and independent group camps, including freedom of movement. This form acknowledges, enables, and may even promote an informal, transient lifestyle, while also prioritizing community building, which supports self-esteem. This form may be an acceptable first stop to persons who may otherwise be reluctant to seek services and return to permanent housing. Zoning restrictions could limit opportunities for projects of this type in denser suburban or urban settings.

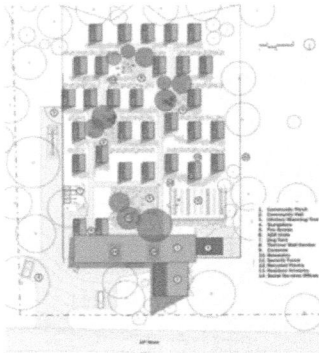

- *Scaling up*: A network of transitional villages could be established to support individuals who regularly move for employment or other reasons. These venues could be searchable on the internet or by means of a smartphone app. Residents could provide labor in lieu of rent by contributing their time to maintenance, gardening, or cottage industries.

13.2
Site plan of a hypothetical transitional village and community porch with kitchen and social services office.

POD ACCOMMODATIONS

Residential pods are a building containing large rooms of partially private bed areas with common bathrooms and other supportive spaces.

- *Example*: Economic pressure and the allure of city living have given rise to "pod living" options for young professionals. The company PodShare has created shared accommodations for travelers and workers at market rates, reacting to the rapid rise in housing costs in urban areas (PodShare, 2020).
- *Intended for*: Urban dwellers seeking affordable, safe, and flexible accommodations at lower costs than hotels or apartments. Historically, these have been most attractive to single men and women, day laborers, factory workers, visitors to the region, seniors living alone, persons with disabilities, and persons of lower means who want to live in cities.
- *Geographic location*: Urban or suburban areas, owing to their typically multistory form.
- *Alternative to*: Single resident occupancy (SRO) apartments, a fully or partially enclosed apartment with a shared bathroom. This boarding house form comprised a large percentage of worker housing in large cities until its elimination in the late twentieth century. No systemic replacement emerged.
- *Description*: Pod accommodations have single beds in communal rooms with shared kitchens and bathrooms. On-site features often include kitchens, laundry, housekeeping services, and secure storage for personal belongings. Interestingly, current market-rate pods often offer less walled privacy than historic SRO forms. Lengths of stay vary from nightly to long-term.

13.3
Market-rate
PodShare
development in San
Francisco.

- *Advantages and hurdles*: With client vetting, proper quality, and economic controls in place, pods could offer physical safety, self-determination, privacy, the ability to come and go without constraint, proximity to work, and access to city amenities and social services (Aberg-Riger, 2018). Sleeping spaces without walls, on the other hand, may introduce concerns about privacy, acoustics, interpersonal disagreements, and potentially inappropriate behaviors. If not handled well, keeping these urban dwelling options affordable could lead to diminished construction quality and harm a neighborhood's reputation, the same issue that led to the elimination of most SRO buildings 60 years ago. That said, entrepreneurs are recognizing the potential for this type of housing for clients who cannot afford market-rate rents. PodShare has announced the formation of a non-profit organization called PodShare for Social Good, whose objective is to raise funds to place sleeping pods in underused commercial buildings (PodShare, 2020).

- *Scaling up*: PodShare and similar organizations are building networks of pod living locations that allow people to move between them easily. National or global networks of locations could further expand this flexibility, accommodating persons who prefer to move in response to work, climatic conditions, or for other reasons. We also see opportunities for pod-style living for family units, and also niche pod communities for groups including members of the LGBTQ community, seniors, veterans, or persons with disabilities. Locating social service providers nearby or on-site would be important for some of these user groups.

DETACHED ACCESSORY DWELLING UNIT CLUSTER SYSTEMS

Detached accessory dwelling units (DADUs) are stand-alone, externally accessed living quarters provided on the site of a single-family dwelling.

- *Example*: The BLOCK Project in Seattle (Lerner, 2019; The BLOCK Project, 2020).
- *Intended for*: Persons exiting homelessness in conjunction with homeowners seeking to participate in solutions by leveraging backyards to host DADUs. Vetting of participants (both host and residents) to achieve compatibility is important for success. BLOCK homes (DADUs) are integrated in backyards throughout Seattle neighborhoods. Residents have agency in how long they stay and can define success themselves with support from neighbors. Single adults and small families are eligible. This housing form provides physical safety needs, self-determination, privacy, and social integration. DADU integration into established neighborhoods increases density, supports cross-class integration, provides an opportunity to live/work in the neighborhood of choice, and socially enriches hosts, neighbors, and residents.
- *Geographic location*: Suburban and urban.
- *Alternative to*: Tent cities, living in vehicles, traditional transitional shelters, segregated housing.
- *Description*: The BLOCK Project's approach emphasizes increased proximity and social connection among neighbors with differing backgrounds throughout Seattle. The program provides support in the form of neighbor and host orientations, social events, educational programs, and partnerships with social service agencies. BLOCK Homes are designed to achieve Living Building Challenge certification, providing healthy environments built with sustainable, toxin-free materials, and are constructed largely by community volunteers under the guidance and supervision of BLOCK Project staff. Some argue that DADUs preserve community architectural styles. Homes provide full-time access, whereas shelters or similar congregate living facilities often require guests to exit with their belongings each day around sunrise. This usually puts the displaced overnight guests on the streets around the same time permanent residents in the neighborhood are leaving for work and school. Integrated housing through DADUs blunts objections on the basis of losing neighborhood character (Lerner, 2019).
- *Advantages and hurdles*: The idea of renting rooms within an established home has a long history. DADUs leverage a home's backyard and provide more privacy between the homeowners and the DADU resident than a room inside a larger home. Attendance to neighbors' needs and expectations, combined with the decentralization of persons in crisis, can create living conditions less prone to trauma, but also contribute to isolation for some. Proximate social service providers and community support are important to holistic models of success.
- *Scaling up*: The BLOCK Project's strategy could be extended to other cities, systematizing a network of DADUs coupled with a vetting process to gauge clients' and hosts' suitability and increase the chances of success. Incentives for potential DADU hosts such as tax credits are being explored in pilot programs (Los Angeles County Department of Regional Planning, 2017).

13.4
The Seattle BLOCK Project detached accessory dwelling units are stand-alone micro-apartments in the backyard of an established home.

13.5
Interior of BLOCK Home – detached accessory dwelling unit.

CONCLUSION

The organizers of the 2020 Venice Architectural Biennale recently posed the question, "how will we live together?" Alongside them, we urge the special examination of the word 'we'. On any given day, all of us are living in communities that include hundreds, thousands, or even tens of thousands of unhoused persons. These are persons for whom architecture often means only a surface to rest against, or a shadow to sit beneath. For far too long, thoughtfully designed buildings have been for those who are 'normal' and can afford such amenities. Homelessness has been a 'social problem' that brands its victims as outcasts, criminals, or degenerates. The very premise of 'designing for unhoused persons' was unheard of. Intentional design fully nourished with time to think, funds that permit places to be built that move beyond subsistence, and decision-making that prioritizes human well-being and potential have not been the way of things.

Housing is a human right, housing is healthcare, and housing is how we signify respect to all members of our society (and, we might add, day centers and other support spaces are similarly critical components of an enlightened culture). The word 'design' implies thought, consideration, and user-centeredness. It implies efficiency, but not at the expense of effectiveness. Designs may not always be good, but good design can make the world better.

We began this book by asking, "For whom has housing design not been working? Whose world would be made measurably better by housing designed especially for them?" There are, of course, many answers to these questions. The readiest answer, however, is persons with no housing at all – for whom, we further argue, thoughtful design has perhaps the most to offer. We hope that, through the ideas, insights, and examples collected in this book, the number of such persons will diminish over time, and that we all will find ourselves living in communities in which housing for every person is permanent, supportive, and well designed.

NOTES

1. Community Corp. is a non-profit organization that restores, builds, and manages affordable housing in Santa Monica, California (Community Corp., 2020).
2. Plant Prefab is a design and construction company that manufactures high-quality prefabricated modules for single and multi-family homes (Plant Prefab, 2020).

BIBLIOGRAPHY

Aberg-Riger, A. (2018, February 22). When America's basic housing unit was a bed, not a house. *Bloomberg News*. Retrieved from www.bloomberg.com/news/articles/2018-02-22/the-rise-and-fall-of-the-american-sro

Auckland Council & Mana Whenua. (2020). Auckland design manual. Retrieved from www.aucklanddesignmanual.co.nz/design-subjects/maori-design/te_aranga_principles#/design-subjects/maori-design/te_aranga_principles/guidance/about

Australian Institute of Health and Welfare. (n.d.). Canadian national occupancy standard. Retrieved from https://meteor.aihw.gov.au/content/index.phtml/itemId/386254

Birdsall-Jones, C., Corunna, V., Turner, N., Smart, G., & Shaw, W. (2010). Indigenous homelessness, final report. Melbourne: Australian Housing and Urban Research Institute

(AHURI), Western Australia Research Centre. Retrieved from www.ahuri.edu.au/sea rch?collection=AHURI&query=Birdsall-Jones%2C+C.%2C+Corunna%2C+V.%2C+T urner%2C+N.%2C+Smart%2C+G.+%26+Shaw%2C+W

Bornstein, D. (2018, June 5). A growing drive to get homelessness to zero. *The New York Times*. Retrieved from www.nytimes.com/2018/06/05/opinion/homelessness-built-for-zero.html

Bourdeau, C. (2018, July 10). Auburn University Rural Studio's 20K initiative: the key to affordable home ownership. Retrieved from https://ocm.auburn.edu/newsroom/news_articles/2018/07/101004-rural-studio-20k.php

Brooks+Scarpa. (n.d.). The Nest Toolkit. Retrieved from https://brooksscarpa.com/the-nest-toolkit

Central Land Council. (n.d.). Kinship and skin names. Retrieved from www.clc.org.au/articles/info/aboriginal-kinship

City of Refuge. (2020). Retrieved from Programs & Partners: https://cityofrefugeatl.org/programs

Community Corp. (2020). Who we are. Retrieved from Community Corporation of Santa Monica: www.communitycorp.org/who-we-are/

Community Solutions. (2020). Built for zero. Retrieved from www.joinbuiltforzero.org/

Fantin, S. (2003). Housing Aboriginal culture in North-East Arnhem Land. Ph.D. thesis, St Lucia: Aboriginal Environments Research Centre, School of Geography Planning and Architecture, University of Queensland.

Gifford, R. (2007). *Environmental psychology: principles and practice* (4th ed.). Colville, WA: Optimal Books.

Grant, E., Greenop, K., Refiti, A. L., & Glenn, D. J. (2018). *The handbook of contemporary indigenous architecture*. Singapore: Springer. Retrieved from https://books.google.com/books?id=rS9iDwAAQBAJ&printsec=frontcover&source=gbs_ge_summary_r&cad=0#v=onepage&q&f=false

Green, R. (2009, June 9). Florida tent city offers hope to homeless. Retrieved August 2020, from Reuters: www.reuters.com/article/us-usa-homeless-tentcity/florida-tent-city-offers-hope-to-homeless-idUSTRE55G01Z20090617#:~:text=The%20Pinellas%20Hope%20camp%2C%20250,it%20opened%20two%20years%20ago

Holmes, K. (2020, October 3). How bad design perpetuates harmful stereotypes. Retrieved from Medium.com: https://medium.com/s/story/how-bad-design-perpetuates-harmful-stereotypes-759c0e4ba2b3

ICON. (2020, March 6). ICON Delivers Series of 3D-Printed Homes for Homeless in Austin. Retrieved from www.iconbuild.com/updates/icon-delivers-series-of-3d-printed-homes-for-homeless

Lerner, J. (2019, August). Home away from no home. *Landscape Architecture Magazine*, 68–75. Retrieved from https://landscapearchitecturemagazine.org/2019/08/27/home-away-from-no-home/

Los Angeles County Department of Regional Planning. (2017). Second dwelling unit (accessory dwelling unit) pilot program. Retrieved from Los Angeles County Department of Regional Planning: http://planning.lacounty.gov/secondunitpilot

Luoni, S. (2019). Permitting a homeless transition village: transactions between the informal and the formal. *The Plan*, *4*(1), 137–157.

Memmott, P. (2015). Differing relations to tradition amongst Australian Indigenous homeless people. *Traditional Dwellings and Settlements Review*, *26*(2), 59–72. Retrieved from http://iaste.org/category/tdsr/page/2/

Memmott, P. (2018). The re-invention of the "behavior setting" in the new indigenous architecture. In E. Grant, K. Greenop, A. Refiti, & D. Glenn, *The handbook of contemporary indigenous architecture* (pp. 831–868). Singapore: Springer. Retrieved from https://books.google.com/books?id=rS9iDwAAQBAJ&printsec=frontcover&source=gbs_ge_summary_r&cad=0#v=onepage&q&f=false

Memmott, P., & Keys, C. (2017). The emergence of an architectural anthropology in Aboriginal Australia: the work of the Aboriginal Environments Research Centre. *Architectural Theory Review, 21*(2), 218–236. doi:10.1080/13264826.2017.1316752

Memmott, P., Long, S., Chambers, C., & Spring, F. (2003). *Categories of Indigenous "homeless" people and good practice responses to their needs.* Melbourne: Australian Housing and Urban Research Institute, Queensland Research Centre.

Peters, A. (2019, March 11). 3 cities in the U.S. have ended chronic homelessness: here's how they did it. Retrieved from FastCompany: www.fastcompany.com/90316607/3-cities-in-the-u-s-have-ended-chronic-homelessness-heres-how-they-did-it

Plant Prefab. (2020). Company. Retrieved from www.plantprefab.com/about

PodShare. (2020). As Angelenos we must do our part. Retrieved from Podshare.com: www.podshare.com/use-the-pods-to-house-the-homeless

Price, M. (2009, December). More than shelter. *Monitor, 40*(11), 58.

Reser, J. (1979). A matter of control: Aboriginal housing circumstances in remote communities and settlements. In M. Heppell, *A Black reality: Aboriginal camps and housing in remote Australia* (pp. 62–95). Canberra, Australia: Australian Institute of Aboriginal Studies.

Swenson, K. (2018, May 9). CityViews: we need innovative designs – and open minds – to solve the housing shortage. Retrieved from https://citylimits.org/2018/05/09/cityviews-we-need-innovative-designs-and-open-minds-to-solve-the-housing-shortage/

Taylor, J., & Bell, M. (2004). *Population mobility and indigenous peoples in Australasia and North America.* London: Routledge.

The Block Project. (2020). I gave a little part of my back yard and it opened a much bigger world. Retrieved from the Block Project: www.the-block-project.org/

TEACHING MATERIALS

Lauren Trujillo

Key Terms

Accessory dwelling units

Avoidance behaviors

Circular mobility

Cultural constructs of privacy and
crowding

Dysfunctional mobility

Exteriority in design

Modular buildings

Pod accommodations

Synomorphic

Transition villages

Discussion Questions

1. Take a moment to do some blue sky thinking of your own, perhaps related to your industry or area of specialty. What additions would you make to this chapter?

2. Reflect on the architectural typologies introduced in this chapter (transition villages, pod accommodations, and ADU cluster systems). Would any of them work in your neighborhood? Why or why not? Which typologies would you prefer to inhabit if you found yourself experiencing homelessness?

3. In the expert opinion section of this chapter, Paul Memmott proposes that privacy and crowding are cultural constructs. How many people could you share a room with before you would feel crowded or that your privacy was not being maintained? What factors might cause you to increase the number of people with whom you could share a room? What avoidance behaviors might you incorporate to help you tolerate sharing a space or room with more people?

Credits

6.3   Summarized by the authors from multiple sources: Card, Taylor, & Piatkowski, 2018; Center for Health Design, 2018; Farrell & Weeks, 2019; Hopper, Bassuk, & Olivet, 2010; Trauma and Justice Strategic Initiative, 2014

6.4   Images by Jonathan Farrell. Architecture by Duncan Wisniewski Architecture.

6.5   Images by Jonathan Farrell

7.1   Image by Jill Pable

7.2   Architecture by Holland Harvey Architects. Photography by Nicholas Worley

7.3   Table courtesy of Yelena McLane

7.4   Adapted from Shepley & Pasha, 2013, pp. 18–19

7.5   Image courtesy of Jill Pable

7.6   Image courtesy of Jill Pable

7.7   Image courtesy of Norix Furniture

7.8   Image courtesy of Jill Pable

7.9   Image courtesy of Jill Pable

7.10 Bakhita Gardens, Seattle. Catholic Housing Services, design by Environmental Works Community Design Center. Image courtesy of Jill Pable

7.11 Concept for the Atlanta Mission courtyard at the Shepherd's Inn. Design by Jill Pable and Lindsey Slater, Design Resources for Homelessness

7.12 Bakhita Gardens, Seattle. Catholic Housing Services, design by Environmental Works Community Design Center. Image courtesy of Jill Pable

7.13 Design by Jill Pable and Kenan Fishburne. Photo courtesy of Jill Pable

7.15 Summarized by the authors from multiple sources cited in text of table.

7.14 Concept for the Atlanta Mission Ethel Street Women's Shelter by Jill Pable

7.16 Architecture by Killefer Flammang. Photo courtesy Jill Pable

7.17 Concept for the Shepherd's Inn courtyard for Atlanta Mission. Image courtesy of Jill Pable, designer

7.18 Trinity Winchester House, Winchester, United Kingdom. Photo courtesy of Jill Pable

7.19 Architecture by Killefer Flammang Architects. Interior design team: Collaborative House, LLC. Photographer: Mary E. Nichols

7.20 Project for the Shepherd's Inn. Atlanta Mission. Design by Jill Pable and Lindsey Slater

7.21 Photo courtesy of Jill Pable

8.1   Image courtesy of Yelena McLane

8.2   Photos courtesy of Bob Glatt, photographer

8.3   Photos courtesy of Jill Pable

8.4   Architecture by Holland Harvey Architects. Photography by Nicholas Worley

8.5   Image courtesy of Yelena McLane

8.6   Image courtesy of Yelena McLane

8.7   Image courtesy of Yelena McLane

9.1   Architecture by HKS. Photography by Garrett Rowland

9.2   Architecture and Interior Design by Camillin Denny Architects. Photo courtesy of Camillin Denny Architects

9.3   Image courtesy of Yelena McLane

10.1   Table courtesy of Yelena McLane. Adapted from Substance Abuse and Mental Health Services Administration, 2010

10.2A   Photo by Ben Rahn/A-Frame. Architecture by LGA Architectural Partners

10.2B   Architecture by Brooks + Scarpa. Photography by Tara Wujcik

10.2C   Image courtesy of Lorcan O'Herlihy Architects by Paul Vu

10.2D   Image courtesy of Cas Allan, under creative commons license by its publisher, CitizenJ: http://citizenj.edgeqld.org.au/brisbane-homeless-find-common-ground/

10.3   Photo by Ben Rahn/A-Frame. Architecture by LGA Architectural Partners

10.4   Images courtesy of Yelena McLane

10.5   Architecture by Brooks + Scarpa. Photography by Tara Wujcik

10.6   Image courtesy of Lorcan O'Herlihy Architects by Paul Vu

10.7   Image courtesy of Common Ground Queensland

10.8   Table by Yelena McLane

10.9   Image by Yelena McLane

11.1   Image courtesy of Yelena McLane

11.2   Architecture by Shopworks Architecture. Photography by Matthew Staver

11.3A   Architecture by Shopworks Architecture. Photography by Matthew Staver

11.3B   Architecture and images by Shopworks Architecture

11.3C   Architecture and images by Shopworks Architecture

11.4A   Architecture by MGS Architects. Photograph by Trevor Mein

11.4B   Architecture by MGS Architects. Photograph by Chris Matterson

11.4C   Architecture by MGS Architects. Photograph by Andrew Latrielle

11.4D   Architecture by MGS Architects. Photograph by Andrew Latrielle

11.5   Architecture by MGS Architects. Photographs by Trevor Mein

11.6   Image courtesy of Yelena McLane

12.1   Image courtesy of Nicolas Boullosa, www.flickr.com/photos/faircompanies/14760104695

12.2   Table courtesy of Jill Pable

12.3   Image courtesy of Elemental

12.4   Table courtesy of Jill Pable

12.5   Image courtesy of Nicolas Boullosa of Vina Lustado's socal tiny house + studio – Ojai, unincorporated Ventura County, California

12.6   Table courtesy of Jill Pable

12.7   Architecture by Environmental Works Community Design Center. Photo and graphics by Jill Pable and C. Nilon

12.8   Table courtesy of Jill Pable

12.9   Client: Synapse. Architecture by People Oriented Design and Indij Design. Construction by Hutchinson Builders. Photo by Michael Marzik

13.1   Image courtesy of Brooks + Scarpa

13.2   Image courtesy of the University of Arkansas Community Design Center

13.3   Image courtesy of Podshare

13.4   Image courtesy of Facing Homelessness and the BLOCK Project

13.5   Image courtesy of Facing Homelessness and the BLOCK Project

Index

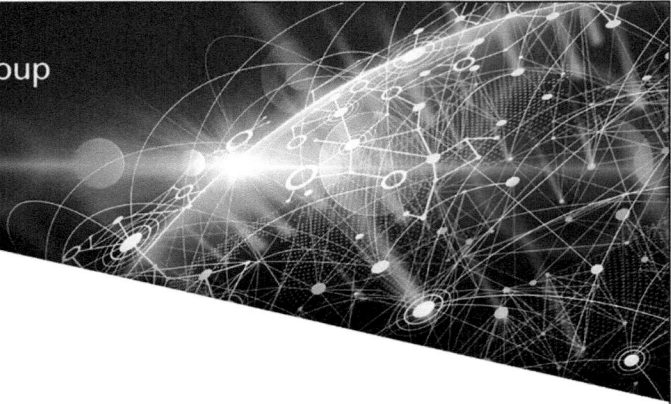